THE WAR IN GA

Thanks to dialectical and historical materialism, Marx and Engels placed at the disposal of the human race the possibility of extending their scientific method to the analysis of history and society. This is already an extremely important result; but Marxist science is much more than that. Applied to human society, Marxist science explains the processes that make communism a historical necessity, allows the scientific definition of the strategy for the communist revolution, and ensures the superiority of the proletariat over the other classes, a superiority ensured solely by this scientific strategy.

All the Marxist literary works are born as weapons in the revolutionary battle for communism and are only able to survive as such. In one and a half centuries, the fighting of numerous generations of Marxists has led to the accumulation of a scientific patrimony that unfortunately is little known and even less used today.

Arrigo Cervetto, who considered science as the salient feature of Lenin's party and founded his attempt to transfer the Bolshevik experience from tsarist Russia to post-WWII imperialist Italy on this hypothesis, defined the patrimony of Marxist science as a largely unexplored lode.

To bring a part of this theoretical treasure trove back into the light for the English-speaking reader is one of the tasks our publishing house has set itself, not with the aim of spreading culture but with the aim of providing the theoretical weapons with which to fight the revolutionary battle for communism.

The reality of this 21st century as a whole reveals how much of scientifically-founded revolutionary strategy was contained in the final appeal of the "Manifesto" – *Workers of all countries, unite!* An international proletariat that has swollen to huge dimensions has more than ever an urgent need to rediscover Marxist science and, in view of its future battles, to anchor its revolutionary preparation in it.

The work that lies before us is immense. Our catalogue is the measure of the contribution that we, as the Éditions Science Marxiste, have succeeded in making so far.

The War in Gaza
An Internationalist Response

Science
éditions Marxiste

Marxist Science Publications

For information about our publications please contact
Éditions Science Marxiste SARL
10, rue Lavoisier – 93100 Montreuil-sous-Bois – France
e-mail : info@sciencemarxiste.com
http ://www.sciencemarxiste.com

Translated from Italian
First published as: *La Guerra di Gaza*
Una risposta internazionalista
Edizioni Lotta Comunista, Milan, Italy

ISBN – 978-2-490073-72-6

Publisher's note:

This volume collects articles published in the newspaper *Lotta Comunista*, translated into English and published from 2003 to 2024 in the *Bulletin*, *Internationalist Bulletin*, *Internationalism*. Apart from the correction of misprints, they are presented integrally. The division and chapter headings are the work of the editor.

Introduction

In Israel "there is a bourgeoisie and a proletariat". In the Arab countries, "there is a bourgeoisie and a proletariat".

We must never tire of repeating this. At the very moment when fanaticism flares up, it is vital to remain anchored to our internationalist principle. Precisely in the darkest hour, after the 1,200 massacred in the South of Israel on October 7th, Jews but also Asian immigrants in the *kibbutzim*, and in the face of the 40,000 victims of the Israeli retaliation amidst the rubble of Gaza, horror must not cloud reflection.

In June 1967, at the outbreak of the *Six-Day War*, the class criterion was the cornerstone of the internationalist strategy of Lotta Comunista, at that time a small group in which the first young people were joining the group of workers and partisans who, having fought in the Resistance, had come to Leninism passing through libertarian communism.

In our newspaper of that time, in the editorial "Against War, Revolution!" we wrote: "The Arab and Israeli workers have no conflict of interests"; on the contrary they share "the same fate" of being exploited by their bourgeoisies, in their turn "linked by the tightly-woven web of capital invested in the Middle East. This is channelled through the old and new Meccas of imperialism: Washington, London, Paris, Bonn, Rome, Moscow and Tokyo". Today we can also add Beijing and, increasingly, New Delhi. The war revealed the "imperialist potential" of Italian society. Alongside a pro-Israeli interventionism, there emerged "left-wing interventionism alongside the Arab bourgeoisie" in support of the Mediterranean policy of the Italian bourgeoisie.

At the end of this book, the reader will find the texts of that political battle during the 1967 war, together with others which have again proposed and enriched that original outline of the situation in the following decades. We draw attention to one of their aspects. Their reflection on the transformations of the *national question* throughout three different phases of communist strategy, beaten out by the progress of the world's capitalist development, is crucial. Fanaticisms and mortal ideologies cling to the principles of *sovereignty* and *national self-determination*; this holds true for the Gaza tragedy, but it also holds true for the other *wars of the crisis in the world order*, present and future. The Ukrainian bourgeoisie wanted to be *sovereign* in 1991 following the dissolution of the Soviet Union, but it denied the Russian populations of Donbass and Crimea their *self-determination*; Russia denies Ukraine's *sovereignty* and claims it on the basis of the historical space of the New Russia ("Novorossiya"), colonised since the times of Catherine the Great, but in doing so it exploits the *self-determination* of Donbass and Crimea. The bourgeoisie of Western Ukraine is willing to *yield sovereignty* to the European Union, while that of Eastern Ukraine has yielded to Russia and the Eurasian Economic Union: this confirms that imperialist partition is the real characteristic of the war, and the *national question* is caught up in this. Along the Taiwan Strait, the next potential conflict, Beijing claims *sovereignty* over the island; in Taipei, the political currents wanting independence from China are prevailing; those requests for *self-determination* are being brandished in Washington by those who believe Chinese imperialism can be curbed.

The *crisis in the world order* is demonstrating that without a serious grounding in Marxist theory and internationalist strategy, proletarians end up as foot soldiers on the war fronts of imperialism. In the 19th century of bourgeois rise, Marx and Engels backed the national democratic revolutions in Europe wherever the advent of big states, free from the particularisms and dead weights of the old absolutist and feudal regimes, would create vast national markets, accelerating the development of large enterprises and concentrating a modern proletariat in large masses.

Lenin updated that strategy for the 20th century of imperialism as capitalist development, moving eastward, swept over the Slav area and the Near and Far East. The Bolsheviks brandished national self-determination against the Tsarist Empire, the *prison of peoples*; The Communist International, before being overwhelmed by Stalinism, supported the anticolonial movements of the young Asian bourgeoisies. The era of bourgeois-democratic revolutions, which had ended in Europe, was proposed again in the Slav area and Asia on "new bases", argued Lenin. As had been the case for Marx and Engels in Old Europe, now in the new areas of global capitalist development the bourgeois-democratic demands which favoured the proletariat's international strategy were to be supported. With one difference: where those demands had been "merely an instrument of the clerical or financial-monarchist intrigues of other countries", then they should have been rejected. The clergy, "Pan-Islamism" and "mullahs", as well as every attempt at using national movements in a reactionary way, were to be fought, Lenin wrote to the International in 1920. Support for national self-determination was a strategic choice, and not a matter of principle.

The third period began in the 1960s with the end of the movement of anti-colonial independence and the entrenchment of capitalist development all over the world. Communism backed the bourgeois-democratic revolutions because they develop productive forces, Arrigo Cervetto argued: the democrats "had themselves supported with the aim of eliminating us". Now that capitalist relations of production are predominant and widespread everywhere, communism is no longer "obliged" to support bourgeois democracy. All the more so since the national questions which have remained unresolved are seized upon as "a pretext" in the struggle between regional powers and among the powerhouses of imperialism.

The crux of the matter is that *there can no longer be a national solution to the question of nationality*. The drama of the Palestinian populations, as of every other oppressed minority, will only be dealt with and truly resolved by internationalist strategy, now that a mature class contraposition has created the conditions for this.

This is at the root of that internationalist battle in the face of the 1967 war: precisely, in Israel "there is a bourgeoisie and a proletariat", and in the Arab countries, "there is a bourgeoisie and a proletariat"; the Arab and Israeli workers must unite in order to prevent war and to transform it into revolution, and not let themselves be sent to slaughter by their ruling classes hand in hand with imperialism.

This raises a question. Over half a century after that seminal battle, what has changed? The struggle for communism is not a generic ideal aspiration, nor can it lose its vitality in a lazy repetition of principle. Marxist science lives if it knows how to be a party, if in faithfulness to revolution it knows how to grasp changes and transformations. How can those foundations of its political position and internationalist strategy be verified and updated? The starting point can only be the condition of the contention between imperialisms and its consequences for the regional theatres. The irruption of China as well as the laborious *federal/confederal* definition of the European Union have opened up a *new strategic phase* in global relations, in which large powers and great, continent-sized powers face each other. The United States, China, Europe, Russia, Japan and Brazil:

it is first of all between these giants of capital that the contention for the world markets is being played out, flanked tomorrow by other big demographic concentrations, such as Indonesia, or, the day after tomorrow, by some African giant.

This has profound consequences at the regional level, starting in the Middle East, which, because of its energy resources, has never ceased to be a *nerve centre* of that contention. In the third chapter we follow the century-old contention *for oil* and *through oil*, punctuated by the two world wars and subsequently by the long series of regional conflicts. For a century, the Middle Eastern bourgeoisies, incited by the great powers' jostling for influence, have fought to consolidate their national states and to participate in the share-out of gas and oil revenues. They are state entities crisscrossed by very intricate ethnic and religious fault lines and enclosed within arbitrary borders, the legacy of the collapse of the Ottoman Empire and of colonial rule. With the failure of the attempts at regional aggregation and the end of *Pan-Arabism* with Nasser's defeat in 1967, the new condition of a continent-sized power is all the more out of reach. This, moreover, holds true for all the balances of power, whether global or regional: a *fourth period,* defined by the insufficiency of the "19th-century nation-State" in the face of the size of the Asian giants, is to be added to those three periods of internationalist strategy regarding the national question.

On the one hand, this means that the imperialist powers' battle for influence will remain a determining factor in the Middle East, and that it will indeed be complicated by China's entry as a new pretender. On the other, precisely because China is emerging as a new locus of power in opposition to the declining West and United States, this may paradoxically increase the *medium-sized powers'* margins of action. The *crisis in the world order* may become an opportunity for defining regional relations or for some miscalculated adventurism. The *wars of the crisis in the world order* are also of this kind: they are the proxy wars of great powers, but they are also the effect of *medium-sized powers'* sorties, in the interregnum between declining Western hegemony and rising Chinese influence.

The latest *war in Gaza* has its origin in this, in the contention between Iran and Saudi Arabia; we deal with this in the articles collected in the second chapter. Tehran and Riyadh have introduced Beijing into their game, but the Iranians are only a step away from the atomic bomb and are on the *nuclear threshold*, while the Saudis think that, with the *Abraham Accords*, they can follow the same path with the Americans' assent. In order to prevent this or to impose negotiations, Tehran has mobilised or allowed its clients, Hezbollah in Lebanon, the Houthis in Yemen and Hamas in Gaza, to act.

For the Saudis, the *Abraham Accords* should include a national solution for the Palestinians which may be mediated by a revitalisation of a discredited Palestinian National Authority (PNA), but it is hard to see how the question of the Jewish colonies in the West Bank, a potential armed mass base for an intra-Israeli civil war, can be resolved. For the moment, the Iranians are insisting on playing a game of interdiction, which has its precedents in the *Rejectionist Front* which has opposed every negotiation with Israel since the 1970s. Hamas's demand for a Palestine unified "from the river to the sea", i.e., wiping out Israel, is a mirror image of the ambitions of the Israeli right wing and of Jewish religious fundamentalism for a *Greater Israel* which would reclaim the Biblical regions of Judea and Samaria, i.e., complete colonisation and annex the West Bank occupied territories.

The game being played between the Middle Eastern powers, and between these and the powerhouses of imperialism, exploits and keeps open a contradiction which has centuries-old roots. In the first chapter we give a broad overview of the currents which have interpreted it: the two leading figures of Zionism embodied at the beginning by David Ben-Gurion's labourists and by Vladimir Jabotinsky's *revisionist* right wing; and the currents of the PLO and political Islamism contending Palestinian nationalism, which are in turn influenced and exploited by Arab and Iranian nationalism.

Over the decades, this has revealed two recurring patterns. The first is that every power which has had ambitions in the area or has felt itself frustrated and excluded by the agreements of others has brandished the Palestinians' drama by organising and financing their factions, pushing them at a political, confessional, military and often terrorist level. This has been the case, in turns or in variable alliances which have used and then abandoned the Palestinians, with Egypt, Syria, Jordan, Iraq, Lebanon, Algeria, Libya, Tunisia, Kuwait, Qatar, Saudi Arabia and Iran. Today it is Tehran's turn, but we can be sure that without an agreement which would bring all the players to the negotiating table, if that is ever possible, there will be forces ready to rekindle a conflict which in and of itself has been made almost unsolvable precisely by the entrenchment of hundreds of thousands of settlers in the West Bank.

The second pattern concerns the imperialist powers, which have brandished those national and confessional rivalries in their share-out agreements or have stirred them up into dozens of conflicts, in order to prevent the unity or hegemonic control of the region.

There are three further aspects of the internationalist battle which require attention. The first regards our class forces. In comparison with 1967, wage-earners in the North African and Middle Eastern area which extends from Morocco to Iran, including Turkey, have risen in number from 20 to 120 million and amount to two thirds of the working population, with a quarter of those belonging to the industrial proletariat. This interweaves in the Gulf petro-monarchies with sizeable Indian and Asian immigration, often forming the absolute majority of the labour force. It is understandable that only an internationalist position can conceive of the unity of such a vast proletariat in North Africa and the Middle East, but it is also possible to glimpse the force it could express if organised and oriented by a revolutionary strategy.

In 1967, Arrigo Cervetto rejected the objection that the relations of force were not favourable to the proletariat in the Middle East. Wage-earners already accounted for a considerable share of the working population and there were "large masses of proletarianised peasants"; in any case, a Leninist strategy could not be built solely on the Middle Eastern proletariat but would need to be welded to "the revolutionary struggle of the European proletariat". Only an internationalist battle, and certainly not "interventionism" in support of the various Nassers and the social-national myths of the Arab bourgeoisies, would be able to entrench that class strategy in Europe.

Half a century later, 120 million proletarians along the southern shore of the Mediterranean, six times as many as in 1967, could count on 200 million class comrades in Europe, if only a communist strategy knew how to coordinate them. Undoubtedly, we can see with our own eyes the delay of the world party, the lack of an International founded on the *class principle*, but even more openly revealed is the failure, after a whole century, of the *national principle*, in the ineptitude of bourgeoisies drenched in oil revenue, incapable of any kind of regional agreement and degraded to the point of supporting the worst fanaticisms.

The second question requiring an updating is, precisely, the relationship between the Arab bourgeoisie and the Palestinian bourgeoisie. Commenting on the tragic defeat of the PLO in Lebanon in

1982, hard-pressed by Israel but abandoned by the Arab countries, Cervetto observed that the PLO was "a heterogeneous collective of dozens of organisations in constant conflict, sometimes armed", a "sum of military groups coming directly under the various Arab bourgeoisies which financed them, from the Saudi to the Iraqi". Moreover, only the Palestinian populations of the West Bank and Gaza, under Israeli occupation, were stably entrenched, with a social stratification in which "a property-owning bourgeoisie" in its turn, influenced some PLO currents with one hand, while with the other it collaborated economically with the Israeli bourgeoisie, in a market "in full expansion" in spite of the permanent state of war.

Yasser Arafat himself, Palestinian historians report, recognised that the various organisations gathered in the PLO were part of the "conflict of the Arab nation" and were "linked to Arab countries"; hence, facing them would have meant facing those countries; his attempt, or his illusion, was a continual oscillation between the different influences in order to avoid depending on them.

Edward Said, one of the greatest Palestinian intellectuals, defined Palestinians as "victims of victims", thanks to the unique situation of the millions who found themselves exiled or in refugee camps at the hands of a State, Israel, which carries imprinted in its moral factor centuries of anti-Semite pogroms and the horror of the Shoah. It is Said himself who claimed in a 1978 book that the Palestinian diaspora has given birth to one of the "regional elites" in the Middle East, an important part of the "Arab upper middle class", with "key positions in the bureaucracies or in the oil industry" or "roles as advisers in the economic field or as counsellors of various Arab governments".

What must be added today is the following: the dependence of the Palestinian bourgeoisie of the diaspora on the various sectors of the Arab bourgeoisie was its original sin; it exposed the PLO's fragility when the trickle of oil revenue devoted to it was redirected to the Islamist currents and Iranian influence also became part of the game. The first Gulf War in 1991 was an about-turn, the Arab powers siding with Washington while the PLO continued to support Saddam Hussein. The decisive boost to Hamas dates back to that time, when it was subsequently encouraged by the right-wing Israeli governments themselves, who saw in it the opportunity to split the Palestinian front while the colonisation of the West Bank was proceeding. This is why the Israeli government is also to be numbered among the ruinous bourgeoisies, in the sorcerer's apprentice game regarding Hamas which overwhelmed it on October 7th, while the atrocious fury of its retaliation on Gaza, in the era of *social media* and TV carnage, will leave an indelible mark on its reputation.

The consequence of the slow annexation of the West Bank was the weakening of the PNA, while Gaza ended up in the hands of Hamas: a failure for the old secular and social-national roots of the Palestinian representation, a mirror image of the political setback suffered by the Israeli currents which were still amenable to the formula *two peoples, two states.* And there was a division of Palestine's future prospects along two lines of influence: that of Tehran, which aims to become a nuclear power, and that of Riyadh, which would like to emulate it via the *Abraham Accords* with Israel. There could not have been a more tragic and derisive epilogue for the Palestinians than to be left exposed, with 40,000 victims, to Israel's retaliation in the name of the atomic ambitions of the Iranian mullahs, and of having as an alternative a downward compromise with Israel itself in the shadow cast by the Saudi petro-monarchy. It is difficult to say, in this framework, what fate will befall the Beijing Declaration, by which fourteen organisations, including Fatah and Hamas, recognise the PLO as "the sole legitimate representative" of the Palestinians; what is certain is the role that China is confirming in the area, which has already emerged with the mediation attempt between Iran and Saudi Arabia.

Finally, the third question regards the prospects of internationalism. In 1985, taking stock of the *principle of class struggle* in dealing with the national question, Cervetto wrote that the Leninist party which complied with this principle would not be dragged into "social-imperialist positions" by the transmission belt of the national question: it could "be reduced to extreme isolation" but it could not "be distorted".

That condition of "extreme isolation" brings us back to the reality which a line advocating Arab-Israeli class unity has to face today in both Israel and the Arab world. This is nothing new: even the simple positions of economic-trade union unity in the 1920s were opposed and often physically liquidated in both the Jewish and the Arab-Palestinian camps. Moreover, this has been the case throughout history for every internationalist minority which has found itself facing the fanaticisms stirred up in war mobilisations: the Bolsheviks were forced into living outside the law or taking refuge abroad, accused of being agents of Germany, before that war itself shattered consensus within the country and in the trenches, and opened up the way to revolutionary defeatism.

And yet, in this half-century the possibilities of consolidating a class position, of rebuilding an internationalist strategy, albeit along a narrow and arduous path, have grown. Let's deal with the question starting from another Cervetto article, written in 1986, regarding the "poisoned seeds of Mediterranean politics". One of these "poisoned seeds" was terrorism, which from a highly-developed Middle East and "incandescent hotbed of wars", and therefore a "chaotic hothouse of bombs and bombers", spilled into the Italian and European metropolises. Another poisoned seed was the conditions of the immigrant labour force, with low wages and "without any kind of protection"; the Italian metropolis drew on "a new source of surplus value from the Mediterranean basin" which increased "its imperialist maturity and the wage-earning aristocracy's possibility of corruption".

In these decades, this same progress of capitalist development, of the disintegration of the peasantry and of demographic growth which has sextupled the proletariat along the southern shore of the Mediterranean, the periphery of European imperialism, has pushed tens of millions of migrants into the Old Continent's big cities. It goes without saying that this fact alone makes our internationalist battle in Europe indispensable; our opposition to the poisons of nationalism, which inevitably spread through a multiethnic proletariat, accompanies our struggle against every kind of racism and every kind of discrimination.

The vast majority of immigrants is by now undoubtedly part of Europe's wage-earning stratification and also ends up being assimilated into the metabolism of the social scale; hence, the questions of class defence now prevail over distinctions by migratory origin. Nevertheless, such a vast pool of immigrant labour force, destined to grow, to a certain extent opens the way to the representation which wants Europe as the rearguard of the Middle Eastern conflicts. The ruling class is discussing this with ample doses of hypocrisy and cynicism. After October 7th, Henry Kissinger went so far as to state on *Welt TV* that "it was a grave mistake to let in so many people of totally different culture and religion and concepts because it creates a pressure group inside each country that does that". With a bourgeoisie which cannot do without immigration but must reassure public opinions which have grown old and afraid, the pretexts for hateful discrimination and xenophobic campaigns are multiplying: we need only think of the suspicions raised against French people with dual nationality, or the controversies in Germany over the new right to citizenship which accelerates naturalisations.

However, that same presence of tens of millions of immigrants from the southern shore of the Mediterranean, with the entrenchment of the second and third young generations, may prove to be a breach for our internationalist battle. If the margin of action for a communist minority in the Middle Eastern tangle is limited to "extreme isolation", the possibilities of clarification and internationalist entrenchment in the European rearguard are much greater.

We Leninists are no longer that small group which was seeking to consolidate internationalist positions in 1967. Every year, thousands of young people now have the possibility of knowing the positions of revolutionary Marxism; in the growing share which has its roots in immigration, there are increasingly those who find in internationalism the solution – almost a revelation – in the face of a century of failures on the part of the Middle Eastern nationalisms. The same holds true – while the conflict is again raising the spectre of anti-Semitism in the Old Continent – for the young Jews, Arabs, Arab-Israelis, Iranians or whoever living in Europe for studies. Removed from the climate of fanaticism of the *union sacrée* of war, and to a certain extent safe from the obtuse ferocity of retaliation, they can come to terms with Marxism and internationalism; this is why the young people of our Workers' Clubs are carrying on their battle in the universities, rejecting the boycotting of Israel's universities and those of any other country.

Here, too, pages of the history of the revolutionary movement, which should be read, act as confirmation. The First International, starting from Marx and Engels, was powered by the immigration of Europeans and political émigrés to London. In the early 1920s, whole sectors of the Third International, before being engulfed or annihilated by Stalinism, were recruited among the young people who were in Paris, London or Berlin from all over the world for studies or for work.

This is the practical way that half a century of political battles has opened up since those *six days* in 1967. We do not know what *wars of the crisis in the world order* will shake the next decade, nor to what extent. What is certain is that very many young people and very many proletarians, in Europe and in the world, will find themselves facing fundamental questions regarding the barbaric future which this society promises new generations. It is therefore a matter of rooting Leninism in Europe and throughout Europe, among European young people and proletarians as well as among those of every origin.

This is a work which requires the patience to rebuild internationalism youth by youth, and worker by worker, but also promptness in grasping about-turns and sudden accelerations which may shake class consciousness. Is this a narrow path? Take a look at what is believed to be the broad way, the highway of bourgeois rule, that of nationalism or of the share-outs of imperialism: that is a dead end paved with millions of victims, and promising further millions the same future.

G.L. - July 2024

Chapter One

Israel and Palestine

The Origins of the State of Israel*

Eli Barnavi is a historian and a former Israeli ambassador to Paris. In his book *Storia d'Israele* [1996], he writes that modern European anti-Semitism, the mainspring of the formation of the Zionist movement, originated in the second half of the 19th century, when "nationalism" ceased to act as a "liberal force" and instead took on a "conservative and reactionary fallback position". This was no longer a "revolutionary" and emancipatory force as it had been for Judaism during the French Revolution. The "Michelets" gave way to various characters such as "de Gobineau and Chamberlain", who were theorists of racism. From it they would derive a "biological anti-Semitism".

During the Second World War, this anti-Semitism found its most heinous expression in Nazi ideology, giving rise to the mass extermination of the Jewish population via industrial methods. The six million Jewish victims of Nazism and its allied regimes accounted for approximately 10% of the total number of deaths during that world conflict.

The plurality of Zionist currents

Barnavi's analysis of the reactionary character of bourgeois nationalism coincides with what Marxism describes as the emergence of imperialist maturity. If Zionism as a political movement found its theoretical elaboration in the writings and practical activity of Theodor Herzl [1860-1904], with a first world congress held in Basel in 1897, in Barnavi's opinion part of its roots can be traced back to 1848-49 uprisings, thus with a secular matrix. However, both in the Jewish communities in Eastern Europe and in those in the Middle East and North Africa, the religious aspirations of a "return to Zion", i.e., Palestine, emerged.

According to the historiography, for Herzl the need to create a "Jewish State" was dictated by a "defensive" necessity: to provide

* Gianluca De Simone, April 2024

refuge and protection in the face of the recrudescence of the "Jewish question" and of anti-Semitic outbreaks picked up by some mass political movements. In Herzl's opinion, the prospect of the "assimilation" of the Jewish diaspora within individual European nation-states had failed. Barnavi speaks of a "nationalism that came too late", which, with its own religious specificity, was mirrored in other national claims of the time within the Austro-Hungarian and Tsarist empires. The Zionist movement would find its mass base in the emigration processes from the Tsarist Empire between 1881 and 1914, marked by regular outbreaks of anti-Semitic violence; this component would make up the majority of those who emigrated to Palestine and created the State of Israel. In its settlement of Palestine from 1881 onward, Zionism clashed with, and in some ways acted as a catalyst for, the rise of Arab nationalism within the Ottoman Empire.

As it developed, Zionism would see a dialectic between its political centres, first in Vienna, then in Berlin and London and finally in Palestine. Its prevailing mass base, at least until the 1930s, was represented by the emigration of the Eastern-European diaspora, which redefined Herzl's secular-liberal framework in the direction of a "national socialism", according to the historian Zeev Sternhell's formula: this would become the ideology of the State of Israel and its "State capitalism" [*Aux Origines d'Israël: Entre Nationalisme et Socialisme*, 1996].

From 1925, especially in Poland, the Zionist right-wing current started to grow: a national-liberal ideology, but with marked sympathies for Kemal Ataturk's authoritarian orientation, Irish nationalism, Garibaldinism, as well as Italian fascism and the authoritarian regime in charge of Poland between 1919 and 1939. Right-wing Zionism had two major competitors: the Jewish workers' movement of "The Bund" and its internationalist positions, which criticised Zionism, including left-wing Zionism, as a "nationalist and petit-bourgeois movement" which would divide the proletariat; and religious anti-Zionism, of orthodox origin, which considered "the return to Zion" as a sign of divine will and as an enabler of the coming of the messiah of Jewish tradition [Arturo Marzano, *Storia dei Sionismi*, 2017]. The Bund fell victim to Stalinism and Nazism; as for religious anti-Zionism, it is still present in some *haredim* ["orthodox"] components in Israel and the diaspora. Right-wing Zionism, left-wing Zionism and national-religious parties would constitute the main Israeli political formations after 1947.

"Hundred Years' War"

When examining the moral force of the State of Israel, one must consider the process of its formation which, in addition to thousands of years of religious persecution, was heavily influenced by the tsarist *pogroms*, *fin-de-siècle* European anti-Semitism, the anti-Semitic persecution in Ukraine during the Russian civil war between 1918 and 1921, and the exterminations carried out by Nazi-fascism and Stalinist persecution. Other events such as the mass expulsions from Arab countries after 1948 and the immigration of the 1990s after the collapse of the USSR played an important role.

On the level of international relations, the birth of the State of Israel is combined with the "question of the East": the decline of the Ottoman Empire, between 1856 (end of the Crimean War) and 1922, passing through the hairpin bend of the first imperialist conflict and leading to the establishment of the British Mandate for Palestine. The so-called Jewish-Palestinian "Hundred Years' War" stemmed mainly from the actions of rival powers in the region: first between colonial powers to the detriment of the Ottoman Empire, and later between the two superpowers, the USA and USSR, and the declining colonial empires; it also affected the formation of the area's nation-states, including Israel [Ilan Pappé, *A History of Modern Palestine*, 2004].

The birth of the Jewish State – as both Barnavi and Dan Vittorio Segre have pointed out – is contemporaneous with the process of decolonisation, hence the formation of many Arab states, but also of countries such as India, Indonesia and Pakistan. It was achieved by both military and diplomatic means against the British power, and through a Palestinian civil conflict in 1947-49. According to Dan Segre, the first four Arab-Israeli conflicts – 1947-48, 1956, 1967 and 1973 – can be considered "wars of construction" in the sense that they resulted in the internal consolidation of both the Jewish State and its adversaries. They also produced a "second Zionism", Palestinian nationalism, which so far had the lower hand [*Le Metamorfosi di Israele*, 2006].

This intertwined process has produced both an inextricable knot of contradictions and a modern proletariat thanks to the extension of the capitalist mode of production in the region. The modern proletariat is the only protagonist, if united on class and internationalist positions, that could break the vicious circle of national, ethnic and inter-religious conflicts – a smouldering fire which is continually stoked by the regional and international bourgeoisies.

The three ways of Zionism: diplomatic, practical, and synthetic

In its actions between the end of the 19th century and 1947, Zionism can in turn be distinguished into "diplomatic Zionism" and "practical Zionism". The first variant – embodied by Herzl and Chaim Weizmann, subjects of the Austro-Hungarian and British empires respectively – sought the creation of a Jewish State with the consent and protection of the great powers. Herzl examined the intentions of Wilhelmine Germany, the Ottoman Empire, the Vatican and finally London, seeking their diplomatic support for the creation of a Jewish State settlement. In combination with what can be called "philanthropic Zionism", expressed by Jewish big finance, he considered the possibility of founding it in Argentina or even, within the British empire, in Kenya. However, this philanthropic expression of Zionism had already financed the establishment of Jewish agricultural colonies in Palestine from 1881, the *moshavot.* Herzl had also considered the option of a settlement in Cyprus. He was outvoted by Russian Zionist currents, which imposed a Jewish State settlement in Palestine. These currents were centred around personalities such as David Ben-Gurion and his rival Vladimir Ze'ev Jabotinsky – the founder of the *revisionist* Zionist current – an exponent of the so-called "practical Zionism", which sought the establishment, through mass emigration, of the State of Israel on the territories that had hosted the ancient Jewish monarchies.

A "brilliant publicist" and skilful orator (according to Barnavi), Herzl created the symbolism of the future State of Israel, starting with the flag, "recovering the thousand-year-old historical-religious culture" which united the communities of the Jewish diaspora and made them a people. He was an offspring of *Mitteleuropa*, born in Budapest and at ease in the "intellectual circles of Viennese liberalism" at the turn of the century, according to Michel Abitbol – a renowned orientalist and a professor at the Hebrew University of Jerusalem. During his stay in Paris as political correspondent for the Viennese daily *Neue Freie Presse*, Herzl witnessed the emergence of a new "social political phenomenon": "an amorphous and uncontrollable crowd of sympathisers of the new mass parties", often stirred up by demagogues such as, in the French case, the anti-Semitic Édouard Drumont [*Histoire d'Israël*, 2024].

The members of practical Zionism, Abitbol continues, constituted the bulk of the second *aliyah* (literally "rise" in Hebrew). This a was a flow of 35,000-40,000 migrants, who flocked to Palestine from 1903 to 1914 (out of a total Jewish emigration of about 2 million people from the tsarist empire, most of whom landed in Western Europe and the Americas), with an "important number" of *japonitzki*, the "deserters from the Russian army during the conflict with Japan". They were younger, urban, artisans and poor workers, animated by the desire to achieve "a synthesis between their adherence to the socialist revolution and their attachment to the Zionist ideal". They were characterised by a romantic nationalism and a scorn for the "bourgeois spirit" of the *moshavot*, which had morphed into capitalist enterprises with large numbers of Arab manual workers, modelled on the French colonial economy in Algeria.

Diplomatic Zionism, as mentioned above, aimed at cultivating relations with the great European powers of the time, since, in Herzl's conception, a Jewish State could only exist with an "international guarantee" offered by the concert of powers. This was the case for the various Christian religious minorities in the mosaic of the Ottoman Empire. Apart from the promise to direct the flow of capital, the offer to the Sublime Porte of Istanbul was to act as an instrument for the modernisation of the empire. If the Palestinian notables, both Arab and Christian as well as Greek Orthodox, were open to the sale of land to Jewish settlers, they nevertheless also perceived it as a vector for European penetration and meddling. This view was also shared by the Ottoman bureaucracy. Both in Berlin and later in London, Herzl presented the Jewish settlement as a "European outpost" in the Levant. Berlin was more interested in preserving its relationship with the Turkish Empire and Germany's direct projection towards the Persian Gulf, so it declined the offer. London was more favourable due to its presence in Egypt and interests in Iran's oilfields.

It was Chaim Weizmann – the future president of Israel and naturalised British citizen – who expressed the new Zionist leadership in the diaspora. Between 1914 and 1917, he was able to realise Herzl's goal of gaining British support, achieving a "synthesis" between the diplomatic and the practical Zionist lines.

The Creation of the Modern Middle East*

"The Middle East became what it is today", wrote David Fromkin in *A Peace to End All Peace* [1989], "both because the European powers undertook to reshape it" between 1911 and 1922, "and because Britain and France failed to ensure that the dynasties, the states, and the political system they established would permanently endure". During and after the First World War, "London and her allies destroyed the old order in the region irrevocably; they smashed Turkish rule of the Arab-speaking Middle East beyond repair". In its place they "created countries, nominated rulers, delineated frontiers" and introduced a European-style state system, but without taming the significant local opposition to these decisions. This process, conducted during the first imperialist conflict, may have ended "Europe's Middle Eastern question", but it gave birth to the "Middle Eastern question in the Middle East itself".

After the "1922 settlement", the problem of what (and who) would succeed the Ottoman Empire was solved as far as the European powers were concerned, but the problem of its legitimacy was left unresolved. This assessment highlights the series of Arab-Israeli conflicts that took place after 1947 and the creation of the *Palestinian question*, a constant *national pretext* for regional and international confrontation between world powers. It is on a par with other national questions that have remained unresolved since then, starting with the Kurdish and Armenian questions. All three resurfaced with the Syrian conflict that began in 2011, the Nagorno-Karabakh incidents in 2020-23, and today's war in Gaza. These are conflicts that the crisis in the world order has once again re-ignited.

The "1922 settlement" was the product of the *breakdown* of the world order, which found its expression in the Imperialist First World War, although, after 1911, its harbingers had manifested themselves in the form of the wars in the Balkans and Libya.

During the First World War, the key decisions taken on Palestine, Syria, and Turkey had much wider reverberations, though in terms of the military confrontation it was a theatre of secondary importance. According to Fromkin, the extension of the European conflict

* Gianluca De Simone, May 2024

to the Ottoman Empire in October 1914 meant that Britain, still the world's leading power, had "in a little less than a hundred days [...] completely reversed the policy of more than a hundred years". This radical change can be summarised in three stages.

From the McMahon Papers to the Balfour Declaration

The first was London's probing of the possibility of using Arab nationalism to destabilise the Turkish empire. To this effect, Arthur H. McMahon – the high commissioner for Egypt – was in correspondence with al-Husayn ibn Ali, the emir of the Hejaz and Sherif of Mecca and Medina. These contacts took place between July 1915 and March 1916, straddling the Anglo-French offensive in the Gallipoli peninsula. London had hoped that the offensive would quickly put the Ottoman Empire out of action, thereby supporting Russia (Britain's ally) and breaking the stalemate on the Western Front. The second stage was represented by the Sykes-Picot Agreements, negotiated by France and Britain between November 1915 and March 1916. They laid out the Allies' war aims concerning the Ottoman Empire, which amounted to its pre-agreed partition between the spheres of influence of Paris, London, St Petersburg, and Rome. Finally, the third stage was the Balfour Declaration of November 1917, which expressed British support for the Zionist movement and the idea of a "Jewish National Home" in Palestine.

The British "third empire"

These were all decisions that, at least in the case of the British Empire, were defined by the dialectic between the various centres of imperial interests and decision-making, such as Egypt and India, South Africa and Australia, and no less than "eighteen British government agencies": from the War Cabinet to the Foreign Office, from the War Office to the Colonial Office. In 1917, the "Arabists" or "Anglo-Egyptians" – an expression of the British governorate in Egypt – were granted the creation of an "Arab Bureau" (the Department for Arab Affairs) following a "centralising measure". After 1918, Fromkin writes, "British commitments and objectives underwent a series of adjustments and attempts to strike a balance between overall imperial interests, the internal political cycle, economic conditions, and the maintenance of Britain's obligations".

By 1918 the extension of the British Empire had reached its zenith, adding a "third empire", the Arab one, to those it had in Africa

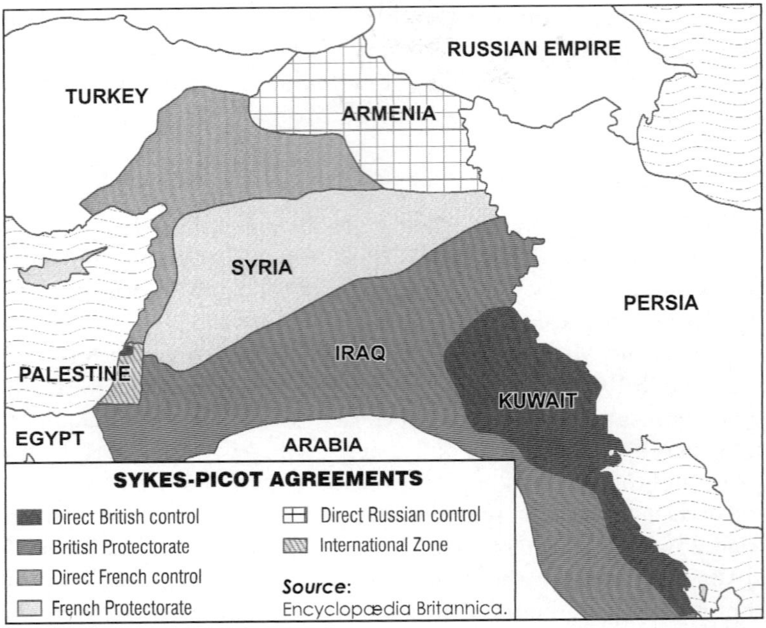

and the Indo-Pacific region. This "imperial archipelago, strung across the world", was held together by the Royal Navy and British trade and finance [John Darwin, *The Empire Project*, 2009]. As the French Arabist Henry Laurens writes, it was also a dominion "imposed by a British moment" between West Asia and the Indian Ocean [*Les crises d'Orient*, vol. 2, 2019]. According to Fromkin, between 1919 and 1922 London was "overextended", which was made worse by demobilisation and the post-war economic crisis. The UK was forced to follow a policy of financial retrenchment, and soon came to consider as burdens both its support for the Hashemite dynasty and the support for the "Zionist programme it had vigorously espoused in 1917". The result was that British policymakers "imposed a settlement upon the Middle East in 1922 in which, for the most part, they themselves no longer believed", not least because many of their earlier decisions "had taken on a life of their own".

"Jihad made in Germany" and Zionism in the imperialist contention

The Zionist political movement, while having a religious component, was born as an expression of secular nationalism. According to Theodor Herzl's intentions, its aim was to create a secular-liberal State, with "militarism confined to the barracks and rabbis to the synagogues". The support it received from London – and to a lesser extent, from Paris – transformed it into a *national pretext* utilised for various purposes in the context of the conflict. The same can be said for the support offered to Arab nationalism and the support that all powers offered to national minorities or various religious denominations for war and political purposes. This was nothing new in historical terms, except for the global dimension of the conflict.

Both Fromkin and Laurens emphasise how, from 1870 onwards, during their imperial expansion, the major European capitals developed an "obsession" with Pan-Islamism, a phenomenon that spanned the enormous Ottoman-Islamic space, stretching from the Atlantic to Central Asia. Britain, France and Russia – Laurens argues – became configured as "Muslim powers" as a result of their colonial subjects' Islamic faith. When the Anglo-Indian Empire was formalised in 1876, Prime Minister Benjamin Disraeli claimed that the British Empire was "an Islamic empire": by 1922 it would encompass over 50% of the world's Muslim population. However, being a caliphate and hence claiming the spiritual leadership of the Muslim world, the Ottoman Empire was the only "remaining sovereign" Islamic power. As a matter of fact, the Ottoman Empire was a sovereign State recognised by the 1856 Treaty of Paris, which ended the Crimean War [1853-56].

The various European powers portrayed themselves as *protecting powers* of the Ottoman Empire's Christian minorities, which was also a means of interfering in the policies of the Sublime Porte. Germany's rise from 1871 onwards and mutual power rivalries gave rise to a fear of Pan-Islamic ideology as an instrument of influence. Paris – Laurens continues – considered it necessary to create a "French Islam" through a "western caliphate" in Morocco, given that the Sherif dynasty in Rabat boasted of being directly descended from Muhammad. This hypothesis was contested by the exponents of the French colonial party in Algeria and the so-called "Syrian party", to which François Georges-Picot [1870-1951], the former French consul in Lebanon, belonged.

For London, the issue revolved around its rivalries with Russia in Central Asia and with Germany in the Ottoman domains. From 1829 onwards – Fromkin writes – "British strategy thereafter was to employ the decaying regimes of Islamic Asia as a gigantic buffer between British India and its route to Egypt" against the Russian threat. This policy was especially associated with the figure of Lord Palmerston. The strategic epicentres in West Asia were Constantinople and the Dardanelles, while in Central Asia it was Afghanistan. In Tory governments, this strategy was summarised in the formula of supporting the "Turkish bulwark" against Russia.

Liberal governments, however, particularly those of William E. Gladstone, promoted a *moralpolitik* based on "their abhorrence of the corrupt and despotic Middle Eastern regimes". In 1880-85 the Gladstone government withdrew its "protection and influence from Constantinople", prompting it to seek support from Bismarckian Germany, which "took Britain's place at the Sublime Porte". Subsequent Conservative governments proved unable to reverse course.

London, Cairo, Shimla and the "buccaneer gang"

Horatio Herbert Kitchener became the leading figure of the "Anglo-Egyptian" current in the imperial debate. After distinguishing himself for his command of Anglo-Egyptian forces in Khartoum, he would become the commander-in-chief of the Anglo-Indian army and later was appointed as Secretary of State for War in 1914. He promoted the strategy of backing Arab national claims against the Ottomans, creating an "Arab kingdom" under British protection, and "moving the Caliphate south". This line of support to Cairo's ambitions found opposition from the "Anglo-Indian" current, the government in Shimla – the summer capital of the British imperial administration in India. The outcome was the McMahon-Husayn correspondence mentioned prior, with the Emir of the Hejaz claiming that he could lead an anti-Ottoman Arab movement. Cairo, according to Fromkin's reconstruction, wanted to believe the information that the numerous secret societies of Arab nationalists, particularly present in Damascus, could sow dissent among the Ottoman troops, which did not happen. Until 1918, the Arab troops, albeit with significant desertions from 1917, remained loyal to the sultan in Istanbul and the Young Turk regime, established in 1908.

Throughout the negotiations – adds Fromkin – London, Cairo and Husayn exchanged "counterfeit coins": England was unsure of the emir's real strength and had already negotiated with France about commitments in Syria. In reality, Husayn sought subsidies from London, Paris, and Constantinople and was convinced to launch the revolt only when he realised that the Ottomans wanted to sack him. According to Laurens, France was counting not only on its traditional Maronite allies in Lebanon, but also on the Syrian-Palestinian frenchified urban notables, in whose eyes the Hashemite "Bedouin dynasty" was "backward" and an "intruder in the Levant". London, for its part, considered Hashemite "traditionalism" to be a useful tool *vis-à-vis* the Arab peasant masses and considered the urban elites to be a little too French and therefore "spineless". For the "Anglo-Indians" and the Foreign Office, it was preferable to keep the Caliphate within the Ottoman dynasty, which would rule over a kind of Arab-Turkish confederation. As George Nathaniel Curzon – the viceroy of India and later foreign minister in London from 1919 to 1923 – put it, this was an "aggregate of Islamic states" fulfilling an anti-Russian function. This aggregate also included Persia and, with the Russian civil war, the various Khanates of Central Asia.

For Shimla especially, a key aim of the war was the partitioning of the Ottoman provinces of what is now Iraq, particularly Basra, which the "Anglo-Indians" wanted to annex to the Indian Raj. In the memoirs of Edward Grey – the Liberal foreign secretary in office until December 1916 – the discussions at No. 10 Downing Street about the partitioning of the Ottoman domains "had resembled that of a gang of buccaneers" [D. Fromkin, *op. cit.*].

In December 1916, with the establishment of the government of David Lloyd George – serving as the minister of War in the previous cabinet – the line of the "Orientalists", advocating a greater war effort against the Ottomans, was strengthened in London, whereas the line of the "Westernists" wanted to focus on the French theatre. Laurens points out that Lloyd George was under no illusions about the possibility of driving Germany out of the Middle East, but he did believe that this theatre of war, as well as providing greater territorial acquisitions, would "save forces" to be brought to bear on the European table at the time of peace negotiations. A devout Protestant, like Foreign Secretary Arthur J. Balfour, Lloyd George believed that London had conceded too much to Paris with the Sykes-Picot accords and that it "would be an outrage to let the Christian Holy Places in Palestine fall into the hands of 'Agnostic Atheistic France'".

Chaim Weizmann's "door of hope"

Fromkin writes that Mark Sykes, a man of "fierce imagination", with strong anti-Semitic prejudices, considered "mercurial" and "a novice in government" – particularly by Anglo-Indian exponents – was introduced to the Zionist movement in early 1917. He began to consider that a Jewish settlement in Palestine would represent, together with an Arab kingdom based in Damascus, a counterweight to the French presence in Syria. For Lord Balfour – writes the historian Lorenzo Kamel – as was the case for many exponents of the British establishment, deep anti-Semitic prejudices coexisted with a "pro-Zionism of a Protestant religious matrix": promoting the "redemption" of Palestine. In other words, the return of the Jewish confession to the biblical lands, was in line with messianic designs [*Terra Contesa*, 2023].

Chaim Weizmann – a naturalised British chemist and the head of the British Zionist organisation, who had a close connection to Sykes – said that the Zionist movement had found "in the anti-Semites its best allies". The Weizmann-Sykes relationship opened to the British Zionists the "door of hope" represented by Balfour's Foreign Office. For London and Paris, the importance of the Zionist card was increased by two factors: the Russian Revolution of February 1917 and the American pro-Zionist orientation.

According to Michel Abitbol [*Histoire d'Israël*, 2024], both England and France took it for granted that there was "great Jewish influence" over the White House and Congress. Above all they counted, as did Russia, on the "Jewish banks in New York" to "finance the war effort". However, the American Jewish community rejected any support for the Entente because of "pathological Russian anti-Semitism" and felt "natural sympathies towards the central empires", from which "many of the leaders of American Jewry" originated. They espoused "American neutrality" and showed gratitude for the interventions of Germany and Austria in "favour of the Jews in Palestine", as opposed to the repressive measures taken by Constantinople. Being of Russian origin, these Jews were regarded as suspect by the Ottoman authorities, who in 1915-16 had already conducted the vicious repression of the Armenian minority, which the Ottomans considered to be a "Russian fifth column": an ethnic cleansing bordering on extermination.

As early as 1914, tsarist war plans included supporting the uprisings of Christian minorities (like the Armenians) and Kurdish minorities against the Ottoman regime [Michael Reynolds, *Shattering Empires*, 2011]. Up to 1920, London had also believed it could pursue the same policy, airing plans for the creation of independent Armenian and Kurdish states as well as Arab and Jewish states in Ottoman territories. Supporting the Zionist movement in Palestine – Abitbol continues – was also considered a means of influencing Russian "Jewish revolutionary circles" and preventing a separate peace with

Germany. Less well known is the fact that the Balfour declaration was modelled on the May 1917 declaration by Jules Cambon – the secretary-general of the Quai d'Orsay [French foreign ministry]. In the declaration, France "pledged to help the rebirth, through the protection of the Allied powers, of the Jewish nationality" on lands from which "it had been driven out for many centuries". Paris, whose Jewish community was not particularly supportive of Zionism, deplored the "cynical British game" of backing "both Jews and Arabs", but nevertheless understood the need to "keep Russia in the war". Additionally, it saw no advantage in turning the Zionists, who were "perhaps the victors of the future", into "irreducible enemies" on the frontier of the French possessions in the Levant.

Balfour presented the British declaration on November 2nd, 1917, not to Weizmann, but to Lionel Walter Rothschild, who headed the British branch of the renowned financial dynasty and later supported Zionism. The Paris declaration – Abitbol points out – also served to weaken the resistance of the current in the London cabinet opposed to supporting the Zionist movement. This current was led by Curzon and Edwin Montagu [1879-1924] – the Secretary of State for India and leader of the Liberal party until 1916. Curzon considered a Jewish settlement impracticable because it would arouse Muslim protests against London. Montagu, for his part, was a proponent of Jewish assimilation into British society, and feared that establishing a Zionist State would be to the detriment of the Jewish diaspora, who would thereafter be held in suspicion for their "dual national allegiance".

Ben-Gurion's Ottoman sympathies

Laurens notes how the world war threw European Zionism, an "international movement", into a "condition of paralysis", as its various national components committed themselves to the service of the war effort in their respective states, including a "mobilisation of propaganda towards neutral countries". In Sykes's depiction, Zionism could operate as "the nationalist antidote to Jewish internationalism". It may be added that the Young Turk regime was a manifestation of nationalism within the Ottoman body politic; London, however, saw it as conditioned by international Jewish finance and Freemasonry, factors that supposedly contributed to its pro-German orientation [D. Fromkin, *op. cit.*; S. McMeekin, *The Ottoman Endgame*, 2017].

Pro-Ottoman sympathies were present in the ranks of Zionism in Palestine. David Ben-Gurion celebrated the 1908 revolution with demonstrations in Jerusalem, arousing the anxieties of the Sephardic Palestinian and Turkish communities, who were fearful that the enthusiasm of Russian immigrants would end up disturbing a five-century coexistence with the Ottoman regime. He even offered to enlist a Jewish militia to fight the British, recruiting men in the United States, where he had landed in 1917 after his expulsion from Palestine [T. Segev, *A State at Any Cost*, 2019]. Later, like his great political rival Vladimir Jabotinsky – the founder of right-wing Zionism – Ben-Gurion decided to enlist in the Jewish Legion in Palestine, alongside British troops, in 1918.

Ben-Gurion's pro-Ottoman sympathies were based on the belief that Germany would win the conflict and that collaboration with Constantinople would enable Jewish settlement as one of the empire's "nationalities". Furthermore, the Austro-German armies, advancing into the Polish territories of Russia, emancipated the Jewish population from Moscow's anti-Semitic measures. More than 400,000 Jewish soldiers fought in the ranks of the tsarist army but were viewed with suspicion by their commanders because of their linguistic commonality with the Jewish populations of Austrian Galicia – Yiddish being a lingua franca with Germanic roots [Jeffrey Veidlinger, *In the Midst of Civilised Europe*, 2022].

The rise, decline, and recycling of Arab nationalism

London made the Balfour Declaration public on November 9th-10th, 1917, i.e., two days after the Bolsheviks had taken Petrograd. The USA had entered the war in April 1917 while, in December, British troops entered Jerusalem, accompanied by a delegation of British Zionists. The taking of the city, described by Lloyd George as "the Christmas present to the British nation", marked the end of Ottoman rule over Palestine. British financial support for the Arab revolt was worth £11 million, $1.3 billion in real terms and at today's exchange rate, with Thomas E. Lawrence – the renowned "Lawrence of Arabia" of Allied propaganda and champion of the Arab cause – playing the role of London's "great benefactor" to the Hashemites.

The Palestine campaign – writes Laurens – had a secondary significance in the conflict: Lloyd George, "an excellent connoisseur of the psychology of the masses", exploited its "symbolic significance" to bolster British morale, while the Allied forces in Europe were being killed in the bloody, drawn-out Battle of Passchendaele. Damascus fell on October 1st, 1918: as the city had surrendered to an Australian cavalry contingent, Lawrence organised a "mock conquest" by the Hashemites to allow Faysal to proclaim himself king of Syria. On October 30th, at Mudros, the Ottoman Empire signed the armistice. Faysal was the only Arab representative to attend the Versailles conferences obtaining an endorsement from the victorious powers. Weizmann was also present with the aim of supporting the Zionist cause.

Both Paris and London were opposed to the participation of delegations from colonial countries in the peace conference, since the principle of national self-determination, promoted by Wilson's presidency and contested as an objective of war by France and Britain, clashed with their respective colonial domains. There was therefore no Palestinian delegation at the Paris conference, which would have supported the incorporation of Palestine into "Greater Syria", the nominal Arab kingdom of Faysal. The Arab opinion carried no weight in the revision of the Sykes-Picot agreements: Palestine and Mosul were claimed by London, which accepted French control over Syria and Lebanon. The issue was settled with the secret Clemenceau-Lloyd George agreements at the end of 1919 and the introduction of mandated regimes over Syria and Palestine at the San Remo conference in 1920. It was a second diplomatic victory for Zionism, as the terms of the Balfour Declaration were preserved in the British Mandate. In 1918-19, London had considered giving the United States the mandate over Palestine. This option collapsed when the USA refused to join the League of Nations and steered toward isolationism. For Ilan Pappé – an anti-Zionist Israeli historian – America's absence made the League of Nations an "Anglo-French creature": it was impossible for the Arab, and specifically Palestinian, side to obtain a revision of the British mandate on Jewish settlement, except from London itself [*The Rise and Fall of a Palestinian Dynasty*, 2010].

Paris liquidated the Hashemite Arab kingdom in Damascus and the dynasty's Pan-Arab ambitions between July and September 1920. With the "settlement of 1922", entrusted to Winston Churchill, London recycled the Hashemites into the so-called "Sherif's realms" of Iraq, Transjordan and the Hejaz from which they were exiled in 1924, losing Mecca and Medina to their Saudi rivals. In dividing Palestine from Transjordan, London effectively created the territory of present-day Israel and Jordan. As a result, one of the dimensions of the *Palestinian question* surfaced.

The Political Families of Zionism and Palestinian Nationalism*

Until the "arrangement of 1922", writes Henry Laurens [*Les Crises d'Orient,* vol. 2, 2019], despite growing friction over Jewish settlement, Arab nationalism started from a "regionalist identity", which defined itself under five centuries of Ottoman domination. These are "the facts of history", evoked in 1899 after the first Zionist congress in Basel, by the former mayor of Jerusalem Yusuf Diya al-Khalidi, who came from a dynasty of Palestinian local nobility, in a letter to the Chief Rabbi of France Zadoc Kahn. In the letter, al-Khalidi wrote that "historically" Palestine "is your country, [...] but the destinies of nations are not governed by abstract concepts, [...] but by concrete facts". "Palestine is an integral part of the Ottoman Empire and, more seriously, is inhabited by others who are not Israelites. This reality of concrete facts, of the brutal forces of circumstances, leave Zionism no geographical space in which to realise itself [...] besides endangering the situation of the Jews in Turkey. [...] Achieving the goals that Zionism proposes will require [...] guns and battleships. And which power would put them at Herzl's service?" [M. Abitbol, *Histoire d'Israël*, 2024].

When two rabbis were sent on an exploratory mission to Palestine, organised in 1897 by Max Nordau, secretary to Theodor Herzl, their response upon returning was that: "the bride is beautiful, but she is already married to another man". It was an explicit refutation of Herzl's propagandistic thesis that Palestine was "a land without a people for a people without a land". This phrase was actually first used by British exponents of Zionism during their pilgrimages to Palestine in the mid-19th century. Both Herzl and the currents of left-wing Zionism relied on an economicist solution: the inflow of skilled labour and Jewish and European capital would increase overall productivity and also benefit the population of ethnic minorities, solving the "Arab question".

Zionism and the Arab question

This thesis was criticised by an exponent of so-called "cultural Zionism", Asher Ginsberg [1856-1927], for whom Jewish rebirth

* Gianluca De Simone, June 2024

had to take place through the recovery of its past. Ginsberg challenged the perception of Palestine as an "abandoned land". Not only was it not "abandoned", but its population would be ready to defend itself if it felt threatened: "Should the time come when our people in Palestine develop to the point of usurping [...] the place of the local population", he wrote in 1891, "the latter would not easily surrender" [Arturo Marzano, *Storia dei sionismi*, 2017].

Ber Borochov [1881-1917] and Aaron David Gordon [1856-1922] – the former a Marxist, the latter indebted to Tolstoyan thought – represented the main theoretical influences on the "socialist Zionism" adhered to by David Ben-Gurion. In 1906, Borochov asserted that the "liberation of the Jewish people" would only come about "by means of the labour movement" through "the class struggle". Writing in 1905, he envisioned peaceful relations with the Arab population, based on the "racial affinity" between the Jews of the diaspora and the *fellahin* (the Palestinian peasants), who were considered to be "the direct descendants of the Jewish agricultural community which had remained". Economic factors, Borochov continued, would encourage an assimilation of the Palestinian population, thanks to the development of productive forces. The Arabs, after all, were not and would not be a nation for long. Should the Palestinian minority not assimilate culturally, a "Jewish democratic society" would grant the Arabs "a cultural autonomy" within a Zionist "territorial autonomy".

Gordon, imbued with a "populist mystical vision", bequeathed the exponents of the second *Aliyah* (Jewish immigration from the diaspora) two pivotal concepts: *kibush ha-'Avodah,* the *conquest of labour*, the means of physical and spiritual regeneration of the Jewish people, and *kibush ha-'Adamah*, the *conquest of land*. For the new waves of Jewish immigrants, in practice this translated to: "Jewish land – Jewish labour – Jewish product" and the removal of the *fellahin* from the "lands they cultivated and felt were their own", even though they belonged to the *ayan,* the landowners, who were often absentee landowners residing in cities like Jerusalem. This was the case with the family clans of the Husseini and the Nashashibi, historically rivals, who in the 1920s vied for the leadership of the nascent Palestinian nationalism.

The instrument of Zionist agrarian colonisation was the Jewish National Fund (KKL), whose task was to buy land from the landowners. It was prohibited from reselling the land to non-Jews. It suited the *ayans* to sell land, at a premium, which was often located in difficult or malaria-prone areas. Once purchased, the land was fenced off and the Palestinian farmers removed. Although this was not an expropriation, since the peasants did not own the land, the population was nevertheless uprooted and forced to go elsewhere [Georges Bensoussan, *Une histoire intellectuelle et politique du Sionisme (1860-1940)*, 2002]. Until 1947, however, the Zionist movement had only managed to acquire 6% of the land in Palestine [Benny Morris, *Righteous Victims*, 1999; Ilan Pappé, *A History of Modern Palestine*, 2004]. In 1908, the Palestine Land Development Company (PLDC) was established, the brainchild of the German Arthur Ruppin [1876-1943], with the task of supporting and training Jewish workers for the land acquired by the KKL.

Ruppin hoped to create "a Jewish closed economy", in which producers, consumers and intermediaries should all be Jews [A. Marzano, *op. cit.*]. A model from which the *kibbutzim,* the agricultural colonies, arose, and which the historian Gershon Shafir defines as an "ethnic plantation colony", based on the colonisers' control of the land and their employment of immigrant labour from the motherland. "The struggle for the 'conquest of labor' in fact transformed the Jewish workers into militant nationalists who sought to establish a homogenous Jewish society in which there would be no exploitation of Palestinians [...] because there would be no Palestinians" [Gershon Shafir, *Zionism and Colonialism*, 1989].

Ben-Gurion's social-national theory

Ben-Gurion came to Palestine in 1906 as a militant of *Po'alei Tzion*, which was founded in Russia in 1903 and then spread to the Austro-Hungarian Empire. Its goal was to bring together the Jewish masses in Palestine, from which to conduct the class struggle. In 1919 *Po'alei Tzion* split into two factions and Ben-Gurion took over the leadership of its right wing: from it arose *Ahdut ha-'Avodah* ("Labour Union"), which in 1920 would give birth to the *Haganah* ("Defence") – the paramilitary force the Israeli army stems from – and the *Histadrut,* the trade union head office of which Ben-Gurion became general secretary.

According to Zeev Sternhell's critique, Ben-Gurion had begun to revise his socialist positions towards national ones, pointing to the "nation" as one of the engines of history alongside "class struggle".

The idea of Arab-Jewish class co-operation was abandoned in the late 1920s, with the emphasis shifting to the role of "national edification" by the Jewish working class. According to Sternhell, "socialism had become [...] a means for the realisation of Zionism" [Zeev Sternhell, *Aux origines d'Israël: entre nationalisme et socialisme,* 1996; Benny Morris, *op. cit.*; Zachary Lockman, *Comrades and Enemies,* 1996]. The title of Ben-Gurion's 1933 collection of essays points to this change: *From Class to Nation*. According to Élie Barnavi, "in the Zionism/socialism pair" the former prevailed: "the aims of the national struggle" took priority [*Storia d'Israele,* 1995]. The consequence was the exclusion of Arab workers from the main trade union organisation, which had become one of the pillars of state-building in Palestine. Despite this, there were Arab-Jewish trade unions, such as the railway workers' union that arose in 1919, in which a "common solidarity between Arab and Jewish workers" developed [Z. Lockman, *op. cit.*].

Berl Katznelson [1887-1944] was one of the founders and ideologists of the *Histadrut*, an anti-Marxist and fierce opponent of the Labour left. According to Sternhell, Katznelson was one of the main exponents of "neo-socialism" or "constructivist socialism", which drew on the experiences of the Italian "national syndicalism" of Filippo Corridoni, a follower of Mussolini, and those of the Belgian Maurice Déat. Katznelson initially advocated a peaceful coexistence with the Arab population, but in 1937, at a congress of the *Histadrut,* he argued: "I have always been of the opinion that this is the best solution [...] I have always thought that [the Arabs] should be transferred to Syria and Iraq" [Israel Shahak, "A History of the Concept of Transfer in Zionism", *Journal of Palestine Studies*, 1989].

Sternhell recalls how Déat's positions were also popularised by *Devar,* a daily newspaper of the Betar youth movement.

Chaim Arlozorov [1899-1933], a Marxist-trained exponent, contested Ben-Gurion's approach, condemning the "segregation" of the Arabs and advocating the line of Arab-Jewish integration. He was murdered in 1933 in Tel Aviv, possibly by members of the Zionist right. According to Tom Segev, one of the reasons for his murder was also that he was responsible for negotiating the "Haavara Agreement" ["transfer" agreement] with Nazi Germany. Signed in 1933, with a central role played by the President of the Reichsbank Hjalmar Schacht, this agreement allowed the emigration of German Jews to Palestine as a means to promote the export of German goods to the country. The agreement was harshly contested by the Betar, a youth organisation of the revisionist Zionist Party of Vladimir Jabotinsky, Ben-Gurion's great national-liberal opponent [Tom Segev, *The Seventh Million*, 1999; *One Palestine, Complete*, 2001; Edwin Black, *The Transfer Agreement*, 1984].

The revisionist Zionism of Vladimir Jabotinsky

Jabotinsky [1880-1940], born in Odesa into an "assimilated" Jewish middle-class family, advocated a return to Herzl's vision of a Jewish State in Palestine. He challenged the other two currents of secular Zionism, that of Labour and Chaim Weizmann's liberal centrism, also known as *general Zionism*. In his 1923 essay, *The Iron Wall*, he argued that Jewish and Arab nationalism were irreconcilable and needed to be separated, enforced by a "steel wall of Jewish bayonets", claiming one or both banks of the Jordan for the State.

According to the San Remo Accords of 1920, the *Yishuv*, the Jewish settlement, was limited to Western Palestine, the coastal strip.

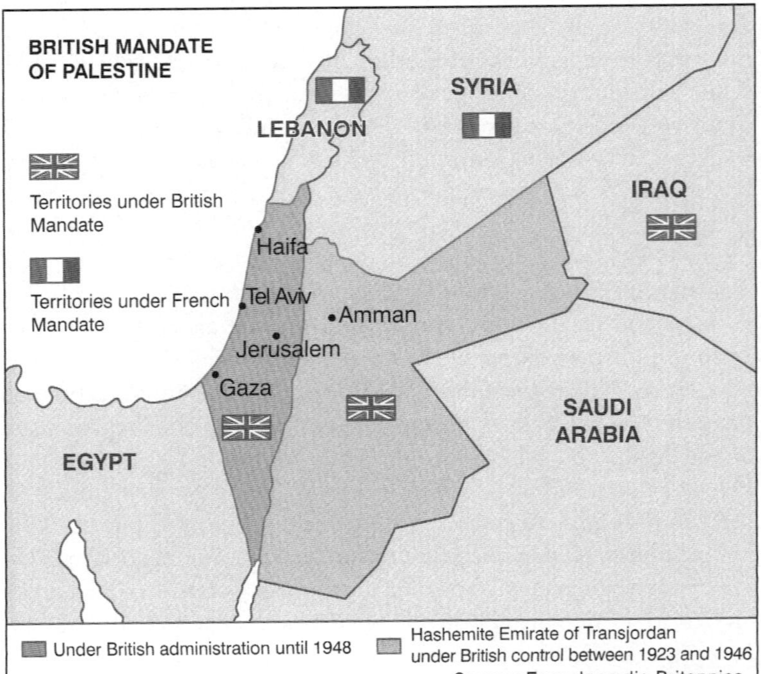

According to Pappé, a historian and exponent of the anti-Zionist Israeli left, the "settlement of 1922" and the division of Palestine from Transjordan created the "western shore", today's West Bank, which would later be annexed by Amman in 1950 and occupied by Israel in 1967. Churchill's partition had assigned it to the Hashemite kingdom, but the "demographic reality made the enlarged kingdom a de facto Palestinian State". Palestinian nationalism, emerging, from the second half of the 1930s, believed it could use this fact to challenge the legitimacy of the monarchy, at least in the West Bank [Ilan Pappé, *The Rise and Fall of a Palestinian Dynasty*, 2010].

Jabotinsky's revisionist concept aimed, at least until the 1930s, at the "revision" of the British mandate on Palestine, in collaboration with London. Jabotinsky, a cosmopolitan personality, studied in Italy from 1899 to 1903, calling it his "spiritual homeland". He was an admirer of both the *Risorgimento* experience, in particular of Mazzini and Garibaldi, with whom he identified, and the idealism of Benedetto Croce. He wrote several articles for *Avanti!*, an Italian socialist newspaper, on Russian affairs and was a pupil of Antonio Labriola. According to the writer Arthur Koestler he was a "national-liberal [...] in the revolutionary tradition of 1848"; in Walter Laqueur's opinion he was "a Sorelian who may have never read Sorel" [*A History of Zionism*, 2003]. He also expressed a certain admiration for Mussolini's fascism, in particular his growing hostility to socialism and communism after 1917.

Pro-fascist sympathies were most pronounced within the "maximalist" current of revisionist Zionism, from which emerged the paramilitary organisations Etzel (or Irgun) and Lehi (known as the Stern gang), both splits of the Haganah (the Labour militia). Jabotinsky, an admirer of British parliamentarianism, contested the hegemony of Zionist Labourism and aimed at a Jewish State supported by a middle class of Ashkenazi origin and rooted in small and medium-sized industry. He fiercely opposed what he called the "union dictatorship" of Labour. In 1925 and 1935, disagreements with the Zionist leadership led him to form *Ha-Zar*, the World Union of Revisionist Zionists, and *Ha-Zach*, the New Zionist Organisation.

The antagonism between revisionists and Labourists became, Barnavi writes, "without limits": the former described Labourists as "red swastika"; the latter called Betar activists "fascists and brown shirts" shirts" [*Storia d'Israele, op. cit.*]. Betar accused the Labour leadership of compromising with the Nazis over the Haavara Accords; Labour accused Betar of a tactical alliance with the movement of Symon Petljura [1879-1926], who was considered responsible for the anti-Semitic pogroms in Ukraine during the civil war and was murdered by a Jewish anarchist in Paris [T. Segev, *op. cit.*; Jeffrey Veidlinger, *In the Midst of Civilised Europe*, 2022]. According to Sternhell, the "class collaboration" in Palestine between Labour and the Jewish bourgeoisie, entangled in a symbiotic relationship, prompted Jabotinsky to seek a "mass base" in the petty bourgeoisie in Poland, as a section of the Polish Jewish masses was not always supportive of "the elitism of the Labour pioneers and their disdain for traditional Yiddish culture". Jabotinsky also realised that Labourism, in its work of national edification, had become "financially dependent" on funds from Jewish diaspora communities. It was Betar and the revisionist right that took control of Jewish emigration from Poland, but also from Germany.

Palestinian nationalism

Barnavi, Abitbol and Dan Vittorio Segre [*La Metamorfosi d'Israele*, 2006] point out that a major advantage of Zionism over Arab nationalism was its European matrix, with its nation-State models. Palestine in Ottoman times was a backward rural province whose territorial definition took place from 1856 onwards. Its ruling class took the form of urban local nobility, linked either to the Ottoman administration, the *effendiya*, or to the *ayan,* the landowners, via clan relations. In the Palestinian sphere, proto-nationalist formulas were borrowed from similar Egyptian and Syrian-Lebanese ones, often produced by the Arab-Christian minorities, which also recycled French and European anti-Semitic theories. [M. Abitbol, *op. cit.*].

As mentioned, the main figures of Palestinian nationalism were the Husseini and Nashashibi clans, both settled in Jerusalem and marked by centuries of rivalry. Between the 1920s and 1948, the leading figure of Palestinian nationalism was Hajj Amin al-Husseini [1897-1974], uncle of Yasser Arafat, the future leader of the PLO. From 1921, Husseini occupied the position of Grand Mufti of Jerusalem, the highest religious authority in Palestine, which is highly important in the Islamic world. Trained partly in Cairo and partly in Istanbul, in the school of administration, he was enlisted as an artillery officer in 1914. From 1918 he was close to the circle of Faysal's ephemeral kingdom of Syria and a partisan of Pan-Arabism.

An anecdote gives an idea of the contradictory relations between the various factions and the British authorities. In April 1920, following the confessional clashes at the Tomb of Moses, which according to Pappé were triggered by the concentration of the Jewish Passover festivities and half a dozen Christian denominations in Jerusalem, Husseini had to go into hiding with a Jordanian Bedouin tribe after being sentenced to ten years in prison for holding fiery rallies against the British administration and the Zionists. Jabotinsky was also arrested for illegal possession of weapons. Herbert Samuel, the first British governor of the mandate, met Husseini by chance during a visit to the same tribe. He was dissuaded from arresting him by Bedouin elders, who reminded Samuel that the tribe had "a thousand guns" and was bound to protect Husseini by the "laws of hospitality". Samuel allowed Husseini to move to Damascus.

In May 1921 there were new and more violent clashes in Jaffa, later extended to other areas of Palestine, triggered by incidents during May Day marches between Labour militants and Jewish communists, with the latter demanding the establishment of a Soviet republic. The clashes between demonstrators and British police spread to the Arab community, causing about 100 deaths and injuring some hundreds more in six days. Samuel saw this as a nationalist confrontation and imposed a brake on Jewish immigration to Palestine, the increase of which was linked both to the pogroms that occurred in Ukraine and Poland between 1919 and 1922 and to the anti-immigration laws in the USA passed in 1922-24. The death of Grand Mufti Kamil al-Husseini in 1921 prompted Samuel to choose his successor from within the same family, appointing Hajj Amin on May 8th, soon after the uprisings. This office provided the new Mufti with considerable financial resources, including those allocated to the Supreme Islamic Council, which he headed from 1922 to 1938, increasing his political-religious role in Jerusalem and Palestine.

The Grand Mufti between anti-Zionism and real estate deals

Husseini is remembered as the instigator of the violent riots of 1929. These were linked to the mutual provocations between Muslim and Jewish confessions, especially by Betar, around the Temple Mount and the Esplanade of Mosques. Arab social conditions also weighed heavily, with the development of large slums around urban centres. Husseini then played a role in the 1936 uprising and collaborated with fascism and Nazism in the 1940s. But his relationship with the British and also with the Jews was not always dictated by hostility. Personal and family interests often counted.

At least until 1936, Husseini pursued a policy towards London aimed at obtaining a revision of the Balfour Declaration, while being careful not to damage British approval, which he and his family depended on to stay in power. Pappé recalls that one of his projects, the creation of a luxury hotel, the "Palace Hotel", to accommodate religious tourism in Palestine (both Jewish and Christian) was carried out by the construction company headed by Tuviah Dunya, Chaim Weizmann's son-in-law. On the second day of digging the foundations, the contractor found ancient Islamic tombs. The Mufti ordered him to proceed with the work, but to keep it secret, as the Nashashibi family would not hesitate to accuse him of "desecration".

Dunya became a personal friend of Husseini, who used him as a channel to communicate with the Zionist leadership, letting it be known that his opposition to the partition of Palestine was "not personal but political": "If I announced to my people that I had reached an understanding with the Jews, based on concessions, the entire Arab people would ostracise me and I would be denounced as a traitor who had sold out his homeland". The "Palace Hotel" was closed in 1934 for the construction of the rival and more luxurious "King David".

Sheikh al-Qassam and the Arab revolt

The real figurehead of the Arab revolt of 1936-39, mainly against the British occupation, was not Husseini, who according to various sources was taken by surprise and only later assumed leadership, but Sheikh Izz al-Din al-Qassam [1882-1935]. Born near Latakia, Syria, al-Qassam studied at the al-Azhar University in Cairo where he initially embraced Salafist ideology, which opposed Ottoman institutional Islam. In 1911, he supported *jihad* ("holy war") against the Italian invasion of Libya. In 1914, he joined the Ottoman army and led guerrilla actions against the French in the early 1920s. Repatriated to Haifa, he worked as a preacher and social reformer, even setting up an Arab trade union. Borrowing the model of the Muslim Brotherhood in Egypt, which had arisen in 1928, he built up a large following among the popular as well as the urban strata of Haifa, especially among the newly urbanised landless peasants.

Between 1921 and the early 1930s, al-Qassam cooperated closely with the Grand Mufti, but their relationship worsened considerably, according to various sources, due to his independent activism, critical perhaps of Husseini's more cooperative approach which refused a decisive break with the British [Élie Kedourie, *Zionism and Arabism in Palestine and Israel*, 1982]. Al-Qassam also started a secret society, the "Black Hand", through which he organised and conducted guerrilla and terrorist actions against the British and Zionists. He was killed in November 1935 by a section of the Anglo-Palestinian police. The affair triggered massive demonstrations and strikes throughout Palestine.

For Ben-Gurion, the death of al-Qassam represented "an educational myth" for the younger generations of Arab-Palestinians, not unlike that of Iosif Trumpeldor [1880-1920], who founded the "Jewish Legion" with Jabotinsky in 1915 and who was killed in a clash with Arabs in Palestine. The militia of al-Qassam's followers, the Qassamiyun, unleashed a series of attacks against Jewish settlers five months later, starting the Arab revolt of 1936-39. It was the largest British colonial crisis since that of 1919-21 in Ireland and represented a civil conflict that would anticipate that of 1946-47 in Palestine, a presage of the first Arab-Israeli war.

The Partition of Palestine and the Formation of the State of Israel*

The period of Palestinian history ranging from 1929 to 1947 is often described in the historiography, especially following the outbreak of the Arab revolt, as a long, creeping civil war, characterised by tension and clashes both within the Zionist component – where rivalry between currents intensified – and within the Arab component. For the British Empire, Palestine had become an important component of its "imperial defence", serving as a territorial junction between the eastern Mediterranean, the Persian Gulf, and the Indian Ocean. Doubts, however, were growing as to whether the commitments made to the two nationalisms during the first imperialist conflict could be kept [Dan Diner, *Ein Anderer Kreig*, 2021].

The world economic crisis and the storm clouds of a new conflict – the first crack in the post-war order in 1931 with the Japanese occupation of Manchuria, then the rise of Nazism in Germany and the Ethiopian War in 1935 – heightened Britain's sense that its mandate in Palestine was more of a "burden" than a "benefit". According to the assessments of both the armed forces and the Colonial Office, London faced an "insoluble conflict" in Palestine, like the one they had faced between Catholics and Protestants in Ireland between 1919 and 1922 [D. Diner, *op. cit.*; T. Segev, *One Palestine Complete*]. The repression of the Arab revolt cost some 2,000 lives, of which 400 were Jewish and 150 British; London, in particular with the deployment of Marshal Bernard Montgomery from 1938, used methods not dissimilar to those that France would apply during the Algerian war [1954-62]. According to Segev, competition between the revisionist and Labour currents increased "to hegemonise not only the movement, but also the future Jewish State".

In the Arab camp, the Grand Mufti of Jerusalem, Hajj Amin al-Husseini, conducted an internecine conflict with the Nashashibi dynasty, involving contract killings [I. Pappé, *A History of Modern Palestine*, 2014]. Nevertheless, both Zionists and Arab nationalists tried to avoid a break with London. Husseini was forced into exile, first in Beirut, then in Damascus, and finally in Baghdad, following an attempt to get the

* Gianluca De Simone July-August 2024

Arab countries that had gained formal independence from England (Egypt, Iraq and Saudi Arabia) to intervene, in order to induce London to disavow the Balfour Declaration and stop Jewish immigration to Palestine. This Pan-Arab solicitation troubled London in the light of growing Arab sympathies for fascist Italy and Nazi Germany.

The Peel Commission and the "forced transfer"

According to Segev, the pro-German and pro-Italian positions in the Arab world and Palestine from 1939 onwards mirrored those of the Zionist movement towards the British government in 1917. London drew up no less than "ten partition plans" for Palestine in the 1930s and 1940s. The most famous was that of the Peel Commission in 1937, which envisaged the creation of two states and an international administration of Jerusalem. The Zionist leadership greeted it with caution, while it was rejected by the Arabs.

David Ben-Gurion, however, considered it the "declaration of independence" for the Jewish State, since it introduced the formula of the "forced transfer" of the Arab population. The commission referred to the precedent of the population exchange that had taken place between Turkey and Greece in 1923, at the end of the Greco-Turkish war, with Athens supported by London and opposed to Kemal Ataturk's nationalists. Since the early 1930s, Segev continues, the Jewish leadership had been drawing up plans for the transfer of the Arab population, debating whether it should be "forced or voluntary"; voluntary transfer, however, was understood not as based on "individual will", but rather on the basis of an "agreement between states".

The idea of a population transfer gained support in the 1940s. Before he died of a heart condition, Vladimir Jabotinsky, active in the USA, argued that "the world has become accustomed to the idea of mass migrations and has almost become fond of them", adding that "Hitler – as odious as he is to us – has given this idea a good name in the world" [T. Segev, *One Palestine Complete*]. The position was also reinforced by growing Arab refusals to accept a Jewish State in Palestine. This made the proposals ephemeral for a "bi-national solution" put forward by the currents of "moderate Zionists", such as the Brit Shalom ("Peace Alliance"), which found sympathisers, for example, in the Schocken family, of German origin, who became the owners of the daily newspaper *Haaretz* in 1935 and still own it today.

In a book with a tragically effective title, *The Seventh Million*, Tom Segev addresses the question of *how the Holocaust marked the history of Israel*. We will not go into a delicate and inevitably controversial debate;

we will simply consider his basic argument. Segev challenges the thesis that the Holocaust was Israel's founding event. In Segev's view, the Holocaust was wielded as a *diplomatic tool* by a now *Palestine-centric* Zionist leadership, which had supplanted Chaim Weizmann and the priority he had given to the relationship with London. Both Ben-Gurion and the revisionists considered, "pragmatically", that neither the *Yishuv* (the Jewish settlement) nor the belligerent powers could do much to *save the Diaspora* from Nazi extermination: the priority objective was the creation of the State of Israel. The issue, Segev goes on to say, marked a "rift" between the Labour leadership and the survivors of the Nazi extermination, most of whom were driven to emigrate to the future Israel by both the victorious powers and the recruitment activities of Zionist agencies. If it took the Zionist leadership a decade to absorb the survivors of the death camps, they became part of the Israeli moral factor and approach to the state's foreign relations.

London, which on the eve of the Second World War had reiterated its proposals for partition, which were then postponed until 1949, maintained a policy of appeasing Arab public opinion. Prime Minister Neville Chamberlain, in approving the 1939 White Paper, in which any further Jewish immigration was frozen, emphasised that if London was to "arouse the displeasure of anyone, it had better be of the Jews" [T. Segev, *The Seventh Million*, 2001].

The march to independence

The Arabs, in the opinion of Segev and other historians, made a "grave tactical error" in rejecting partition, since the British proposal would have allowed them to "gain time" to prepare for a war that, by then, was considered "inevitable" by everyone. A second Arab mistake was to seek collaboration with the fascist regimes. In 1941, the Grand Mufti obtained an audience with both Mussolini and Hitler, without obtaining any concrete commitment from the two powers. In April-June 1941, Diner recalls, the British overthrew the Iraqi and Iranian governments for their pro-Nazi positions, just as they did with the Vichy forces in Syria and Lebanon. Husseini, who had received support from pro-Nazi soldiers in Iraq, was forced to flee, first to Rome and then to Berlin. He soon became involved with Heinrich Himmler in facilitating the recruitment of Bosnian and Albanian Islamists into the ranks of the SS, who played a role in the anti-partisan struggle in Yugoslavia and the massacres of Jewish minorities in Albania. Having fled Berlin shortly before the arrival of Soviet troops, Husseini then found refuge in Cairo, where the Arab League had been established in 1944 on British initiative. The British waived his arrest in order to avoid conflict with the Egyptian monarchy and the Arab world in general. The outcome of the Second World War, which was tragic for the European Jewish diaspora, accelerated the economic and industrial development of Palestine: being the main logistical base in the eastern Mediterranean furthered the development of "hundreds of industrial enterprises" [D. Diner, *op. cit.*]. London, between 1918 and 1939, had already invested in infrastructure projects, for example the expansion of the port of Haifa, the road network towards Iraq and the Gulf, and the railway network. With the development of the refineries and their pipelines from the Gulf, as Benny Morris recalls, Haifa was also the metropolis where Arab-Jewish workers" solidarity was greatest, especially in the refineries of the British-owned Iraq Petroleum Company. It was a class solidarity shattered by the blows of Arab and Jewish terrorist reprisals [B. Morris, *Righteous Victims*, 2001; I. Pappé, *op. cit.*].

The "saison" and the war of independence

The Zionist congress held in May 1942 at the Biltmore Hotel in New York was the Labour Zionist leadership's turning point from a pro-British standing to a pro-American one. Ben-Gurion was convinced that the outcome of the conflict would determine the birth of the Jewish State [D. Diner, *op. cit.*]. Nevertheless, as in 1917, he offered military personnel for the Allied effort, also weighing up the support for the British Empire expressed by other anti-colonial movements, e.g., that of Mahatma Gandhi and the Indian Congress Party. As the *Lehi* (the so-called Stern gang) and the *Irgun* launched an anti-British terrorist campaign from 1944 onwards, Labour adopted a balance of cooperation and conflict with the British authorities, fearing above all that London's withdrawal, decided upon in 1947, would create an administrative "power vacuum" in Palestine. Both Segev and Colin Shindler [*The Rise of the Israeli Right*, 2015] point out that to a large extent the nationalist confrontation between the Jewish currents, while at times heading towards the risk of a "civil war", was a competition over "patriotic credentials".

In 1944-45, the Labour leadership supported the British repression against Irgun and Lehi, in what is remembered as *la saison*, or "the hunting season". But Labour also tacitly supported Irgun and Lehi in their "counter-terrorist" actions against the Arab element, helping them with its own special units, the *Palmach*. The *Palmachniks*, Segev writes, were animated by an ethos that combined the egalitarianism of the *kibbutzim* (members of agrarian cooperatives), "puritanical customs" and a "great admiration for Stalin". He also points out how by 1947 London had come to believe that the strategic value of the mandate had declined. Britain had not been driven into Palestine by "economic interests", but by a combination of factors: it was "economic reasons", the decline of its global position, accelerated by the Second World War, that dictated its "exit from the scene".

The Palestinian "catastrophe"

Palmach, Haganah, Irgun and Lehi were integrated into the national army in 1947. However, the right-wing paramilitary formations, Morris recalls, were considered "hostile" to the Haganah during the 1947-48 Arab-Israeli conflict [Benny Morris, *1948*, 2004]. In a confidential report submitted to the government, the Haganah intelligence services reported that "15 to 20% of the Arab population" had been driven out of their villages due to the activities of Irgun and Lehi.

The conflict was divided into two phases. In February 1947, London announced its withdrawal from Palestine and in November the UN General Assembly announced the adoption of Resolution 181 for partition, with the support of the major powers, but not of London and the Arab League. From December a substantial civil war began, with Arab attacks and Jewish reprisals. In January 1948, irregular Arab militias began to flow into Palestine, and managed to besiege Tel Aviv and Jerusalem in March. The Haganah began to receive arms shipments from Czechoslovakia and the Zionist leadership drew up the so-called Dalet Plan, which envisaged the defence of the borders and the possible destruction of Arab villages, inside the Jewish State, which were considered difficult to control. Pappé [*The Ethnic Cleansing of Palestine*, 2008] and numerous Palestinian historians considered it the plan for the expulsion of the Arab majority. Morris, an exponent of the Israeli "new historians" current, who later adopted a neo-conservative position, attributes the *Nakba* (literally "the catastrophe": the exodus of 700,000 Palestinians) to the dynamics of military confrontation, with the populations closely intertwined. He acknowledges that Jewish forces committed no less than 40 massacres, the most infamous of which took place in the village of Deir Yassin, in addition to the deliberate destruction of hundreds of others.

PALESTINE: THE PARTITION PLAN OF THE PEEL COMMISSION, JULY 7TH, 1937

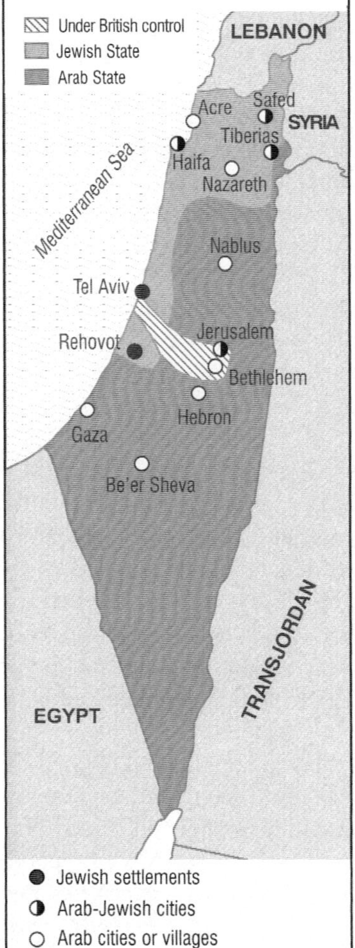

Source: Encyclopedia Britannica.

PARTITION PLAN APPROVED BY THE UN GENERAL ASSEMBLY, NOVEMBER 29TH, 1947

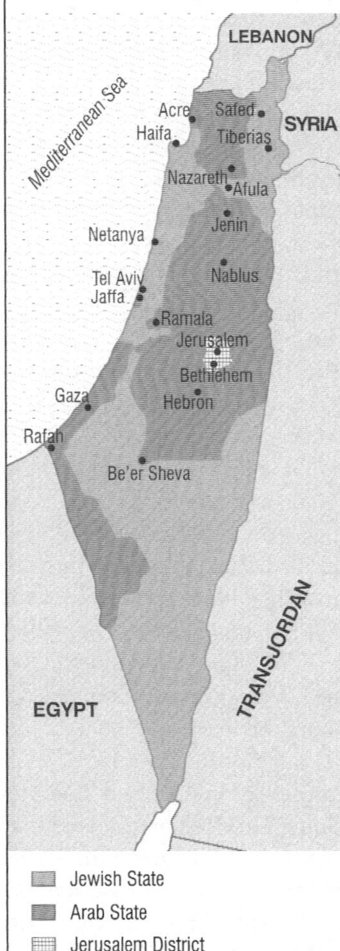

Source: Encyclopedia Britannica.

In the affair of the "concept of transfer", Morris admits the role of Zionist thinking, namely the need to obtain a "demographic majority" for the newly-born State of Israel. Similarly, he highlights the fact that Ben-Gurion did not issue "written instructions" or formal endorsements that could incur political or moral responsibilities for the State of Israel. He also emphasises how the Zionist leadership had, as a precaution, examined historical precedents, from the Greco-Turkish population transfer in 1923 to that of the Armenian and Kurdish question between 1915 and 1926. The practice of expulsion, he adds, provoked a lively debate within the various currents of the Mapai, the Workers' Party [B. Morris, *Righteous Victims*, 1948]. Eli Barnavi speaks of decisions dictated by Ben-Gurion's "realpolitik", in the face of an Arab component that could act, even with regard to the minority remaining on Israeli territory after partition, as a "fifth column" of hostile Arab countries [*History of Israel*, 1995].

The second phase of the conflict began with the intervention of Arab regular forces [May 1948-July 1949]: their poor coordination and the better preparation and numerical supremacy of the Jewish forces, which had swelled in the course of the fighting, led to Israeli victory.

The 1947-48 conflict was the bloodiest for Israel: around 6,000 dead, military and civilians, or 1% of the Jewish population. Casualties on the Arab and Palestinian side are estimated at 5,000 to 15,000. The Rhodes Armistices, signed separately between February and July 1949 with each of the warring Arab countries, defined the borders until the 1967 conflict, leaving Israel with 78% of the territory of Mandate Palestine, with the remainder occupied by Egypt and Transjordan. Compared to the UN plan, Israel acquired 30% more territory.

Segev points out that the same partition plan adopted by the UN implicitly endorsed a dynamic of territorial expulsion of populations. This had manifested itself at the end of the Second World War not only for 12 million Germans, but also with the "forced repatriation" of Poles, Ukrainians and other minorities in Eastern Europe, both before and after the Yalta Accords [K. Lowe, *Savage Continent*, 2013]. Between 1947 and 1950, the newly founded State of Israel, in addition to integrating the survivors of the Nazi extermination, negotiated with countries such as Poland, Romania and Hungary for the transfer of their Jewish minorities, "at a high economic price" in the form of trade concessions.

Israel in the contention for the Middle East

Between 1949 and 1956, as Morris recalls, Israel conducted its "long border war", in particular with "reprisals" in Jordanian territory, not only to hinder the infiltration of Palestinian peasants, not always motivated by guerrilla actions. The Palestinian and Arab defeat in the 1948 war can be attributed both to the lack of real leadership, with the figure of the Grand Mufti overwhelmed by the outcome of the conflict, and to the divergent calculations of the Arab countries.

The thesis of Avi Shlaim, another exponent of the Israeli school of new historians, refers to the dynastic interests of Jordan, and to its substantial "collusion" with Israel over the partition of Palestine, with the West Bank annexed in 1950 to the Hashemite kingdom. He also points to the rivalry for the leadership of Pan-Arabism between Iraq, Jordan, Egypt, Syria and Saudi Arabia, and to the territorial interests of Israel's neighbouring states. In Shlaim's opinion, each State tried to bilaterally negotiate peace agreements, only to be often hamstrung by their "Pan-Arab constraint" into the non-recognition of the Jewish State [A. Shlaim, *Collusion across the Jordan*, 1988; *The Iron Wall*, 2001]. In other words, both the Palestinian national pretext and the Jewish national pretext were used by the Arab bourgeoisies in their mutual rivalry as well as in the dispute between the various imperialisms.

The second Arab-Israeli conflict, in October 1956, saw the collusion between France, Israel and Britain in the context of the Suez crisis, the nationalisation of the Canal by Gamal Abdel Nasser's regime. For Israel it was a pre-emptive war, fearing the military reinforcement of Egypt, a country that, according to Barnavi, Ben-Gurion considered "the only true State" in the region, similarly to Turkey and Iran: the other Arab regimes were mere clusters "of tribes and clans". The Franco-Israeli-British "collusion" aimed at destabilising or overthrowing Nasser, who supported the struggle for independence in the Maghreb, especially in Algeria, and threatened not only Anglo-French control of the Suez Canal, but also the British position in Jordan. However, the operation met with joint opposition from Washington and Moscow, which blocked it, leading to the fall of Anthony Eden's government. For James Barr, London had misunderstood the degree of Washington's hostility towards Nasser, when the Eisenhower administration had authorised the CIA to consider his removal. London's initiative was a gamble in the middle of the American election campaign and during the Russian suppression of the Hungarian uprising. Washington forced Britain to back down, prompting a sterling crisis and threatening an oil embargo. Moscow threatened military action [J. Barr, *Lords of the Desert*, 2018; W. Bass, *Support Any Friend*, 2003].

The period 1945-57, according to many Israeli historians, was also the apogee of Franco-Israeli relations and of a line of connection with Europe, pursued by Shimon Peres and Ben-Gurion himself. In addition to nuclear collaboration with the Jewish State, France was also its main supplier of armaments. The 1956 conflict, despite Egypt's military defeat, gave Nasser a leadership role in the Arab world, creating the preconditions for the 1967 conflict. However, for both Barnavi and Dan Vittorio Segre [*The Metamorphosis of Israel*, 2006], it determined a decade of pause for the Jewish State, which was busy absorbing a million Sephardic diaspora immigrants from Arab countries (Yemenite Jews, Iraqis, Moroccans) and from Iran, after negotiating the post-war reparations agreement with Federal Germany.

The "mizrahi" immigration and "gush emunim"

Ben-Gurion's agreement with Konrad Adenauer aroused fierce protests in Israel, led by Menachem Begin, who succeeded in 1943 to the leadership of the revisionist current and secretary of Herut, the centre-right formation. It was not until 1960 that the revisionist current joined the Histadrut central union. Until 1967, with the accession of the government of national unity that arose on the eve of the Six-Day War, the Israeli political order had a centrist orientation, centred on the alliance between Mapai and the religious Mafdal party. The economic structure was largely consolidated in the State-capital or strongly dirigiste form, also due to the need to ensure the development and absorption of the new immigrants, called *mizrahi* or *mizrahim* ("orientals") by Israeli sociology.

This component, with different customs and characteristics to the Ashkenazi bloc of Central and Eastern European origin, emerged during the 1960s and 1970s as the main mass base of the Israeli centre-right, also helped by the confrontation for the succession to Ben-Gurion within Mapai. The mizrahim, writes Abitbol, contested the dominance of the Ashkenazi establishment in the institutions, representing large sectors of the Israeli proletariat, which experienced substantially worse economic conditions and even discrimination. *Haaretz*, for example, described immigrants of Yemenite and Moroccan origin in almost racist tones, as "more Arab than Jewish", due to rituals, customs and a lumpen-proletarian background. For Barnavi, the "Moroccan immigrants" in particular were the most intolerant of the social discipline imposed by Labourism. In the early 1970s, a movement of social demands was led by the *mizrahi* component with the so-called "black panthers", in which Pappé himself militated, an explicit reference to the Afro-American militantism that arose in the American ghettos.

The second force that emerged in the aftermath of the 1967 victory was the national-religious movement of the *gush emunim* ("faith bloc"), whose social background was the Labour middle class: it adopted a national-Messianic conception of the State of Israel, promoting the colonisation of the occupied territories. This current was viewed with sympathy by Labour exponents such as Shimon Peres and Moshe Dayan, who considered it a new incarnation of the spirit of early 20th century "Zionist pioneer-ism". In 1965, the two exponents of the "young Labour Guard", considered by Ben-Gurion as his successors, followed him in seceding from the Mapai, giving birth to the Rafi. The *gush emunim* was formed in 1970 and was dominated by the former disciples of Rabbi Zvi Yehuda Kook, for whom all the events that happened to the Jewish people, from the Shoah to the creation of the State of Israel up to the victory of 1967, were "the premises of redemption", hence the fulfilment of biblical prophecy [M. Abitbol, *Histoire d'Israël*, 2024; I. Zertal, A. Eldar, *Lords of the Land*, 2007].

The Palestinian Question in the Chain of Conflicts in the Unstable Middle East*

The four Arab-Israeli wars from 1947 to 1973, the Lebanese conflict between 1982 and 2000, and the second Lebanese war of 2006, together with the two *Intifadas* of the 1980s and 2000s are said to have caused, according to an estimate by the daily newspaper *Maariv* in 2007, around 20,000 deaths for Israel and 60,000 for Arabs and Palestinians. The subsequent conflicts, the five wars in Gaza including today's, bring the Arab total to around 100,000 victims. The estimate of deaths from what Dan Vittorio Segre calls the "Arab civil wars" (the Jordanian conflict of 1970-71, the Syrian civil war of the 1980s), the Lebanese civil war [1975-90] and the post-2003 Iraqi war is around 300,000 [Dan Vittorio Segre, *Israel: A Society in Transition*, 1971]. In the ongoing Syrian and Yemeni conflict which started in 2011, it is estimated that around 400,000 have been killed. The Iran-Iraq war [1980-1988], with much of the Sunni Arab world aligned in support of Saddam Hussein's regime, still remains the bloodiest inter-State conflict in the Greater Middle East, with about one million dead.

Roughly speaking, the costs of defining state structures in the region can be calculated at almost two million victims in three quarters of a century; conflicts that are amply funded by the various imperialist powers, both in arms and capital.

The Palestinian question in the Middle Eastern power game

Since 1948, the *Palestinian question*, has emerged both as a rallying point between the Arab bourgeoisies to oppose European colonial presence, and as a national pretext to stir up, manipulate, or conceal conflicting and often rival regional interests. For Segre, the clash over Palestine was in its essence a territorial clash, but due to the "revolutionary Pan-Arab pretensions" and the internal contradictions within Pan-Arabism it took on a "symbolic character" that ultimately made it "intractable" [*op. cit.*].

Segre looked at the connection between the Arab-Israeli conflict and the different state traditions that emerged after decolonisation,

---

* **Gianluca De Simone, September 2024.**

identifying three types of State. First, those founded on a "tribal-religious union", such as Yemen and Saudi Arabia, but also Morocco. Then there are those that preserved pre-colonial power structures, such as the emirates of the Gulf, but also Algeria and Egypt: hinged on a military structure with an Ottoman matrix, the *Mamluks*, they then evolved, in relation with the European powers, into "dynastic-republican" structures that, due to the centrality of the armed forces, drew on the Turkish Kemalist model. Finally, states such as Israel, Jordan, Lebanon, Iraq and Syria: their dominant feature has been the search for a "national identity", often by what Henry Kissinger calls "dominant (ethnic or confessional) minorities". The reference is to the Iraqi case, which can also be extended to Lebanon, Syria and Jordan. Israel, a multinational State with a 20% Arab population, also experiences a contradiction between Israeli and Jewish identity in the Zionist national ideology.

This process of states seeking consolidation, of dominant nationalities and stateless minorities, as well as of atavistic religious conflicts, is inseparable from the rivalry between the imperialist powers in the area. The Middle East remains an epicentre of contention well beyond the period of colonial domination and geopolitical stakes for London and Paris, given the crucial importance of oil in the post-war global development cycle. The struggle *for oil*, and the power confrontation *through oil*, based on the control of its transportation and of the Persian Gulf *energy artery*, have become permanent features of Middle Eastern wars and crises. Hence Arrigo Cervetto, in the editorial "Against War, Revolution!" [cf. p. 245] on the Arab-Israeli conflict of 1967, wrote:

> "Raised and nourished on intrigues with the European and American imperialists, the Arab bourgeoisie has long added the Soviet card to its hand. The Israeli bourgeoisie played and used the Stalinist card well in 1947, when the Soviet Union and the United States supported Zionism to oust from the Middle East the exhausted Anglo-French powers that were even dusting off Pan-Arabism, arming and organising it in order to stay afloat... on oil. The State of Israel was born not with the blessing of Jehovah, but with that of Stalin and Truman. Then, in 1956, it abandoned its godfathers, allied itself with Eden and Mollet, and marched towards Suez. The Sixth Fleet blocked the operation.
> The Middle East has now become an American sphere of influence, in which the Russians enter only to play the game of the United States. In fact, the Stars and Stripes waves over nearly all its oil. It will take ten years before the reinforcement of European capitalism attempts to return to the Middle East as a competitor and provokes another imbalance in the international and internal relations of the area. The

> alignment of the states resumes: the Soviet Union has room for its manoeuvres, and the United States expands the contradictions of its hegemony.
> The Arab and Israeli bourgeoisies play a secondary but indispensable role in all this process. Incapable, through weakness and rivalry, of seizing the oil, they can, however, as go-betweens, prepare the troops for a war from which only the great imperialist powers could profit today. Skilled at bartering favours and capital, they are quick to turn both into ideologies with which to stuff the heads of the workers, who are not even different as regards race, but only as regards the opium of their religions" [*Unitary Imperialism*, Vol. 2].

Here we find the relative weakness of the Arab and Israeli bourgeoisie emphasised, also with regard to the distribution of the oil rent, and the dominant role of the US and the defensive role of the USSR. Cervetto also points to European imperialism's attempt to "competitively reinsert" itself into the region as one of the triggers of the new crisis. Charles de Gaulle had initiated his "great Arab policy": in that context, in 1967 he suspended military supplies to Israel and warned it not to engage in pre-emptive war. According to Raymond Aron, Nasser would not have decreed the blockade of the Gulf of Aqaba, the trigger of the war, "if he had not believed he had France's backing" [*Le Figaro*, August 31st, 1967].

The fact remains that, in the years to follow, Europe would struggle to make its way back into the fold, caught between its energy dependence on the Middle East and its lack of strategic-military autonomy vis-à-vis the United States. As for the division of the energy rent, the situation would change radically with the war of 1973 and the *oil shock* that would shake the world economy. The colossal shift of revenue to the Middle Eastern bourgeoisies was equal to a few points of world GDP: more than enough to motivate and feed the sequel of conflicts and regional tensions, including the fostering of terrorist currents and religious radicalism.

The transformation of the "1922 arrangement"

Let us return to the post-World War II period. The arrangements that emerged in the Middle East from the outcome of the First World War, with the "1922 arrangement", changed between 1945 and the late 1950s [David Fromkin, *A Peace to End All Peace*, 1990]. In 1952 the Egyptian monarchy was deposed by the armed forces, which were dominated from 1954 by the figure of Gamal Abdel Nasser. The Ba'ath ("Resurrection") party was founded in Syria in 1947, a proponent of an Arab national socialism and Pan-Arabism, with Iraqi, Yemeni and Jordanian branches. From 1954 the Ba'ath entered the Syrian executive, which was marked by strong instability; in 1956, with the Suez crisis and the rise of Nasser as the main Arab leader, Damascus was balancing relations with the USSR, which had made a clearly pro-Arab turn.

Syrian instability and Nasserist influence led to the creation of the UAR, the United Arab Republic, between 1958 and 1961. Damascus, intolerant of Egyptian tutelage, seceded in 1961 and, in 1963, the Ba'ath, whose Pan-Arab ambitions competed with Nasser's, assumed the role of sole party in Syria. In 1966, however, the military component of which Hafez al-Assad, an Alawite official, was also a member, overthrew the "old guard" of the party, leading to a schism with the Iraqi branch.

In Baghdad, the pro-British monarchy had been overthrown in a military coup in July 1958 by General Abd al-Karim Kassem, a nationalist of Shia confession. The latter was in turn overthrown and killed by local Ba'athists in 1963; the consolidation of the Ba'athist regime did not take place until 1968, with the establishment of Saddam Hussein. Historian and diplomat Michael Oren [*Six Days of War*, 2002] writes that between 1949 and 1967 Syria experienced "sixteen different governments, almost one a year"; the feuds between Ba'athist, Nasserist and nationalist currents produced continuous purges, with fierce rivalry between the Syrian and Iraqi branches.

The Arab Cold War

The various socialist-national regimes in the Arab world, clients of Moscow and rivals of Pan-Arabism, including Algeria and Libya from 1969, in the context of the imperialist rivalry in the region found themselves engaged in the so-called "Arab Cold War". They were in a conflictual relationship with the so-called "moderate" and more pro-Western countries: Saudi Arabia, the Gulf emirates, Lebanon and Jordan. The latter was forced to balance its relations between Western powers, traditional Saudi dynastic rivals, Pan-Arabism and the Palestinian issue, having a 70% Palestinian population, some of whom were expelled from Israel in 1948.

Great power rivalry and the "Arab Cold War" were welded together in 1957, with the establishment of the "Eisenhower doctrine" for the Middle East [Eugene Rogan, *The Arabs*, 2009; Yevgeny Primakov, *Russia and the Arabs*, 2009]. Among of the fallout of this "cold" conflict was Egypt's participation in the Yemeni war in 1962-67, an "Egyptian Vietnam", according to Nasser himself. Cairo was forced to send around 70,000 men to confront local Shiite religious guerrillas, supported by the Saudis, the British, the Iranian Shah's regime and Israel itself. The intervention also led to a prolonged crisis in the Egyptian economy, which was heavily dependent on American grain supplies. These were not propitious conditions for the *rais* ("leader") of Cairo to open a conflict with Israel.

The 1967 conflict

According to his biographer Jean Lacouture, one of Nasser's greatest political limitations was his "inability to distinguish between imagination and reality", which made him a prisoner of both his own rhetoric and of that of others. The need to defend his prestige as the leader of the Arab world drove him in 1967 to a "show of force", according to both Primakov and Oren, an assessment that was also expressed by Yitzhak Rabin himself, then Israeli Chief of Staff. Nasser, alarmed by the possibility of an attack by Israel against Syria, according to information he had received from Moscow, deployed almost 100,000 men in Sinai after a succession of border clashes and the intensification of Palestinian guerrilla warfare. After demanding the withdrawal of the UN contingent, he imposed a blockade of the Strait of Tiran, the Jewish State's sea outlet on the Red Sea at Eilat and a terminal for Iranian oil supplies.

The conflict led to disaster and, with the Arab defeat, also to the decline of Pan-Arab ideology.

Although he baptised Palestinian nationalism, which arose in 1954 with the birth of al-Fatah and then developed with the creation of the PLO in 1964, Lacouture continues, since 1957 Nasser "had endeavoured to put the Palestinian question in the freezer" and preserve the *status quo* with Israel, barricading himself behind the position of "neither peace nor war". The French historian argues that Nasser's Pan-Arab ambitions were based on the pretence of pooling Arab oil revenues, especially those of Saudi Arabia, of which Egypt was almost totally deprived. This confirms our judgement on the "oil-soaked Arab bourgeoisies", as such now unable to perform a revolutionary function in the bourgeois-democratic sense.

According to Oren, Nasser made a "gamble" in 1967 that aimed to obtain a "diplomatic victory without any war". It was also the product of inter-Arab and internal rivalry between the *rais* and his Chief of

Staff Abd Hakim Amer for control of the Armed Forces: the latter vastly overestimated the capabilities and organisation of forces whose training was deficient and whose armaments were only 70-75% operational. For Oren, the Russian game was very ambiguous: to increase local tensions in order to "remind Arab countries of their dependence" on Moscow's support.

On the Israeli side, Oren recalls that David Ben-Gurion's main objective in the war of 1956 was to "deflate Nasser" and to also obtain assent from London and Paris to a rearrangement of the region: the creation of a Maronite State in Lebanon, the partition of Jordan between Israel and Iraq, and the Israeli annexation of South Lebanon up to the Litani river. A plan that neither London nor Paris was willing to go along with [Oren, *op. cit.*; Benny Morris, *Righteous Victims*, 2001]. In fact, in 1956 Israel only obtained the guarantee of the Red Sea outlet with the port of Eilat and the interposition of UN forces in Sinai.

Israel's decision to launch a pre-emptive strike in June 1967 was dictated by a condition of panic in Tel Aviv. The premiership of Levi Eshkol was strongly contested by Ben-Gurion, who did not want any war after the split of his party, Rafi, from Mapai in 1965, in the conflict over the internal succession to Ben-Gurion himself. But military top leadership was also decisive. According to Tom Segev, Oren and Morris, "the generals' putsch" in June 1967 imposed Moshe Dayan in the Defence Ministry, taking it from Eshkol [Tom Segev, *1967: Israel, the War and the Year that Transformed the Middle East*, 2007].

Jordan's decision on May 30th to establish a unified command with Egypt, Iraq and Syria was the occasion that allowed Tel Aviv to "realise the goal missed in 1948", Morris writes: the complete takeover of Jerusalem and the acquisition of the West Bank and part of the Golan Heights, as well as control of the source of the Jordan river, one of the elements of friction with Syria.

On the Arab side, all this came to confirm that Israel acted as a "western sentinel" in the region and reinforced the weight of the Palestinian card in inter-Arab politics. With the occupation of the West Bank and Gaza and the new wave of refugees, according to both Morris and Dan Segre [*op. cit.*], a Palestinian national identity was consolidated. The PLO always remained an umbrella organisation, traversed by a multiplicity of currents – Yasser Arafat's al-Fatah was one of the main ones – variously used by the Arab powers. The victory of 1967 affirmed Israel's role as the main military power, but animated, says Morris, a "nationalist chauvinism" even in Labour currents, although the path of territorial exchange to gain Arab recognition remained open.

The Yom Kippur conflict and the fall of Labour hegemony

Nasser, who died in 1970, had obtained at the Khartoum summit of the Arab League in September 1967 the "declaration of the three no's": no peace, no negotiations and no recognition of Israel. And the commitment to the constitution of a Palestinian State, accompanied, until 1970, by the so-called "war of attrition" between Egypt and Israel along the Suez Canal.

The Middle East *status quo* determined by the 1967 war was broken by the next round of hostilities in October 1973. According to Morris, Egypt and Syria "did not aim to destroy the Jewish State [...] aware that such an objective was beyond their reach and that, if

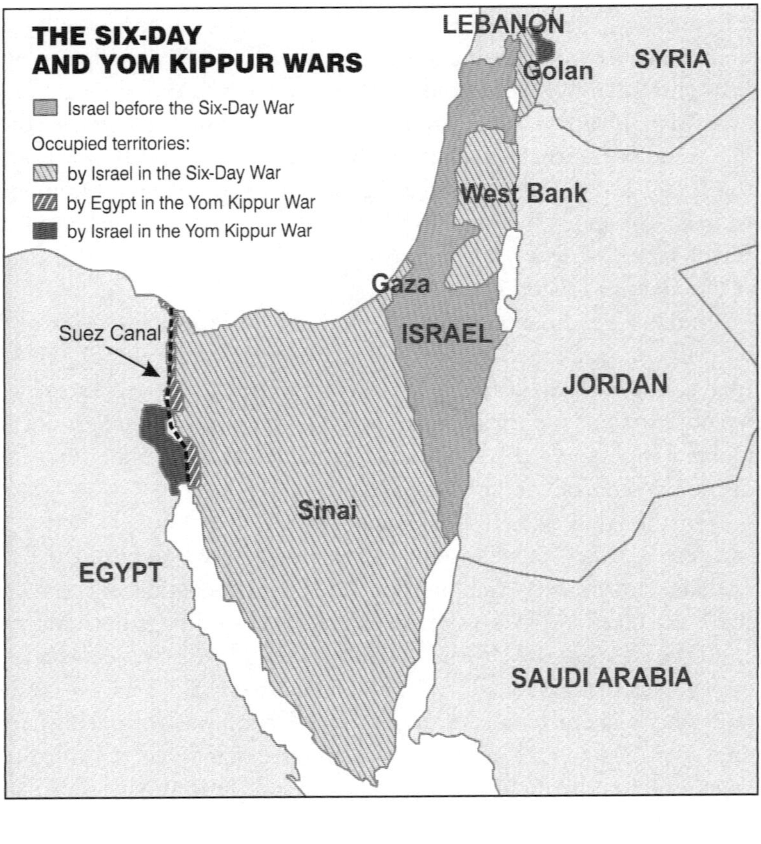

threatened with annihilation, Israel could use the atomic weapons it already possessed". It may be added that even in 1967, the nuclear dimension, i.e., the Israeli fear that Egypt might target the Dimona power plant, was a factor that drove Tel Aviv to conflict. In 1966, Oren recalls, Nasser had even warned Washington about the possibility that Cairo would engage in "a suicidal conflict" to prevent Israel from acquiring nuclear weapons, although he did not raise the issue again [*op. cit.*].

The Egyptian goal, Morris continues, was to acquire a strip of territory on the eastern shore of the Suez Canal and shake "the diplomatic immobility of Israel and the international community", the great powers. Damascus' goal was to take back the Golan Heights. Above all, for both, it was to "wash away the dishonour of 1967", which "would bring both regimes rich rewards", including "financial contributions from the rich oil monarchies". In any case, neither country nor their Arab allies stood for Palestinian nationalism. For both the Syrian regime and that of Anwar al-Sadat, Nasser's successor, national interests prevailed.

Israel won the conflict militarily, but politically its status of superiority was reduced. The war was also functional to Egypt's switching of allegiance, undertaken by Sadat to move Cairo from the Russian orbit to the American one, an achievement widely claimed by Henry Kissinger, then Secretary of State. The long wave of the conflict, in March 1977, brought about the end of Labour hegemony in Israel and the rise of the Likud, a centre-right coalition created in 1973 by Menachem Begin [1913-1992], which General Ariel Sharon joined.

The rise of Likud and the Lebanon War

Born in Belarus, Begin initially joined the socialist movement Hashomer Hatzair ("The Young Guard") that arose in Galicia in 1913. In 1929-30 he switched to Betar, the revisionist youth movement, and became its organisational head. In 1939-41, as a member of the Polish army, he was interned in a Stalinist *gulag*. Freed after the Allied accords for the reconstitution of the Polish army under the command of General Anders, Begin stayed in Palestine in 1942, becoming the head of the Irgun: as such, he was among the organisers of the 1946 attack on the King David Hotel, seat of the British military command in Palestine. In 1948 he refused to disband the Irgun, which in April had been responsible for the Deir Yassin massacre, one of the major massacres of the first Arab-Israeli conflict. In an attempt to get arms to the Irgun, Begin found himself embroiled in the "Altalena Affair", from the name of a ship christened with the pseudonym of Vladimir Jabotinsky, sunk by the Haganah on the direct orders of Ben-Gurion.

The "political earthquake of 1977", writes Michel Abitbol [*Histoire d'Israël*, 2018], led to the emergence of the Israeli Right as a government bloc, where the political balances defined by Ben-Gurion had ensured the dominance of Labour in connection with the religious Mafdal party. The turnaround was precipitated by Likud's ability to attract the vote of the *mizrahi* component with a national-populist discourse, including the Sephardim, as well as, progressively, the national-religious component, which arose after 1967. It was with Begin that Sadat drew up the Camp David Accords in 1978 and the peace with Egypt.

It was still under Begin that Israel slipped into the Lebanese civil conflict in 1982. The declared motivation was to purge from the country the "parallel State" created by the PLO and the various Palestinian factions. These factions had been expelled from Jordan in 1970-71, for the attempt, apparently supported mainly by Assad's Syria, to overthrow the Hashemite monarchy and establish a Palestinian State. This option was viewed favourably, Avi Shlaim recalls, by Likud exponents like Sharon, as a variant of the so-called "Jordanian option", intended to favour the final annexation of the West Bank to Israel [*Lion of Jordan*, 2008]. The Jordanian conflict, which has gone down in history as "Black September", saw a harsh repression of Palestinian guerrilla formations, costing between 5,000 and 15,000 lives.

The Lebanese conflict, with the siege of Beirut, was conceived by Sharon along the lines of Ben-Gurion's intentions in 1956, i.e., to create an allied Lebanese state with a Maronite leadership. The war succeeded in its objective of expelling the PLO from Lebanon, forcing it to retreat to Tunis. It was, however, one of the factors that led to the emergence of Hezbollah, the Shiite party-militia that arose from Palestinian factions of Maoist orientation, but entrenched among the largely rural populations of southern Lebanon, with the support of the Islamic republic of Iran [Christophe Ayad, *Géopolitique du Hezbollah*, 2024; Joshua Gleis and Benedetta Berti, *Hezbollah and Hamas*, 2012]. In the course of the siege of Beirut, the Maronite militias were responsible for the massacre of the Palestinian refugee camps of Sabra and Shatila, an equally bloody repetition of those committed in 1976. This led to Sharon's resignation as Defence Minister.

The Lebanese conflict, which turned into a quagmire for Tel Aviv's forces in 1983, also due to the country's growing economic difficulties, forced Begin to pass the baton to Yitzhak Shamir. From 1984, the latter had to launch a coalition government with Labour led by Shimon Peres, Rabin's eternal rival, who led the government between 1974 and 1977. In 1974, with the Rabat Congress, the Arab states recognised the PLO as the sole legitimate representative of the Palestinian people. In 1988 King Hussein of Jordan proclaimed the administrative separation of the West Bank, while in 1974-75 he had already envisaged a Jordanian-Palestinian federation. In fact, says Shlaim, Hussein's decision closed the prospect of a Jordanian option in the sense of a federal or confederal union. One factor was the outbreak of the first Palestinian Intifada in December 1987, which according to historians was a spontaneous movement of the West Bank population, which took both Israel and the PLO itself by surprise. It was also an opportunity for Hamas, the movement for Islamic resistance, which arose in Gaza and has been tacitly supported by Israel since the 1970s, to establish itself as a religious current of Palestinian nationalism, competing with Fatah and the PLO. In 1988 the leadership of the PLO recognised the legitimacy of the State of Israel and the creation of a Palestinian State in the West Bank and Gaza. The American endorsement, in fact, enabled the establishment of direct negotiations that would result in the Oslo Accords of 1993.

Fragmented and Rival Nationalisms in the Middle Eastern Maze*

The Zionist project, as a Jewish nationalist movement with a heterogeneous mass base, was a belated experiment in a national solution to the "Jewish question" in Europe. It set out to recover, both in an ideological and practical sense, the historical sovereignty of the Jewish people in Palestine, one of the cultural links of the diaspora, especially in Europe. It took root through two world wars, playing on the shift in the international balance of power and the process of decolonisation, i.e., the retreat from and decomposition of previous European imperial positions, and obtained the backing of the US and the USSR and later of the European imperialist powers. Palestinian nationalism, which was still immature and weaker, came out the loser.

The irreconcilable principles of the bourgeois theory of the State

Arrigo Cervetto pointed out that this also applied to other nationalities, e.g. the Armenians and the Kurds. Also, in Cervetto's analysis of the Falkland-Malvinas conflict between Argentina and Great Britain, we find a clarifying reflection: "The two irreconcilable principles of the bourgeois theory of the State", sovereignty and national self-determination, have "quarrelled over the centuries and reconciled only at the expense of those who did not have the strength to claim them". "The democratic theory of the State has never succeeded in reconciling them and the final verdict has always been up to the weapons whose deeds are commemorated in the history of each State".**

Claims to the right of national sovereignty, "besides clashing with those of other States, do not coincide with the right of peoples to self-determination upheld by a number of minorities". This is a condition in which all states find themselves, and is

> "the fruit of internal and external wars, multiform alliances, infinite historical circumstances, uneven relations of economic strength, and

---

* Gianluca De Simone

** "La nuova contesa imperialistica raggiunge il Sud Atlantico", June 1982, in *Opere*, vol. 4.

the use of organised violence. Most of the states recognised by the UN were formed in the last 35 years. Almost all of them incorporated populations of various ethnic origins and acquired their rights to national sovereignty by using the violence that colonialism and imperialism had used against them. Many of these States inherited borders drawn administratively by the old powers. Some of these States have already broken up or are on the point of doing so" [Cervetto, *op. cit.*].

From Beirut to Oslo

We find this theoretical framework again in the analysis done one month after the Israeli invasion of Lebanon in 1978. With regard to Palestinian nationalism, Cervetto wrote, it was crushed by the "storm of multiple and conflicting interests" that emerged around the Lebanese conflict: it was abandoned by all and left at the mercy of Israeli military supremacy, after having been cultivated and instrumentalised. By eliminating the PLO as a military entity, Israel aimed, among other things, to support "the pressure of the Palestinian bourgeoisie of the occupied territories towards integration into a market that was already proceeding rapidly in that direction" and make this the prevalent trend. The result, Cervetto continued, was not, however, a foregone conclusion, even though such a tendency towards integration existed in the Palestinian bourgeoisie.*

Opponents of the formation of a Palestinian State, particularly the Likud currents, such as Ariel Sharon, supported (and to some extent still support) the thesis that such a State already existed in the Kingdom of Jordan. The so-called "Jordanian option" was promoted by Labour currents, such as Shimon Peres, in the form of a regional common market and a customs union between Israel, Jordan and the Palestinian territories. This hypothesis was pursued with the Oslo Accords of 1993 between Yitzhak Rabin and Yasser Arafat and in the framework of a possible regional market. Cervetto evaluated it in the aftermath of the Camp David Accords between Egypt and Israel in 1978 and as a possible evolution of the Oslo Accords, which saw the agreement for the creation of a Palestinian entity. It was resurrected by the *Abraham Accords* of 2017-20 and was supported by Joe Biden's administration until the outbreak of the Gaza war.

It can be observed that the Oslo Accords were propitiated by changing international balances (the collapse of the USSR) and regional balances, the agreements on the conclusion of the Lebanese

---

* A. Cervetto, "L'invasione del Libano riapre la sanguinosa partita nel Medio Oriente", July 1982, in *Opere*, vol. 4.

conflict and the effects of the Gulf War of 1991. Two conditions of relative weakness weighed heavily. Israel was grappling with a crisis and with the economic transition from the previous state capitalist structures, which Likud, despite its liberist stance, had not touched. It also had to accommodate the latest wave of migrants from the former USSR, over 500,000 people. This offered Washington negotiating leverage in support of the conflict settlement, a $10 billion package which was wielded by the Bush administration. Finally, the first Palestinian Intifada in the West Bank and Gaza, from 1987 to 1990, highlighted the costs of occupation for Israel.

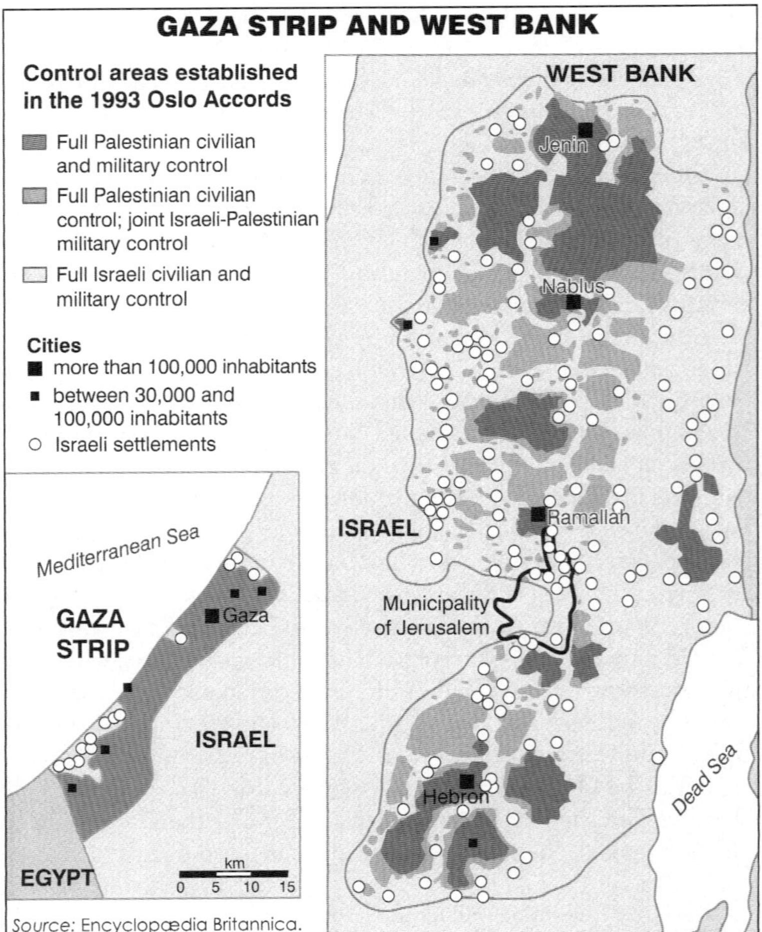

Source: Encyclopædia Britannica.

The other, greater weakness was that of the PLO. Exiled to Tunis after 1982, it gained American recognition at the end of the decade as its regional supporters faded away. Jordan formally renounced its role in the administration of the West Bank. Arafat's support for Saddam Hussein's Iraq in 1990-91 led to a reduction in funding by the Arab petro-monarchies. The Intifada itself, determined by economic issues, exposed the PLO to increasing political competition from Hamas and Islamist nationalism. The process of creeping colonisation of the West Bank by Israel, the competition between Palestinian currents, with the progressive assertion of Hamas, and the Gordian knot of Jerusalem determined first the crisis and then the stalemate of the 1993 agreements. This stalemate became a progressive collapse, in part due to the Palestinian civil war in Gaza in 2006-07, which saw the expulsion of Fatah from the Strip and the further subdivision of the Palestinian territory between the two nationalist currents; the West Bank went to the PLO and the Gaza strip to Hamas.

Benjamin Netanyahu's governments in 1996-99 accepted the withdrawal of the colonial settlements in some areas of the West Bank, such as in Hebron; Ariel Sharon implemented the withdrawal from Gaza in 2005, splitting the Likud to give birth to the centrist Kadima party ("Forward" from the slogan of the Israeli parachute units, commanded by Sharon in the mid 1950s). But from 2009 until today, the Netanyahu executives' choice has increasingly been to support the settler movement and play on internal Palestinian rivalry. Since then the number of players, from Qatar to Turkey to Iran, resorting to the Palestinian card as an instrument of influence and projection has also multiplied. Today, the two-State solution, with a Palestinian entity that would still be an economic satellite of the Jewish State and with limited sovereignty, is conditioned on the security arrangements negotiated between Washington and Riyadh: the Saudis would like the signing of a defence treaty with guarantees similar to those existing between Washington and Tokyo and support for the development of its own nuclear programme. Israel, in turn, would like a bilateral defence treaty with the US: in return it would have to accept a concession of sovereignty to Palestine. However, two open issues remain: Jewish colonial settlements in the West Bank and the question of a Palestinian capital in East Jerusalem, which is one of the most intractable issues in the Palestinian tangle.

A confederal or economic union solution, fertilised by international capital and the Gulf's oil revenues, has its own objective rationale and material basis, with the intersection in the region of various economic corridors: from China's Silk Road to the IMEC corridor between Europe and India. By the same token, however, there are just as many sources of tension between powers: from Iranian interests to those of Turkey, from Chinese to Russian interests.

Sharon's realism and cunning

Rivalries also run between the currents of the "two Zionisms", as Dan Vittorio Segre describes them [*Le metamorfosi di Israele,* 2006]: in the Jewish one, between the historical secular current and the national-religious one, to which the national-populist variant has been added during Netanyahu's twenty years in power; and in the competing Palestinian one, between ANO-Fatah and Hamas. The "from the river to the sea" slogan, wielded by Hamas, is also, in the opposite sense, a traditional claim of the Israeli right, nationalist since the 1930s and then national-religious since the 1970s. In the most extreme versions it becomes "from the Nile to the Euphrates", i.e., a reading of the "promised land" according to the biblical text.

Both Anwar Sadat in 1981 and Rabin in 1995 paid with their lives, the former a victim of the terrorist currents that emerged from the Muslim Brotherhood, the latter of the extremism of the national-religious right. Sadat for having signed the peace treaty in 1979, Rabin for the Oslo Accords. For Dan Segre, the latter did not realise that signing these agreements would lead not only to the "death of the PLO", but also "the end of the dream of greater Israel".

Paradoxically, Segre continues, it was Sharon who was "one of the big culprits" of the "trap" represented by the territorial expansion of 1967. He was "a war technician and a chieftain, stocky and crude", but also endowed with qualities that would allow the Jewish State to emerge. Among these was the gift of "cunning", defined in the Talmud as the quality of a man "who knows how to disentangle himself from situations that the wise man would never have entered". Although the opposite of Charles de Gaulle, Segre continues, Sharon had in common with him the quality of "political realism". It was what induced the General to abandon Algeria and Sharon the Gaza Strip: in both cases, "the demographic growth of the colonial territories" would have "distorted French and Jewish national identity". This capacity of Sharon was one which, according to Segre, his successors would not be able to emulate, not least because of the trauma caused by Rabin's assassination. According to Anshel Pfeffer, a columnist for *Haaretz* and biographer of Netanyahu [*Bibi*, 2020], that act had matured in a "civil war climate" in the Jewish State since 1993.

The civil war of Palestinian nationalism

On the Palestinian side, writes Paola Caridi [*Hamas: From Resistance to Regime*, 2012], the Fatah-Hamas competition was exacerbated. The Islamist movement had been entrenched in Gaza since the late 1930s, with a refugee population made permanent after the expulsion from the Israeli territories in 1948 and subsequently swelling in 1967. The personnel that emerged from the "second generation of refugees" had a close relationship with the "Palestinian diaspora in the Gulf monarchies", for example in Kuwait. It could count on a widespread network of aid organisations, as well as mosques and universities, set up with the help of the charitable organisations of the Arab world. From the 1970s onwards, Hamas benefited from the rise of political Islamism. Cervetto emphasised how the PLO was the sum of "military fractions", shared by different Arab bourgeoisies and with a "mass base represented by an uprooted population". Arafat himself, born in Cairo, claimed to be a native of Gaza.

The entrenchment of Hamas, as Israeli commentators themselves have recalled, was favoured by the political and military leadership in Tel Aviv after 1967. The aim was to have an Islamist, conservative and until the mid-1980s "quietist" competitor to the secularism tinged with the "Arab socialism" of the Nasserist and Ba'athist PLO brand. In some ways, according to the Indian analyst Brahma Chellaney, it was a move conceived along the lines of American policies towards the Afghan Islamist resistance against the USSR.

In the Fatah-Hamas conflict between the two specular currents of frustrated Palestinian nationalism, Fatah has sought both international and Israeli tacit support against its Islamist rivals. It suffered electoral defeat, in 2006, and then military defeat, with the hegemony of Hamas in the Gaza Strip and the expulsion of Fatah's military wing. The rivalry spread to the West Bank and Jerusalem. Hamas engaged in a maximalist race with its rival, with the tacit assent of Tel Aviv, but also of the Arab governments.

For the latter, Hamas has been an interlocutor and an instrument of influence. Egypt has repressed the Muslim Brotherhood at home, but has always used its branch in Gaza to support its role as regional mediator and exploit it in its triangular relationship with Tel Aviv and Washington. Some Gulf monarchies, such as Qatar and Kuwait, financed it and, during the Syrian war, Emiratis, Qataris, Saudis and Turks tried to use it against the Assad regime. Iran, via Hezbollah, has provided its military wing with ballistic capabilities and training. Hamas has an audience in Jordan, where 75% of the population is Palestinian and the devastating Gaza war puts pressure on the Hashemite dynasty, with growing calls to denounce the 1994 peace treaty with Israel.

"Frustrated lovers of Zion"

For Pfeffer, Netanyahu's political journey should be read through the lens of a dual ambition. The first is to establish himself as the new federator of the Israeli right, in a traditionally fragmented political landscape. This condition has been exacerbated by the relative decline of Labour and Likud as major parties, aided by massive Jewish immigration from the former USSR since the late 1980s. By introducing a kind of de facto presidentialism in a hyper-proportional electoral system, wrote Ran Halévi of the CNRS and commentator in *Le Figaro*, Netanyahu has given small parties, especially the national-religious ones, a "strong capacity for blackmail" and, often, a role as the balancing vote in government coalitions. The other ambition, Pfeffer continues, has been to establish themselves among the "founding dynasties of Zionism", like the Dayans or the Weizmanns. Originally from Lithuania, the Netanyahu family, for Pfeffer, typified the "frustrated lovers of Zion": figures of intellectual depth, but marginal in Jewish nationalism. The grandfather advocated a religious Zionism and was a "gifted orator", but did not develop a particular following. The father, Benzion, born in Warsaw, was an academic with ambitions as a political leader. As Vladimir Jabotinsky's secretary in the US, he had seen himself as his possible *dauphin*, but was eclipsed by other figures of "maximalist revisionism", linked to the Irgun. Faced with the continuing Labour hegemony in Israel, Benzion came to the conclusion that Zionism was "a failed project", advising his sons to pursue American careers. Which Benjamin did until the mid-1970s.

It was in the USA, however, that Netanyahu discovered the effectiveness of the television medium and his own oratory skills, tools that he translated into Israeli politics at the beginning of the 1990s when Likud was in a deep organisational and financial crisis; he thus managed, as an outsider, to make his way in the party hierarchy, dominated by the so-called "princes", the sons of historical right-wing exponents. Together with Rabin, Netanyahu can boast the fact that he is one of Israel's native-born premiers, as well as his record for political longevity.

In the crisis surrounding the Oslo Accords, with massive street agitations and a polarised confrontation, Netanyahu supported the settler movement, as did Sharon himself and other right-wingers, marching in the squares in rallies accusing PM Rabin of "treason", "selling off" the State of Israel, accompanied by death threats. A "forced" choice, writes Pfeffer, due to the fact that Likud "did not have enough militants" to "preside over the squares"; on the other hand, the settler movement, also cultivated by Shimon Peres and with roots in the Labour body, had been developing a significant mobilising capacity since the 1970s, as well as having sympathisers within the American right.

Rabin's assassination, reminiscent of Chaim Arlozorov's murder in 1933, which the Left attributed to revisionists, branded Netanyahu as the "inciter-in-chief" of the hate campaign, even though, Pfeffer acknowledges, other right-wingers, including Sharon, had launched "even more vitriolic" rants against Rabin. This branding, for Pfeffer, may explain Netanyahu's "deep-seated resentment" towards the mainstream media and the Israeli liberal world.

His emergence as prime minister in 1996 against Peres, himself unloved in the Labour ranks and Rabin's fierce rival, came about by only 30,000 votes, in the midst of a terrorist campaign and in spite of an international opinion – the Clinton administration and the EU – which openly supported the Labour candidate's victory. But, as the biographer of Peres, Michael Bar-Zohar [*Shimon Peres*, 2007], points out, international and Arab chancelleries "did not vote in Israel". Peres, again according to Zohar, became an interlocutor with Netanyahu, conducting regular evening visits to the premier's residence. Rabin, for his part, harboured "a visceral antagonism" towards Peres, whom he called "the saboteur-in-chief" when he was his minister of foreign affairs, and also "contempt" towards Netanyahu, considered politically "a lightweight".

Two Israels: Tel Aviv versus the "Kingdom of Judea"

The criticism traditionally levelled at Netanyahu is that he has navigated among what are called today's "tribes of Israel", resorting to a securitarian populist stance. The expression "tribe" was used by Reuven Rivlin, president from 2014 to 2021, in a speech in 2015.

Israeli politology defines five electoral blocs: the secular *askenazis*, an expression of the traditional Israeli establishment; the *mizrahim*, with the Sephardic component, who immigrated in the 1950s and became one of Likud's mass bases in the 1970s; the "Russians", who immigrated in the 1990s; the religious; and the Arab-Israeli bloc, a vote bank for Labour up until Rabin. Finally, there would be a transversal bloc called *haredim*, the national-religious or national-messianic component.

The other accusation against Netanyahu, made in particular by sources in the French diaspora, is the use for electoral purposes of the opposition between "Jews" and "Israelis" or between *Eretz Israel*, the Land of Israel in the biblical sense, and *Medinat Israel*, the State of Israel. Alon Pinkas, a former diplomat and columnist for *Haaretz*, goes so far as to speak of "two States of Israel" that are mutually "incompatible". On the one hand, the "State of Israel", "secular, high-tech and globalised", whose expression is the Tel Aviv area, with its almost four million inhabitants, about half the country's population, and which produces a large part of the Israeli GDP. On the other hand, the "kingdom of Judea", a "Jewish and supremacist theocracy" with "messianic tendencies" that encourages isolation.

Pinkas refers to two precedents: the first between 796 and 586 BC, the date of the destruction of the first temple and the so-called "Babylonian exile" in the Old Testament narrative; and the second between 140 and 63 BC, with the reign of the Hasmoneans and the Roman conquest. Divisions that became "more acute with the first Jewish revolt in 66 AD, which led to the destruction of the Second Temple" by Roman legions in 70 AD, "producing the diaspora and the disappearance of a Jewish State until 1948".

Internal division and political "sectarianism" are fuelled, for Pinkas, by the almost 60 years of occupation of the West Bank, which from "temporary" has become a "permanent feature of Israel's political and geopolitical ecosystem". The exercise of "a condition of occupation over nearly five million Palestinians" fuels a condition of "civil war". The "kingdom of Judea" that Netanyahu is "stitching together as an electoral bloc", composed of right-wing, far-right, ultra-Orthodox people and "followers of his personal cult", does not represent "the majority", but is in power. If it prevailed, Israel would no longer be the State created by "Zionism" because, as the critics claim, an ethno-religious conception of the State would be affirmed, and to the detriment of the 20% of the Arab-Israeli population, largely Palestinian.

The two-State solution appears to be a difficult obstacle even for centre or centre-left governmental structures. For Efraim Inbar, director of the Jerusalem Institute for Security Studies (JISS), who is close to Likud, such a solution, envisaged by Washington in the context of the extension of the *Abraham Accords* to diplomatic normalisation between Israel and Saudi Arabia, is "wishful thinking". On the one hand, Tel Aviv has no guarantee that "a Palestinian entity" will not be shaken by a "civil war" as happened in Syria, Iraq and Yemen, with renewed fighting between "Palestinian factions", becoming a "failed State". On the other hand, a security agreement between Riyadh and Washington, in an anti-Iranian sense, would see an American assent to the development of a Saudi nuclear sector: "a strategic nightmare" for Israel, which does not want "a multipolar nuclear order in the Middle East", since such a development would drive a regional "nuclear race".

It is not just about rival Iran, which, according to *The Jerusalem Post*, is "one or two years" from making the nuclear warheads operational. For Inbar, participation in the nuclear race by Turkey and Egypt would also be encouraged, confirming that the conflict promises to remain as inextricable as it was over a century ago. The only thing that can unravel it will be proletarian internationalism.

The PLO Taken Hostage by Arab Nationalism and Petro-Monarchies*

Few independence movements have been as "massively dependent" on external assistance as the Palestine Liberation Organisation (PLO), "whose survival has been conditioned by preserving its unity at any price". This is because of the characteristics of Palestinian nationalism during the process of its formation, between the 1930s and the 1950s, which distinguished it from other similar movements, such as the Algerian National Liberation Front (FLN).

This is what Alain Gresh, deputy editor of *Le Monde Diplomatique*, wrote in the introduction to the English edition of his history of the PLO [*The PLO: The Struggle Within: Toward an Independent Palestinian State*, 1983]. The PLO, founded in 1964 as an umbrella organisation to regroup the currents of Palestinian nationalism, was headed from 1969 to 2004 by Yasser Arafat [Mohamed al-Rahman al-Rauf al-Qudwa al-Huseini, 1929-2004]. For 40 years, it was the main representative of secular-oriented Palestinian nationalism.

Since the mid-1980s, Hamas, the Islamic resistance movement responsible for the October 7th 2023 massacre in Israel and the hegemonic political force in the Gaza Strip, has become the PLO's main competitor. The war in Gaza, which has cost up to 40,000 lives, making it the most devastating in terms of human losses in the history of Israeli-Palestinian conflicts, represents a tragic setback and a confirmation of what we have called the "strategic bankruptcy" of both Palestinian and Israeli nationalism.

The riddle of Arab and Palestinian nationalism

Alain Gresh is a sympathiser of the Palestinian national cause. Maxime Rodinson, among the doyens of French Arabism, sees his preface as a "serious and solid effort" to clarify the "contradictions underlying Palestinian and Arab nationalism". They are theoretically "complementary" forces, but in the course of almost a century, i.e., since the "Palestinian question" arose, they have often found themselves in opposition. Arab *raison d'état* had prevailed over Palestinian demands: this was the judgement of Abu Iyad [Salah Khalaf,

* Gianluca De Simone.

1933-1991], one of the founders – alongside Arafat – of Fatah (meaning "conquest", an inverted acronym of "Movement for the Liberation of Palestine") the main Palestinian nationalist party and the majority force within the PLO.

Born to a Russian mother of Jewish faith and a Coptic Egyptian father, Gresh was a militant in the Egyptian left and later in the French left, in the French Communist Party (PCF). His father, Henri Curiel [1914-1978], was assassinated by Secret Army Organisation (OAS) agents linked to the French secret services, due to his prominent militancy among the Jeanson Network (also known as the "suitcase carriers"), a French network who supported the Algerian National Liberation Front. Although he was accused of having links with the USSR and its Arab policy, in 1976 he initiated a series of meetings between members of the PLO and the Israeli left, under the chairmanship of Pierre Mendès-France, former French prime minister of the Fourth Republic.

Gresh, in his 1983 book as well as in later interventions, argued that the creation of a "Palestinian mini-State" in the West Bank and Gaza was the only realistic solution to the conflict, and sees the rejection of the UN resolution for the partition of Palestine in 1947 as a missed opportunity for Palestinian nationalism [*Palestine 1947: Un partage avorté*, 1992]. Gresh admits, however, that such a solution was difficult to pursue at the time, given the "balance of power" between a "subordinate Palestinian nationalism" and the Arab states, in the rising tide of ideology and Pan-Arabist political currents, and with the "Palestinian trauma" of the *Nakba* ("catastrophe"), the military partition of Palestine in 1948.

In his memoirs, Abu Iyad mentions the thesis of Hajj Amin al-Husseini, Grand Mufti of Jerusalem, from a conversation in Beirut in 1974. As the Grand Mufti saw it, the Arab states, both due to the convictions of their leaders and to British pressure, "put forward obstacles to the foundation of a Palestinian State in the West Bank and Gaza, territories that the Jewish army had not been able to conquer. King Abdallah of Transjordan had [...] no interest in favouring the creation of a Palestinian entity, as he intended to annex the West Bank to his kingdom, which he did after the war of 1948. King Faruk, for his part, did not seek to annex Gaza to Egypt; he convened a Palestinian congress in the city in September 1948, which appointed a government under the leadership of Ahmed Hilmi, whose main objective [...] was to assert his effective authority over Gaza and the

West Bank. But the Egyptian government prevented the Palestinian government from setting up in Gaza so as not to provoke the Israeli army, risking the occupation of the enclave. The Palestinian government had to install itself in Cairo, where Hilmi", a Jordanian banker, "was more concerned with his own affairs than those of his ghost government". Betrayed by the Arab states, Gresh continues, Husseini was abandoned by the majority of Palestinian leadership, which split into two groups, the pro-Jordanian and the pro-Egyptian.

The new nationalist generations of the diaspora

The majority of historians, including the Palestinian ones, recognise the long-term effects, lasting for at least "a generation" according to Gresh, of the political vacuum created in the 1930s in the Palestinian nationalist movement, which was mown down by British repression during the "Great Arab Revolt" of 1936-39. The group of men that was to take over the leadership of Fatah, in fact, belonged to the next generation. They were born in the 1930s and began their political activity, like Arafat, in connection with the Egyptian Muslim Brotherhood and the historical Palestinian establishment, embodied by Hajj Amin al-Husseini. In the 1950s, the group entered into a conflictual relationship with the Pan-Arab ideology of Gamal Abdel Nasser's Free Officers.

According to the American Arabist William Quandt, who played a role in the Camp David negotiations of 1978-79, the nationalist currents that later converged within the PLO were an expression, in the case of Fatah, of "the well-to-do, conservative and religiously observant Gaza bourgeoisie", which in the case of Arafat, who was born in Cairo and lived in Jerusalem for a short period of his childhood, had not suffered the loss of his possessions in 1948. The other main current, the Arab Nationalist Movement (ANM), was composed of exponents of the "Christian middle-classes", from the central and northern regions of Palestine, trained at the American University of Beirut [see *The Politics of Palestinian Nationalism*, 1973]. Strongly Pan-Arabist and pro-Nasser, the ANM also welcomed non-Palestinian political exponents.

The difference between Fatah and ANM currents, according to Gresh, is among the specificities of Palestinian nationalism, summarised in five main characteristics. The first is the "territorial dispersion" that followed 1948. The military partition of the British mandate in Palestine meant that the majority of the Palestinian population was under "Jordanian, Israeli or Egyptian sovereignty", while the diaspora ended up in Lebanon, Syria, and the Persian Gulf. This dispersion, says Gresh, also led to a "socio-economic differentiation", with the "Palestinian bourgeoisie" deprived of direct contact with the mostly peasant population in the "refugee camps" and in Palestine. The only connection was through the so called "Jordanian establishment", i.e., the section of the traditional notables loyal to the Hashemite monarchy in Amman.

The second characteristic was the different formation of the nationalist leadership. Its ideological orientation ranged from the "Pan-Arabist Palestinian nationalism" of Fatah, which took as a model the Algerian National Liberation Front (FLN), to the ANM's "Pan-Arab national socialism", from which several formations competing with Fatah, such as the Popular Front for the Liberation of Palestine (PFLP) and the Democratic Front for the Liberation of Palestine (DFLP), would arise once the movement had joined the PLO.

A third specific characteristic were the strong individualistic and particularistic traits of the leadership. These were very pronounced among the Palestinians, whose traditional social structure involved a considerable weight of clan, family and regional ties. A fourth factor were the ideological divergences, accentuated by the high level of education of the Palestinian bourgeoisie: Arafat studied in Cairo, like other Fatah leaders; and the leadership of the Arab Nationalist Movement, as mentioned above, studied in Beirut, at the American University.

Forms of Arab interference

Finally, the fifth and most important factor: "interference from Arab countries". According to Gresh, it manifested itself in two forms. Openly, through the creation of "organisations directly dependent on Arab regimes": for example the *Saika* ("storm"), created by Syria in the late 1950s; the Arab Liberation Army (ALA), created by the Iraqi regime; and the Islamic Liberation Front (ILF), linked to Saudi Arabia. Interference could also take an "indirect form", through the "alliances" concluded at a given moment with one or another organisation within the PLO. Historically, there are a dozen Palestinian organisations of varying sizes, at least six of which were "recognised by the PLO".

Gresh argues that, starting in 1968, Arafat chose the "Vietnamese way", i.e., the creation of a broad front of nationalist organisations gathered within the PLO, instead of the "Algerian way", characterised by the hegemony of the FLN. The relative dominance of Fatah was certainly affirmed, but the "armed liquidation" of the other currents – as had happened in the Algerian independence movement – was ruled out [Alistair Horne, *The Algerian War*, 2012]. In the Vietnamese case, although the weight of the Hanoi regime, which had been independent since 1954, was decisive, the *Vietminh* in the South also incorporated currents that came from outside the Vietnamese Communist Party.

In an interview in 1970, Arafat himself argued that the different organisations within the PLO were part of the "conflict of the Arab nation", which also included Palestine; they were organisations "linked to Arab countries" and "confronting them militarily" would mean confronting those countries. In his biography of Arafat, the Palestinian Christian journalist Said Aburish [*Arafat*, 1998] points out how the Fatah leadership, while admiring the figure of Nasser, distrusted him, and blamed the Arab countries for "the stab in the back" the Palestinian nation had received in 1948, both for their state interests and for the "incompetence and corruption" in their armies. It was a criticism wielded by Nasser himself against the Egyptian monarchy, which was overthrown in 1952. Moreover, Fatah feared Nasser's willingness to use Palestinian nationalism as an instrument of Egyptian foreign policy, through the formulas of Pan-Arabism. Nasser, for his part, was suspicious of the affiliations of many Palestinians in Egypt with the Muslim Brotherhood, with which they had fought as volunteers around Gaza in 1948. In 1954, after an assassination attempt, Nasser made the Brotherhood illegal.

The "Kuwaitis" of Fatah

The founding nucleus of Fatah, including Arafat, thought it wiser to emigrate to Kuwait, at the height of the oil boom. It was a choice, according to Aburish, which allowed the Fatah men to come into contact with exponents of the Palestinian bourgeoisie close to the local monarchy, as well as with that of Qatar. From there came the sources of funding to create, in the late 1950s, a newspaper in Beirut, and to recruit, especially in Lebanon, men for the military wing.

In Kuwait, Palestinian exponents headed the petro-monarchy's sovereign wealth fund, and in Qatar they headed the Central Bank. Men from the family of Abu Mazen (Mahmoud Abbas), the current president of the Palestinian National Authority (PNA), were among the advisers of the Qatari monarchy. Arafat's connections also included Ahmed Zaki Yamani [1930-2021], the former Saudi oil minister from 1962.

Arafat and the Fatah leadership, says Aburish, were aware of the need of Arab support for the Palestinian cause; they believed, however, that they could negotiate it without "making themselves dependent" on any "single Arab country". Drawing on oil revenues, however, also entailed a substantial "ideological vagueness": in Fatah's programme, apart from the liberation of Palestine, there were no demands for "social reform" or "Arab politics", unlike the currents linked to Nasserism or the Syrian and Iraqi Ba'ath parties. Such centrism did not arouse the concerns of the conservative Gulf sheikhs, who could also use the funding of Fatah as a "political counterweight" to the demands of national socialism in the Arab republics (Egypt, Syria and Iraq). This did not prevent Fatah from obtaining, from 1962, financial and military assistance from Algeria, a powerhouse of Arab radicalism.

The apogee of the PLO and Fatah, according to Barry Rubin, an Arabist at Johns Hopkins University, was during the 1970s and 1980s; those multiple relationships made it one of the "best-funded" nationalist movements in the world, thanks to generous funding from the petro-monarchies and other Arab states; this even included a 7% "national tax" taken from the wages of Palestinian workers in the Gulf [*Revolution Until Victory?: The Politics and History of the PLO*, 1996].

Palestinian manipulation and Arab leverage

According to Rubin, by "avoiding domination by a single patron or conflicts with Arab states" – and maintaining a line of non-interference in their internal affairs, as long as the Arab states did not interfere with the Palestinian cause – "Arafat gained a considerable degree of autonomy for the PLO", but also realised "that having Arab rulers as friends would make it necessary to have others as adversaries". Therefòre, Arafat operated like "a tightrope walker", balancing "every favour he received by leaning in the opposite direction" in order to preserve his independence. The Arab leader himself repeated that "those who had shot him would kiss him the next day, and vice versa".

Arafat's ploy was to manipulate and exploit Arab contradictions, dragging along the heterogeneous Palestinian fractions, between whom he continuously mediated. It was an exercise that, according to the Israeli journalist Danny Rubinstein [*The Mystery of Arafat*,

2003], on at least two occasions saw the Palestinian leadership first "walk to the edge of the cliff", and then, abetted by international circumstances, plunge into disaster. Granting or withholding support, Rubin argues, gave the Arab regimes "enormous leverage over the PLO", with Syria and Egypt preventing it throughout the 1960s from using their territory to attack Israel. In 1970-71, the establishment of a Palestinian quasi-State on Jordanian territory, with the anti-Hashemite radicalism of the PFLP and DFLP, led to a military stand-off with the Jordanian monarchy. The climax was "Black September", which cost the PLO militias between 5,000 and 10,000 fighters and resulted in their expulsion from Jordan.

In 1975-76, the alliance with the Lebanese National Movement, headed by the Druze leader Kamal Jumblatt, involved the PLO in the Lebanese civil war and pitted it against Syria, leading to a massacre in a Palestinian refugee camp by Maronite militias, which were allied with Damascus at the time. In 1982-83, at the time of the Israeli invasion of Lebanon, the PLO was first driven out of the south and Beirut, with the massacre of the Sabra and Shatila camp, again by the Maronite "phalanx", this time allied with Israel. In the autumn of 1983, the PLO was expelled from Tripoli, after a siege led by the Syrian army; and in 1985 the remaining refugee camps still suffered attacks by Amal's Shiite militias. Those belonging to the PLO were evacuated to Tunisia, escorted by the French navy.

From 1977-79, with the separate peace with Israel, signed by Anwar Sadat at Camp David, Egypt de facto abandoned its support for the PLO, which was forced to re-establish relations with Jordan, then Syria and finally Saddam Hussein's Iraq. The tail end of the Lebanese affair, Gresh points out, was the fragmentation of the PLO into three components: one led by Arafat, a second led by Abu Nidal, supported by Syria and Libya, which conducted "a war of extermination" against the Fatah leadership through terrorist attacks; the third was a Libyan component. Support for Baghdad's invasion of Kuwait in 1990 cost the PLO the support of the petro-monarchies. Only on two occasions, in Jordan in 1970-71 and in Lebanon until 1982-83, did the PLO succeed in establishing itself as a "quasi-State". This was not the case in the West Bank and Gaza, where the guerrilla take-over had failed since 1968.

The "State in exile" in Beirut and the Lebanese civil war

According to Robert Fisk, *The Times*' famed Middle East correspondent, the PLO had created a kind of "State in exile" in Lebanon, threatening the country's political and confessional balance, with its "seventeen confessions and seven recognised ones" and, since the 1960s, "over seventy armed militias" [*Pity the Nation: Lebanon at War*, 2001].

According to Aburish, in Lebanon, the PLO had not only enjoyed a territorial sanctuary but had also set up economic groups such as the SAMED (Palestine Martyrs Works Society), entering into direct and autonomous liaison with the financial flows that passed through Beirut. Arafat, in particular, established close relations with the "Beirut Palestinians": "men of the world" with dual passports, more inclined to Levantine trade than to guerrilla warfare. The presence of over 300,000 Palestinians in refugee camps, without Lebanese citizenship, created a recruitment pool for the guerrilla war against Israel and, later, for the long Lebanese civil war [1975-1990].

According to a Palestinian estimate, until 1990, "three quarters of Palestinian victims" were the result of Arab action rather than Israeli repression. In Lebanon, Fisk recalls, Palestinians were part of local feuds, caught up in the massacres of Tel al-Zaatar by Christian Phalangists in 1976, which was followed by a vicious reprisal against the Maronite village of Damour. Thousands of Palestinian refugees were massacred in Sabra and Shatila in 1982 by Maronite Phalangist militias; during the "War of the Camps", in 1986, on behalf of Syria, it was the turn of militiamen of the Shiite Amal party.

Today's Gaza conflict, with its almost 40,000 victims, has shifted this bloody toll to the government in Tel Aviv, in what is the latest of the "seven wars" in Gaza between Hamas and Israel. The premise, however, had been the military confrontation between Fatah and Hamas in 2007, for supremacy over Palestinian nationalism.

Confirmation of the "national pretext"

The painful and bloody experience of Palestinian self-determination, even in its dimmed form of the mini-State that emerged from the Oslo Accords, is proof of how Middle Eastern bourgeoisies and great powers have used the Palestinian "national pretext" for their own ends, abandoning it today, under the rubble of Gaza. The same flow of petro-dollars that provided the PLO with ample financial means, and enabled it to gain international recognition, also thanks to the use of the oil weapon by the Gulf countries, has also fuelled, alternatively in cooperation and competition, the currents of political Islamism.

An instrument of influence of the petro-monarchies, both in the context of the contest over the Middle East and in the rivalry of Iranian Shia confessional nationalism, oil revenue has financed both the Islamic militias in Afghanistan and the various *poisoned seeds* of reactionary terrorism. This includes Hamas, whose entrenchment is also the result of the policy of *divide and conquer* practised by the Israeli bourgeoisie.

As recalled by the daily newspaper *Haaretz*, Hamas, until the 7th of October, though held in suspicion for its affiliation with the Muslim Brotherhood, moved between the various Arab capitals, still enjoyed the hospitality of Qatar and even Kuwait, and was allied with Marshal-President al-Sisi's Egypt in the fight against the terrorist fractions of ISIS and Al Qaeda, active in Sinai. Aburish claims that Kuwait, Saudi Arabia and Qatar, in 1991, in order to punish the PLO for its support of Saddam Hussein's Iraq during the first Gulf War, not only expelled a large number of Palestinian workers, but also blocked the flow of financial aid and directed it towards "Palestinian Islamist currents".

Various observers believe that as early as 1973 Arafat had become convinced of the impossibility of reversing the outcome of 1948. Therefore, also under pressure from the "money men", the component of the Palestinian diaspora that acted as an interface with the Arab monarchies and as a funding channel, became convinced that they had to pursue a "diplomatic solution", in conversation with Amman and Washington. The competition between Palestinian fractions forced Arafat to move through confidential channels to avoid a split in the PLO. The emergence of a nationalism in the occupied territories also weighed heavily, fuelled also by the integration of the Palestinian labour force into the Israeli economy, hostile to Jewish settlements in the West Bank and Gaza as well as to Jordanian tutelage, given the break produced by the "Black September" of 1970. This radical current in the territories began to call for the creation of an independent state based on 1967 borders, a solution that was endorsed by the Arab monarchies of the Gulf and Egypt.

Since 1979, following the signing of the Camp David Accords, the Carter administration itself advocated for "Palestinian national determination". However, it took the Lebanese defeat and the eruption of the first Intifada, the popular uprising in the territories, together with the end of the Cold War and of the USSR's influence over a section of Arab nationalism, to enable Arafat to establish the

PLO as the political leader. According to Aburish, the Arab monarchies and Egypt considered that Arafat's charter was useful to "contain" the Palestinian uprising and to avoid the contagion of *Intifada* spreading to other Arab countries.

This seemed to make the mini-State solution viable, with the Oslo Accords of 1993. Part of the same currents of the PLO began to denounce those agreements as the product of the influence of the "money men" and their contacts in the Gulf. The policy of co-optation conducted by Arafat by centralising Arab funding, in order to manipulate the various currents, also weighed heavily. Edward Said [1935-2003], one of the best-known Palestinian intellectuals, disavowed the Oslo Accords as a "sell-out" of Palestinian nationalism to Israeli and American diktats, accusing Arafat of managing power like "an African tribal chief of the 19th century". For Aburish, Arafat's actions reflected a "bazaar merchant's" conception of power, traditional to both Palestinian and Arab society. In any case, Gresh emphasises, the position of weakness stemming from the Oslo Accords, the rise of Hamas' competing nationalism, fostered by Israel itself, and Tel Aviv's policy of the creeping annexation of the Palestinian territories, rarely questioned by Washington, led to the "slow wreck" of the Oslo Accords and to their demise from 2006-2007, with the outbreak of the civil war between Fatah and Hamas and the subsequent "Gaza wars" between the Islamist party and Tel Aviv from 2008 onwards. According to Gresh [*Israël, Palestine*: *Vérités sur un conflit,* 2024], it was precisely the penultimate Gaza war, in 2021, that sanctioned Hamas's dominance within Palestinian nationalism, with the decomposition of Fatah's, undermined by Abu Mazen's declining leadership in the PNA and the exercise of *divide and conquer* by Israeli governments.

If the outcome of the war has once again changed these relations, it will be a new game between the powers that determines the fate of Palestine, this time in the confrontation between Saudi Arabia, which would like to bring the *Abraham Accords* with Israel and the United States to a successful conclusion, and the Iran of the *mullahs*, which has mobilised its proxy militias to prevent it. Iran may also wish to use the conflict to negotiate a new understanding that includes recognition of its nuclear status.

Chapter Two

Abraham Accords and the War in Gaza

Risky Bets and Calculations in the Unstable Middle East*

There are several interpretations made by international observers about the objectives of what could go down in history as the "Trump declaration": the decision, made on December 6th to formally recognise Jerusalem as the capital of Israel and move the US embassy from Tel Aviv to West Jerusalem. Since 1949, the latter has been declared capital and since 1980 named "inseparable capital" of the Jewish State with a vote in the Knesset, the Israeli parliament, claiming also the majority-Arab part, East Jerusalem, which was under Jordanian administration up to June 1967.

In short, the comments tend to credit a calculation of the White House tenant strongly marked by contingent rather than strategic motivations, honouring the promises made during the campaign with a symbolic and unilateral gesture. But there would also be a strategic dimension: achieving the diplomatic normalisation between the Jewish State and Saudi Arabia and strengthening their political-military convergence in the direction of anti-Iranian containment. A third hypothesis is elicited in an elliptical way by the *Financial Times*: appeasing the pro-Israeli American groups with a symbolic gesture and freezing the threatened denunciation of the nuclear agreement with Iran. This threat, bounced between Congress and the White House, could remain pending until the end of Donald Trump's presidential term, in 2020, keeping the pressure on Iran.

On both issues – Jerusalem and the nuclear agreement with Tehran – the US position finds opposition from both the EU, the main donor of funds to the Palestinian Authority (PA), and China and Russia. Predictably, Trump's decision has provoked a mobilisation of the Palestinian factions, with clashes in the West Bank and Gaza, but also the protest of the Arab League and the OIC, the Organization of Islamic Cooperation.

* Gianluca De Simone, December 2017

Founded under Saudi Arabia's leadership in 1972, the OIC brings together 57 Islamic countries. At its summit in Istanbul, thanks to the rotating presidency of Turkey, it approved a Turkish-Malaysian-Iranian motion that recognises East Jerusalem as the Palestinian capital. Recep Tayyip Erdoğan's presidency has announced Turkey's intention to open its own embassy in East Jerusalem.

"Alabama song"

Formally, the Trump presidency complies with a congressional law passed in 1995, which all his predecessors have waived every six months. The State Department was quick to point out that the transfer of the diplomatic headquarters will take place, in practice, not before 2020, given the "logistical difficulties". The American diplomacy seems to buy time, also thanks to the substantial vagueness of the presidential declaration on the other aspects of the Israeli-Palestinian conflict. At the same time, the calendar is intertwined with the Election calendar of the administration: not only the race for the senatorial seat in Alabama, where the Republicans came out defeated, but above all the midterm elections of 2018.

Le Monde points out how the recognition of Jerusalem as the Israeli capital has been part of the electoral programs of presidential candidates for both parties since 1972. Trump's announcement, according to the newspaper, represents "a rape of diplomacy", liquidating 70 years of international efforts on the Israeli-Palestinian conflict and consecrating the "politics of faits accomplis" pursued by the Israeli governments, especially those of the national-conservative Benjamin Netanyahu.

Since 1967, about 200,000 Israelis have settled in East Jerusalem, then entirely Arab, further complicating the question of the status of the city. According to *Le Monde*, Trump's unilateralism would not even take into account international law: it is guided by his own "imperatives of domestic politics", pandering, according to convenience, to evangelical Christians and various pro-Israeli lobbies. However, the effect is to create "a dangerous destabilization". The international community, as it did on the Paris climate agreements, must acknowledge and "learn to circumvent" Washington.

The commentary of *Le Figaro* is similar: one cannot avoid the suspicion that the "fate of the Middle East is being decided in some small town in Pennsylvania" and that the decision is "a stroke of domestic politics" to reward "part of the political base and donors" of the White House tenant. On this topic, several sources cite the casino owner Sheldon Adelson, financier of the Trump campaign and closely associated with Israeli extremist religious nationalism. If Trump's decision appears above all to be symbolic, it affects "one of the strongest symbols", says the Dassault group's daily newspaper, given "the enormous political and religious value of a three-time-holy city" to the Christian, Jewish and Islamic faiths.

Bets and calculations

The Japan Times, often an informal channel of Tokyo's diplomacy, offers a good summary of the possible "strategic calculation" of Washington as a "bet" on the decline of the importance of the Palestinian cause in the Arab-Sunni world and on the significant weakening of the Palestinian factions, mainly Hamas, a branch of the Muslim Brotherhood, and Fatah, a secular faction.

The two main souls of Palestinian nationalism reconciled last October, after more than a decade of conflict. That conflict, like the political rise of Hamas, was triggered in 2000 by the "second Intifada", the Palestinian uprising. The trigger was the visit of Ariel Sharon (future Israeli premier) to the Haram al-Sharif (Temple Mount) in East Jerusalem. For the Islamic religion, this place, on which stands the al-Aqsa mosque, indicates the point of Muhammad's ascent to heaven. For the Jewish faith, it is the site of Solomon's Temple. Sharon's act was considered by the Palestinians to be a claim of Jewish sovereignty. Concluded in 2005, the second Intifada caused about 6,000 deaths among Palestinians and Israelis and consolidated the hegemony over Gaza of Hamas, hostile to the 1993 Oslo Accords.

From 2008 to 2014, the Israeli armed forces conducted three military interventions against Hamas in Gaza, which with 1.5 million inhabitants represents 40% of the total Palestinian population in the areas nominally administered by the PA, controlled by Fatah. Israeli military action, embargo and change in regional balances, in particular the Syrian war and the establishment of the military regime of Abdel al-Sisi in Egypt, seriously undermined Hamas, both economically and militarily. The "symbolic victory" given by Trump to Israel, continues *The Japan Times*, humiliates the leadership of the PA, which remains the main Palestinian interlocutor, and deprives Washington of negotiating incentives with the leadership of Tel

Aviv. Using the axe to untangle one of the most intricate knots of the Middle Eastern chaos does not appear to be a "prudent decision, neither on the tactical nor on the strategic level".

Role of Jordan and Egypt

According to Peter Van Buren, an American career diplomat, Trump's intemperate move gives a blow to two US allies in the region. First of all Jordan: since 1924, the monarchy of Amman, which boasts a direct descent from Muhammad, has been managing the Temple Mount through a foundation, thus compensating for the loss of custody of Mecca and Medina, passed to the Saudi family after the exclusion of the Hashemites from the Arabian Peninsula.

By 1950, the Jordanian monarchy had annexed, as a trustee, the territories of the West Bank and East Jerusalem, which were then conquered by Israel in the Six-Day War of June 1967. If Jordan with the 1994 peace treaty with Israel has renounced its territorial claims in favour of the PA, nevertheless it takes part of its legitimacy from the formal protection of al-Aqsa. Moreover, the Palestinian component is 3.2 million people, about half of the Jordanian population. In the territories of the former British mandate of Palestine, there are about 7 million Israeli citizens, 20% of whom are of Arab-Palestinian ethnicity; Gaza, West Bank and East Jerusalem are estimated to have about 4.5 million Arabs. The Palestinian diaspora in the Middle East amounts to another two million, mainly in Egypt, Syria, Lebanon and Saudi Arabia. Another two million are scattered in the Americas, the EU (around 100,000) and Asia.

The other ally involved is Egypt, which, with Gamal Abdel Nasser and his Pan-Arab policies, baptised the PLO in 1964. According to Van Buren, the leadership in Cairo will not be able to ignore Egyptian public opinion on the role played by Jerusalem, also because of the "canon of Islamic radicalism". Furthermore, Trump's decision coincides with "a preliminary agreement" between the Egyptian government and Moscow to grant the use of air space and Egyptian bases to Russian military aircraft for the first time since 1973.

It can be observed that President Anwar Sadat's exulsion of advisers from Moscow in 1972, marked the pro-American turn of Egyptian politics. In 1978, with the Camp David Accords, Egypt was the first Arab State to sign a peace treaty with Israel, a treaty in which the question of the status of Jerusalem was left pending.

The "Arabian nights" of Jared Kushner

According to Alastair Crooke, a former MI6 executive and former counsellor to Javier Solana on the Palestinian and Middle Eastern question, "the bone thrown by Trump to Israel" is part of the "tectonic change" under way in the region: the return of Russia, with the Syrian conflict and the "defeat" suffered by Riyadh and Wahhabism in the Levant. To rebalance the Russian-Iranian role in Syria and the consolidation of Tehran's role, Riyadh would aim to strengthen its convergence with the US-Israel axis.

Crooke, often a guest of the Kremlin-sponsored *Valdai* forum, echoes Russian positions, particularly on the role of Moscow in ending the American "unipolar moment". The statement according to which Trump would have accepted the picture proposed by his son-in-law Jared Kushner – the conflict around Jerusalem as "a real estate dispute" – should be considered with a grain of salt. It is certainly true that it is a "symbol that agitates the blood and passions of every Muslim: there is no home in the region in which the image of the al-Aqsa mosque in the Haram al-Sharif, the sacred sanctuary, is not present". This should also induce caution in the Saudi monarchy.

According to *Reuters*, Riyadh expressed a harsh rhetorical condemnation of Trump's statement; but for the Palestinian leadership there could have been a Saudi-American "backroom agreement" whose foundations could have been laid in long nocturnal secret meetings between Kushner, to whom Trump could have entrusted part of the Middle Eastern dossier, and the Crown Prince Mohammad bin Salman, shortly before the purge of the Saudi elite last November. According to *Reuters*, Palestinian officials fear, and "many Arab officials suspect", that Washington could close the door on East Jerusalem as the Palestinian capital, offering "limited self-government inside disconnected patches of the occupied West Bank", without any right of return for the refugees of the wars of 1948 and 1967 and keeping the Jewish settlements.

Le Monde evokes the possibility of a sop in the form of a "mini-capital" in a suburb of Jerusalem. According to a Saudi source, reported by *Reuters*, "the businessman in Trump, who has always spoken of a definitive agreement, should not be underestimated. It is unlikely that Riyadh would accept it if it had not included something that would allow Prince Salman to sweeten it and sell it to the Arab world. That is, the Palestinians will have their State".

"The deal of the century"

Russian Foreign Minister Sergei Lavrov has declared, with more than a hint of sarcasm, that the US is imagining "the deal of the century", an image contrived by Secretary of State Rex Tillerson; in the intentions of the Americans, it "will solve the Israeli-Palestinian conflict in one stroke". Russia "certainly would like to know how that would work", Lavrov said.

On this subject, *RIA Novosti* reported the statements of the Israeli intelligence minister Yisrael Katz, deputy of Likud, considered very close to Netanyahu. According to Katz, "the US is shaping a peace plan but they are not telling us what it includes. They say it will have something creative and they will not impose any agreement". Riyadh, "as the leader of the Arab world, should take the initiative, come to Palestine and offer to sponsor the peace plan" and seize this opportunity to normalise diplomatic relations with Israel, with an exchange of State visits. Both the Iranian "Twelver Shia government" and "Saudi Wahhabism", he concludes, claim "the exclusive legacy of the message of the Prophet" and leadership over the Islamic community.

Since 2013 and with the intensification of the conflict in Syria and around the Iranian nuclear issue, several analysts have proposed a strategic convergence between Tel Aviv and Riyadh, even with a nuclear guarantee dimension extended by the Jewish State to the Saudi monarchy and the Persian Gulf. The nuclear arsenal of Israel is about 100 warheads and can boast its own "triad" of vectors: ballistic missiles with long-range and very long-range air components and, it is believed, also a naval component, boarded on conventional submarines. Since the 1970s, Riyadh has been among the financiers of the Pakistani nuclear program, with Islamabad deploying a military contingent to protect Mecca and Medina. But the Saudi monarchy would no longer be so certain of Islamabad's willingness to play, in the words of Henry Kissinger, the role of "nuclear armorer". Pakistan has resisted the Saudi attempts to drag it into power and religious struggles with neighbouring Iran.

Taking advantage of the alliance with Washington, Tel Aviv has often conducted a skilful and unscrupulous balance policy, exploiting inter-State disputes and the game of regional balances. During the 1970s and 1980s, it coordinated with the Shah's Iran. But Israel also intervened in favour of Khomeini's Iran during the 1980-88 Iraq war. According to the French military historian

Pierre Razoux, out of $24 billion of war supplies to Tehran during the conflict, Tel Aviv with $2 billion was the fourth largest supplier after China, North Korea and Libya and before Russia [*La guerre Iran-Irak*, 2013].

In the Syrian conflict, Israel restricted itself to targeted interventions, designed to contain the presence of Hezbollah and Iranian militias. The most recent operation took place at the beginning of December, against a Pasdaran base under construction near Damascus. A weakened Assad regime is a strategic advantage for Tel Aviv. Israel may fear that the presence of Moscow, which has announced a reduction of its military contingent, is not a sufficient guarantee to contain the entrenchment of the Iranian presence from the Mediterranean to the Gulf.

The Gulf confrontation, which sees the Saudis and the Emirates against Qatar, offers margins of intervention to the Jewish State with the establishment of a bilateral agreement separate from the Gulf Cooperation Council (GCC), which finally broke up on the issue of relations with Tehran. The strategic substance of the Tillerson-summoned deal of the century, therefore, could be a diplomatic normalisation between Israel and Saudi Arabia as an anti-Iranian coalition, with the Saudi seal of approval, as leader of the Sunni camp, to the Israeli-Palestinian peace plan. This would be a sort of re-edition of the agreements of Camp David, with the monarchy to take the role played by Sadat – a step that would also endorse, it seems, the reformist turn of Prince Salman, repudiating the image and the role of headquarter of Salafist-Wahhabi radicalism. Such a programme would be vast indeed, to use the ironic expression of Charles de Gaulle, in light of the regional dynamics and the often-poisoned historical heritage of the region, and in the context of the political stature displayed up to this point by Trump.

Scientific prudence suggests, however, that we take into account what Marx wrote about Napoleon III in *The Eighteenth Brumaire of Louis Bonaparte*: "the class struggle in France created circumstances and relationships that made it possible for a grotesque mediocrity to play a hero's part". The possibility of Trump becoming the protagonist of a Great Middle Eastern agreement as a specific expression of the imbalance that led him to the presidency cannot be ruled out. Another matter is to see if that is actually sustainable, given the multiplication of the actors, their growth in size and the relative American decline.

The ghost of Balfour

It can be noted that the reactions of the regional powers did not miss the analogy, even temporal, with the Balfour Declaration of November 1917 in which London committed to supporting "the establishment in Palestine of a national home for the Jewish people".

For the historian Eugene Rogan, this was the last in the series of "partition plans" of territories of the Ottoman Empire, negotiated with Paris, St. Petersburg and the Arab potentates since March 1915. London's decision was based on "wartime considerations", i.e., the intention to use the Zionist movement to "channel Jewish influence into the British war effort", which he believed could "gain the support of influential Jewish personalities in the United States and Russia", and to keep the two powers actively engaged in the conflict.

It was also considered a way to downsize the territorial concessions made in Paris with the Sykes-Picot agreement and to secure the vital imperial artery of the Suez Canal. Without the support of a great power, the Zionist national ambitions "were inconceivable"; therefore, the offer of a national home by foreign minister Balfour, was deemed by Prime Minister David Lloyd George as functional to putting Palestine "under English sovereignty".

Finally, the propagandistic aspect was important: the entrance of General Allenby's troops in Jerusalem on December 11th, 1917, was defined by Lloyd George as "the Christmas present for the British nation" [Eugene Rogan, *The Fall of the Ottomans: The Great War in the Middle East*, 2015]. A success that followed the bloody battle of Passchendaele, defined by the military historian Basil Liddell Hart as "the saddest drama of British military history" [*The Real War, 1914-1918*].

African contentions

The search for Saudi support is not limited to a possible convergence with Tel Aviv. Last October, King Salman made a historic trip to Moscow, reiterating the truce in the oil price war that began in 2013-14, perhaps expanded to some agreement on Syria. The question of the listing of Aramco is always open, and China is also in the competition with its Shanghai market.

Adel Al-Jubeir, Riyadh's Foreign Minister, has sent signals to the EU and to Emmanuel Macron: a contribution of €130 million to the training and equipment of the task force created, with European initiative, by the G5 countries of the Sahel (Niger, Burkina Faso,

Mali, Mauritania and Chad). Among the functions of the African task force, there would also be the role of controlling migratory flows to the EU.

It is worth remembering that since the 1970s the projection of Paris in *Francafrique* has availed itself of the cooperation of the *petro-monarchies*. The formula used by French intelligence was: "Paris plans, Morocco executes, and Saudi Arabia finances". At the time it was a question of containing the adventurism of Muammar Gaddafi, the manoeuvres of the USSR and, later, a certain Iranian penetration, particularly from Sudan. Not secondary in importance was the recycling of the Gulf's petrodollars which, in the opinion of Gilles Kepel, involved turning a blind eye to the spread of the "Wahhabi madrassas" in areas of Africa [*Jihad: The Trail of Political Islam*, 2006].

In the opinion of Bernard Hourcade, a specialist in Iranian issues, Africa is a stage for the Iranian-Saudi power struggle. Although Africa has a limited weight in Tehran's foreign policy, Iran plays the card of religious proselytism. Over the years a "thin but effective Islamist network (*Shiite*) [has been created] in West Africa", with a constant presence in the Horn of Africa [*Géopolitique de l'Iran*, 2010].

Iran is not the only regional power of which Riyadh must be wary in the new contention. There is also Turkey, which on the question of the alleged alignment with the US and Israel is running an anti-Saudi campaign. For the Indian diplomat M.K. Bhadrakumar, Erdoğan's presidency sees the opportunity, similarly to Iran, to "undermine the Saudi dominance in the Middle East". Therefore, Riyadh will have to be careful not to show excessive "coordination with Israel or to dance to Trump's tune". The road to "the deal of the century" not only looks bumpy but also threatened by a large number of other players.

The fact remains that national issues that are unresolved and unsolvable in the absence of an internationalist unity continue to be exploited in the game of power, and weigh on the whole of the Middle Eastern, Arab, Hebrew, Kurdish, Turkish and Iranian proletariat.

Segregated Proletariat and Illusory "Deal of the Century" in Jerusalem*

The Israel-Palestine conflict is often defined by diplomats as "the most intractable" among the Middle Eastern conflicts. It is the origin of five wars and of a low-intensity confrontation between Palestinian and Israeli nationalisms that has dragged on for over a century. Every American administration, particularly after 1967, has tried to find a solution. Starting in 1978, the Camp David Accords between Egypt and Israel, the Madrid Conference of 1991, the Oslo Accords of 1993 and the peace treaty between Israel and Jordan of 1994 have produced an agreement on paper for a "two-State" solution: Palestinian and Israeli. It is the same solution proposed in 1937 by Great Britain, then the mandatory power in Palestine, and in 1967 by UN resolution 242. It also had a variant, the so-called "Jordanian option": a confederated Jordanian-Palestinian State, when from 1950 to 1967 the Hashemite kingdom annexed the West Bank and East Jerusalem but received only British and Pakistani recognition.

With the June 1967 war, Israel tripled the extension of its territory, incorporating the Syrian Golan Heights, the West Bank, the whole of Jerusalem, Gaza and the Sinai peninsula, obtaining strategic depth and territorial bargaining chips with neighbouring Arab countries. However, while it has never made a *de jure* annexation, except by decreeing, with a vote in parliament, that Jerusalem is the "undivided capital" of the Jewish State, it has been operating an indirect administration of the Arab portion. Since the 1970s, especially with the national-conservative Likud governments, it has favored the creation of military outposts followed by settlements or colonies in the occupied territories.

The logic, mainly military, was to create a "buffer zone" along the border with Jordan, which then turned, from the 1980s onwards, into peri-urban belts or residential areas of major industrial centres, not only a destination for migrant flows from the former USSR or from Eastern Europe. To date, approximately 600,000 Israeli citizens (9% of the population of Jewish faith) reside in nominally Palestinian territories.

---

* Gianluca De Simone, February 2020

Asymmetrical concessions

The Oslo Accords of 1993, orchestrated with American and European support according to Israeli historiography, marked the surrender of Palestinian nationalism represented by the PLO, with the formal recognition of the Jewish State. It was a turning point determined by the new international balances, in particular by the structures that emerged from the First Gulf War: the PLO's backing of Saddam Hussein's Iraq cost them the support, including the financial backing, of the Arab oil monarchies [Ian Black, *Enemies and Neighbors*, 2018].

On January 28th this year, after the blaze of tensions with Tehran and about a month after the new electoral round in Israel, the third one in twelve months, Donald Trump presented his peace plan, announced in 2017 as "the deal of the century". Prepared by his son-in-law and special envoy for the Middle East Jared Kushner, it aims at overcoming the political "stalemate" with a view that wants to be realistic. In practice, as stated by Secretary of State Mike Pompeo, it starts from the "matter of fact", that is the recognition of the Israeli *de jure* sovereignty not only on Jerusalem but also over the settlements created after 1967 and over the Golan Heights, annexed by the Netanyahu government before the September election round.

Real estate logic, electoral calculation, historical dimension

According to the deal, on a territorial level, the Palestinian National Authority (PA) should forgo almost 30% of the West Bank territory, including the entire Jordan valley. In return, the Palestinian administration – without Gaza, which has been politically controlled by Hamas (a wing of the Muslim Brotherhood) since 2006 – would receive a mini-capital in Abu Dis, a suburb outside the municipality of Jerusalem, and the promise of $50 billion in investments over a decade, half of which would come from Egypt, Jordan and Lebanon; it would also obtain state recognition, but with limited sovereignty on six territorial enclaves, under the security protection of Israel. A sharp loss compared to the conditions of 1993, from which, however, a state entity with limited autonomy was supposed to emerge.

Trump, reports *Haaretz*, a newspaper close to the Israeli centre-left, told Mahmoud Abbas, president of the PA, to think like "a real estate entrepreneur", taking a "unique and unrepeatable" opportunity. It also reports how Pompeo admitted privately that he considered the plan "unworkable". Kushner, who curbed Benjamin Netanyahu's intention to have the annexation of the Jordan valley voted on before the elections, diplomatically ditched his tone, speaking of the proposal as a "negotiating starting point".

David Gardner, in the *Financial Times*, stresses that Trump's plan is unacceptable and represents an unnecessary humiliation for the Palestinian leadership, making a two-State solution "physically unfeasible". Its sole purpose is "to greenlight Israel's annexation of the West Bank", a mere "real estate deal" in which the payment for the "surrender of land" is "a collection of scattered cantons" and, at best, a "supra-municipal government".

For *Le Monde*, the plan represents an "electoral gift as big as Manhattan" for Netanyahu, but also a "poisoned meatball" for Tel Aviv. The Palestinian "Lilliputian State", made up of "mini-baronies", favors the creation of "a single State between Jordan and the Mediterranean", which would include Israelis and Palestinians. This would impose two alternatives on Israel: to renounce being a democratic State, practicing a form of apartheid at the expense of the Arabs; or create a "binational entity" in which the Jewish component would no longer necessarily be in the majority. In both cases, according to *Le Monde*, "it would be the end of the Zionist dream".

According to Gardner, the Israeli territorial annexation would end up eroding its legitimacy both in Israel and in the occupied territories, with the Palestinians pushed to lead "an anti-apartheid struggle for equal rights". Although for the main Arab governments the Palestinian cause, used for decades in the regional dispute, has become "irrelevant", it remains "an emotional issue" for their peoples.

For Henry Kissinger, American pragmatism tends to evaluate political problems in quantitative terms, believing that they can solve them by "drowning them in resources". However it seems unlikely that some theme park for religious tourism, glossy brochures, a real estate attitude and a few billion dollars, handed over by Arab sheikhs or the EU, will be enough to solve the Palestinian puzzle.

Anti-Iranian coalition and regional strategies

According to some assessments, Trump's plan is part of an overall strategy in the Middle East based on four directives: fight against jihadism; strengthen the alliance of Sunni States – in particular Egypt, the UAE and Saudi Arabia – with Israel, where there would also be space for a commercial agreement; contain Iran within which, both economically and militarily, aiming at reducing its influence in the "Shiite Crescent"; adjust the American regional balance, carried out by the air-naval projection, allowing a reduction of the land troops.

During the visit to Riyadh in 2017, the Trump administration evoked a sort of "Middle Eastern NATO" in an anti-terrorist and anti-Iranian sense. Regional free trade agreements were envisaged in the plan for Palestine between Jordan and the planned Palestinian State, possibly extendable also to Israel and Egypt, perhaps with the lubricant of offshore oil in the eastern Mediterranean. For *Le Monde* the explicit lack of opposition from the Arab countries to Trump's plan shows the priority they assign to the "Iranian threat": the Palestinian dossier could be used to manage the dosage of American retrenchment in the region.

Palestinian "Bantustan" and Israeli Arab proletariat

Around the time of the Camp David accords, Arrigo Cervetto considered, in the Marxist scientific laboratory, the hypothesis of a "Middle Eastern Zollverein" – a "free trade zone of Saudi-Iranian capitals, Israeli managers, peasant disintegration of 50 million Egyptians and Sudanese" – given the failure of a "Prussian solution" for unifying the region. We noticed that this "strategic variant" did not materialise, as the course of the regional dispute has alienated "not only any hypothesis of a confederation, but also any form of truce between regional actors". The Middle Eastern bourgeoisies are unable to achieve the "new level of continental State power" required by the new strategic phase; unless a "catastrophic breakdown of the world order shatters the imperialist balance of power" [*Reactionary Terrorism, Imperialist Europeanism, Communist Internationalism*, éditions Science Marxiste, 2017].

The tonnage of local actors has doubled, both demographically and economically, increasing their ability to influence the balance. In line with this trend the army of the Middle Eastern proletariat has largely expanded. This also applies to Palestine, in which there is an Israeli proletariat of about 4 million workers and a Palestinian one of 1.5 million. Palestine had about 3.5 million inhabitants in 1967. Today there are 9 million Israelis, including about seven of Jewish faith and two of Islamic faith; Palestinians are around 4.8 million, with a diaspora of another 5.6 million.

The Israeli military annexation has partially integrated the Palestinian territories into the economy of Tel Aviv, including through a customs and monetary union, since the early 1970s. If in 1967 40% of the Palestinian labour force was agricultural, today the share is 6%; 30% are in manufacturing and 64% in services. In Israel, agricultural workers are less than 1%; 16% are in industry and 83% in services. In Palestine, 74% of the 800,000 employed workers surveyed are wage earners. In 2018, around 130,000 were employed in Israel or in settlements, particularly in construction.

For World Bank economist Leila Farsakh, Israeli policy has oscillated between a "maximalist" line of territorial but not demographic annexation, and a "centrist" one, in which a tacit annexation would have favored a more "efficient economic integration" of the territories, diluting nationalist pressures. The result, unwanted or relatively wanted, was to create Palestinian *Bantustans*, i.e., commuting labour pools, similar to the structures used by the apartheid regime in South Africa, but without Israeli ethno-racial legislation [*Palestinian Labour Migration to Israel*, 2012].

The asymmetrical integration of the Palestinian proletariat, whose flows are negotiated with the Palestinian bourgeoisie, and the respective nationalist ideologies are however useful tools to segregate the respective proletariats. Regarding the recent workers protests in Iran, David Ignatius, an authoritative commentator at *The Washington Post*, wrote that "organised industrial workers remain a powerful, bedrock force" for a "fundamental change in society": this is true "in Iran, China and even Donald Trump's America" as "in other modern nations". It is ironic that it is one of the newspapers of the ruling class which acknowledges this. If class struggle is not outdated in Tehran, nor is it in Nablus, Gaza, Haifa and Tel Aviv. The same is true for internationalism.

Missiles, Ballot Boxes and Coalitions in the Gaza War*

In *Jerusalem: The Biography* [2011] Simon Sebag Montefiore, a British historian, evokes the so-called "Jerusalem syndrome": a "psychological" but also "political" condition, where the confrontation between "devouring passions and intransigent feelings, impervious to reason" means that the "law of unintended consequences" often prevails. A condition that, perhaps, can be extended to the entire history of the Middle East.

Last May, the trigger for the "eleven-day war" – the fourth low-intensity conflict in Gaza – was a disputed ownership connected to real estate: the eviction of a few dozen Palestinian families in the city's Arab quarter "Sheikh Jarrah" was demanded by an association of Jewish settlers on the basis of a sales contract signed with the Ottoman authorities in 1876, at the time of the very first Jewish immigration to Palestine. The district is named after the personal physician of Saladin, the Kurdish military leader who recaptured the city from the Crusaders in 1187. At the time of the British Mandate, the Grand Mufti of Jerusalem, Amin al-Husseini, resided in that district, and in 1944-1945 the first headquarters of the Muslim Brotherhood, of which Hamas is an offshoot, was opened there too.

According to Jewish tradition, a cave on the edge of the neighbourhood contains the tomb of Simon Hatzadik (Simon the Just), an important religious figure in the 3rd century BCE. For Montefiore, this is just a legend since the tomb is actually Roman, built five centuries later. History, myths, beliefs and passions have piled up over almost 3,000 years. This is a further demonstration of the crassness of Donald Trump's approach in the much-trumpeted 2017 "deal of the century".

Hamas's electoral missiles

Several other issues have become enmeshed with that of Sheikh Jarrah: the demonstrations of the Jewish religious right to celebrate the conquest of East Jerusalem in 1967; the predictable Palestinian counter-demonstrations, culminating in access to the Esplanade

* Gianluca De Simone, June 2021

of the Mosques being blocked; and then the arrival of the Israeli police to clear it out, resulting in hundreds of injuries and arrests. Mahmoud Abbas, president of the *Sulta* (the Palestinian National Authority which administers the West Bank), took the opportunity to suspend the legislative and presidential elections. These elections, in which Hamas (the Islamist movement that controls Gaza) had also agreed to participate, would have been the first since 2006.

Among Abbas's motivations is the exclusion of Palestinian citizens of Jerusalem from the vote. But, according to observers, the crux of the matter is the growing dissidence within Fatah, Abbas's party. This is combined with the fear that, as in 2005-2006, Hamas will emerge as the winner in both Gaza and the West Bank. At the time Hamas, the Islamic resistance movement (the acronym in Arabic means "zeal" or "dedication"), obtained 56% of the votes against 44% for Fatah. This year about 30 electoral lists were presented, with Fatah itself divided into three.

Excluded from the ballot box, Hamas operates on the streets and, as the *Hindustan Times* of Delhi writes, has chosen to conduct "an electoral campaign of sorts for the West Bank" with "a salvo of its Qassam missiles": about 4,000 of them were launched. They opened the confrontation, symbolically, with the first barrage towards Jerusalem, then against the major Israeli urban centres, including Tel Aviv, and this eventually triggered the military reprisal. In the jargon of the IDF, the armed forces of the Jewish State, the "war at a distance" against Hamas – conducted with drones, air raids and artillery strikes – is called "mowing the lawn". The strategy is essentially to hinder Hamas's military capabilities and, to a certain extent, its economic ones. Hamas's strategy switched from the use of suicide terrorism employed in the Second Intifada of 2000-2005 to ballistic guerrilla warfare. A large number of the Hamas missiles, allegedly 90%, were intercepted by the "Iron Dome" anti-missile system. The entire episode resulted in 260 victims, the overwhelming majority of whom were Palestinians.

"Cynical synergy"

"Calm for calm" is the formula used by Benjamin Netanyahu's government to define the relationship with Hamas, i.e., a tacit armed coexistence. Tel Aviv, which unilaterally withdrew from Gaza in 2005, does not intend to dismantle the Islamists' entrenchment in the Strip, which has a population of 1.8 million, leaving it under the management of Hamas. From 1948 to 1967, Gaza was under Egyptian military administration. Israel, in peace negotiations with Cairo between 1978 and 1981, tried to return it to Egypt, which rejected the offer: "the Egyptians left the fishbone down our throats", was the comment of Israeli diplomats at the time [Ahron Bregman, *Cursed Victory: A History of Israel and the Occupied Territories*, 2014].

The Islamist presence in Gaza and the West Bank dates back to the 1940s. It expanded in the 1950s and 1960s, with Jordanian and Saudi financial support and a substantial Israeli assent: Tel Aviv saw in the charitable efforts of the Muslim Brotherhood a conservative counterbalance to Palestinian nationalism, which was influenced by both Nasser's Pan-Arabism and its Ba'athist variant of Syrian and Iraqi influence. It was indeed Sheikh Ahmed Yassin [1937-2004], a refugee in Gaza since 1948 and educated at the University of al-Azhar in Cairo, who gave life to Hamas at the time of the first Intifada, in December 1987, starting from a charitable and religious base. Between 1967 and 1987, the number of mosques created by the Palestinian Brotherhood had increased from 200 to 600.

One historic reason for the rivalry with Fatah dates back to 1957-1958, due to the Brotherhood's refusal to join the PLO and the armed struggle against Israel [Paola Caridi, *Hamas*, 2009]. This choice was reversed in 1987 and 2000, at the time of the second Intifada, partly triggered by Ariel Sharon's [1928-2014] provocative visit to the Esplanade of the Mosques, a gesture claiming sovereignty which was functional in determining his return to the political scene: he went on to win the premiership in 2001.

The Hamas-Fatah confrontation for hegemony over Palestinian nationalism led to the armed secession of Gaza in 2007, with Hamas's electoral success in 2006, triggering a low-intensity civil war. It ended up favouring the policy of Palestinian cantonisation operated by Israel and was used by Likud, the main faction of the Israeli centre-right, with the aim to capture the electoral support of "settlers" and religious Zionism, as well as the securitarian vote. This "cynical synergy", as the *Hindustan Times* called it, has also gripped the Israeli political fragmentation.

The debate over Hamas's missiles, in fact, entered the negotiations for the formation of the new government in Tel Aviv, where a heterogeneous coalition, with a majority of only one vote in the

Knesset (Israel's parliament), put an end to the long political reign of Netanyahu, who had been in power for twelve years.

Arabs holding the balance of power in the "coalition of eight"

The revolt was led by a former ally of the outgoing Prime Minister and exponent of the religious right, Naftali Bennett, who became the first Orthodox Jew to lead an Israeli government. The Ra'am party's role was decisive in breaking the electoral deadlock, with four elections in two years: the United Arab List is the first Arab party to be part of a government coalition, which is formed of eight parties, from the extreme right to the extreme left.

Founded in 1996, Ra'am derives from the Islamic Movement in Israel, created in 1971 by Arabs and Circassians. One of its components, called the "northern branch", was excluded from the elections in 2015, because it was suspected of links with Hamas. Mansour Abbas, head of the "southern branch", considered moderate, is a dentist from Maghar, an Israeli province with a strong Druze presence. Abbas was also willing to join a majority led by Netanyahu, in exchange for economic measures to support the Israeli Arab minority.

As *Le Monde* points out, it was Netanyahu himself who broke the "cordon sanitaire" around the Arab vote in the 1990s, on which the Israel Labor Party in the 1990s "tacitly cashed in". Netanyahu tried to use the confrontation with Hamas to prevent the agreement between Ra'am and the alternative coalition. Abbas's change of horses in midstream, however, was determined by the inter-communal clashes in Israel. These were triggered by the events in Jerusalem, but probably caused by the economic fallout of the pandemic of the century and the processes of social advancement of the Arab-Israeli component.

The Arab "middle class"

Arrigo Cervetto pointed out in the early 1980s how, in the Palestinian populations of Gaza and the West Bank, there is a process of "social stratification that culminates in a property-owning bourgeoisie"; its exponents "influence some currents of the PLO with one hand", while with the other "collaborate economically with the Israeli bourgeoisie". The Jewish State had an interest in letting "the pressure of the Palestinian bourgeoisie of the occupied territories" prevail for integration into a single market, but also in preventing it from forming an independent Palestinian State. Israel also had the problem, not easy to solve, "of the political representation of the Palestinian bourgeoisie in the State of Israel, characterised today by complete Jewish supremacy". The European and American historical experiences, however, offered examples of states "with multi-denominational cohabitations held together by emerging industrial and financial bourgeoisies" [*Opere* (Complete Works), Volume 4].

Last April, the *Haaretz* newspaper underlined the social mobility within the Arab-Israeli component. The "Arab middle class" has a per capita income between 75% and 125% of the median disposable income, and between 2007 and 2018, increased from 16% to 23% of the Israeli Arab population; the "upper-middle class", with incomes between 125% and 200% of the median, grew from 5.4% to 6% of the Arab population. In the twelve years of Netanyahu governments, the rate of Arab enrolment in high school has tripled, reaching about 20%, as did employment in hi-tech sectors, which rose to 3%. In particular, female proletarianisation and schooling have increased, with a drop in birth rates. However, inequalities remain high, with a poverty rate of 50% – three times the national average – and youth unemployment is still at 50%.

For *The Economist*, Israel, by opposing a two-State solution, determines by default that of a single State. In such a way it strengthens both the grip of Hamas nationalism and the Palestinian claim to "equal rights" against an "apartheid state". This produces internal social tensions, especially with the approximately one million Jewish immigrants of the 1990s from the former USSR: they populate the suburbs of Israel, often coinciding with the settlements, and are an electoral pool for both Likud and "religious Zionism".

From a working-class perspective, any nationalist or religious, denominational tangle is a trap. Only an internationalist position can unravel it.

In the "Twenty Years' War", an Understanding on the Gulf Is Reached in Beijing*

In the opinion of Camille Lons, Middle East specialist at the London-based International Institute for Strategic Studies (IISS), the agreements that took place in Beijing on March 10th between Riyadh and Tehran are to be read, from a Saudi perspective, as "sending a message to the US". It is not by chance that this message came a few days before the 20th anniversary of the 2003 Iraq war. For the Saudis, the agreements are part of "the search for a provision" in case the US no longer provides the monarchy with "sufficient guarantees". For its part, Tehran has not yet given up hope of bringing the US and other powers back to the negotiating table on the nuclear dossier.

According to the Japanese newspaper *Nikkei*, the Chinese diplomatic sortie signals "the West's waning influence over the world's most unstable region", where Beijing maintains "a consistent and strategic approach" in contrast to American oscillations. In order to avoid the "worst-case scenario" of "having to compete with China in appeasing the Middle East", America's partners, such as the EU and Japan, may be forced to "help fill the vacuum" in leadership left by the Americans.

Tokyo's warnings, like China's strategic consistency, make it clear that securing the Persian Gulf's energy artery is a matter of preeminent interest to the Asian powers. An article in *Kompas*, Indonesia's largest daily newspaper, describes the diplomatic normalisation agreement between the two rival Gulf powers as "a new geopolitical chapter" and a "historic milestone" that may help ease regional tensions. Indonesia is the largest Islamic country in the world, with a plurality of ethno-religious minorities, and it is likely that the religious dimensions of the confrontation between Riyadh and Tehran also factor into the Indonesian perspective.

Regional effects

According to Georges Malbrunot – *Le Figaro*'s Middle East correspondent – the "confidential clauses" featured in the Beijing agreement might see a mutual commitment to reducing the support to

---

* Gianluca De Simone, April 2023

proxy agents: on the one hand, the People's Mujahedin Organisation of Iran (MEK), an Iranian anti-regime militia present in Iraq, and on the other Sunni groups in Iranian Balochistan, which were active during social protests against the Tehran regime. There might also be provisions for a reduction in military supplies to the Shia Houthi movement in Yemen and an increase of pressure on Shia Iraqi militias to refrain from attacks against Saudi oil infrastructure, such as the one that occurred in 2019.

In Yemen, Riyadh is reportedly negotiating a political agreement to freeze the military crisis. According to *Le Monde*, the monarchy has effectively recognised the Houthi military victory and is looking for a way to extricate itself from the conflict, which began in 2015, while "saving face". In the opinion of several observers, Yemen seems destined to be "the sacrificial lamb" of the rapprochement between the Saudis and the Iranians, with a de facto tripartition: the North under Houthi control and the South-West divided between Saudi and Emirati spheres of influence. For the daily *Asharq al-Awsat*, the semi-official organ of the Saudi monarchy, Yemen itself will be a measure of the success of the agreement.

In the opinion of several French diplomats, a major beneficiary will be the regime of Bashar al-Assad in Damascus, with Saudi Arabia and the Emirates (UAE), but also Egypt, Tunisia and Turkey, working to normalise diplomatic relations there – an operation that has the discreet support of Moscow. In Beirut, the agreement in Beijing could resolve the political stalemate preventing the election of a new president. Less discussed, but significant, is the re-establishment of ministerial contact between Turkey and Egypt on March 18th. These talks between the two foreign ministers are important for agreements on Turkish recognition of Egyptian interests in Cyrenaica and Egyptian recognition of Turkish interests in the eastern Mediterranean.

Prince Salman's "Saudi priority"

Most commentators see the Gulf agreement as a recalibration of the foreign policy pursued by the crown prince, Mohammed bin Salman. In 2015, at the moment of intervention in Yemen, the prince had defined a "Salman doctrine" intended to assert Saudi military primacy within the Gulf Cooperation Council. He intended to counter the expansion of Iranian influence, also hinting at a willingness to pursue nuclear status to balance Tehran's position as a "virtual nuclear power". Present in the "Salman doctrine", however, was also an ambition to grow "strategic autonomy" from Washington, the traditional guarantor of Saudi security. A third element was the so-called "Vision 2030", a programme to modernise the country in order to cope with the energy transition [Gianluca De Simone, *Il Grande Medio Oriente* (Greater Middle East), Edizioni Lotta Comunista, 2016].

According to *Le Monde*, in order to pursue a programme of "modernisation from above", Salman, who is preparing to reign, needs a relatively stable neighbourhood. In turn, this is needed to make the monarchy attractive to foreign investment and open it up to tourism, with the ambition of making Saudi Arabia one of the top ten global economies. The adventurism in Yemen has turned into a quagmire for Riyadh. Now, above all, Riyadh seeks the security of its own borders, which have proved vulnerable to Houthi missile guerrilla warfare modelled on that waged by Hezbollah against Israel. Nevertheless, the monarchy is continuing in its quest for strategic autonomy, a search which takes the form of a multi-alignment: it joins with Moscow and Beijing, as does Iran, in the Shanghai Cooperation Organisation (SCO); it pursues an active neutrality on the Ukraine conflict; and it affirms a "Saudi priority" in parcelling out oil production quotas within OPEC+, in which Russia is also a member. Finally, Saudi Arabia does not renounce the security nexus with Washington, even though it has long been negotiating the acquisition of medium-range missiles from China in a tradition dating back to the 1980s and the Iran-Iraq war.

According to an opinion in *Foreign Affairs*, "Riyadh wants close and independent ties with the United States, as well as with Russia and China" and believes it can play "a crucial role in the region, balancing Egypt, Iran, Israel, and Turkey to protect its own security and wield regional influence". According to the analysis of various sources, in Riyadh's view, détente with Tehran does not exclude a possible normalisation with Israel. In Malbrunot's opinion, Tel Aviv appears at the moment to be the "big loser" of the Beijing agreements.

A strategic surprise for Tel Aviv

According to sources close to Mossad, Tel Aviv's foreign intelligence agency, the Beijing meetings between the heads of the Saudi and Iranian national security councils and their respective services "went unnoticed by all Israeli intelligence agencies". The media and analysts see the agreement as a severe setback for Prime Minister Benjamin Netanyahu, who is grappling with a difficult domestic political-institutional crisis.

In 2021, the ambitions Tel Aviv expressed to transform the *Abraham Accords* – the diplomatic normalisation arrangements with the UAE in which Morocco, Jordan and Egypt also participate – into an "Arab NATO" organised against Iran were already considered "premature" by the UAE and Egypt. Moreover, Cairo is an observer in the SCO, as is Turkey. A diplomatic normalisation with Riyadh, in addition to having an anti-Iranian valence, would have been important for Israel with respect to the Palestinian question and East Jerusalem. For the INSS – a think tank close to Aman, Israel's military intelligence agency – the Beijing agreements, like China's willingness to conduct discussions with Moscow on "Gulf security", signal a growing Chinese diplomatic activism. In today's international situation and in light of a regional "tendency towards détente", Tel Aviv must avoid moves that could cause an escalation in the Palestinian and regional context, which would risk leading to its diplomatic isolation.

For *Haaretz* as for the *Jerusalem Post*, the fact is that dependence on the American ally, while remaining indispensable, in the framework of Sino-American rivalry conditions the relationship between Israel and the Chinese Dragon.

Israeli polarisation

However, internal political polarisation also weighs heavily, with the mass protests in March against the government's plans for judicial reform. The executive is considered to be a hostage of the national-religious parties, which are minority members in a coalition that holds 64 of the Knesset's 120 seats. The confrontation over judicial reform has exposed tensions in Likud itself, Netanyahu's party, and brought to the fore critical positions in the security and military apparatus. This has also opened a clash with the judiciary, as the government could overturn its rulings, limiting legal protection for the Arab-Israeli component and benefiting the "Israeli settlers' party". The military and security apparatuses also contest the creation of a "national guard", a paramilitary force under the Ministry of Security and not the police.

According to *Le Monde*, the anti-Netanyahu faction includes "part of the Israeli secular elite" in Israel – who are in the "Ashkenazi majority", i.e., originally from Eastern Europe – and who find the coalition formed with the "ultra-nationalist and religious parties" that came out of the polls last November "repulsive". The coalition's provocations on the Esplanade of Mosques fuel Palestinian militancy and tensions with the Arab-Israeli minority.

The assessment of the "Twenty Year's War"

Hamas's launch of about 40 rockets from the Hezbollah-controlled region of South Lebanon, with limited retaliation by Israel, was read by Saudi sources as a "code signal" by the Lebanese party-militia: they wanted to remind Tel Aviv of its "red lines", hence its deterrence capacity, but in the context of the Beijing agreements signed by its own Iranian sponsor. Often Middle Eastern political logic is more elliptical than rectilinear; for *Le Monde*, Hezbollah's attitude of "leaving it to Hamas" is an indirect warning about its capacity to raise or lower tension in response to Israel's actions.

If China's entry into the Gulf represents a "major step" that, with Beijing's exercise of a "double pillar" policy, erodes the Carter Doctrine (see "Tirpitz and Kautsky in Beijing", *Internationalism* May 2023), on the regional level, the détente between Riyadh and Tehran marks a moment, perhaps a transitory one, in what we can define as the *Twenty Year's War*. Opened with the American invasion of Iraq in 2003, this war has profoundly altered regional alignments and sharpened the traditional power rivalry between the two shores of the Gulf. In the perspective of the petro-monarchies – particularly Riyadh – both the overthrow of Saddam Hussein's Sunni minority regime in Iraq and the subsequent oscillations in Washington's policy from 2011 onwards have fuelled existential threats. In particular, the petro-monarchies are concerned with the expansion of Iranian influence as far as the Mediterranean Sea, alongside Turkey's ascent to power – which recently operationalised its first light aircraft carrier *Anadolu* – and the activism of the wealthy Emirates.

The consequences of the 2003-2023 period were the cantonisation of four regional states – Iraq, Libya, Syria and Yemen – and, on the human level, between one and two million dead and some tens of millions of refugees, who have been displaced both within and outside the region.

The Strategic Bankruptcy of Arab and Israeli Nationalisms*

The surprise attack of October 7th along the border between Israel and the Palestinian enclave of Gaza was described by *Le Monde* as a "politico-securitarian earthquake" in the Middle East. The attack has had the effect of throwing a "grenade" onto the negotiating table of ongoing attempts, instigated by the USA, to normalise diplomatic relations between Riyadh and Tel Aviv. The offensive by Hamas, an Islamist political-military movement, is unprecedented for the form it took, that of a massive incursion into Israeli territory, and for its "brutality", killing over 1,000 people and taking about 200 hostages.

Feuding brothers over surplus value and segregated proletariats

It is not only civilians who have been killed: almost 300 soldiers have died. This was a level never before recorded, neither in previous clashes with Hamas in Gaza nor with Hezbollah in the 2006 Lebanese conflict. Jewish lives are not the only ones to have been taken: the *reactionary terrorism* unleashed by Hamas has also claimed victims among Arab-Israeli wage-earners, Palestinians or Druze, as well as among Thai, Filipino and Nepalese immigrant workers, employed as labourers in today's *kibbutzim*. In 2022, according to data from the International Labour Organization (ILO) and the Tel Aviv government, there were almost 140,000 migrant workers in Israel and another 140,000 from the Palestinian territories, including 15,000 – 20,000 from Gaza. Since 2018, Israel has established bilateral agreements overseeing the importation of foreign workers from several Asian countries, including Thailand, the Philippines, Nepal, India and even China, to staff sectors such as agriculture, construction, manufacturing, and healthcare.

The use of work permits, both in the West Bank and in Gaza, brings together the Israeli bourgeoisie and the Palestinian bourgeoisie which, via its terrorist faction, takes advantage of the de facto segregation of the Arab proletariat. Wages paid by the Israeli bourgeoisie become tax revenues for their counterparts in Ramallah and

* Gianluca De Simone, October 2023

Gaza. This is one of the planks of the modus vivendi established between Tel Aviv and Hamas, along with Israel's agreement, at least since 2009, to allow Qatari funds to pay the salaries of Hamas officials and administrative staff in Gaza, amounting to about $1 billion a year. At the time of writing, the retaliation unleashed by Israel in response to Hamas's slaughter has claimed over 5,000 lives and displaced about 600,000 people out of a total population of 2.2 million.

The "pressure cooker"

In an interview with *Le Grand Continent*, the former French ambassador to Israel Gérard Araud compares Gaza to a "pressure cooker", that regularly erupts into violence every three to five years. The dynamic is as follows: a more or less successful attack by Hamas triggers a "heavy Israeli response"; then, after a while, there is a mediation, usually led by Egypt, with calls for a ceasefire – a *hudna* (Arabic for "truce") – until the next explosion restarts the cycle. On this occasion the "pressure cooker" ended up exploding with greater violence than usual. The difference lies in the complexity of the operation which, in its "undeniable tactical success", has inflicted "an incredible psychological shock" on Israel and left the government looking surprised and helpless. The capture of over 200 hostages, Araud adds, "is an unprecedented shock" that will make the Israeli retaliation more difficult. The increase in Palestinian casualties in Gaza puts the various Arab countries, in which public opinion is mostly pro-Palestinian, in a position of "extreme embarrassment", complicating the secretive activities for diplomatic normalisation between Riyadh and Tel Aviv. If the two "are not married, they have been sharing a bed for at least ten years", Araud continues, based on the geopolitical axiom that "the enemy of my enemy is my friend". In this case, Saudi Arabia and Israel's common adversary is Iran.

The 2020 *Abraham Accords* are "Trump's great diplomatic success". The "megadeal" that the Biden administration is working on – its extension to Saudi Arabia – poses a "delicate challenge for Riyadh". The Saudi dynasty is the custodian of the holy sites of Medina and Mecca and cannot neglect Jerusalem, where a "far-right government" has been installed. This government's "radical elements are calling for the reconstruction of Solomon's Temple" on the ruins of which the Al-Aqsa mosque was built. An agreement between Riyadh and Tel Aviv, he continues, "would be a historic rupture". It is therefore understandable that Hamas and Tehran have a common interest in "derailing the agreement". The current crisis, like previous violent reaffirmations of the unresolved Palestinian question, will hinder Riyadh's intentions of rapprochement.

Hamas's little Yom Kippur War

The Hamas attack coincided with the 50th anniversary of the Arab-Israeli war known as the Yom Kippur War [6th-25th October, 1973]. According to *Le Monde*, because of its "undeniable hold on the Arab imagination", the latest action – the breaching of the high-tech security barrier surrounding Gaza, which the Israeli Defence Force (IDF) touted as "insurmountable" – was reminiscent of the Suez Canal crossing and the breaching of the Israeli defence system in the Sinai Peninsula, the "Bar-Lev line".

In the opinion of Élie Barnavi – a historian and former Israeli ambassador to France – Hamas's "little Yom Kippur War" is likely to "upset the regional balance", as it did in 1973. Furthermore this war is, as it was then, a "predictable event" and not "a divine plan". Rather, it is the result of two factors: "a fanatical Islamist organisation" and "an imbecilic Israeli policy", to which a "succession of governments" have clung and which the current one has brought "to incandescence". Over the years, in the process of defining power relations, Hamas was granted the "right of initiative", being able to decide the "heat level" of the confrontation based on its own interests. When, for example, Qatar's funding was felt to not be generous or prompt enough, it was sufficient to set off a "salvo of rockets" to drag Israel into a confrontation, which ended with an ephemeral ceasefire after a spiral of casualties.

According to Barnavi, a solution would have required an Israeli government that could "rehabilitate politically the PNA (Palestinian National Authority) and economically Gaza", rather than allowing Hamas to consolidate its power by dividing "the Palestinian territory in two sections". This is the goal sought by Tel Aviv for which Hamas has proved useful. Benjamin Netanyahu, for his part, has "made a Faustian pact" with "messianic-religious nationalists" in order to extricate himself from his legal entanglements. For Barnavi, the nationalists even resemble "the Jewish version of Hamas". This pact triggered "civil insurrection in Israel", in a climate of "latent civil war", and has eroded the cohesion of the armed forces and security services. All of this is being closely monitored by Hamas, Hezbollah and Iran.

On the eve of the attack, Barnavi adds, an entire army battalion was deployed in Nablus, in the West Bank, to protect "a Bible lesson and a public prayer", when it would have been more useful to protect the settlements around Gaza. As in the 1973 war, Israel showed arrogance and complacency, but this time it has been punished with a "greater humiliation", because the clash then was between over-armed regular armies, whereas today, although Hamas has much experience, it does not have strength comparable to that of the IDF, the most powerful and advanced army in the region.

Realpolitik and the "cynical synergy"

According to the political analyst Ran Halévi, "in the name of jihad" (holy war), Hamas has forgotten the realpolitik and pragmatism that it inherited from the tradition of the Muslim Brotherhood. However, the majority of Israelis "oppose a lasting occupation of the Gaza Strip". And it is hard to see who could replace Hamas if it were wiped out. The best solution, in a "war with no real solution", would be to "weaken it enough to prevent it from acting", but "without annihilating it".

A similar assessment was expressed in *The Economist* by Ehud Barak, a former prime minister of Israel, according to whom Israel should aim at eliminating the military wing of Hamas, now 35,000 militiamen strong compared to 5,000-10,000 in 2009-2014, and then entrusting Gaza to "an Arab peacekeeping force". Both *Haaretz* and the conservative daily *Jerusalem Post* doubt that Tel Aviv can, by militarily occupying the Gaza Strip, impose an administration of the PNA, which would be "supported by IDF's bayonets". The *Financial Times* evokes the additional risk that Gaza could become the equivalent of Afghanistan or Somalia, controlled by armed gangs and *warlords*, like Mogadishu during the last 30 years.

Our analysis has described the exercise of realpolitik by Hamas, as well as Israel, as a "cynical synergy" between the two bourgeoisies: terrorist attacks, rocket salvos, and bombs have served both Tel Aviv's divide-and-conquer strategy and the electoral fortunes of the Israeli right [see also pp. 105-9]. As *Le Monde* notes, all this has served to create the political space for Hamas to assert itself as the sole repository of "Palestinian nationalism", largely thanks to the degradation and discrediting of the secular nationalism of Fatah and the PNA, which many observers now regard as an "appendage" of the Jewish State.

The Sorcerer's Apprentice and his Golem

If the Palestinian proletariat ends up under the ferule of reactionary terrorism, manipulated by the *oil-soaked Arab bourgeoisie*, and left to foot the bill with their blood, the same is true for the Israeli proletariat, which is paying the price for the incipience of its own bourgeoisie. The historian Ian Black writes that at the turn of the 1930s the *Histadrut,* the Zionist trade union centre, abandoned the "old idea of a joint Arab-Jewish trade union federation", which "had never been very successful" [*Enemies and Neighbours*, 2018]. It was only from 1966 onwards, recalls the historian and political analyst Samy Cohen, that "Arab-Israeli workers were admitted into the ranks of the trade unions [...] in which they represented one of the most combative components" [*Israël, une démocratie fragile*, 2021].

Nicknamed *Hakosem* (the magician) by his own supporters, Netanyahu's ruthless exercise of power and cynical synergy with Hamas has ended up creating a *Golem* straight out of Jewish folklore: a creature with human features, made of clay and believed to be able to protect the Jewish people from their persecutors, but also capable of escaping their control and unleashing destructive forces. *Haaretz*, a well-known Zionist newspaper founded in 1919, recalls what the PM had said in March 2019 at a party with the Likud leadership. These statements were published at the time by the *Jerusalem Post*: "allowing [...] Qatari funds to be transferred [to Hamas] is part of a broader strategy to keep [...] a separation between the Palestinian Authority in the West Bank and Hamas in Gaza. [...] Whoever is against a Palestinian State should be for transferring the funds to Gaza". This statement was echoed, in May 2019, by Reserve General Gershon Hacohen in an interview with *Yedioth Ahronoth*, founded in 1939 and among the most widely circulated Israeli newspapers: "We need to tell the truth. Netanyahu's strategy is to prevent the option of two states, so he is turning Hamas into his closest partner. Openly Hamas is an enemy. Covertly, it's an ally".

Throughout his political career, Netanyahu has unscrupulously ridden *two tigers*. The first is the settler movement which, in Netanyahu's race to succeed Ariel Sharon at the head of Likud, has emphasised a "securitary populism" that has amplified Israeli political polarisation. The second is the aforementioned *cynical synergy* with Hamas. The current crisis has forced him to accept the formation of a "war government" with the participation of the head of the largest opposition group, Benny Gantz, a former general who entered politics in 2018, and to exclude far-right ministers from the "war-making decisions". There is no shortage of pressure on Netanyahu, whose political career appears to be at an end, to resign. The precedent of the 1982-85 Lebanese conflict is cited, which led to the resignation of Menachem Begin, who was replaced by Yitzhak Shamir. This happened when the war turned into a military quagmire for the IDF and because of the massacres in the refugee camps of Sabra and Shatila by Maronite phalangists, in the presence of Israeli troops. For this, Sharon – who was defence minister at the time – was held "indirectly responsible" and forced to resign.

The 1973 precedent

According to the historian Benny Morris, in 1973 Egypt and Syria "did not aim to destroy the Jewish State [...] conscious that such a goal was beyond their reach and that, if threatened with annihilation, Israel could use the atomic weapons it already possessed". The Egyptian objective was to acquire a strip of territory on the eastern bank of the Suez Canal and shake "the diplomatic immobility of Israel, the international community", and the great powers, while Damascus aimed to take back the Golan Heights. Most importantly, "washing away the disgrace of 1967" and the entirety of Arab history since 1948 "would bring both regimes rich rewards", including "financial contributions from the rich oil monarchies". In any case, neither of the two capitals or their Arab allies were motivated by the cause of Palestinian nationalism.

This conflict was a "cold shower" for Israel which had become accustomed to "dazzling victories and the comforting certainty of the military and political ineptitude of its adversaries". For the first time, many Israelis questioned how long the occupied territories could be kept by force, and whether "a peace-territory barter should be seriously considered" [B. Morris, *Righteous Victims*, 2001]. On the domestic political level, both the triumph of 1967 and the shock of 1973 gave rise to the settler movement, along with the crisis of the Israeli Labour Party and the birth of Likud – the party of the Israeli nationalist right founded by Sharon and Begin shortly after the conflict. The Likud is an offshoot of both "Zionist labourism and the religious extreme right". It went from being a minority force to becoming, in some of its variants, decisive in the formation of governing coalitions, thanks to the highly proportional electoral system [G. Gorenberg, *The Accidental Empire*, 2006; I. Zertal, A. Eldar, *Lords of the Land*, 2007].

Several sources have recalled that the forerunners of Hamas – who settled in the Gaza Strip, strewn with refugee camps since 1948 – were viewed positively by Labour governments after 1967, as "a religious conservative element" to be pitted against the Palestine Liberation Organization (PLO). When Hamas became unmanageable with the outbreak of the second Intifada in 2000, it became a further factor in the fragmentation of a Palestinian nationalism that had already been largely defeated in 1993 [J.P. Filiu, *Histoire de Gaza*, 2012; A. Bregman, *Cursed Victory*, 2014].

The great massacre carried out by Hamas may prove to be a *fatal gamble* in its ambition to establish itself as a Palestinian national Islamic party, but it is already proving to be a poisoned chalice for the Jewish State and its annexationist policies, which have accentuated its *political imbalance* and triggered internal sectarian clashes.

SHORT-SIGHTEDNESS, POPULIST OPPORTUNISM AND STRATEGIC DISASTER

"Netanyahu must resign, today. [...] He said over and over again (most recently just 10 days ago) that Hamas is deterred and does not want war because it does not want to risk its economic achievements – namely the large sums that Bibi made sure were handed over, whether through Qatar or by increasing the number of workers in Israel who pay tax to Hamas. The tragedy is that with this money, Hamas bought pick-up trucks, machine guns, paragliders and rockets, and used them to kill us. [...] It is exactly that thinking that led the army to transfer its forces from the quiet Gaza border to the turbulent West Bank. After all, someone needs to protect the Haredi nationalists, [...] the pilgrims going up to Mount Ebal, the visitors to Joseph's Tomb, the hundreds of deluded fanatics who went up to the Temple Mount. [...] All of that is of course a thousand times more important than a few people living in the Gaza-area communities. [...] The real existential threat to Israel is leaving the fate of the country and the hostages to a government of incompetents and corrupt. Once the situation stabilises at the front, the need for emergency government will cease. Netanyahu and others responsible for the disaster will be removed and brought to justice".

Haaretz, October 10th.

"The October 1973 attack was caused by the generals' arrogance and the government's over-reliance on their opinions. The October 7th attack was the product of the government's perverted list of priorities created last January, with its unnecessary focus on judicial reform and its capitulation to the financial and political interests of its ultra-Orthodox members. It does not take a political scientist to realise that this coalition has paid less attention to border security with Gaza than that expressed on the law to prevent Netanyahu's removal as PM. [...] The government saw the threat of Hamas in the south as a distraction from important issues such as weakening the judiciary or exempting the ultra-Orthodox from military service. The conclusion is clear: leave! Those responsible for the catastrophe must not remain in power. Their exit is vital for winning the war and rebuilding the economy and society when it is over".

Yedioth Ahronoth, October 10th.

"Benny Gantz and Yair Lapid must enter the national unity government, even if many ask them not to do so, [...] fearing corrupt double-dealings. [...] Many want to dissuade them from lending legitimacy to the national security buffoons. In normal times, they would be right. [...] Israel needs unity, so that IDF does not have to distrust the leadership in combat, or fear its decisions. [...] Anyone who thinks about his personal situation, now that Israel is at war, does not deserve leadership".

Maariv, October 11th.

"Israel is hostage to extremist politicians [...]. It would be better if they were removed from the decision-making centres. Any reasonable person could have seen that disaster was imminent and sounded the alarm, [...] but Netanyahu would not listen. [...] The bottom line was [...] that things could be kicked down the road; that the Palestinian problem has been solved because the Emiratis, Bahrainis, and Moroccans signed normalization agreements with us (and that soon Saudi Arabia will do the same). [...] Israel chose to ignore the fact that the Palestinians are here and are not going anywhere. That they won't show up in Washington, London, or Riyadh in the morning, but in Gaza [...]. And that whoever doesn't solve the problem will eventually have to deal with a much bigger problem. This policy (or more accurately, absence of policy) has accompanied Israel facing the Palestinian arena for 56 years and Gaza for the past two decades. Worse than that, Israel chose to weaken the Palestinian Authority and strengthen Hamas. It saw it as a partner, refrained from crushing it, and ensured it received money, workers, and status. [...] Hamas got what it wanted and attacked; Israel gave it what it wanted and suffered. This vacuum of strategic decision-making enters the political chaos of the past few months in Israel".

Israel Hayom, October 11th.

"This war is Netanyahu's fault. He cultivated Hamas as a strategic partner and led the illusion that it could be bought with Qatari cash. Moreover, Netanyahu replaced ministers of defense like socks, thus sowing in the defense system the same instability he sowed in the political system while inflating and devaluing the government, mutilating the public service, and assaulting the courts. Worst of all, Netanyahu divided Israeli society, and thus led the enemy to believe it had become ripe for its assault. [...] It takes no prophet to predict that what has befallen us will ultimately unseat him, and punctuate his career".

Amotz Asa-El, former editor of _The Jerusalem Post,_
The Jerusalem Post, October 13th.

"Following Operation Protective Edge in 2014, and more so later, we kept hearing that Hamas had gone through some kind of metamorphosis and that it has reined itself in and that its function is ruling Gaza. That's what it does.

It governs. [...] One of my blind spots, that of the army and others, is that we weren't seeing what was right in front of us – Hamas's ideological commitment. [...] It's not like they were hiding it. We just chose not to see it very well. [...] Since 2009, the political leadership has been telling us that we must strengthen Hamas and weaken the PNA. [...] We've created a monster – the strongest force in the region – and they hit us very hard – like nothing before".

Avi Issacharoff, former editor-in-chief of *Haaretz* for Gaza and author of the TV series *Fauda*, interviewed in *Yedioth Ahronoth*, October 16th.

Regional Diplomacies in the War in Gaza*

The joint summit of the Arab League and the Organisation of Islamic Cooperation (OIC) was held on November 11th in Riyadh. The OIC brings together 57 countries, including Iran, Turkey, Malaysia, Indonesia and Pakistan, while the Arab League has 22 members. Saudi Arabia is faced with an internal fracture within the Arab League between the more extremist anti-Israeli positions, led by Algeria, and the more moderate positions of the Arab monarchies and Egypt. In response, it has lessened this confrontation by merging the two summits and creating the formula of a *common Islamic position* on the Palestinian question.

Arab divisions and the return of the Abdullah Plan

According to *Le Monde*, the unanimity at the Riyadh summit with regard to the condemnation of Israel and the relaunch of a two-State solution to the Palestinian question serves to "mask the differences" between the various Arab-Islamic powers, as well as their "undeniable responsibility" for the ongoing tragedy. In fact, the OIC joint communiqué re-proposed the 2002 plan of Abd Allah bin Abdulaziz Al Saud [1924–2015], the grandfather of Saudi crown prince Mohammed bin Salman Al Saud (MbS), which offered diplomatic normalisation with Israel in return for the creation of a Palestinian State on the basis of Israel's 1967 borders.

That initiative, in the opinion of *Le Monde*, was doomed in 2020 with the announcement of the *Abraham Accords*, since these agreements contained "not the slightest quid pro quo", without even "symbolic" attention paid to the Palestinians. Encouraged by Washington, MbS can now "take the big step" of normalisation between Riyadh and Tel Aviv, after "a decent interval". In doing so, he may deprive the Arab states of the "negotiating leverage" that the Palestinian question gives them, even if they have largely distanced themselves from it. Several countries would not mind the "eradication of Hamas" from the Palestinian political arena, which is Tel Aviv's "manifest goal". However, paralysed by their divisions, they express "a guilty impotence", ranging from the Saudi "wait-and-see" attitude

* Gianluca De Simone, November 2023

to the "extremism" of their "Arab brothers", while "death and destruction are increasing" in Gaza.

Iran and Turkey in MbS's "big tent"

The assessment of Israeli sources such as *Haaretz* is very different. In today's crisis, they seem intent to position themselves halfway between the currents in Tel Aviv – be they political or military – and those in the American administration. In the analysis of Zvi Bar'el, the editor-in-chief for the Middle East, MbS's decision to merge the two summits was a "wise move": Riyadh is trying to engage Tehran in a policy of normalisation with the Arab countries and is encouraged by Chinese mediation. Pragmatically, one might add, Saudi Arabia has opted for a *big tent* approach which has counteracted attempts by non-Arab regional powers to make use of the Palestinian question. This approach has indeed granted Iran and Turkey the "diplomatic achievement" of being hosted at an "Arab summit", and hence of having a seat at the negotiating table around the Palestinian question. In the words of Machiavelli: "keep your friends close, keep your enemies closer".

Bar'el points out that the joint OIC resolution calling for a two-State solution contains two clauses on a future diplomatic solution to the crisis. One emphasises the role of the Palestine Liberation Organisation (PLO) as the "sole legitimate representative of the Palestinians", in which "all Palestinian factions" should be "united". The other is the call for "an international peace conference" in the near future. According to Ghassan Charbel, the editor-in-chief of the Saudi daily *Asharq al-Awsat*, the convergence at the Riyadh summit between countries that have "different interests, alliances, friendships and calculations" concerns the creation of an "independent Palestinian State". If the Arab-Islamic world has "never been able to be an effective protagonist in the international arena", today, in a changing world order, those countries possess the capabilities to "defend their interests" and exert influence in a region in which "the West has vital interests".

Kim Ghattas, a commentator for the *Financial Times*, underlines the balancing act carried out by Tehran and Riyadh: the Saudis "hope that since they have not yet normalised" relations with Israel, having a "channel with the Iranians will offer them some protection". The same goes for Tehran, which, along with the Lebanese Shiite party-militia Hezbollah, is said to have opted for a "decoupling" between its regional interests and the Gaza issue.

Nasrallah's "support front"

As the Riyadh summit unfolded, the secretary-general of Hezbollah, Hassan Nasrallah, spoke out for a second time on the conflict in Gaza. Nasrallah assessed the OIC summit positively: "The expectation of the Palestinians was not a summit decision to send troops to break the siege in Gaza [...] but the adoption by the Islamic and Arab world of a unified position" demanding that the USA act and put an end to the Israeli offensive. Regarding the confrontation in Gaza, he evoked "the support front" for the Palestinians, the series of actions led by Hezbollah and Iraqi, Syrian and Yemeni militias, backed by Iran. Nasrallah stressed that the Palestinian victory will be decided "cumulatively, on points, not with a single massive attack".

In Bar'el's opinion, the Hezbollah leader has stopped short of full military involvement. This position reflects the "Iranian directive" to Hezbollah: they must "operate within a narrow boundary of measured and precise responses" with Israel, avoiding the risk of drawing Tehran into a direct conflict with Washington. This position is symmetrical to Washington's "support front". The US objective is indeed to "restrain Israel" to avoid being dragged into a regional war. This eventuality is envisaged only in the event that Iran acquires nuclear weapons, but not for a "local conflict", however tragic, like the one in Gaza.

The Ankara "guarantors" proposal

For Burhanettin Duran – a commentator for the daily *Sabah* and one of the advisors to the Turkish presidency – Ankara's position at the OIC aimed at achieving the following: a ceasefire in Gaza; a two-State solution; and an increased pressure on Israel and its supporters, by mobilising "the Western and non-Western world". In Turkey's view, in order to reach a "just and permanent solution" to the Israeli-Palestinian conflict, the proposal put forward by Turkish Foreign Minister Hakan Fidan must be accepted. This proposal is based on a "guarantor system": several countries, including Turkey, acting as guarantors for the Palestinian National Authority (PNA) and Israel. For the time being, Fidan ruled out the possibility of Ankara deploying troops as an international peacekeeping force in Gaza, a hypothesis circulated by American and British sources, in order to avoid a new Israeli military occupation and to create the conditions for a return to a PNA administration.

According to Abdulrahman al-Rashed, the former director of *Al Arabiya* and *Asharq al-Awsat*, the peace process has been hampered by the de facto collusion between Israeli Prime Minister Benjamin Netanyahu and Hamas. Neither will emerge victorious from the Gaza war. However, the "political wing abroad" of Hamas has declared itself in favour of the two-State solution. Hamas's "politicians abroad" would like to reap "political dividends" from the events of October 7th. In al-Rashed's opinion, with the military wing besieged in Gaza, the political wing could have had a "guaranteed chair at the table of the ongoing negotiations", i.e., that of normalising relations between Israel and Saudi Arabia, in which the Palestinian issue is a major point of discussion. He argues that Hamas's military leadership disavowed the political wing as early as 2017 and, with its attack, tried to "nip the negotiations in the bud". While Israel has promised to "annihilate Hamas", this feat would appear to be impossible without "terrifying casualties", particularly among civilians. But even in that eventuality "Hamas could not be ignored". The PLO, he recalls, was militarily defeated by Israel in the war in Lebanon, but it was necessary to negotiate with it in order to achieve the Oslo Accords, transforming it into the PNA.

The Israeli maze

On the Israeli side, there are essentially three questions: the objectives of the war in Gaza, the time frame needed to achieve them, and the internal political balances required to resume negotiations with the Palestinians. Interviewed by *Haaretz*, James Clapper, the director of the US National Intelligence Council from 2010 to 2017, believes that "only Israel can answer the question" of what constitutes a victory in Gaza: if the goal is to destroy Hamas, it can only be achieved by razing the Gaza Strip to the ground. Several international observers noted that the implicit consequence would mean the *forced exodus* of a large number of Gaza's inhabitants. According to Clapper, given the "emotional" condition generated by the conflict in Israel, Washington's ability to influence Israeli choices "is very limited", as are the chances of a two-State solution emerging from the conflict.

Both the representatives of Likud, the national-conservative party, and those of the extreme national-religious right evoke a "Nakba 2023" for the Palestinians: "forced relocation" or the mass displacement and dispossession of Palestinian population from Gaza and the West Bank, analogous to what happened in 1948, as acknowledged by the historical accounts emanating from Tel Aviv [Benny Morris, *1948 and After*, 1994; Élie Barnavi, *History of Israel,* 1995; Tom Segev, *A State at Any Cost*, 2019].

The historian Benny Morris reports in his book that, at the time, the Israelis looked to historical examples such as the displacement of populations between Greece and Turkey, between Pakistan and India, and to what happened to the Armenians and the Kurds. This was also done to "remind other nations of their own crimes". For the historian and diplomat Élie Barnavi, the right-wing and religious currents may have been excluded or marginalised in political arrangements between 1948 and 1967, but they did not give up brandishing the threat of a "latent civil war". The assassination of Prime Minister Yitzhak Rabin in 1995, after the signing of the Oslo Accords, is considered by both Barnavi and political analyst Samy Cohen to be the realisation of that threat. In Cohen's opinion, this assassination was the "most resounding and baleful success of the fundamentalist circles", which "derailed the peace process". In 1996, he adds, "the settlers mobilised en masse for Netanyahu" in order to "bar the way for Shimon Peres", the other architect of the Oslo Accords. Since then, no Labour leader has ever dared to curb the expansion of settler settlements, in order to "preserve internal peace".

Cohen points out that the withdrawal of Israeli forces from the Sinai produced the formation of a "terrorist network", with members hailing from the "best families" of settlers, whose attitude was reminiscent of that of "the OAS towards De Gaulle and the French withdrawal from Algeria". The troop withdrawal was carried out by Menachem Begin's Likud government starting in 1979 as part of the implementation of the peace treaty with Egypt [*Israël, une démocratie fragile,* 2021].

Today the number of settlers stands at about 700,000, or around 10% of the Jewish population. Those in the territories that nominally belong to the Palestinians, according to a potential agreement formulated by former premier Ehud Olmert, account for about 200,000, or 2.5%. It seems doubtful, given historical precedents, that moving them out in order to implement a two-State solution can be achieved peacefully.

Trouble Spots Triggered by the War in Gaza*

Speaking in November 2023, John Raine, a former Foreign Office civil servant and adviser to the International Institute for Strategic Studies (IISS) – a British think tank – described the war in Gaza as confirming how, in the Middle East, "non-State actors ranging from militias to political and religious movements", have a "disproportionately large share of power" which, in spite of "the strength of their states", "remains outside of the State-based system". If they have not dominated the State agenda, they have in any case remained a "permanent feature of the region's geopolitics".

Over the decades, continued Raine, many of these groups have received "moral and material support from state backers" or from "sympathisers" within the State. Kurdish and Palestinian groups have been powered "by nationalist aspirations and decades of grievances", and Islamic extremists by "radical ideologies", while players in Lebanon, Syria, Iraq and Yemen have received "financial and operational sponsorship" from Iran. Tehran remains the "excluded power" in the attempts at regional cooperation which, in Raine's opinion, are also "a function of the global rise of China". On this occasion, the regional states, including Iran, have sought, to varying degrees, "to sympathise with the Palestinians [...] without risking becoming embroiled in military conflict with each other or with Israel".

Tehran's combination of ideology and pragmatism

"An unstated but implied objective" of these states, Raine concluded, was "retaining control of their own and the region's agenda". His assessment recalls our analysis of "the Middle Eastern bourgeoisie's terrorist splinter groups, reactionary terrorism, the poisoned seeds of Mediterranean politics, i.e., the effects of the imperialist lines deployed in the region for over a century" [*Grande Medio Oriente*, Edizioni Lotta Comunista, 2016] and the use of the *national pretext* as a tool of political action on the part of the various powers.

Regarding the regional policy mixes, there are some echoes to be found in the theses of Vali Kaleji, a Tehran researcher close to Iran's security policy circles. In his opinion, both the diplomatic

* Gianluca De Simone, January 2024

normalisation between Saudi Arabia and Iran, brought about through China's mediation, and the war in Gaza have weakened the American effort to isolate Tehran, at least *pro tempore*. A war limited to Gaza is exactly "the war (Tehran) wants": Iran's support for Hamas is not the same as seeking a more widespread war, "at least at this stage". Concerning this, he quotes the policy mix pursued by Hezbollah. By combining "ideology and pragmatism", Tehran is trying to keep the war "limited to Gaza" – an attempt which Kaleji admits is complex.

Emile Hokayem, the director of Regional Security and senior fellow for Middle East Security at the IISS, argues the same thing. According to him, wars in the region don't tend to remain "within state boundaries". "The underlying emotions and grievances, foreign interference, absence of a regional security process and persistent weakness of local diplomacy combine to make spillover more likely than not". Whether the war in Gaza remains "a competition for regional influence" or becomes an "open war", will depend on the specific combination of actions and reactions on the part of Israel and Iran. Israel's targeted killings against the Pasdaran and Hamas leaders in Damascus and Beirut, claimed *sotto voce* by Tel Aviv, as well as the American intervention against the Houthi militias in Yemen, could "change [Iran's] perceptions" and lead Tehran to measures designed to keep its own dissuasive means credible. In any case, the Islamic republic is taking recourse in *strategic patience* for now. Hezbollah, like the other pro-Iranian militias and organisations in the so-called "Shiite Crescent", "offers (Tehran) a strategic depth" and represents a "backup card" for dissuading both Israel and the United States from the possibility of a "future existential struggle". This is an oblique reference to the Ayatollah regime's nuclear programme and its possible acceleration towards military nuclear capability.

This is an element being debated by Riyadh and Washington within the framework of diplomatic normalisation with Israel. According to various American sources, Riyadh would like agreements similar to those granted to Tehran with the Joint Comprehensive Plan of Action (JCPOA) agreement, signed by the Obama administration in 2015 and repudiated by the Trump administration in 2018, with a non-secondary role on the part of Israel.

Israel in the labyrinth of Gaza's ruins

Tobias Borck, a Middle East expert at the Royal United Services Institute (RUSI), the British armed forces' think tank, believes that the repercussions of the war in Gaza will define the regional order beyond 2024, with three sets of problems for Israel.

First of all, in order to restore the credibility of its own deterrence, shattered on October 7th, Tel Aviv will not stop operations until it has obtained the "removal from power" of Hamas and destroyed the group's capacity to threaten it. Given the "intangible nature" of these aims, Israel, whose internal consensus depends on the outcome of the war, will also have to seek "symbolic victories" such as the elimination of Hamas's top leaders. Secondly, it will have to solve the issue of how it "intends to deal with an almost completely destroyed Gaza", a field of ruins which recalls Grozny, Mosul, Al-Raqqah and Aleppo, just to mention recent examples: directly, i.e., by occupying it again, or via a Palestinian or international administration. Finally, the risk is that the violence in the West Bank, at its height since the second Intifada [2000-2005], may end up leading to a third one, deepening Israeli political polarisation, which the war in Gaza has not removed.

Unexpected Ethiopian activism

According to the RUSI and others, the Anglo-American intervention against the Houthi militias in Yemen aims to "contain and degrade" the actions carried out against commercial shipping in the Red Sea in order to prevent the convergence of the Palestinian theatre with that of the energy arteries. According to Borck, however, the Houthis and their Iranian sponsor have succeeded in their aim of shifting part of the regional geopolitical panorama, by making it obvious that they have the means to "hold at risk" two "of the world's most important maritime chokepoints", Suez and Hormuz. Iran's ability to influence, as well as its nuclear programme, concludes Borck, will not only have to return to the priorities of American and European decision-makers, but also those of the Arab and Asian capitals.

Nevertheless, as we have seen, the crisis in the world order is also offering opportunities for territorial revisions and claims in regions which are experiencing both the Middle Eastern tensions and the action of the various big and middle powers. If the Houthis are stirring up the waters of the Red Sea, in the Horn of Africa the Ethiopian demographic giant is seeking an outlet to the sea which, for Addis Ababa, is "vital" for its own economic development. It has therefore reached an agreement with the self-proclaimed Republic of Somaliland, a former British colony which became part of independent

Somalia but broke away unilaterally in 1991 with the crisis of the Somali State and the subsequent civil war. This Ethiopian decision awakens fears about the blurred borders of the African Continent, but has not yet been met with much international opposition. This year, like Saudi Arabia, the United Arab Emirates and Iran, Ethiopia, a major recipient of Chinese but also Middle Eastern investment, has joined the BRICS forum, presented as a kind of emerging powers' counterbalance to the club of those of the old order.

"Zollverein solution" and "Jordanian option"

Last month [Guido La Barbera, "Ukraine and Gaza in Europe's Social and Political Cycle" in *Wars of the Crisis in the World Order*], our analysis recalled Arrigo Cervetto's hypothesis of a "Zollverein solution" to the Palestinian question, i.e., a regional economic integration: these are hypotheses which are to be found again in the theses of the Trump and subsequently the Biden administrations within the framework of the 2020 *Abraham Accords* and of their extension to Saudi Arabia. We quoted Shimon Peres [1923-2016], David Ben-Gurion's former right-hand man as Defence Minister, who crafted Israel's nuclear programme with French assistance in 1955-63 and was subsequently Foreign Minister, Premier and President of Israel: as regards the Oslo Accords and the peace treaty with Jordan, he called for a regional "common market" modelled on the ECM and the EEC.

His biographer Michael Bar-Zohar reports that Peres was both in favour of the "Jordanian option" and of relations with Europe. This was due to his personal relations within European socialism and with Jean Monnet, François Mitterrand, Konrad Adenauer and the Bavarian Franz Josef Strauss. Until the early 1970s, Peres believed that Israel should seek an economic integration in Europe and not in the Middle East. From 1974, faced with the Jordanian monarchy's proposals to create a Jordanian-Palestinian federation, he put forward formulas of a customs/economic union for Palestine, reproposed in 1993 [*Shimon Peres*, 2007].

When the cold war ended, it would have been possible for Peres to attract "great quantities of American, European and Asian capital to the region", thus avoiding by economic means the Arab-Israeli conflict which began with the "partition of Palestine" in 1947. This was a partition, as the Israeli historian Avi Shlaim recalls, which saw the substantial "collusion" between the nascent Jewish State and the Jordanian Hashemite monarchy, with British and subsequently

American support. Amman was the main beneficiary, together with Israel, of the "Palestinian civil war", or the "war of independence" for Zionist historiography. Lesser beneficiaries were Syria and Egypt, which, from the Palestine of the British mandate, itself snatched from the Ottoman Empire, obtained the Golan Heights and the Gaza Strip until 1967. For the Arabs, writes Shlaim, the Palestinian question became more an element of inter-Arab ideological and political competition than a "symbolic tie" for the various competing formulas of "Pan-Arabism" [*Collusion over the Jordan*, 1988; *Lion of Jordan*, 2008].

The Jordanian monarchy was not in favour of an independent Palestinian State, since it would have been a potential threat for its dynasty, and could not, at least until 1988, renounce its territorial claims on the West Bank: until 1967, the latter had accounted for 50% of the kingdom's GDP and for 30-40% of its skilled labour; the custody of East Jerusalem, the third Islamic holy place, also contributed. Even if it was not opposed to Peres's formulas, Amman nevertheless believed they were too optimistic and based on his conviction of being "the best manipulator". What also weighed in the balance was Israel's "economic protectionism" of the occupied territories, underpinned by its colonial settlements. This is an enterprise which, according to some sources, cost about $60 billion from 1967 to 2007, with substantial investment in infrastructure, real estate, agriculture, and in the enhancement of land market value [Dan Vittorio Segre, *Le Metamorfosi di Israele*, 2007]. In 1994, a free trade agreement, ardently desired by Amman, did not accompany the peace treaty with Jordan.

Missiles and Corridors in the Conundrum of Gaza and the Pakistani Crisis*

"I have spent much of the last four decades working in and on the Middle East, and I have rarely seen it more tangled or explosive", says William Burns – a career diplomat and the current CIA director – in *Foreign Affairs*. What is happening in the area is an effect of the crisis in the world order: "The post-Cold War era came to a definitive end the moment Russia invaded Ukraine"; China seeks to "reshape the international order"; "the middle powers diversify their external relations, collaborating with the United States and China simultaneously"; and the war in Gaza has strengthened the Iranian regime, which is "ready to fight to its last regional proxy". This will make a "negotiation with Tehran" crucial to ensure regional and Israeli security.

According to Burhanettin Duran – the director of the Ankara-based think tank SETA, which is very close to Recep Tayyip Erdogan's presidency – Burns's position reflects the limits of America's ability to manage or define a new order in the region.

The "battle of deterrence"

The indirect confrontation with Tehran – in the Red Sea, Iraq and Syria – represents a "battle of deterrence" waged by means of missiles, local militia groups and drones; and it also ended up involving Pakistan, a nuclear power in which elections with a contradictory and potentially chaotic outcome took place on February 8th.

In Duran's view, Washington's ambitions to establish "a big strategic realignment in the Middle East" – the so-called "Biden Doctrine", as per Thomas Friedman in *The New York Times* – discount the fact that the United States "cannot have a strong enough presence in the Middle East to create order"; equally, "Russia and China's interests won't suffice to promote stability". It is therefore up to regional powers such as Turkey, Saudi Arabia, Egypt, Qatar, and the UAE to "launch new initiatives and build new mechanisms to end the fighting in the Middle East and to create a peaceful new order". Moreover, Ankara has recently strengthened its economic ties with Tehran (with an official visit by President Ebrahim Raisi in January), maintains relations with Israel (despite Erdogan's heated pro-Palestinian rhetoric), and continues its détente with the Gulf powers.

---

* Gianluca De Simone, February 2024

Tehran's "ring of fire"

As we noted a few months ago, one of the effects of the crisis in Gaza has been to assert the role of non-Arab regional powers around the crux of the Palestinian issue and, thus, regional balances ["Regional Diplomacies in the War in Gaza", *Internationalism*, December 2023]. In the fourth month of the conflict the death toll has reportedly reached almost 30,000, while the Israeli government, despite pressure from Washington, seems unwilling to stop its operations in the Gaza Strip, partly because of Tel Aviv's internal contradictions. Several observers therefore expect a favourable outcome for Tehran.

According to Ali Vaez – the director of the Iran programme at the International Crisis Group (ICG) – in an article in *Foreign Affairs*, the war in Gaza has undoubtedly allowed Iran to reap benefits: "The conflict has, at a minimum, delayed the normalisation of relations" between Riyadh and Tel Aviv, and "could have reisolated Iran" after the diplomatic rapprochement with Saudi Arabia. Furthermore, "the axis of resistance has used the conflict to burnish its capabilities and wide reach". The main architect of this axis, Pasdaran General Qasem Soleimani – who was killed by an American drone strike in Baghdad in 2020 – called it Iran's "ring of fire" around Israel. This has been an instrument of both Tehran's will to influence and its "advanced deterrence" to protect its national territory, in particular its nuclear infrastructure.

However, says Vaez, the Iranian leadership is following a practice of "strategic patience": it wants to avoid any direct conflict with Washington and does not at all intend to sacrifice Hezbollah or its regional network "for the sake of saving Hamas". Tehran was surprised by the attack on October 7th, which halted attempts at a possible détente with Washington that had commenced in 2021. Iran is thus "a reticent actor on its back foot". In an effort to restrain Israel by preventing it from conducting a pre-emptive strike in Lebanon against Hezbollah, Washington has been forced to exercise deterrence by deploying its forces in the eastern Mediterranean and intervening in Yemen and Iraq. While Tehran has a mighty and increasingly sophisticated ballistic arsenal and the ability to ignite hotbeds of crisis in the region, it is aware of its relative military weakness, with internal social tensions characterised by a confrontation among political currents. Iran is also about to hold an election to renew the *Majles*, its parliament.

Political deterrent and "just in time"

Iran, warns Vaez, could be very close to what proliferation specialists call "breakout": it may take a short time for it to produce enough enriched material to build five operational nuclear warheads with a yield of approximately 10-20 kilotons. This payload could be mounted onto its medium-range ballistic launchers (2,500 km), derived from North Korean models. In 2021, other American sources spoke of Tehran's posture for a "just in time" arsenal, i.e., which can be assembled as needed. Vaez highlights that this would be, first and foremost, "a political weapon", which Tehran could be induced to use if it felt that the US deterrence exercise overreached.

In March 2023, Mark Milley – the chairman of the US Joint Chiefs of Staff – told Congress that Washington's policy remains to disallow Iran to "have a fielded nuclear weapon". A formula that suggests American tolerance for a *de facto* but not *de jure* Iranian nuclear State. It is the same condition endorsed for Israel having "the bomb in the basement", i.e., capable of employing it only as a strategic last resort (if the Jewish State faced an existential threat).

The "Biden Doctrine" between Tehran, Riyadh and Gaza

This is a condition that could apply in the future to agreements with Saudi Arabia. To expand a Saudi-American security alliance is one of the "three tracks" of the "Biden doctrine" evoked by Friedman. The other two are a strong stance against Iranian regional influence and the normalisation of relations between Riyadh and Tel Aviv, conditional on Israel's formal commitment to a two-State solution. This is a substantial agenda. The American linkage between recognition of the Palestinian State and normalisation with Riyadh represents both the stick and the carrot used to condition Israel's attitude, but it is also one of the most complicated pieces of the Middle East puzzle.

"Buried after the failure of the 1993 Oslo accords", comments Isabelle Lasserre – *Le Figaro*'s diplomatic correspondent – the two-State hypothesis is "exhumed" by the crisis in Gaza, with the Israeli-Palestinian war wrongly considered a "semi-frozen conflict". Benjamin Netanyahu's government is against the two-State solution and has encouraged the "colonisation of the West Bank", turning it into "Swiss cheese" with the presence of 450,000 settlers to make it infeasible. According to Élie Barnavi – Israel's former ambassador to France – the conflict in Gaza "amplifies the rift between the West and the Global South". This allows the revisionist powers "China,

Russia and Iran" to "go toe-to-toe with the American pawn in the region", Israel, while Washington struggles "to create a regional coalition". However, the two-State solution is better than the alternatives: "apartheid" towards the Palestinians, including 20% Arab-Israelis, or "civil war" in the Jewish State.

Missiles, corridors and ballot boxes

In American intentions, the regional reorganisation of the Middle East also passes through the Sino-Indian rivalry. At September 2023's G20 in Delhi, Biden supported the India-Middle East-Europe Economic Corridor (IMEC), by adding it to the extension of the *Abraham Accords* to Saudi Arabia. The IMEC is the "Cotton Corridor" in competition with Beijing's "Silk Road". Through the Adani group, India is already present in the seaport of Haifa, with Israel also showing interest in Chinese capital.

According to Bruno Tertrais, the deputy director of the Foundation for Strategic Research (FRS) in Paris, in its multi-alignment and rivalry with Beijing, Delhi aims to exploit China's economic rise to create space for its own. However, India offers its availability for greater convergence with Washington towards South-East Asia, in exchange for "increased influence" in the Persian Gulf and the Middle East, areas jealously "garrisoned" by Centcom – the United States Central Command with responsibilities in these regions. Here, Beijing's projection passes through the "strategic triangle" established since the 1980s with Saudi Arabia and Pakistan [*La Guerre des Mondes*, 2023], but also, one might add, through China's linkage with Iran.

The missile exchange on January 16th-18th between Iran and Pakistan took place in the border region of Balochistan. This is an area divided in 1947 between Iran, Afghanistan and Pakistan and since the 1970s the scene of irredentist tensions of the Baloch ethnic group: a Persian-speaking population, but of Sunni Islamic denomination, fighting against the government in Islamabad, but also against that in Tehran. On the Iranian side, the military action was ostensibly intended to retaliate against those allegedly responsible for the bloody attack on January 3rd in Kerman, but was overall seen as a signal *tous azimuts*.

For the International Institute for Strategic Studies (IISS) in London, Pakistan's "calibrated" retaliation "indirectly served as a reminder to India": Islamabad suspected Delhi of encouraging

Baloch irredentism in order to hinder the China-Pakistan Economic Corridor (CPEC), a project centred on the port of Gwadar in Pakistani Baluchistan. According to Zhao Minghao – a senior fellow at the Charhar Institute – India considers CPEC as part of a strategic encirclement by the Chinese Dragon. However, Chinese economic penetration "alters the internal relations between different ethnic, religious groups and local forces". One example is the port of Gwadar, which alters the relationship between the Balochistan province and Punjab – the backbone of the Pakistani State [*One Belt, One Road*, 2020]. According to *The Straits Times* in Singapore, India's countermeasure is to support the development of the port of Chabahar in Iranian Balochistan as a "potential competitor to the port of Gwadar".

The election eve has certainly impacted the decisions of Islamabad, which faces a political crisis which began last spring with the removal from government and subsequent arrest of the populist premier Imran Khan, accused of corruption. This was an operation orchestrated by the armed forces, the historical arbiter of power in the country. Khan's party, the PTI, won a relative parliamentary majority, with about 100 MPs out of 265. The generals in Rawalpindi, headquarters of the general staff, can play the card of a coalition government, but this will have a problem of legitimacy. For Pakistan's major newspapers it would be wiser, in a country of 244 million inhabitants with an average age of 20, to opt for "national reconciliation", in order to avoid "a protest vote" turning into "hostility to the State". In the intertwined crises in the world order, a major crisis in Islamabad, a nuclear power, could have far-reaching consequences.

Choreography of Deterrence between Iran and Israel*

The missile exchange between Iran and Israel between April 13th and 19th was described by most international commentators as having been carefully "choreographed" by the two rival Middle Eastern powers, meaning that it was designed to re-establish mutual deterrence without triggering a major conflict in the region.

The certainly spectacular military-political exercise, at least on the Iranian side, was brought about by Israel's attack on Iran's diplomatic compound in Damascus: a "targeted killing", a tactic that Tel Aviv has practiced for decades now, which on April 1st killed seven Pasdaran officers. Among them there were some senior ranks, who were responsible for logistical coordination with the networks of pro-Iranian Shia militias operating between Lebanon, Syria, Iraq and Yemen.

A parallel "shadow war"

The "shadow war" parallel to the conflict in Gaza – in the words of *Financial Times* commentator Kim Ghattas – sees Iran opposed to Israel and the USA in an undeclared form or with "plausibly deniable participation". Since October 7th, the State of Israel has reportedly eliminated 18 Pasdaran officers in several targeted killings, without triggering an Iranian response. However, Tehran considered the attack on Damascus to have crossed a "red line" and as a direct attack on its interests and national sovereignty. Iran had already conducted a missile exchange with neighbouring Pakistan in the border region of Balochistan in January.

According to observers, Benjamin Netanyahu's government and Israeli intelligence wanted to make clear to Tehran that they could target Iranian activities anywhere and everywhere. According to Jonathan Eyal of the British think-tank RUSI (linked to the Ministry of Defence in London), Iran's backing of Hezbollah in Lebanon – revitalised in part by the conflict in Gaza along with its limited support for Hamas – has created a "buffer zone" within the northern regions of the Jewish State. For the past seven months, the rocket skirmishes on the Lebanese border, in addition to engaging a part

---

* Gianluca De Simone, April 2024

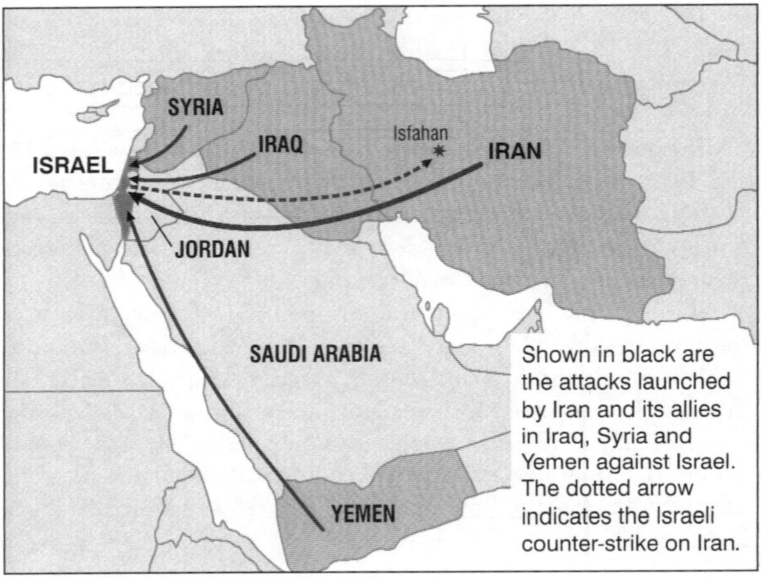

of the Israeli military apparatus, have led to the evacuation of some 80,000 people from the territory. This has created an uncomfortable situation for the Israeli government, with a conflict on their hands in Gaza that seems to have become a stalemate both at political and military levels, along with the enormous degree of destruction and number of casualties in the Palestinian enclave – about 34,000 dead at the time of writing.

With the attack on Damascus, Israel allegedly underestimated the possibility of an Iranian response. For both domestic and international reasons, Iran chose to abandon, at least temporarily, the line of "strategic patience" set out by the Supreme Leader, Ayatollah Ali Khamenei, and reiterated in the aftermath of October 7th.

The search for "détente" and missile exchanges

It is worth noting that this line has been recognised by Washington, which as part of its balancing act in the Middle East is seeking détente with Iran, as are the Sunni countries in the region, with the Gulf petro-monarchies in the lead. This détente has manifested itself through the UAE-Iran diplomatic rapprochement in 2022 and the Saudi-Iran normalisation agreement, which was mediated by Beijing in March 2023. In an effort to prevent the Gaza conflict from spilling over into the rest of the region, Washington obtained Iranian mediation in ending Shia militia attacks on the remaining US forces stationed in Iraq and Syria, after a series of skirmishes in late January and early February. Washington also apparently obtained a reduction in attacks by Yemen's Houthi militias. However, the United States was forced to launch targeted raids against bases in that country and deploy naval forces, which was done without the participation of the Gulf countries and independently from the separate European and Indian missions undertaken in the Red Sea. Washington, through its intelligence apparatus, distanced itself from the attack on Damascus, saying it had not been forewarned. It attributed the attack to Tel Aviv, which did not claim responsibility.

Tehran's response was massive, with the launch, according to US estimates, of over 300 drones and missiles on the night of April 13th-14th. The vast majority were reportedly intercepted by the combined action of the USA, Israel, the UK, France and Jordan, activating the Middle East Air Defence alliance (MEAD). The *Frankfurter Allgemeine* reports that Germany contributed to the in-flight refuelling of French aircraft. As for MEAD, which emerged almost as a surprise out of the crisis, this regional defence architecture was put in place as a consequence of the 2020 *Abraham Accords*, the normalisation of diplomatic relations between Israel and a number of Arab countries, in particular the UAE. Israel joined MEAD in the summer of 2022, moving from the operational purview of US European Command (EUCOM) to that of Central Command for the Middle East and Central Asia (CENTCOM). Apparently, only nine Iranian ballistic missiles, possibly of the Shahab 2 model, made it through the coordinated defensive bubble, causing light damage to an Israeli airbase in Nevatim, in the Negev desert region, 20 kilometres from the Dimona nuclear compound. According to various sources, part of Tel Aviv's airborne nuclear arsenal is stationed at Nevatim. Criticised by the Arab and even Western press as a failure and described as a "noisy fireworks display", the attack was nevertheless also acknowledged as "a carefully calibrated action", which raised the level of confrontation whilst leaving Israel with the possibility of de-escalation.

According to *The Jerusalem Post*, a daily newspaper close to Netanyahu's Likud party, Tehran had warned both Dubai and Riyadh of the operation about 48 hours earlier. None of the weapons launched were aimed at urban areas in Israel. Tehran limited itself to a single wave, despite possessing more sophisticated devices and a vast arsenal.

According to *Yedioth Ahronoth,* Israel's leading daily, "with about 60 tons of high explosives" the Iranian missiles "could have flattened the two targeted airbases". According to the Japanese newspaper *Nikkei*, the great effectiveness of the "zone" or "multilayered" anti-aircraft and anti-missile system used to defend Israel deserves to be studied by other countries, for example for the integrated air defence project between the USA, Japan and Australia. But it also turns out to be extremely expensive: April 13th was "the most expensive day in the history of Israel's defence", with the cost of intercepting the attack far outweighing the cost of launching it. The defence system requires "high production volumes" to cope with large missile arsenals.

The myth of a "Middle Eastern NATO"

The US-Israel coordinated defence exercise, with the participation of London, Paris, Berlin and Amman, directed and conditioned the Israeli retaliation with a demonstrative and limited strike: Tel Aviv used one or two "Blue Sparrow" ballistic missiles, launched from fighter jets from southern Syria towards the Isfahan airbase, not far from the uranium enrichment site of Natanz. According to Amos Yadlin – a former air force officer and former director of military intelligence in Tel Aviv – Israel sought to "restore deterrence", as this was the first direct attack on the country since the Iraqi Scud launch in 1991 and the first ever by Tehran: "without escalation, the equation was Isfahan for Nevatim", thus a symmetrical response, allowing "the two sides to stare each other down and de-escalate the conflict".

It is important to note that the missile exchange, on both sides, threatened their respective nuclear capabilities: operational but undeclared nuclear deterrent on the Israeli side, and a *latent* nuclear deterrent for Tehran. As *Le Figaro*'s diplomatic editor Isabelle Lasserre puts it, "the ghost that haunts" Middle Eastern geopolitics manifests itself "with each regional crisis". The only thing needed for it to emerge, according to IFRI's Héloïse Fayet, is a "political decision" on Tehran's part.

In various international and Israeli commentaries, the coordinated interception seems to envisage the emergence of a "Middle Eastern NATO" or an anti-Iran "strategic alliance". *Le Monde* is more sceptical: from the perspective of the Gulf countries, such an alliance would be a "chimerical prospect". As Emile Hokayem – the senior fellow for Middle East Security at Britain's International Institute for Strategic Studies (IISS) – also states, the cooperation of the Arab countries was based on their respective "national interests", primarily that of avoiding the escalation of the conflict. If in 2020 Jordan expressed enthusiasm for "a military alliance in the Middle East on the model of NATO", argues *Le Monde*, today the petro-monarchies and Egypt "have got cold feet" about the idea. These countries are already engaged in rapprochement with Iran after the disappointing results produced by the "maximum pressure strategy" applied by the Trump administration, after it unilaterally abandoned the nuclear agreement. In order to pursue such a military alliance, according to Riyadh, concrete and "irreversible" steps will be needed for the solution to the "Palestinian question", thereby relaunching the two-State solution. Moreover, the Gulf monarchies would like to have explicit security guarantees from Washington and an endorsement of their nuclear programmes. That is to say, an American assent to latent nuclear and military capabilities like those of Iran.

"US shield" for Tehran

Following its military show of force, Iran has declared the confrontation to be over. Meanwhile, the USA ruled out support for Tel Aviv's retaliation, based on the overwhelming success of its defences. Tehran has thus shrouded itself with Washington's "protective shield", as several observers have noted. Among them is *Haaretz,* according to which the ayatollahs' Iran is a "brutal regime, but one which acts as a rational actor".

This offers an answer to the question posed by Henry Kissinger, that of whether Iran is "a country or a cause" [*World Order*, 2014]. The answer is that it is both, though the instrumentalisation of the Islamic revolutionary cause for the interests of the Iranian State seems to predominate. Since the 16th century, by making the Shia denomination the State religion, Iran has always used religious minorities for its own foreign policy purposes; as Christophe Ayad – the former Middle East correspondent for *Le Monde* – writes, pro-Iranian Shia militias, above all Hezbollah in Lebanon, are Tehran's "shield and sword" in the region [*Géopolitique du Hezbollah,* 2024]. In Eyal's view, they represent "an instrument of advanced deterrence", protecting Tehran while it develops its "nuclear option", as an instrument of deterrence and power politics, as well as a bargaining chip in negotiations at regional and global levels.

Chapter Three

Oil and Middle Eastern Wars

"Black Gold" in the Century of Imperialism*

Over the course of the 20th century the tangle of the Middle East has knotted up in a series of connections which have made it a crossroads for all the powers. The specific interrelation fed by oil has been – at certain defining moments in power relations – important enough to appear decisive. But to what degree was it actually decisive? In what James Schlesinger, Secretary of Defense under Nixon and Ford and energy secretary under Carter, has called "the most complete and detailed treatment of the oil age" Daniel Yergin seeks a response to this question, following the drama of oil as the common thread linking some of the main struggles of the century. In Yergin's opinion oil is "The Prize" – the sought-after trophy of these struggles.

Rockefeller, Nobel and Rothschild

The cradle of the oil era was Pennsylvania, at the turn of 1860. The first competitors to American oil were the Russian oilfields of Baku, which around 1890 reached four fifths of American production without, however, succeeding in giving the Russian development the American pace. Three great names then dominated the oil sector: Rockefeller in America, Nobel and Rothschild in Russia. In 1890 the first, with Standard Oil, controlled seven tenths of the market and the "Russians" the remaining three tenths. The first attempt to create a world cartel, immediately aborted, was made in 1890 between Standard Oil and the Nobels who partitioned the world market in the proportion 75%-25%. In the 1890s the third oil pole emerged, in the Dutch Indies, with British Shell in Borneo and the Royal Dutch Company in Sumatra. The two firms united in 1907 to form a group with a 60% Dutch majority.

Only on the eve of the First World War did the Persian Gulf begin to emerge as a fourth pole. The Gulf oil cycle began half a century after the American one. While the centre of gravity of financial

* Nicola Capelluto, April 2003

and military power shifted from the Old World to the New World, the oil centre of gravity began a slow shift in the opposite direction. The resulting course of the two movements could not be painless, even though the United States kept its absolute position as the world's first oil producer – and its full self-sufficiency – for another four decades.

The strategic stake of the Persian Gulf

At the beginning of the century the strategic importance of the Gulf was not related to energy, but was geopolitical. Yergin underlines the long rivalry between Great Britain and Russia in Central Asia: Russian expansion threatened British India, conferring absolute importance onto Persia. However, foreign minister Lord Lansdowne's historic declaration of May 1903 – that the British government would regard any "naval base or fortified port in the Persian Gulf by another power" as a "grave menace" to be repelled "by all means" – was not only directed towards Russia. Paul Kennedy's reconstruction of the "Anglo-German Antagonism" highlights the entry of King Wilhelm's Germany into the "Great Game" of the Middle East: the attempt at a joint Anglo-German project to construct the Baghdad Railroad – negotiated between the Barings, Morgan and Deutsche Bank groups and strongly supported by Lansdowne himself – had just failed. His declaration was defined by Lord Curzon, Viceroy of India, as "our Monroe Doctrine for the Middle East". Exactly 100 years later, in the midst of the Iraq War, the demand for a Monroe Doctrine for the Middle East – this time a European Monroe Doctrine – was proposed again by the French ambassador to Washington, Jean-David Levitte: "the Middle East, for Europeans, is what Mexico is for you. Mexico is your backyard. The Middle East is our one". Today this is more a cry of pain than a threat. The direct consequence of the "Lansdowne Doctrine" was the intervention of the Foreign Office and the Admiralty in favor of the first British concessionary for oil prospecting in Persia, William Knox d'Arcy. The operation required years of exploration, loans from the Admiralty, alliance with the Scottish Burmah Oil, the assurance of supplies to the Royal Navy and the Indian market, and in part motivated the Anglo-Russian partition of Persia in 1907, which secured the southeastern drilling sites. The first oil flowed in 1908 and with it began the history of the Anglo-Persian Oil Company, subsequently British Petroleum.

Winston Churchill's battle for oil

Paul Kennedy writes that at the time of the Boer War the German high command became convinced that, without a complete reorganisation of its defences, the British Empire would dissolve in a couple of decades. In the *naval race* between the two empires Admiral John Arbuthnot Fisher, First Sea Lord since 1904, fought for the conversion of the Royal Navy from coal to oil and for d'Arcy's Persian project. He was, however, bogged down by the opposition of the majority of the admirals, faithful to Welsh coal and tradition. This knot was cut by Winston Churchill. Churchill had long been among the supporters of an Anglo-German naval accord which would allow the reduction of naval spending in favor of social reforms. The crisis provoked in July 1911 by the German gunboat "Panther", which entered the Moroccan port of Agadir, shifted Churchill into the naval faction. Having become First Lord of the Admiralty at the end of that year, he found that the greatest battleships still burned coal. The maximum speed, 21 knots, was insufficient. According to Churchill this figure needed to be raised by four knots: "the priority is speed – to be able to attack when, where and how one wants". Speed meant diesel.

Anglo-Persian and Royal Dutch Shell

In 1912 the construction of the Fast Division – five "Queen Elizabeth" battleships – was begun. "The best ships of the Navy, on which our lives depend, are fed exclusively on diesel" wrote Churchill, conscious of the immense risk: Great Britain was forcing herself to procure oil "via sea, in peace or in war, from far away countries...committing the navy to diesel propulsion meant truly to confront a turbulent sea".

That strategic choice sealed the fate of the Anglo-Persian Oil Company, Shell's competitor for the Admiralty's oil orders. In June 1914 Churchill had Parliament approve the government's acquisition of 51% of Anglo-Persian. The British government taking shares in a private company – observes Yergin – had a single precedent: the acquisition of shares in the Company of the Suez Canal on the part of Disraeli in 1875. The joint stock company celebrated the marriage between British geopolitics and geoeconomics.

The Royal Navy and the German Fleet

The gamble was risky: on the eve of the conflict Persia represented less than 1% of world oil production. But this was enough to set the pattern of certain battles in the First World War. As soon as it entered the war Turkey tried to take possession of the Abadan refinery. The English repulsed the Turks and counterattacked, taking Basra in November 1914. The city became the outpost for the defence of Iranian oil. Baghdad was conquered in March 1917. Meanwhile the English fleet, without big battles except for that of Jutland, blocked the German fleet – which had remained stuck to coal – in the northern ports. According to Yergin it was the victory of a naval supremacy founded on oil – a combination of speed, greater range of action, and swiftness of re-supply. Paul Kennedy notes that from 1900 to 1914 the German war fleet absorbed – depending on the year – from a third to a half of all German military spending. If one accepts Yergin's thesis, Churchill's "gamble" annihilated the colossal German naval investment, transforming – one must deduce – the arch-navalist Tirpitz into a sort of unconscious fifth column who only subtracted resources from the German land forces.

The tank as "land ship"

The first battle won thanks to the internal combustion engine was that of Paris: the military governor of the capital, Joseph Gallieni, in September 1914, requisitioned all Parisian taxis in order to send reserves rapidly to the front, halting the German advance. Studying the stalemate of trench warfare, the English colonel Ernest Swinton combined the machine gun tested in the Russo-Japanese War with the farm tractor developed in America, and thought up the first vehicle which was armoured, motorised and propelled by tracks. The British high command rejected the project. Its potential was, by contrast, grasped by an indignant Churchill who committed funds from the Navy to the development of the armoured vehicle. The sponsorship of the Navy was reflected in the first names which designated the new weapon: "land cruiser" or "land ship". When the German high command declared in October 1918 that victory was no longer possible, it identified the introduction of the tank as the chief reason. The victory of the Allies was also the victory of the truck over the locomotive. What had begun as a war of trains and horses ended with more than 150,000 English and American motorised transport vehicle operating on the French front. The conflict marked the definitive takeoff of air power: in four years Great Britain produced 55,000 airplanes, France 68,000, Italy 20,000, Germany 48,000 and the USA – in only 18 months – 15,000.

The industrialisation of war

The English general J.F.C. Fuller, who had masterminded the tank battle at Cambrai, in *Armament and History* [1946] proposed a synthesis, which on one point grasps the substance of these figures better than Yergin. In what he too defines as the "oil age", armies have conquered, beyond new mobility, the "third dimension", by the combination of the internal combustion engine with the propeller, and the "fourth dimension" with the wireless telegraph "which suppresses time as much as it does space". But above all the oil age is the age of the industrialisation of war: "For the first time in the history of war battles were as much struggles between competing firms as they were between rival armies".

The First World War and the post-war period

The "Open Door" in the Partition of Mesopotamia*

In the fourth year of war the Bolshevik revolution deprived the powers of the Entente of Russian oil. From that moment the United States provided 80% of what the Allies needed to continue the butchery. The distribution of American crude oil in Europe was entrusted to the National Petroleum War Service Committee under the direction of the president of Standard Oil of New Jersey: war reconciled Standard Oil with the federal government which, six years before, had succeeded in breaking up Rockefeller's monopoly.

American oil production had risen by 25% between 1914 and 1917, but demand was rising faster. This was true for both war demand and civilian demand – the diffusion of the automobile in the United States doubled between 1916 and 1918. Washington was forced to import oil from Mexico, drain the reserves, keep factories closed on Mondays and appeal to the population for "Sundays without gasoline".

Three parallel wars

The "oil famine" weighed more heavily on Europe because of deadly U-boat attacks on the convoys. The powers included oil among their war objectives. The secretary of the British Ministry of War, Sir Maurice Hankey, wrote to Foreign Minister Arthur Balfour: "The single great source that we can place under our control is that of Persia and Mesopotamia. The control of these oil sources becomes an English war aim of the first order".

At the time Mesopotamian oil was only a hope, but thirst for black gold magnified the mirage situated in the Arabian geo-strategic area. On this mirage turned some of the most fascinating chapters of three "parallel wars": the Anglo-American war for succession to the leadership of the imperialist world; the Anglo-French war for a new partition in Europe and in the colonies; and the Anglo-English war between the Arab Office and the Indian Office of the Empire for the lead in the Middle East.

---

* Nicola Capelluto, May 2003

Two British lines

David Lloyd George, head of government from December 1916, set himself the goal of exclusive hegemony for Great Britain in the Middle East: this meant repealing the Sykes-Picot Accord of January 1916 which assigned Lebanon and Syria up to Mosul to Paris, while to Great Britain went Basra, Baghdad and the Palestinian ports of Acre and Haifa. The accord reflected the vision of the War Minister, Lord Kitchener. The field marshall attributed to the area of French influence, from the Mediterranean to the Iraqi hinterland, the role of a long wall between Russian and English zones of influence. At the same time he envisaged the creation of an Arab State or confederation which, in the form of a caliphate and with powerful English support, would deprive the "Sublime Porte" of its role as Islam's spiritual guide.

American historian David Fromkin, a member of the CFR, observes in *A Peace to End All Peace* [1989] that Kitchener and part of the Foreign Office dangerously manipulated explosive ideas like "caliphate" and "Arab independence", reflecting the mood of the English elite of Cairo which dreamed of a new "Egyptian Empire", substantially Pan-Arabist, as a counterweight to India. This faction felt betrayed by the 1916 accord that gave Basra and Baghdad to the Anglo-Indian administration. A few months later the cruiser transporting Kitchener to Russia hit a mine. Fromkin cites documents made public 70 years later according to which the Admiralty knew that the course was mined but did nothing to save the hero of Khartoum.

The balance imagined by Lloyd George was different from that of Kitchener. For him the Middle East had an intrinsic value, and not only as a middle ground between Egypt and India: England had to have absolute control of it, favouring the disintegration of the Ottoman Empire but not unifying the Arabs, by using Greece in Asia Minor and Jewish aspirations in Palestine as counterweights. The clash at the Versailles Conference between Lloyd George and Clemenceau was fierce, especially over Syria. The "Tiger" became so enraged as to enjoin the English leader to choose between a sword and a pistol.

Even the United States changed its war aims. Washington had thrown its sword and its industry into the balance only after three years of conflict had bled Europe, invoking a defensive war against the sinking of its merchant ships and Germany's attempt to make Mexico enter the war against the United States. It was the

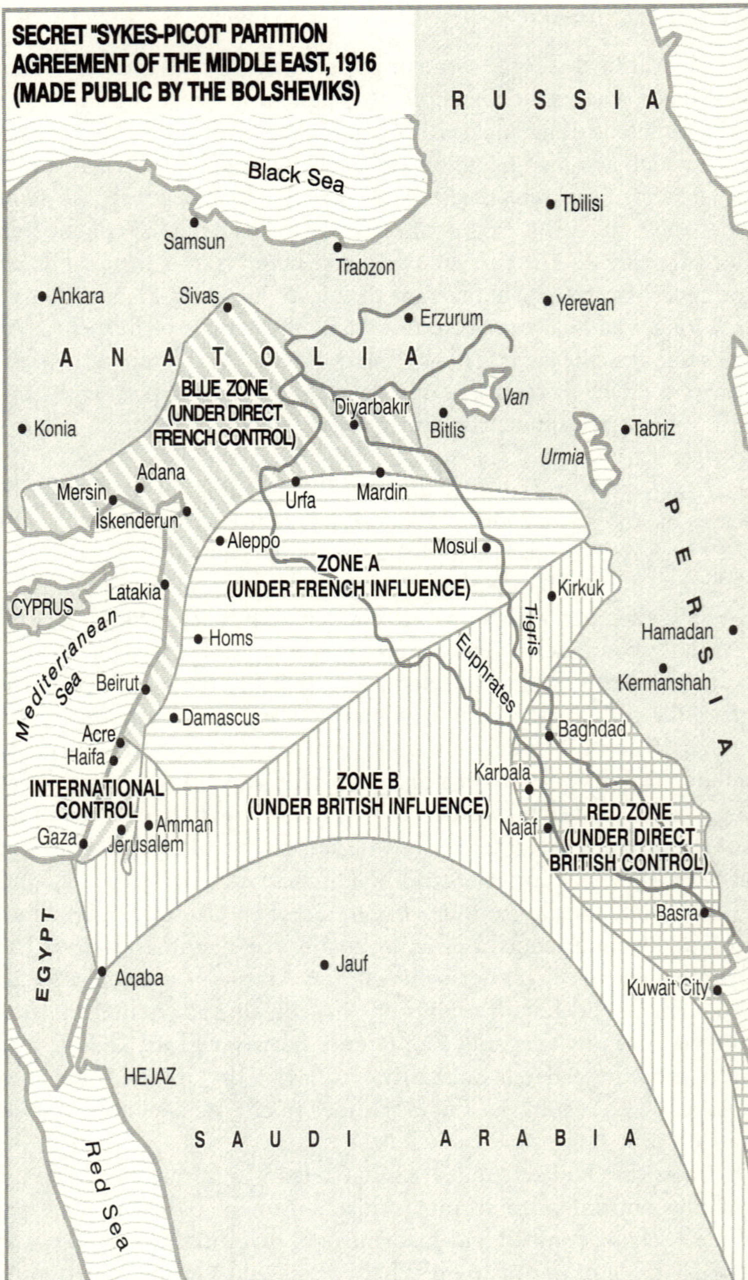
SECRET "SYKES-PICOT" PARTITION AGREEMENT OF THE MIDDLE EAST, 1916 (MADE PUBLIC BY THE BOLSHEVIKS)
RUSSIA
Black Sea
Tbilisi
Samsun
Trabzon
Ankara
Sivas
Yerevan
Erzurum
ANATOLIA
BLUE ZONE (UNDER DIRECT FRENCH CONTROL)
Van
Diyarbakır
Bitlis
Konia
Tabriz
Urmia
Adana
Mersin
Urfa
Mardin
İskenderun
PERSIA
Aleppo
Mosul
ZONE A (UNDER FRENCH INFLUENCE)
Latakia
Kirkuk
CYPRUS
Tigris
Hamadan
Homs
Euphrates
Mediterranean Sea
Beirut
Kermanshah
Damascus
Baghdad
Acre
Haifa
Karbala
ZONE B (UNDER BRITISH INFLUENCE)
INTERNATIONAL CONTROL
Amman
Najaf
RED ZONE (UNDER DIRECT BRITISH CONTROL)
Gaza
Jerusalem
Basra
EGYPT
Aqaba
Jauf
Kuwait City
HEJAZ
SAUDI ARABIA
Red Sea

publication, decided by Lenin, of the secret accords of imperialistic partition that induced the American president, in January 1918, to launch his "Fourteen Points".

Wilson's "Open Door"

Wilson re-proposed the tried and tested objective of the "open door" in the formula of the "removal of all economic barriers" and placed in doubt the partition plans by means of the obscure "principle of equality of the requests of populations and of governments", in a bold balancing act between "sovereignty" and "self-determination". But with regard to the Ottoman Empire he leaned toward the "autonomous development" of the "nationalities now under Turkish domination".

The message was intended more for Great Britain than for exhausted Turkey. Balfour responded by distinguishing between the form and the substance of the confrontation: "I do not care under what regime we succeed in keeping the oil for ourselves, but I am perfectly conscious that it is indispensable that we be able to have it at our disposal".

Balfour proposed a multilateral solution in the Middle East, with the presence of the French and the Americans, which did not compromise the centrality of Britain. An exponent of the imperialist wing like Hankey wanted to cut out the French but include the Americans, conceding Palestine to them. The alliance with the United States was central to the balance advocated by Lloyd George, but not to the point of ceding to it a piece of the Middle East. For the prime minister the involvement of the United States had to be obtained by giving it the mandates for Constantinople, the Dardanelles and Armenia for anti-Russian and anti-German reasons.

Paris in, Berlin out

When the isolationist orientation prevailed in Washington, Lloyd George – declares Fromkin – was forced, in "a sudden change of direction, to seek again the aid of France". "This required the abandonment of the steadfast anti-French policy in the Middle East. But at this point the damage inflicted on Anglo-French solidarity could be only partially remedied".

The San Remo compromise of April 1920 gave France the mandate for Lebanon and Syria (but without Mosul), while Palestine and Mesopotamia went to Great Britain. The accord included the transfer to

France of the German share in the Turkish Petroleum Company, the grantor of exploration rights in the Ottoman Empire. The preceding accord of March 1914 reflected one of the attempts to assuage Anglo-German antagonism: the Anglo-Persian Company held 50% of the consortium, Royal Dutch-Shell held 25% and Deutsche Bank held 25%. Defeated Germany had to resign itself to the Anglo-French metamorphosis of the Turkish Petroleum Company, but victorious America did not. Daniel Yergin describes, in *The Prize* [1990], the climate of fear of the exhaustion of crude oil which was spreading in the United States. The director of the Bureau of Mines predicted that the decline of the national oil industry would begin within 5 years. Scarcity put pressure on prices, which rose by 50% in 1918-1920. Standard Oil of New York was the first to try to force open the door to Mesopotamia but its geologists were arrested; the State Department re-launched the "open door". The English and American foreign ministers dueled in a memorable match of political arithmetic: for Lord Curzon Great Britain controlled just 4.5% of world production of crude against 80% for the United States, which was the first to exclude non-American interests from its areas; Secretary of State Bainbridge Colby replied that the United States possessed only 1/12 of world oil reserves and suffered the greatest gap between demand and supply.

In London suspicions arose that behind Atatürk's movement in Turkey and the Shiite rebels in Iraq were the dollars of American oilmen. But for Allen Dulles, in charge of the Middle East from 1922 at the US State Department, it was clear that the "open door" policy should neither put British preeminence in question nor risk the explosion of the region. Embroiled in the crisis of the postwar period and threatened by the questioning of the legitimacy of the Turkish Petroleum Company's rights, London became more open to dialogue. Standard Oil of New Jersey formed a consortium between the principal American companies for the assault on Mesopotamia.

The Red Line Agreement

Standard Oil of New Jersey – thereafter Exxon – had inherited from the breakup of Standard Oil the greatest sales network in the world but very little production – just 16% of its refining capacity. Its president Walter Teagle had ordered a globalised line of production: "Our policy is to interest ourselves in every area of production, independently of the country in which it is found". In July 1922 Teagle began negotiations with London which would last for 6 years.

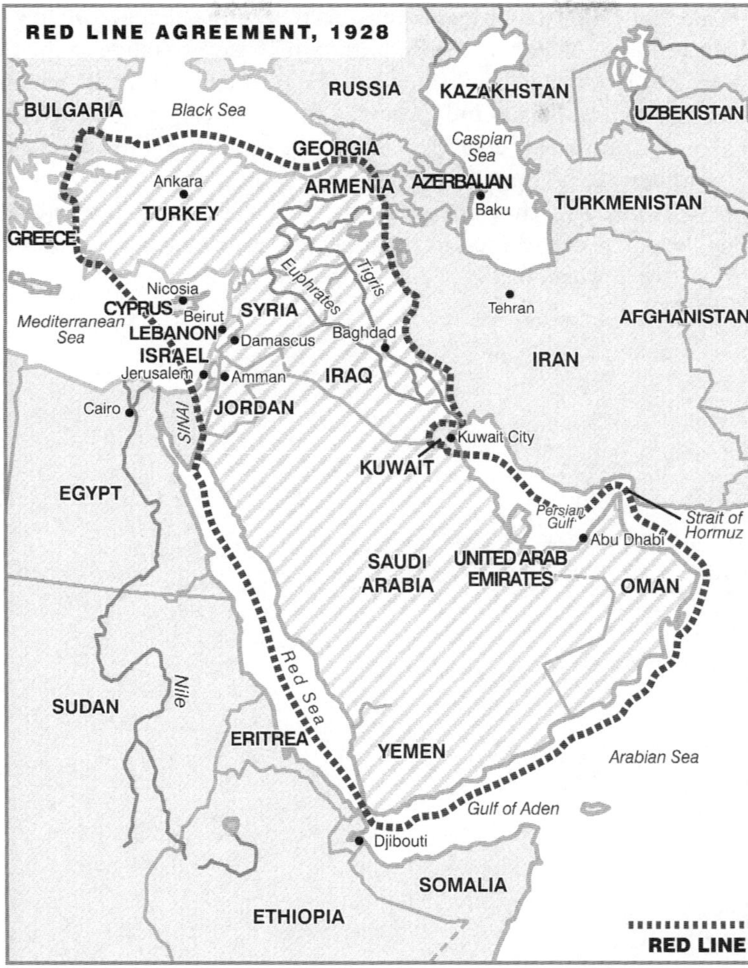

The inclusion of the United States in the stabilisation of Europe with the Dawes Plan of 1924 long preceded the Middle Eastern accord, which was reached only in July 1928. The discovery of oil to the northwest of Kirkuk in October 1927 was decisive. A daily flow of 25,000 barrels pushed the competitors to close the deal. On the Turkish Petroleum Company's new team the four principal partners – Shell, Anglo-Persian, Compagnie Française des Petroles and the American consortium Near East Development Co. – had equal shares of 23.75%. The founder of the Turkish Petroleum Company, the

Armenian Calouste Gulbenkian, a partner with the remaining 5%, had the honor of tracing the Red Line which gave its name to the accord: it surrounded Asia Minor and the Arabian Peninsula, leaving out Kuwait and Persia, and indicated the confines within which the partners committed themselves to respect the "self-exclusion clause" – to undertake no prospecting activities if not jointly.

Not only had the "open door" closed behind the Americans, but the partners had dressed themselves in a straitjacket that would prove to be intolerable.

1920s to 1930s

From the Gulf of Mexico to the Persian Gulf*

The oil glut between the end of the 1920s and the beginning of the 1930s must be considered as one of the main causes affecting the political cycle of the interwar period. It determined the fall in price of oil, but it also increased the popularity of old and new nationalisms, suggested new ways to create an oil cartel, and inspired an extraordinary and direct intervention by the State in the economic regulation.

California, Oklahoma and Texas

In the hectic search for the new oil wells, the great profits of the war, the push of motorisation and of energetic conversion from coal and new prospecting methods came together. Daniel Yergin highlights the role of new geophysics technologies: the scale of torsion that measures the variations of gravity on the terrestrial crust, the magnetometer that finds out the components of the terrestrial magnetic field, the seismograph that allows the identification of saline dams, potentially containing petroleum, through the waves of an explosion, the microscopic analysis of fossils, air photography and the extraction of oil at depth. The discoveries of 1923 around Los Angeles temporarily turned California into the first American oil producer.

In the second half of the decade, new wells were discovered in Oklahoma and in the Permian Basin, between western Texas and Mexico. In 1930 it was the turn of the "Black Giant" in eastern Texas (a truly extraordinary oilfield producing more than 340 barrels a day), discovered thanks to the instructions of a self-taught geologist, and to the chagrin of high-tech geophysicists. In the 1920s a new oil refinement process (cracking), that allowed a double production of petrol, became more and more popular. Between 1920 and 1929, the number of American cars tripled and the consumption of gasoline increased fourfold. In 1929 in the USA there was one car for every five people; the ratio was about 1:30 in the UK and France, 1:100 in Germany and 1:700 in Japan. A typically American contribution to the new abundance of oil was the "rule of capture" established by the courts: small oil producers could exploit their wells without limits,

* Nicola Capelluto, June 2003

even when operating on a common basin with other producers; their neighbours, in order to protect themselves, had to do the same.

Mexico and Venezuela

New producers emerged globally: in these countries the newly discovered oil rent often coincided with the creation of the first modern proletarian concentrations around foreign investments, which became the objective base for radical, and often rather nationalistic, trade unionism.

The Englishman Weetman Pearson, known nowadays for the financial-editorialist empire named after him, was called on by the Mexican President Porfirio Diaz to become the counterweight to the American intrusiveness. His "Mexican Eagle" made its first important oil discovery in 1910. During the war Mexico became the main source of American supplies and by 1925 it was – with 11%– the second world producer. The insertion of the principle of nationalisation of the underground in the Constitution scared foreign investors, not yet used to discussing such matters with bourgeoisies of emerging countries. In 1935, the Mexican share had fallen to 2.5%. Only at this stage, in 1938, the nationalisation suggested by General Lazaro Cardenas was approved, with the purpose of stopping the national oil decline and of inserting it in the geopolitical game opened by the Axis powers.

As a matter of fact, it was the Mexican difficulties that Venezuela took advantage of. General Juan Vicente Gomez's regime allowed American companies to take part in the drawing up of the "Oil Law" [1922] in order to attract foreign capital. But here too British capital had for a certain period of time a very strategic importance: Venezuela became the principle supply source for Shell and in 1932, because of American taxes, became the main supplier for the UK. As the third world producer in the 1930s, behind only the USA and USSR, during the Second World War Venezuela conquered second place, with 12% of the world oil production.

The Achnacarry's cartel pact

The harsh price war completes the scenario. Jersey, Shell and the Nobels had created a united front fighting to get reimbursed for the properties that had been nationalised in 1920 by the USSR. Standard Oil of New York (Socony) took advantage of the situation and obtained the concession for the installation for the production of kerosene in Batum, as a base from which to break into the Indian market.

The manager of Shell, Henri Deterding, started a world offensive on prices against Socony's "communist oil".

Only one month after the Red Line Agreement, in August 1928, the managers of Shell, Anglo-Persian, Jersey, Gulf and Indiana met for two weeks, in the Scottish castle of Achnacarry, in order to put an end to the price war in Europe and Asia. That conclave was part of the line of Winston Churchill, Chancellor of the Exchequer, and Sir John Cadman, president of the Anglo-Persian, to get to a cooperative partition of the markets, together with Shell and Jersey.

Achnacarry's pact, kept secret until 1952, reported "the excessive competition that has been translated into modern hectic overproduction" and promised "the acceptance of the present mass of deals and their dimension in every future increase of production". The pact also established the common use of the plants to avoid the construction of new oil refineries; the exchange of oil between the companies to supply the markets from the wells which were geographically closer; and in the end the popular "Gulf Plus System". Back then, the "Gulf" par excellence was not yet the Persian one, but the Mexican one: oil prices all over the world were decided according to the price of oil in Mexico, the departure point for the American oil export, plus the transport cost from Mexico. American prices were becoming world prices.

The pact failed almost immediately , even though signed and approved by 18 companies, which included also the Seven Sisters: the new Texan wells and the impossibility of letting the majority of the US exports enter the cartel contributed to its failure. In 1930, Jersey, Shell, and Anglo-Persian tried to restore it, but Russian oil, sold at incredibly low prices to finance Soviet industrialisation, did not allow it. New attempts were made in 1932 and 1934. The last pact worked for a few years thanks to the reduced American oil production and to the increased Soviet industrial consumption.

In 1931 more than one million barrels of oil were extracted from Eastern Texas. The price of Texan oil decreased from $1.85 per barrel in 1926 to $1.00 per barrel in 1930 and to $0.15 in 1931. In August 1931, the Governors of Oklahoma and Texas proclaimed martial law and got the National Guard to occupy the wells in order to stop the "competitive suicide". It was at this time that the Texas Railroad Commission (TRC), an obsolete populist organ, came back to life, becoming the institution for the control of oil prices, with a role of global relevance for more than 40 years. The TRC gave out dozens of orders which were obeyed by the troops but cancelled by the courts. The price increased to $1.00 in 1932 but again fell to $0.10 a few months later, in 1933.

The New Deal's oil

The battle in Texas was visibly worsening, but the arrival to the White House of Franklin D. Roosevelt turned it into the battle of the New Deal: fighting against deflation was an imperative in the battle against the Great Depression. Given this task was Harold Ickes, a lawyer from Chicago and manager of Theodore Roosevelt's electoral campaign in 1912. He sent federal agents to Texas to dismantle the clandestine network of oil commerce but moreover he set the goal to create a federal roof to the production of oil of 300 barrels per day, with limits established for every State. In 1935, the Supreme Court repealed a great part of the National Industrial Recovery Act which was one of the bases of authority used by Ickes, but the quotas continued as a voluntary system. Between 1934 and 1940, prices did not vary much from $1.00-$1.18 per barrel.

Saudi Arabia and Kuwait

In 1935 Jersey's vice president, Orville Harden, complained that, at that stage, they had to take into account "nationalistic policies in nearly every foreign country". In the Middle East, the first strong sign came from Iran. The Depression had diminished the oil royalties going to the Persian treasury and the Shah announced in 1932 the repeal of the concession to Anglo-Persian. Cadman had to get back his privileges at a very high price by guaranteeing minimal royalties of £750,000 per year and moreover by conceding 20% of the company's profits at world level.

In 1932-33, Saudi Arabia and Kuwait entered the oil galaxy. Up till then, the Saudi income came mostly from the pilgrimages to Mecca, which the Depression had diminished. The discovery of oil in Bahrain, in 1932, made King Ibn Saud decide to open the search for petrol to foreign investments. The role of Harry Philby was decisive: an ex-civil servant of the Indian Civil Service who, disgusted by English colonial politics in Iraq, had converted to Islam and become a friend of Ibn Saud. He became a consultant of Standard Oil of California (Socal) that was not included in the Red Line Agreement and he let the company get the first Saudi concession, excluding Iraq Petroleum and the hated Anglo-Persian. If Lawrence of Arabia had nourished Arab nationalism with English gold, Philby did it with American gold.

Anglo-Persian learnt its lesson and in the competition for the concessions in Kuwait, realising that it could not overtake Gulf, decided to become its ally in a joint venture, the Kuwait Oil Co. In both Arabia and Kuwait they needed to wait until 1938 to see black gold gushing. With the dollars of Socal, Philby sent his son to study in Cambridge. Here, young Kim Philby was recruited by the Stalinists, in a career that turned him into the most notorious Russian spy within the English and American communities: a splinter of the public and private vices of unitary imperialism.

The Second World War and the post-war period

Roosevelt and Churchill in the Vexed British Withdrawal from the Gulf*

At the beginning of 1943, the final outcome of the war in North Africa and the Middle East was already clear. This speeded up the covert Anglo-American war. California's Standard Oil and Texaco, who had joined forces with Casoc and Caltex in Saudi Arabia and Bahrain in 1936, asked the federal government for its support in keeping the English out in the post-war period and in guaranteeing "purely American initiatives in the area". This appeal to the State was backed up by two "theories": one of "conservation", which feared the risk of using up US oil and pushed for the development of extraterritorial reserves, and the other of "solidification", which drew from the Mexican experience the lesson that private citizens could not stand up to foreign governments on their own.

The war cabinet seized the opportunity. The Secretary of the Interior, Harold Ickes, obtained Roosevelt's assent to including Saudi Arabia in the Lend-Lease Act and proposed, together with the War, Navy and Mobilization Secretaries, the creation of the Petroleum Reserves Corporation, a federal agency that would buy up the American oil assets in Saudi Arabia. Roosevelt gave his approval, despite the opposition of Cordell Hull, the Secretary of State. But the heads of the oil companies rebelled; they wanted to be helped, not gobbled up. "They had come to catch a cod and had caught a whale", was the sarcastic comment of the government advisor, Herbert Feis. It was agreed that the State should hold a minor parcel of shares in Casox, but the agreement fell through because of the opposition of Mobil, Jersey and the independent oil magnates who feared the whole sector would be nationalised. Ickes proposed that the American government should lay a 1,600-km pipeline carrying Saudi and Kuwaiti oil to the Mediterranean, in exchange for a billion barrels of oil for the US Armed Forces, at a 25% discount. The plan was blocked by Congress.

* Nicola Capelluto, September 2003

An attempt to agree on sharing-out

With the failure of direct participation, Roosevelt tried to get the British to agree on sharing-out. In February 1944, the British ambassador, Lord Halifax, reported to London that Roosevelt had advanced this proposal to him: "Iranian oil is yours. Let's share Iraq's and Kuwait's. Saudi Arabia's is ours". Lord Beaverbrook, press magnate and lord of the Privy Seal, wrote to Churchill: "Oil is the only great resource we shall have left after the war. We should refuse to share our last commodity with the Americans".

Washington and London's parallel war

The exchange of letters between Churchill and Roosevelt, on the eve of the D-Day landings, is a model dialogue between imperialist plunderers who, while trying to steal each other's wallets, do not spare frank words, sour pride and meticulous good manners. Churchill warned that "a row over oil would be a poor basis for our tremendous common undertaking" and pointed out fears "that the USA wishes to strip us of our assets in the Middle East, on which the Royal Navy depends for its fuel supplies". Roosevelt retorted that it was Great Britain that seemed to be trying to "meddle" in the American concessions in Saudi Arabia and reassured Churchill: "I beg you to believe that we are not casting sheep's eyes at your oilfields in Iraq and Iran". Churchill retorted, "Permit me to assure you categorically that neither are we thinking of meddling in your Saudi-Arabian interests and assets". But without drawing in his claws: Britain "will not allow itself to be deprived of anything that rightfully belongs to it after having contributed so much to the good cause".

For some time, the "row" was avoided. In August, 1944, shortly after the Bretton Woods Conference, the British and Americans agreed on the creation of the International Petroleum Commission, which was to allocate the world production quotas. The agreement came to a standstill in the American Senate; neither Roosevelt nor Truman was able to get it going again.

The third card played by the USA was that of the oil companies. In 1947 three fundamental agreements were reached. In Saudi Arabia, Aramco (Arabian-American Oil Company, Casoc's new name since 1944) opened its share capital to Jersey-Exxon (which bought 30% of it) and to Socony-Mobil (which bought only 10%). In order to reach this understanding, the famous Red Line agreement, forbidding its partners separate agreements, had to be rescinded. The legal pretext was the "supervening illegality" attributed to the quotas of the French CFP and the old Gulbenkian, domiciled in enemy territory during the war.

Aramco and the ousting of France

With the second agreement, Gulf, owner of 50% of the Kuwait Oil Company, became Royal Dutch-Shell's partner for ten years; the latter owned one of the eastern hemisphere's major commercial networks, guaranteeing 30% of its requirements.

The third agreement was reached in Iran, which had been the stage of one of the first important battles of the cold war. In the spring of 1946, the Russian troops that still occupied northern Iran were forced by Anglo-American pressure to leave, but Moscow kept on pressing through the Tudeh Party and claiming a share in the oil. Anglo-Iranian underpinned its monopolistic position by drawing up two twenty-years business agreements with Jersey and Socony. Great Britain held tightly on to its oil bastion while, in the very same year of 1947, it granted India its independence, handed over the protection of Greece and Turkey to the USA and announced its withdrawal from Palestine.

France was excluded from the agreements. According to the American Senate's "Multinational Report" of 1975, "the French have never forgiven the Americans for excluding them from Saudi Arabia". In July 2003, the French Total's participation in the joint venture for the exploitation of the natural gas in the south-east of Saudi Arabia would be – if brought to completion – of historic value for France.

Parallel foreign policies

The three agreements were looking at the European markets, where reconstruction was already underway. Daniel Yergin emphasises the *synchronisation* between them and the launching of the Marshall Plan, which enabled the industrial furnaces and power stations to change over from coal to oil, and which gave impetus to their transport sector. Anthony Sampson [*The Seven Sisters*] points out, instead, another kind of "synchrony", the one between the agreements and the UN's decision in November, 1947, on the State of Israel: from that moment, the USA firmly recognised "two opposite foreign policies", Washington's, in favour of Israel (also for electoral ends at home), the other in favour of the Arab countries and, in particular, of Saudi Arabia, delegated to the oil companies.

"Through this stratagem, the two policies were kept markedly separate for the next 25 years".

Fifty-fifty between the oil companies and the Arab bourgeoisie

The Middle-East situation was set in motion again by the revision of the agreements between the Saudi monarchy and Aramco. In 1943, Venezuela had forced Jersey and Shell, with the open collaboration of Washington that refused to repeat the "Mexican" experience, to accept the famous fifty-fifty division of the profits between the oil companies and the revenue – taxes and royalties – of the oil producing countries.

In 1950, Saudi Arabia, too, got its *fifty-fifty* agreements, thanks to the generous application of a 1918 US law that allowed the deduction at home of taxes paid abroad. The taxes paid by Aramco to the American Treasury ($50 million a year) were re-routed to the Saudi coffers, with American consent. A long time later, in 1974-75, during the inquiry by the Church senatorial subcommittee, it was conjectured that the American executive had handed out a massive subsidy to a foreign government, using a tax dodge to get round the authorisations needed from Congress; but, in 1950, the order of priorities was dominated by the Korean War. In 1951, the fifty-fifty agreement was applied in Kuwait and, in 1952, in Iraq.

Fragility of the British Empire

The American Yergin gives a positive evaluation of these agreements, not only because they reflected a balanced compromise, but also because they created a valid model, in contrast with that of Mexican nationalisation: the Venezuelan government, through its fifty-fifty agreement, earned 7% more per barrel compared to Mexico, and with a production that was six times higher.

On the contrary, Sampson criticises them radically. According to the English author, first of all they upset the traditional equilibrium of the big American companies, pushing them to an excessive foreign investment: in 1973, the Five American Sisters made two-thirds of their profits abroad, without paying any taxes. In 1972, Exxon paid only 6.5% of its global profits and Mobil only 1.3% to the US inland revenue.

The second, long-term consequence of the "golden tax dodge" was that it seriously damaged the companies' internal organisation: it was fiscally convenient to transfer most of the profits "upstream" on to the crude oil, and most of the cost "downstream" on to refining and distribution. "They littered the roads and freeways with sales outlets, to attract consumers at all costs. [...] Engineers and geologists dominated the board, while marketing men were at a discount". In the end, the oil-producing countries, becoming partners at 50% of the profits, demanded transparency on the profits and publicity of the prices. "At that moment, it seemed a fair system, but it had serious consequences. The oil-producing countries got used to standard revenues based on fixed prices. And they did not think they could drop, so the 'official price' became an artificially high one on which the companies paid taxes".

The deepest motivation for Sampson's hostility is another: America "oiled" its penetration into the Middle East by making easy concessions that dangerously favoured nationalist tendencies. The dam broke at its weakest point, i.e., that of British imperialism in retreat. The storm of the first post-war oil crisis broke in Iran.

The decolonisation of the 1950s

The British Defeat in Mossadeq's Iran*

On May 1st, 1951, the Shah of Persia announced the official nationalisation of the Anglo-Iranian Oil Company. This was the work of Mohammed Mossadeq, who had been the head of government for only three days. An incredulous London reeled with the shock of a drama that had, nevertheless, been fermenting for a decade. The Shah's father had been deposed in 1941 because he was pro-German. Iranian nationalism had been born anti-British. The Empire's withdrawal from India and the Balkans galvanised it. The battle for the distribution of oil revenues, which had given birth to a variety of models in Latin America, provided it with an economic programme and a unifying target. But why did a "Mexican-style" nationalisation and not a "Venezuelan-style" compromise prevail in the Iran of 1951?

The erosion of London's influence

Geography placed Iran at the crossroads of the second World War victors' zones of influence: it had taken "a hard-fought negotiation at Yalta and later" – writes Anthony Eden in his *Memoirs* – to achieve the withdrawal of the Russian and Western forces from Persia. Great Britain, with Anglo-Iranian, kept its exclusive zone of influence, but it was only apparently so. The pro-Moscow party, the Tudeh, embraced oil nationalisation. The pro-American party – relates Anthony Sampson [*The Seven Sisters*] – "was led by the dynamic ambassador Henry Grady, a first-generation Irish-American who made no bones about his aversion to British imperialism and encouraged the Iranians – very misleadingly – to believe that the Americans would back them up against the English".

Anglo-Iranian's nationalisation

Anglo-Iranian's policy worsened the crisis. From 1945 to 1950, the company had registered profits of £250 million, but Iran pocketed only £90 million of this sum. Eden himself, at that time in the opposition, sided with the Iranian protest, considering it as "Insincere

* Nicola Capelluto, October 2003

that His Majesty's government, as a shareholder in the oil company, should receive ever larger sums in the form of taxes and should refuse to increase the dividends which would have benefited the Iranian government". In June, 1950, after the assassination of an English diplomat, General Ali Razmara, the army Chief of Staff, became Prime Minister. According to Daniel Yergin [*The Prize*] the contemporaneous outbreak of the Korean War pushed the stakes sky-high; Iran produced 40% of Middle Eastern oil, and the Abadan refinery supplied the Eastern hemisphere with most of its aeroplane fuel. The chairman of Anglo-Iranian, Sir William Fraser, refused substantial concessions, and only when Aramco entered into a *fifty-fifty* agreement with Saudi Arabia did he hasten clumsily to initiate it. It was too late: in Tehran the slogan was "nationalisation". In March, 1951, the prime minister, who had tried to block it, was assassinated. Parliament nationalised the company, the first to arrive in the Middle-East in 1908. Mossadeq, until then head of the oil commission, became prime minister.

An anticipation of the Suez Crisis

Dean Acheson, Truman's Secretary of State, in his autobiography [*Present at the Creation*], comments contemptuously on the British executives: "Never did so few lose so much, so stupidly and so fast. [...] Their folly led them into that mess that Aramco had avoided by securing for itself with grace what it could no longer obtain by force". The launching of the National Iranian Oil Company (NIOC) was hailed with the sacrifice of dozens of sheep: the symbolic manifestation of an emerging national bourgeoisie, whose aggressiveness was fuelled by the religious fanaticism of feudal properties and whose courage in the face of the Empire died down on the threshold of the large landed estates; oil was nationalised, but agrarian reform was shelved.

The British Labour government drew up a plan for the military occupation of the island of Abadan, the site of the largest refinery in the world. The defence Secretary, Emmanuel Shinwell, prophesied: "If Persia gets away with it, Egypt and other Middle Eastern countries will be tempted to follow suit. The next move may well be the nationalisation of the Suez Canal". According to Acheson, the English were wrong: the US recognised the right to nationalisation provided that the expropriations were indemnified at a fair price, while the British refused this right. Acheson warned that an intervention was not admissible: it might trigger a "communist" *coup d'état*, or an armed intervention on the part of the USSR. Fearing that Iran might end up in Russia's lap, Washington blocked the military expedition and sent to Tehran, as a mediator, Averell Harriman, the former ambassador to London and Moscow. There was a strong suspicion that the object of the mission was to pave the way for US capital. John Kennedy, at that time a young Congressman, warned that without an agreement "the American companies might do well to step into the breach".

Mossadeq's ploys and quirks

Mossadeq, at that time 70 years old, came from a family of the landed aristocracy, was the great-grandson of the previous dynasty's Shah, had graduated in France and Switzerland and had taken part in the 1906 constitutional revolution. His political theatrics were legendary, his speeches culminated in tears and fainting fits. His negotiations with Harriman, a record of which has survived through the interpreter Colonel Vernon Walters, were often exasperating, sometimes hilarious. He received Harriman lying down in his bed, aching all over yet always nimble. The American wanted to explain the market laws to the Persian: for instance, the price of a barrel of crude oil cannot be more than the sale price of its by-products; the sum of the parts is always equal to the whole. Mossadeq objected: "This is not true. [...] Look, take the fox. Its tail is often longer than the fox itself". It was not for "Old Mossy's" plays and quirks that Harriman stayed in Tehran for two months, but to put a damper on London's ebullience. In the end, he solemnly declared that Mossadeq refused all agreements because any agreement with the British would have put an end to his political career.

Great Britain put an embargo on Iran with the support of the oil cartel. It was an Italian company, Supor, that broke the embargo with the tanker "Mariella", winning a contract for 12.5% of the Iranian oil, thus paving the way for the ENI of Enrico Mattei, who had not yet declared his war of independence from the Seven Sisters. Mossadeq reacted to the embargo by ordering the British to get out of Abadan. According to Yergin, more than this humiliation, what was fatal for the Empire's credibility was having threatened to use force without carrying it out. Eden sees a direct relation between these events and the growth of the nationalist movement in Egypt, leading to the 1952 "revolution" and Nasser's rise to power.

The 1953 coup d'état

In October, 1951, the Conservatives won the election. Churchill, the Prime Minister, and Eden, the Foreign Secretary, went to Washington in January, 1952. Churchill – relates Acheson – threw in Truman's face that the oil controversy would never be settled so long as the Americans continued to support Iran financially; he reproached his predecessors for having climbed down over Abadan when "a single fusillade would have been enough to decide the matter", and stated that he would back the US in the Far East only if Truman backed Britain in the Middle East. The American tactics changed only when the Republicans came to power in 1953. The President, Eisenhower, the Secretary of State, Foster Dulles, and his brother Allen Dulles, the head of the CIA, reckoned that it was time to close the chapter. The opposing parties had almost run out of steam and Washington could play its trumps. The preparation for a *coup d'état* was entrusted to Kermit Roosevelt, President Theodore Roosevelt's grandson. "Operation Ajax" was a palace plot backed by a part of the army and the parliament that Mossadeq had dissolved. A first attempt failed and the Shah fled abroad. A second attempt, backed by a mass demonstration, was successful; on August 18th, 1953, Mossadeq was arrested.

The new Anglo-American cartel

The victory on the ground was American and the search for a compromise was entrusted to Herbert Hoover Jr., the former President's son. The US companies did not want to get involved: Iran's exclusion from the market had favoured them in the rest of the world, but, above all, they feared the Department of Justice and Federal Trade Commission's inquest into the "international cartel", which had been going on for years. The Eisenhower government guaranteed, through a directive of the National Security Council, that "the application of the US antitrust laws against the Western oil companies operating in the Near East must be considered as subordinate to the interests of national security". Hence, the Iranian Consortium was set up, and finalised in October, 1954. Anglo-Iranian, renamed British Petroleum, took over 40% of the shares, Shell 14%, the American Jersey, Socony, Texaco, Socal and Gulf 8% each, together equalling the British parcel of shares. The French of CFP had 6%. Shortly afterwards, the five Americans each handed over 1% to nine independent US companies. National Iranian Oil remained the owner of the oil, while the consortium would see to its production and distribution. BP was indemnified not by Iran but by the partners, to the tune of about $600 million.

Weak Middle Eastern bourgeoisies

In October 1954, Arrigo Cervetto [*Unitary Imperialism* Vol. 1, 2014] placed the conclusion of the Iranian revolution and the "compromise that had been reached" in a strategic class vision: "Here we are face to face with another example [...] of how the bourgeois revolution in the imperialist phase indeed follows the law of the uneven development of capitalism in the world, but is, today, completely determined by unitary imperialism's relations of force". While in Asia, "the national bourgeoisie, favoured by the slackening of imperialist pressure in wartime, conquers positions", in the Middle East and Africa "the national bourgeoisie's attempts take place late, fail, or reach a compromise". "Iran now finds itself at the centre of the interimperialistic struggles for the conquest of markets. [...] France is investing 5 billion francs in it, Germany 60 million dollars, Japan is financing the construction of six sugar refineries. Beside the US and Great Britain we thus find these three rival countries". Beneath the ice of the Cold War, the young internationalist scientist already glimpsed the seeds of the multipolar contention.

The war of 1956

The Watershed of the Suez Crisis*

Raymond Aron, in an article from November, 1955, expressed his admiration for British resilience after the loss of the Iranian oil monopoly. London had supported the creation of the Baghdad Pact through which, during 1955, it had gathered Iraq, Turkey, Pakistan and Iran around itself. "The British recovery is stunning", Aron wrote, but, just a year later, he would have had to eat his words. Egypt had refused to adhere to the Pact. For years, Egyptian nationalism had been seeking full emancipation from London. In 1950, King Faruk's prime minister, Nahas Pasha, had asked for the denunciation of the 1936 Anglo-Egyptian treaty. In July, 1952, Mossadeq's Iranian revolution spawned the revolt of the Egyptian generals, led by Mohammed Naghib, which put an end to the monarchy and proclaimed agrarian reform and the republic.

The third nationalist wave, in the spring of 1954, brought to power Gamal Abdel Nasser, the incarnation of the Egyptian bourgeoisie's regional ambitions. In October, 1954, London and Nasser signed an agreement for the withdrawal of the 75,000 British soldiers within twenty months. In his *Memoirs*, Eden underlines the US role: the US demanded "a quick solution at almost any cost", in the "pathetic conviction that all would be well if an agreement were reached", but also because of "Washington's reluctance to play second fiddle even in an area where the main responsibility was not its own". Eden simplified things too much.

The Aswan Dam and the Suez Canal

In a series of articles written during the second half of the 1950s, Cervetto drew attention to the specific features of the US's "anti-colonialist policy", the "new forms of imperialistic expansion", its "new economic-political techniques" and its "new ideological fronts". The US backed "an inevitable historical development", that of the "emerging national bourgeoisies" that wanted to "ensure political independence for their countries". "But political independence certainly does not give economic independence in countries where the accumulation of capital is still in its early stages; hence, these countries necessarily

* Nicola Capelluto, November 2003

require foreign investments in order to begin their development. The US had such investments to offer", and the replacement of the Anglo-French was the proof that "the United States is the strongest imperialist group which, given its strong economic hegemony, can afford, for the time being, not to intervene directly as the Russian, French or British do". The "fascistic aspect" of many new regimes did not deter American imperialist democracy, intent on the rapid formation of new national markets, a "rapid industrialisation", and, hence, "a large-scale agrarian reform".

The American gamble on Arab nationalism

In this contest, nationalisation was admitted by American imperialism as an accelerating factor of accumulation. Egypt did not have an oil rent to nationalise, but it did have two other potential sources of revenue. The economic content of Nasserism may be summed up in a nutshell: to get from the waters of the Nile and the Suez Canal the rent – absolute and differential – that the Iranian, Saudi and Iraqi bourgeoisies were getting from oil; to force the pace of development, attract capital and take the lead of a Pan-Arab market. The prospect turned out to be unrealistic. The project for the Aswan Dam was "an indispensable planned starting-point". A three-mile-long dam and one of the largest reservoirs in the world (containing 180 billion cubic metres of water) would have increased farmland – and land rent – by a sixth, and guaranteed the production of 10 billion kWh a year.

According to Eden, the cost of the project was $1,300 million spread over 16 years. The United States and Great Britain had agreed to provide an initial funding of $70 million (London would supply one fifth of the sum), while the World Bank would lend $200 million at 5% interest. But in the vicissitudes of imperialism nothing is linear, except for its apologists' fantasies.

The USSR was seeking a foothold in the Middle East and held out hopes of a loan at 2% interest. For his part, Nasser, in order to balance Israel's rearmament (which was backed by France), turned first to the USA and then to the USSR, getting considerable military supplies through Czechoslovakia. Nasser, who had participated in the conference of nonaligned countries in Bandung and who had arrested hundreds of communists in his native land, thought he could use the East's offers and arms to deal with the West on a better footing. But the parallelogram of forces led to a different resultant.

According to Daniel Yergin, the planned funding of the Aswan dam was blocked in Washington by a coalition of friends of Israel, Southern senators defending American cotton against Egyptian cotton, and Republican senators for whom aiding more than one "neutral" country was not admissible and who were pushing for a choice between Tito and Nasser. Egypt had just recognised Peking (modern-day Beijing) and was trading with Moscow. Foster Dulles chose Tito and cancelled the loans for Aswan. A week later, on July 26th, 1956, Nasser announced the nationalisation of the Suez Canal, managed till then by the Anglo-French Company, whose concession ran out in 1968. Nasser declared that he would use the proceeds to finance the construction of the dam. In 1955, the rent from the Canal had been $96 million, but it was necessary to pay also the shareholders' indemnities and the rearmament expenses. The dam had to wait until 1958, when the first Russian funding arrived.

The European energy artery

In 1955, two thirds of the oil consumed in Western Europe came from the Middle East and, of that, two thirds passed through the Suez Canal. Although 70% of the European economy still ran on coal, its most dynamic sectors, the automobile and petrochemical industries, depended on the Suez artery. Its closure meant a reduction of their supplies: the Cape route (11,000 miles) was almost twice that of the Suez one (6,500 miles) and the existing fleet of oil-tankers was already fully used. In April, 1956, Eden had warned Bulganin and Khrushchev on a State visit to London, that "uninterrupted oil supplies were literally vital for our economy. [...] We were ready to fight for them. [...] We could not live without oil and we had no intention of letting ourselves be strangled in a mortal hold". The declaration of war was virtually made before the nationalisation.

London and Paris started to prepare for war. Eden admitted to British military inadequacy. "We did not have airborne troops for such an operation. [...] Neither could we have aircraft and men in a moment by a miracle. Years were needed to make them ready". It was decided to prepare a landing with a base in Malta a thousand miles away. Eisenhower had no intention either to join in the operation or to allow it. The result was a curious kind of drama in which the Americans gained time in order to postpone any showdown until after the 1956 presidential elections, while the Anglo-French sulked at the US temporising; to tell the truth, they themselves badly needed time to prepare the landing, but had decided to exploit the US elections. Dulles called an international conference in London and proposed an international organisation for the management of the canal. Nasser refused. Dulles came up with the idea of a "Users' Club" that would appropriate the canal tolls. Nasser refused.

At the end of October, the drama accelerated to a feverish pace, interwining with the Hungarian crisis. In the last week of October, Russian troops invaded Hungary; Egypt, Jordan and Syria signed the Amman Pact for military cooperation; Israel mobilised and attacked Egypt; France and Great Britain gave an ultimatum, demanding that Egypt and Israel each retreat 10 miles from the canal. According to Stephen Ambrose, Eisenhower's biographer, the president had no doubt that he was faced with a three-part plot: London, Paris and Tel Aviv.

Nasser's refusal of the ultimatum sparked off the Anglo-French operation on October 31st: 240 aircraft bombed the Egyptian airfields, while 130 warships and another 100 cargo ships and landing craft set sail from Malta. At an emergency meeting, the UN's general assembly approved the American resolution for a ceasefire by 64 votes to 5. Only Australia and New Zealand supported the three aggressors. On November 4th, the Russians launched 4,000 tanks against the Hungarian proletariat's revolt. On November 5th, 1,000 French and British paratroopers were dropped on the canal to occupy Port Said.

London bowed by the attack on the Pound sterling

At daybreak on November 6th, the day of the American elections, the Anglo-French fleet reached the Egyptian coast and started shelling. The Russian premier, Bulganin, wrote to Eden: "How would Great Britain find itself if it were attacked in its turn by more powerful States possessing every kind of modern destructive weapons? [...] We are determined to use force to crush the aggressors". He also wrote to Eisenhower: "If this war is not stopped, there is the risk of it becoming a Third World War"; he therefore proposed a joint Russo-American action in order to put an end to it. Eisenhower refused the Russian offer. He decided to cut off all oil supplies to London and Paris until their withdrawal.

What made Eden give in – he writes in his *Memoirs* – was "a more serious threat than Marshal Bulganin's. On the world's financial markets there was a run on the Pound sterling at such a pace that a disaster was to be feared". In the first week of November, Britain lost 15% of its gold and dollar reserves. According to the British historian Hugh Thomas [*The Suez Crisis*], in New York the British currency was offered for sale in million-pound parcels, while the US Department of the Treasury opposed the British request to withdraw capital from the International Monetary Fund. London capitulated. Eisenhower won the elections. Eden retired from politics.

"Europe will be your revenge"

In the double crisis of 1956, imperialism as a whole revealed all the forms of its violence. The cessation of the crisis did not remove its deep causes. The Suez crisis will crop up repeatedly in the following decades, among the open accounts of the multipolar contention. Henry Kissinger [*The White House Years*] denounced Washington's "short-sightedness": it suspended the funding for Aswan, thus triggering "the begining and not the end" of the crisis: it treated "our closest allies brutally" under the illusion of winning Nasser's gratitude; instead, it led to the consequence that "moderate regimes [...], especially in Iraq, were weakened if not condemned"; it ill-advisedly pushed France and Great Britain "to get rid of their remaining international responsibilities", obliging the USA to "fill up the resulting vacuum in the Middle East and east of Suez and thus to take on itself all the weight of difficult geopolitical decisions". According to this estimate, in 1956 Washington opened a Pandora's box whose evil spirits are persecuting it to this day.

In Europe, the most immediate and most strategic assessment was made by Bonn. On the morning of November 6th, 1956, Adenauer met Christian Pineau, the French Foreign Minister, in Paris, and said to him: "France and Britain will never be powers comparable to the United States and the USSR. Neither will Germany. There remains only one way to play a decisive role in the world: unify Europe. Britain is not yet ripe for this, but the Suez affair will help to prepare a more receptive state of mind. We have no time to lose. Europe will be your revenge".

The cartel of the old powers

The Myth of the "Seven Sisters"*

The "Seven Sisters" cartel was born in 1947, when the five major American oil companies (Socal-Chevron, Jersey-Exxon, Socony-Mobil, Gulf and Texaco) merged with one another and with the two European colossi, Anglo-Iranian and Shell, in three separate agreements in Saudi Arabia, Kuwait and Iran [cf. pp. 165-168].

Together with the cartel, the mythology of the "Seven Sisters" was born, spread by a plurality of actors who, rather than overthrowing the cartel, aspired to be part of it. The Middle Eastern national bourgeoisies, in a twenty-year-long battle and through two deep crises, also military ones – in 1967 and 1973 – ended up replacing the Anglo-Saxon cartel with the OPEC one; but during the 1950s and 1960s, in that curious relationship of hostile and warlike symbiosis, independent oil groups, the companies of the big consumer countries, and rival State-controlled groups plotted and lived together.

Anglo-Saxon cartel and the Middle Eastern bourgeoisies

In this period, the oil production map changed radically. The American quota, which, in 1948, was 64% of the world's production, plummeted to 22% in 1972; the Middle East rocketed from 13% to 43% of the production and from 45% to 70% of the known reserves [*The Prize*].

The oil cartel controlled roughly 90% of the Middle Eastern oil but only 40% of that of the USA: hence, it had a minority force, though highly concentrated, in the United States, where three-fifths of the market were in the hands of the so-called "independents". It was no longer a matter of the mass of individual or associated prospectors who had waged a war against John Rockefeller's monopoly when it dominated 90% of the US market at the end of the nineteenth century. On the contrary, among the independents were reckoned also some of the companies that had emerged from the dismemberment of the Rockefeller group. Winnowed out over the decades, some of them were well-structured groups that counted in the price fixing at the Texas Railroad Commission and had political influence in their States and in Washington.

---

* Nicola Capelluto, December 2003

The Texan producers, who controlled 38% of the US oil, had successfully opposed an increase in oil production to supply an oil-less Europe after the Suez crisis; they feared a drop in prices and gave in only after getting 35 cents more per barrel. Some of the independents had enough capital and experience to break into the world market.

The objective condition was the marked increase in oil demand during the post-war period, which pushed up the prices. Yergin illustrates the Middle Eastern oil revenue figures; at the end of the 1940s, the world price for crude oil was $2.50 a barrel. In the Middle East, its production and transport costs were only $0.75; the profit margin was $1.75, while in Texas it was only $0.10. The differential profit of $1.65 a barrel was the battlefield between the companies and between them and the national bourgeoisies.

Sisters, stepsisters and "independents"

The "independents" started to arrive in the Middle East in 1947-48. At an auction, the Aminoil consortium between Phillips, Ashland and Sinclair won the concession in the borderland Neutral Zone between Saudi Arabia and Kuwait, on the Kuwaiti side; on the Saudi side, the auction was won by Jean Paul Getty's Pacific Western. The two groups made bids that dismayed the Seven Sisters, paying $17 million cash in advance. Pacific found oil only in 1953 but in such large quantities that, by 1957, Getty had become the richest man in America.

With the arrival of the "intruders" on the scene, the bourgeoisies of the producer countries had proof of the greed of the "seven headed hydra". The royalties paid to Kuwait by Gulf and Shell were 15 cents a barrel; after hard-fought battles, Aramco paid Saudi Arabia 33 cents, while Getty paid 55 cents. In vain did the cartel's economists argue that the precursors had taken upon themselves risks and expenses that weighed much less on the newcomers. a breach that allowed the spread of the *fifty-fifty* system, the 50% sharing the proceeds between the companies and the national bourgeoisies.

The formation of the Iranian consortium in 1954 represented the officialisation of the Seven Sisters' cartel (together with one stepsister, the French CFP). But it was also the occasion of the independents' second advance: the Eisenhower administration forced the five big US companies to hand over 5% of the Consortium to nine US independents: Aminoil, Sohio, Atlantic and Richfield (which later merged), Signal and Hancock (which also merged), San Jacinto (later bought by Continental), Getty and Tidewater (later merged and then taken over by Texaco).

So, in a single scenario, there were combined the oil cartel, the first oil nationalisation in the Middle East (which had numerous sequels) and a "democratisation" of the cartel which, instead, remained an isolated case. Other independents settled in Libya, which adopted, while still under the monarchic regime, a strategy of small concessions to 17 companies, among which were Continental, Amerada, Marathon and Occidental, outflanking Exxon and BP.

Eisenhower's regard for the independents was confirmed in 1959, when he imposed compulsory quotas and a 9% ceiling on US imports. The president of the "open door" in the Middle East closed the door at home so as to protect the national industry, while the imposition of quotas incited new independents to venture into the Middle East.

Enrico Mattei's revolt

In Italy, in 1946, nine oil companies operated, nineteen in 1956 and 81 in 1972, but, according to an estimation reported by Yergin, a good 350 US companies with various specialisations entered the international oil industry between 1946 and 1972.

ENI's exclusion from the Iranian Consortium was the mainspring of Enrico Mattei's revolt. The Suez crisis triggered it. ENI's 1957 accord with Iran broke the golden *fifty-fifty* rule, established after Mossadeq. Mattei granted the Shah 75% of the future proceeds. Paul Frankel, one of the first biographers of the Italian "corsair", maintained that the "75-25" formula was at least partly deceptive because it did not take into account the quid pro quo, the obligation assumed by Iran to reimburse half of the investments and expenses for past and future prospecting. What was a real innovation was the promotion of an oil-producing country from a mere receiver of royalties to a quasi-partner.

Mattei's formula was immediately imitated – in an attenuated form – by the Japanese of the Arabian Oil Company Consortium, which took on the offshore concessions of Kuwait and Saudi Arabia in the Neutral Zone, and – fully – by Standard Oil of Indiana-Amoco in Iran. The violation of the *fifty-fifty* formula was luckier for the Japanese and Amoco, who effectively found oil, than for ENI, which, betrayed by the subsoil, went hungry.

Eni and imports from the USSR

According to Anthony Sampson [*The Seven Sisters*] and, above all, to Exxon's historiographer Bennett Wall [*Growth in a Changing Environment*], Mattei's biggest challenge was that of his agreements with the USSR, towards the end of 1960.

Khrushchev's attempt at modernisation at the end of the 1950s was largely based on the re-introduction of Russian oil into the world market, thanks to the new, rich oilfields in the Volga-Urals region. Absent from the European market until the Suez crisis, in 1960 the USSR had already captured 8% of it, was again the second oil producer in the world, in place of Venezuela, and declared that it aimed to reach its pre-war quota of 19% of the world's exports.

The Russian offensive, carried out through prices that were 25% lower than the market price, shook the cartel and mobilised the diplomatic chancelleries. With its 1960 contract, at $1 a barrel, the lowest post-war price, in 1961 ENI covered 22% of Italian demand, reaching 31% with its second contract at the end of 1963, following the death of Mattei. According to Wall, the Italian government was the most active in blocking US pressure to fix a ceiling on Russian oil imports in the name of Western security.

German engine and Russian Party

The attempt to "westernise" the Soviet bloc was the raft on which the "Togliatti era" counted to refine the social-imperialist navigation techniques of opportunism. In the marriage of interests between the capitalism of the Russian State and that of Italy, the PCI found fuel for its twofold national and Russian allegiance that was not only ideological.

But it was the deeper nature of the process that was not grasped by the opportunist strategy. The engine of change was neither Soviet nor Italian-made, but German-made. The rhythms of German imperialism's revival quickly modified the European energy structure. The OEEC had forecast that the oil share of Europe's energy demand would pass from 20% in 1955 to 25% in 1965. In reality, already in 1960, the oil share was 32% and reached 60% in 1970. Moscow hitched itself to Bonn's engine. All Mattei did was to follow Adenauer to Tehran – as Cervetto clearly saw in 1957 – and, afterwards, on the road to Moscow, in an economic *Ostpolitik* that anticipated the political one.

All in all, Mattei was a by-product of the process, though sufficiently aware as to try to balance the Russian contracts with a five-year contract with Esso International, signed after his death, but – according to Wall – negotiated beforehand. The Togliatti "firm", instead, remained anti-American and anti-German, resistant to the various versions of the "containment", but destined to wear itself out in the face of the Franco-German free-trade cycle and to collapse together with the Berlin Wall.

The producers' cartel on the rise

The Birth of OPEC*

During the 1960s, the European demand for oil grew at more than twice the rate of Western Europe's total energy demand. The impulse towards economic integration given by the 1957 Treaty of Rome was largely responsible for the thirst for oil, but the pace of the acceleration was closely related to the low oil prices that were pushing coal out of the market. At the end of the 1950s, different factors were acting on the lowering of the oil prices.

The limitation of American oil imports introduced by Eisenhower in March 1959, had diverted more crude oil to the European market. The USSR's spectacular re-entry into the market with aggressive prices had forced the big oil companies to lower theirs. From 1959 onwards, Libya's entry into the market represented a formidable competition, both because of the strong presence of the "independents" in the Libyan prospecting field and because the transport of Libyan crude oil was free from the strategic surprises of the Suez Canal.

In February 1959, British Petroleum reduced its list prices by 18 cents a barrel. So long as the oil companies applied discounts, leaving the lists unchanged, the economic loss was theirs alone, but, since the list prices were the contractual base for profit-sharing, their curtailment led to a reduction in the royalties and taxes collected by the oil-producing countries. The "oil" bourgeoisies discovered that, despite Mossadeq's, Nasser's, Kassem's and Mattei's revolutions, the oil companies had hung onto the unilateral right of fixing prices. The reaction soon arrived.

Nationalism in Venezuela

In April 1959, the Congress of Arabian oil was held in Cairo. It was the occasion of a meeting which "black gold" historians indicate as OPEC's date of conception. Juan Pablo Perez Alfonzo, the Venezuelan Minister for Mines and Hydrocarbons, attended the congress as an observer.

Daniel Yergin [*The Prize*] describes him as the key figure of the Betancourt government, which had returned to power in Caracas in 1958, after ten years of military dictatorship. In 1945, as the

* Nicola Capelluto, January 2004.

Minister for Development, Perez Alfonzo had adopted a line of aggressive cooperation with the international oil groups, obtaining increases in the government's proceeds and, above all, the payment of the royalties in oil which the government would sell directly, thus breaking the taboo according to which marketing was the sole right of the Anglo-Saxons.

During the military dictatorship, he had spent some time in the USA, where he had studied the running of the Texas Railroad Commission, the agency that regulated US oil production and prices. He was a cosmopolitan nationalist. He knew that production costs in Venezuela were higher than in the Middle East ($0.80 a barrel as compared to $0.20) and he pressed the Middle-Easterners to increase their taxes so as to reduce the Venezuelan disadvantage. At the same time, he supported the need for an international quota system like the American one. Eisenhower's oil protectionism and the Russian oil offensive had seriously penalised his country.

Pan-Arabism and Middle Eastern bourgeoisies

In Cairo, the sector's most important journalist, Wanda Jablonski, of Czech origin and the *Petroleum Weekly's* correspondent, organised a private meeting between Perez Alfonzo and his Saudi counterpart, Abdullah Tariki. The latter was a fervent supporter of Nasserist Pan-Arabism; he had completed his geology and chemistry studies in Texas and had married an American, but he had never forgiven the Texans for taking him for a Mexican and treating him accordingly. Initially favourable to Aramco's nationalisation, in 1959 he changed his strategy after the unexpected price cut, converting to the Venezuelan philosophy of price and production control.

The two ministers, in a secret meeting with the representatives of Iran, Iraq, Kuwait and Egypt, signed a gentleman's agreement recommending to their governments: a) the creation of an advisory oil Commission in defence of the price structure; b) the setting up of national oil companies; c) the replacement of the 50-50 principle with a passage to a 60-40 profit sharing in favour of the oil-producing countries; d) the establishment of national refineries that would give more proceeds to the governments and stability to the dealers.

In the following months, all anger seemed to have cooled down and this led Exxon to make a fatal mistake. Its new chairman, Monroe Rathbone, an expert on the American oil world but not on the

Middle Eastern one, decided, in August, 1960, to cut the list prices by 14 cents a barrel, equal to 7%.

Exxon's fatal mistake

The decision was preceded by an internal battle in which the alignment opposing the price cuts was led by Exxon's Middle East negotiator, Howard Page, who had an intimate knowledge of the explosive force of Arab nationalism. This time, the retaliatory initiative was taken by the Iraqi leader, Abd al-Karim Kassem, who had overthrown the Hashemite monarchy in 1958 and who contested Nasser's leadership of the Arab world. Kassim convened a conference, with the double objective of reacting to the Seven Sisters and separating the oil policy from Nasserism, because Egypt was not an oil-producing country.

On September 14th, 1960, in Baghdad, five oil-producing countries representing 80% of the world's exports – Saudi Arabia, Iran, Iraq, Kuwait and Venezuela – founded OPEC (the Organisation of Petroleum Exporting Countries), with the immediate objective of restoring the old list prices, and with three strategic objectives: being consulted on the prices, the introduction of a "regulation of the production" on US lines, and a joint reaction to sanctions against any one of them. The Iranian Fuad Rouhani, was nominated as the organisation's secretary-general.

The oil-producers' cartel expanded to eight in 1962 with the membership of Libya, Indonesia and Qatar.

According to Anthony Sampson [*The Seven Sisters*], the USSR toyed with the idea of joining OPEC, but quickly gave it up with the excuse that it was not interested in keeping up artificial prices. A 1962 study by Washington's National Petroleum Council blamed Russian dumping for the oil-producing countries' $490 million loss in proceeds over five years. From Moscow's point of view, probably, Russian dumping had been the christening of the oil-producers' counter-cartel.

Cartel versus cartel

The Seven Sisters' cartel and most of the chancelleries did not take OPEC seriously. Quarrelsomeness, ineptitude and national ambitions divided the "oil" bourgeoisies from one another more than from the Seven Sisters.

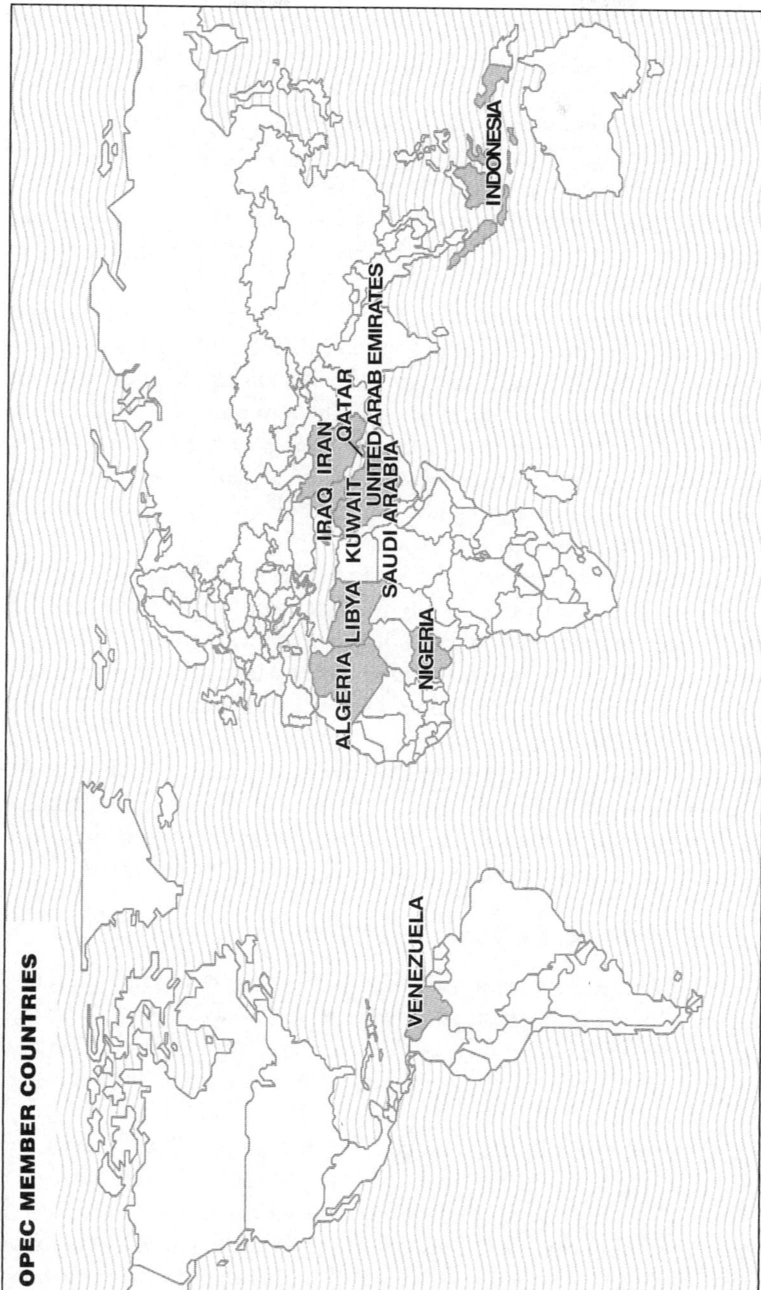
OPEC MEMBER COUNTRIES
VENEZUELA
ALGERIA
LIBYA
NIGERIA
SAUDI ARABIA
KUWAIT
IRAQ
IRAN
QATAR
UNITED ARAB EMIRATES
INDONESIA

In 1961, Kuwait won its independence from Great Britain and Iraq immediately claimed sovereignty over it: the Arab League condemned Kassem's claim, so Baghdad left the League and refused to attend the OPEC meetings. In Saudi Arabia, Faisal, in favour of an alliance with the USA, ascended the throne, and, in 1962, dismissed Tariki, replacing him with Ahmed Zaki Yamani.

Venezuela established friendly relations with the Kennedy administration, and, in 1963, Perez Alfonzo retired, disappointed by OPEC's inefficiency.

Iran, a non-Arab country, cherished the ambition of becoming the world's leading oil-producer and of using the oil-producers' cartel for its own national and regional ends, taking on the leadership of the "moderate" Middle Easterns. Throughout the 1960s, OPEC played a secondary role, torn by the rivalry between Saudi Arabia and Iran who, in order to maximise their revenues, increased their production as much as possible, setting aside the founders' objective, i.e., Texan-style quotas.

All this did not prevent the Seven Sisters' exploitation of OPEC's creation in order to obtain further guarantees from Washington. John McCloy, the World Bank's ex-president, former High Commissioner for Germany, and head of Chase Manhattan's international affairs, during that period took on the political-legal representation of the major oil companies.

In 1961, he obtained from President John Kennedy and the Attorney General, Robert Kennedy, the guarantee that the oil companies would not be prosecuted by the Antitrust Division if they dealt collectively, cartel vs. cartel, with the oil-producing countries.

The Europe and Atlantic of Jean Monnet

The European Community did not take part in these developments. In the immediate post-war period, Jean Monnet and the founding fathers envisaged coal as the basis for reconstruction and created the ECSC, the first nucleus of the European Union around it and steel.

Monnet's biographer, François Duchêne, records that, after the failure of the ECD, inside the ECSC's High Authority, some commissioners like the German Franz Etzel, considered as one of Adenauer's men, the Dutchman Dirk Spierenburg and the Belgian Albert Coppé proposed relaunching the EC process by extending the high authority's competence to all the energy sectors: oil, gas and electricity.

Monnet did not rule out this prospect, but neither did he pursue it. He bet, instead, on atomic energy, also because, since 1953, Eisenhower had declared himself willing to help Europe with "atoms for peace". According to Duchêne, the deciding factor in Monnet's choice was the consideration that, in this sector, there were no lobbies ready to rush to arms in order to defend their markets.

An unborn Europetrol

Eric Roussel, another of the "father of Europe"'s biographers, had published a note dated 1956 in which Monnet renounced any intervention in the oil sector in order to concentrate on civilian nuclear energy: "It is not the possession of Middle Eastern oil that poses a threat of war, since Europe can obtain the quantity it needs from America. It is the fact that Europe does not possess within its territory those sources of energy which are necessary for its growth that poses a danger for peace".

The Euratom treaty, signed together with the Common Market treaty in March 1957, was the translation of Jean Monnet's Euro-Atlantic strategy. Oil policy was left in the hands of the individual European countries. Monnet gave Europe two energy policies, one founded on the fuel of the past, the other on that of the future, rendered uncertain by the vetoes on nuclear proliferation, trusting in an "equal partnership" which, however, left dominion over the fuel of the present to the transatlantic partner. The interimperialistic relations of force, according to Monnet's reckoning, allowed a mature ECSC and an illusory Euratom, but not the unborn Europetrol.

The wars of 1948, 1956, and Yemen

A Never-Ending War from Suez to the Persian Gulf*

For the man in the street, the fight for oil, the Arab-Israeli conflict, and terrorism encapsulate the Middle Eastern question. This triad is insufficient and misleading. During the post-war period, oil and the Palestinian question have at times represented real stakes, at others the pretext and political arms of a plurality of imperialisms and national bourgeoisies, in variable combinations and gradations.

In the twenty-year period between 1947 and 1967, marked by three wars, the battles in the area reveal a variety of typologies: battles over the apportionment of the oil rent between the petro-states and the oil companies; battles among the national "oil" bourgeoisies over shares of the world-markets; battles among and inside the Arab national bourgeoisies for regional hegemony; battles between the Arab bourgeoisies and the Israeli bourgeoisie; battles of the superpowers for hegemony over parts of the area, and battles of the imperialist powers for the preservation or the conquest of influence over one or more national bourgeoisies, within the framework of the global interimperialist struggle. Even when the alignments, catalysed by the wars, buried their differences, these factors have always been present.

Israel and the 1948 war

In November 1947, the UN's General Assembly, in view of Great Britain's relinquishment of its mandate over Palestine, decided to create two states, one Jewish and the other Arab, and an international regime for Jerusalem. In those circumstances, the US and the USSR, Truman and Stalin, enlisted Zionism among their political cards for ousting the decadent French and British imperialism from their colonial areas and as a potential anti-German weapon. The Arabs refused the partition: the civil war that ensued, with atrocities and massacres, turned into a war among states, when the State of Israel was proclaimed in May 1948. Five Arab states, Syria and Iraq in the front line, Lebanon, Transjordan and Egypt marched against the newborn State.

The conflict, which in Israeli historiography is defined as "the war of independence" and in the Arab one as *Nakba* ("the disaster"), led

* Nicola Capelluto, February 2004

to the Israeli conquest of an access to the sea on the Gulf of Aqaba, the port of Eilat. The occupation of Gaza by the Egyptians and the annexation of the West Bank by Transjordan did not mitigate the defeat of the Palestinian Arabs, a defeat to the advantage of friends and enemies. The rendering of accounts for the defeat mingled with nationalist radicalism and struggles between military and tribal clans: in Syria, in 1949, three coups followed in rapid succession and the president, Husni Za'im, was arrested and executed; in 1951, King Abdallah of Jordan was assassinated in Jerusalem by the Palestinians; in 1952, King Farouk was banished from Egypt by General Naghib who, in his turn, was deposed by Nasser.

The 1956 war

Nasser's ascent reintroduced the ideology of Pan-Arabism into the area; this split all the Arab bourgeoisies between an unrealistic prospect of Arab unity and the defence of national or clan ambitions. American and Russian imperialism courted Nasser for a long time just as they had done with Mossadeq in Iran. In the 1956 crisis, the USA and the USSR found themselves together at Nasser's side and against Israel, this time allied with Britain and France that went to war to keep control of Suez.

The 1956 war, called "the Sinai campaign" in Israeli historiography and "the tripartite aggression" in the Arab one, was followed by a long period of internal struggles in the Arab world. In Iraq, in 1958, the Hashemite monarchy was overthrown – King Faysal and the heir to the throne were assassinated – by the revolution led by Abd al-Karim Kassem, who, with a nationalist programme, claimed rights over Kuwait and the Iranian bank of the Shatt-al-Arab river, and took Iraq out of the Baghdad Pact, founded and armed by Great Britain. Kassem was, in turn, overthrown and executed in 1963 by a coup led by the Pan-Arab Ba'ath party, in its turn thrown out of government by a military coup a few months later, returning to power, however, in 1968.

The UAR and the Arab Federation

It seemed that Pan-Arabism had become a reality in February 1958, when Egypt and Syria formed the United Arab Republic (UAR), headed by Nasser. Both countries had rejected the Baghdad Pact and had entered into military agreements with the USSR. The UAR, which for Egypt was the start of a programme of regional hegemony, for Syria largely represented a balance against Russian influence. The immediate response of Jordan and Iraq was the creation of an Arab Federation which had a very short life, ending with Kassem's revolution and the prompt intervention of British paratroopers in Amman. The UAR, on its part, was dissolved in 1961, after the nationalist military coup in Syria.

Between 1961 and 1966 Syria had five coups and ten different governments. Pro-Nasserists, pro-Russians, advocates of "Greater Syria" (in a union with Iraq) clashed in the search of a regional role for a bourgeoisie without oil and scruples. In the 1960s, Syria tried to take an anti-Israeli direction by attempting to deviate the course of the river Jordan and by using the Golan Heights as a bastion of attrition on the Jewish settlements. In Saudi Arabia the clash over Nasserism split the royal family and ended with the crushing victory of Feisal, pro-Western, over his elder brother and King Saud, deposed in 1964. In Jordan the internal struggle between pro-Nasserists and loyalists lasted over ten years, until the eve of the 1967 war. In Lebanon a revolt incited by Egypt and Syria in 1958 was put down by the landing of US toops. In Lebanon and Jordan the Palestinian refugee camps became, for all the Arab states, a recruitment centre, the flag of real suffering but also the fig leaf of fierce internal struggles and adventurism.

Iran and the Saudis

Meanwhile, the two main "oil" bourgeoisies, the Iranian and Saudi, were competing for an increase in the revenue from their oil wells. Iran, with almost 30 million inhabitants, was still, on the eve of the 1967 war, the third Middle Eastern oil producer after Saudi Arabia, with six million inhabitants, and Kuwait. The Shah's objective was to win back the primacy it held before 1951 by accelerating rearmament and public works.

But the oil companies' policy was diversified. British Petroleum which, in the Iranian Consortium, held 40% but was absent from the Saudi colossus Aramco, was in favour of increasing the Persian extraction, supported by the American independents and the Compagnie Française des Pètroles, also absent from Aramco and a partner in the Consortium with only 6%. Instead, opposed to any increase in production, both in Iran and in Saudi Arabia, were Exxon, Socal and Texaco, which each had a 7% share in the Consortium, while each held 30% in Aramco. The three companies, not wishing to create bearish pressures on the prices, sheltered behind the "particular agreements" existing among the partners, secret agreements that foresaw penalties for the company that exceeded its production share. Mobil, a minority partner with 10%, was pushing Aramco to increase its production.

The Shah versus "Arab Imperialism"

According to Daniel Yergin [*The Prize*], in 1964 the Shah, in a meeting with the American president Lyndon Johnson, accused OPEC of having become "a tool of Arab imperialism" and the companies of playing its game. To force the State Department's hand, Iran improved its relations with the USSR and signed an agreement on natural gas with Moscow.

Anthony Sampson [*The Seven Sisters*], quoting the 1974 American Congress hearings, states that CFP and, later, Mobil leaked the secret agreements to the Shah, providing him with further means of pressure.

Yergin concludes that the Shah's pressure worked: between 1957 and 1970 there was a 387% increase in Iranian production, as opposed to 258% in Saudi production. These extraordinary increases were partly possible thanks to the radical Iraqi oil policy that, under Kassem in 1961, expropriated, without any compensation, 99.5% of the Iraq Petroleum Company's concession, leading to a drop in investments and production in Iraq.

A Vietnam for Nasser

From 1962 Saudi Arabia and Egypt intervened on opposite sides in the Yemeni civil war. A pro-Nasserist military coup had deposed the imam Ahmad who led the Yemeni theocratic regime. The civil war lasted for more than fifteen years and the two neighbouring Arab states intervened in it on a massive scale until August 1967.

The fight, which had at first seemed marginal, had, according to the historian of the Six-Day War, Michael Oren, pernicious and unforeseen consequences for Egypt: it kept 50-70,000 of the best Egyptian soldiers immobilised for years, cost an incredible $9.2 billion, bringing the Egyptian economy to the brink of collapse, interfered with Britain's plan to withdraw from its base in Aden and compromised the normalisation of relations with the USA, relaunched by the Kennedy administration with the "big invisible weapon" of wheat, which arrived in 1962 to feed 40% of the Egyptian population. In 1965, the Johnson administration broke off the wheat supplies to Egypt and obstructed the Egyptian attempt to renegotiate its international debt. Nasser went to war with Israel in June 1967 carrying a little Vietnam on his back.

The Six-Day war

The 1967 War*

I

The last fifty years have made the Middle East a veritable testing ground for Clausewitz's concept of war as a continuation of politics, but by other means. Continuation does not mean putting war and politics on the same level, or interchangeability between war and peace. It means bringing the irrationality of slaughtering men back within the rational confines of the political struggle of which war is a tool, but also recognising the impotence of politics in the face of the irremediable traditions of a world divided into classes, nations and religions: the impotence of the potent dominant classes, and not humankind's irrevocable fate.

On average, once every ten years a war has shuffled and re-dealt the cards of the Middle Eastern pack between local and global players. The 1956 war ended without peace treaties. Two "gentlemen's" agreements had finalised the truce. The first, between Nasser and the UN Secretary-General, Dag Hammarskjöld, laid down that Cairo could expel the UNEF's (United Nations Emergency Force) blue helmets, deployed in its territory along the boundary with Israel in the Sinai Peninsula. With the second agreement, John Foster Dulles, the US Secretary of State, together with Golda Meir, Israel's Foreign Minister, pledged that any Egyptian attempt to reintroduce the blockade of the Strait of Tiran, which separates Sinai's southernmost point from Saudi Arabia, would be considered a declaration of war.

These were not so much peace terms as an incentive for a new outbreak of war.

Contradictions among the Arab bourgeoisie

The political victory of Nasserism in the Suez crisis led to a contradictory dynamic between the Pan-Arab rhetoric espoused by all the Arab bourgeoisies and a fierce inter-Arab competition. The birth and failure in 1963 of the Tripartite Union among Egypt, Syria and Iraq was just another in the series of vain attempts. At the beginning

* Nicola Capelluto, March-April 2004.

of 1964 a new flare-up of Arab unity was fuelled by a political crisis in Tel Aviv, resulting in the resignation of Ben-Gurion, the State's founding father, and in the rupture of the Labour Party with the departure of Moshe Dayan, the hero of the Suez War, and of Shimon Peres.

Israeli plans to canalise the waters of the River Jordan from Galilee to the Negev desert roused the fear that the new leadership of Levi Eshkol, Golda Meir and Yigal Allon aimed to make room for another three million Jewish immigrants. Damascus, backed by Amman and Riyadh, incited an Arab-Israeli war. Nasser, pinned down by the war in Yemen, tried to curb the Syrian campaign. The Arab League's summit, held in Cairo decided to finance a project for the deviation of the Jordan at its source, so as to reduce Israel's water supply, and to set up a United Arab Command (UAC) with a ten-year budget of $345 million (almost doubled in 1965), headed by two Egyptian generals. One year later, the Arab leadership set up the PLO (Palestine Liberation Organisation) with the lawyer Ahmad al-Shuqayri, a Nasserist, at its head.

This was not much more than a paper agreement. The divisions flared up again. Jordan refused to let foreign Arab units be deployed in its territory. Lebanon shilly-shallied. Iraq refused to deliver its aircraft to the UAC. The Egyptian command was contested. In 1965 Nasser launched a boycott of Germany, which had recognised Israel, but Morocco, Tunisia, Libya and Saudi Arabia did not adhere to it. Saudi Arabia, Jordan and Iran joined forces in the Islamic League, also known as the Alliance of the Three Monarchies, denounced by Nasser as an American conspiracy. Syria vigorously took up the cause of Palestinian guerrilla warfare: al-Fatah's attacks on the Israeli settlements increased from a few dozen in 1965 to hundreds in 1967. The Nasserist PLO, instead, concentrated its attacks on the Jordanian monarchy of King Hussein. The king had two hundred guerrillas arrested and closed the PLO's premises in Amman, while Nasser jailed all al-Fatah militants in Egypt and Gaza.

Four reasons for the war

The Hamburg historian of the Arab-Israeli conflict, Helmut Mejcher [*Sinai, 5. Juni 1967*] analyses four endogenous courses of the 1967 war. In the first place, the "war over water" in the Jordan valley, and, connected with this, the question of the tillable land, including the borderland demilitarised zone which Israel was beginning to till and cultivate, were a constant motive for clashes with Syria. The question of the West Bank, the main area of the guerrilla attacks but also the seat of Jerusalem, the Biblical capital, was the reason for the the tug-of-war, made up of secret negotiations and reprisals, between Israel and Jordan; the Hashemite king saw himself as the predestined scapegoat of all the Arab pressures on Israel, an earthenware vessel among iron pots.

The third question was the nuclear power station at Dimona, in the Negev, built thanks to Shimon Peres's "French connection": constructed formally for the energy requirements of the desalination plants on the Mediterranean, in reality it was at the centre of Israel's programme for nuclear rearmament. Dimona was crucial in the 1967 crisis: the threat to the power station posed by the Egyptian air force "was actually, from the very beginning, one of the most important factors in the dramatic development of the crisis", i.e., in Israel's decision to launch a pre-emptive attack; according to the German author, when the crisis worsened, Peres proposed "using the nuclear deterrent so as to prevent the outbreak of hostilities", but Yitzhak Rabin, the Chief of Staff, barred him from doing so. However, Eshkol's government ordered that two atomic bombs were to be armed and made ready for use.

The knot of the oil pipelines

The last question was the Strait of Tiran and access to the port of Eilat, which Israel had conquered in 1956. Seven miles wide, Tiran is Israel's communication route, along the Red Sea, with the Indian Ocean and Afro-Asian trade. By the end of 1956 Israel had laid a 257-mile-long oil pipeline connecting Eilat with Haifa, on the Mediterranean, and had an annual flow of nearly five million tons of crude oil, coming mostly from Iran.

According to Mejcher, who places the Eilat-Haifa pipeline among "the real antecedents of the Six-Day War", historians have underestimated the role Israel intended to take on in the energy supply field, in alliance with Iran, threatening the strategic pre-eminence of Syria as the passageway of the oil pipelines coming from Iraq and Saudi Arabia en route to the Mediterranean and even the Suez Canal itself.

De Gaulle's Arab policy

However, it was the change in the relations among the powers that accelerated the race towards the war.

G.H. Soutou, in a note to Raymond Aron's *Les articles du Figaro*, observes that De Gaulle's granting of independence to Algeria had put an end to the Franco-Israeli alliance that had been the linchpin

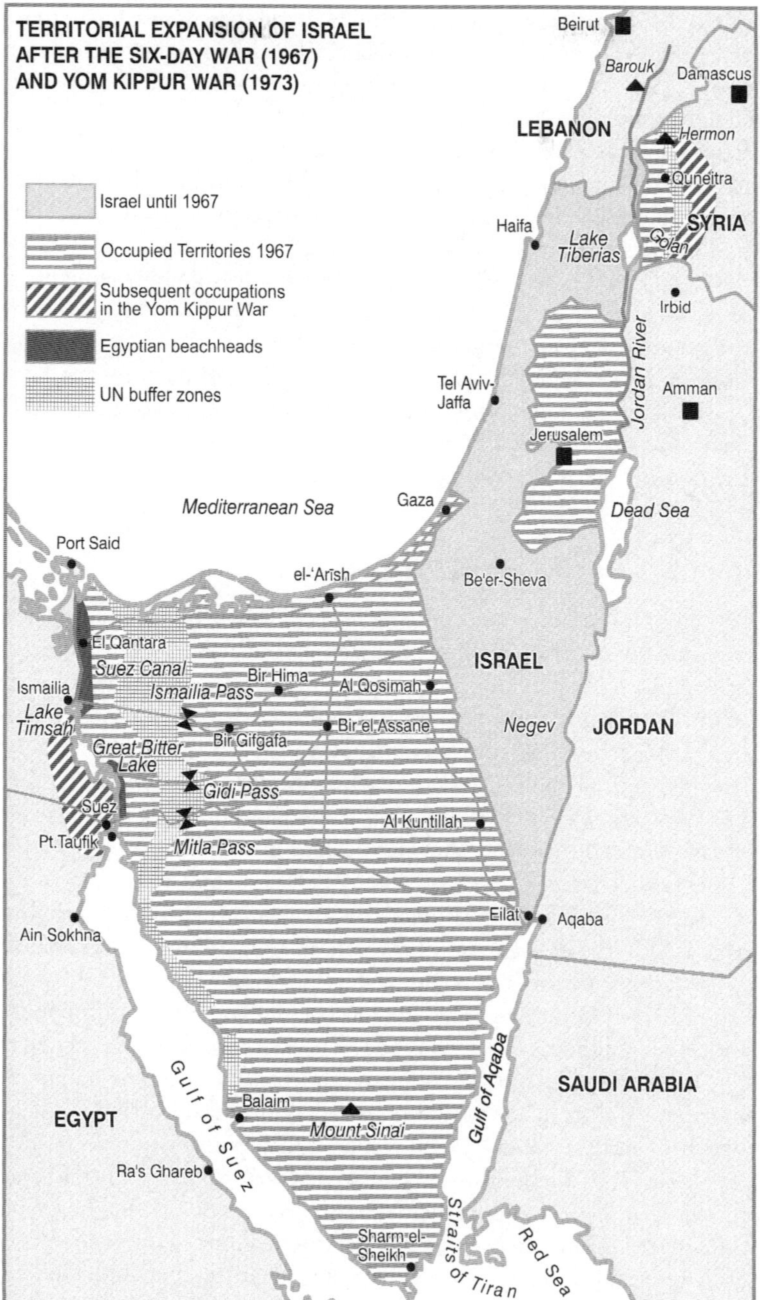
TERRITORIAL EXPANSION OF ISRAEL
AFTER THE SIX-DAY WAR (1967)
AND YOM KIPPUR WAR (1973)
Israel until 1967
Occupied Territories 1967
Subsequent occupations in the Yom Kippur War
Egyptian beachheads
UN buffer zones
Beirut
Barouk
Damascus
LEBANON
Hermon
Quneitra
SYRIA
Golan
Haifa
Lake Tiberias
Irbid
Jordan River
Tel Aviv-Jaffa
Amman
Jerusalem
Mediterranean Sea
Gaza
Dead Sea
Port Said
el-'Arīsh
Be'er-Sheva
El Qantara
Suez Canal
ISRAEL
Ismailia
Bir Hima
Ismailia Pass
Al Qosimah
Lake Timsah
Bir el Assane
Negev
JORDAN
Bir Gifgafa
Great Bitter Lake
Gidi Pass
Suez
Al Kuntillah
Pt. Taufik
Mitla Pass
Eilat
Aqaba
Ain Sokhna
Gulf of Suez
Gulf of Aqaba
SAUDI ARABIA
Balaim
EGYPT
Mount Sinai
Ra's Ghareb
Straits of Tiran
Red Sea
Sharm el-Sheikh

of the 1956 military operation. The General was now aiming to develop an "Arab policy on a great scale". This determined his policy in 1967, when he suspended military supplies to Israel, warning it not to undertake a pre-emptive war: "*Ne faites pas la guerre!*" he repeated three times at Abba Eban. Aron, in an article in *Le Figaro* [August 31st 1967], bears out the thesis that Nasser would not have decreed the blockade of the Gulf of Arabia, which precipitated the war, "if he had not believed he had France's backing".

Israel's other ally in 1956, Great Britain, was going through one of its worst moments. Excluded from the EEC by De Gaulle's veto, in the grip of a deep economic and monetary crisis, in the spring of 1967 London had reached the decision to halve its presence east of Suez. Not only was it unable to play any role in the 1967 Middle Eastern crisis, but the crisis itself became the catalyst for the devaluation of the pound and of the Wilson government's decision to withdraw for good from east of Suez.

The USA bogged down in Vietnam

The United States was getting bogged down in Vietnam. There was no way it could get involved in a second theatre of war either on Israel's side or by imposing a freezing of the crisis. The Johnson administration had tried to create a military balance in the area by increasing arms sales from $44 million to $995 million, of which, according to the Israeli historian Michael B. Oren [*The Six-Day War*], Israel's share was "negligible", while the total military expenditure of the Arab countries in that period had been $938 million a year, almost twice Israel's.

The Soviet Union had been the area's major military supplier. The USSR capitalised on the Vietnam War, which immobilised Washington, in order to reinforce its position in the Middle East, especially – Oren underlines – after its complete loss of influence in Indonesia following Suharto's coup in 1965, and because it needed to counter China's ideological offensive. After 1956 Moscow had made a massive political investment in the Middle East, with $2 billion worth of military aid – 1,700 tanks, 2,400 pieces of artillery, 500 jet planes, 1,400 advisers – 43% of which went to Egypt. It had conferred upon Nasser and his field marshal Amer the title of "heroes of the Soviet Union", an honour never before conferred upon a foreigner. After yet another Syrian coup in February 1966, in which General Salah Jadid and the General of the Air Force, Hafiz Assad, set up a

Ba'athist regime that was more radical than the previous ones, the USSR established strong ties with Damascus. In 1966 alone it supplied financial aid to the tune of $428 million. Russian became the second language in Syrian schools.

The Kremlin's currents

On the Politburo's agenda a war in the Middle Eastern area was not envisaged, but the fear of a war sparked off by Zionism became the refrain of Moscow's diplomacy. The struggle of the factions in the Kremlin, Damascus, Cairo and Tel Aviv imparted an unexpected dynamic to events. In Moscow the Syrian card entered the debate on the intensity with which Washington's Vietnamese venture should be exploited.

Marshal Andrei A. Grechko, the Deputy Minister of Defence, backed by Brezhnev, supported the need for a strong line, encouraging Syria to intensify its guerrilla attacks. Border incidents multiplied. The Syrians used artillery and the air force more often.

Nasser, worried by the increasing Syrian pressure, had recourse to the well-tested method of riding the tiger in order to keep it in check. On November 4th, 1966 Egypt and Syria signed a defence pact, promising reciprocally, in the event of a conflict, to engage Israel simultaneously on two fronts. Syria shut down the Iraq Petroleum Company's (IPC's) pipeline in order to impose an increase in the price of the rights of transit. In Tel Aviv, while the Prime Minister Eshkol, fearing an escalation with Syria and the "Russian bear", wished to contain the clashes along the border and the reprisals, the Chief of Staff Rabin imposed a more energetic reaction. In November, 1966 he organised a reprisal in Jordan territory with the wholesale destruction of Samu, a town with 5,000 inhabitants near Hebron, while in April 1967 he challenged the Syrian air force in the skies above Damascus in an aerial clash involving 130 aircraft and ending with the humiliating loss of six Syrian MiG fighters.

In Egypt, Field Marshal Amer believed that the time to settle accounts with Israel was now ripe: he asked Nasser to regain complete control of the Sinai Peninsula, expelling the UN Emergency Force. Nasser dithered. Moscow diplomacy suggested caution, but meanwhile the Russian fleet was gathering in the Mediterranean. The major protagonists thought that the crisis would stay within the margins of calculated risk, but the danger of every such instance of complex brinkmanship lies in the fact that the red lines are different for each opponent.

II

“Unwanted wars” constitute one of the paradoxes of the “political will”. They reveal the discrepancy between material processes and subjective ones, between real forces and individual and collective psychologies, between calculated intentions and decisions made under the pressure of unprecedented parallelograms of forces or of a stifling impasse. To the subjectivist conception they seem to be “casual wars”, whereas, on the contrary, any “fortuitousness” is only a sum of the factors that shape the bumpy pathway along which “necessities” change into “will” and reach the surface with the explosive force of reawakened volcanoes.

Michael Oren [*The Six-Day War*] compares the process that erupted in the 1967 conflict to the well-known image of a butterfly that sets off a hurricane with a flutter of its wings: “fortuitousness” – he writes – dominated both the genesis and the outcome of the conflict, which spiralled like a “chain reaction”. Similarly, Helmut Mejcher [*Sinai, 5. June 1967*] speaks of the war as the “result of a policy based on wrong calculations, misunderstandings and lack of communication between Tel Aviv and Cairo”.

Currents in Moscow and Cairo

The “flutter of wings” that set off the 1967 hurricane started in Moscow on May 13th. During a visit to Moscow, Anwar Sadat, the president of the Egyptian National Assembly, was informed by the leaders of the Kremlin of the imminence of an Israeli invasion of Syria, between May 16th and 22nd. The information was false. The Kremlin had already “cried the Zionist wolf” various times. According to Oren, the recurrent alarms represented a compromise between those in Moscow who wanted to challenge, in the Middle East, a United States bogged down in Southeast Asia and those who, instead, feared that a war would end in catastrophe for their Arab allies; thus Moscow kept its own role as arms supplier and adviser, but at a reduced risk.

What was new was Egypt’s different reaction. A strong military fraction, headed by field marshal Muhammed Amer and by the general of the air force Sidiqi Mahmud, sought war as a means of atoning for the dishonour of 1956 and the failures in Yemen, convinced that they were now superior to Israel. Nasser feared that this time, if he did not act, his very regime might be overthrown. Hence, he played the card of regaining control of the Sinai Peninsula, demilitarised after the 1956 crisis.

The 1957 accord between Egypt and the UN had given Cairo the right to request the withdrawal of the blue helmets. On May 15th, without any precise plan, the first Egyptian troops crossed the Suez Canal. In 48 hours, Egypt moved 80,000 men, 550 tanks and 1,000 cannons into Sinai, and requested the withdrawal of the UN from the Egyptian-Israeli border. On May 17th, Israel mobilised 18,000 reservists. The UN Secretary-General, the Burmese U Thant, had no doubt about the legitimacy of the Egyptian request and, on May 19th, ordered the 4,500 men of the UNEF to withdraw. Thus the first of the two pillars on which the 1956 cease-fire had been based was removed.

Nasser's casus belli

On May 22nd, Nasser announced the restoration of Egyptian sovereignty over the Gulf of Aqaba. With the blockade of the Tiran Strait and the port of Eilat, Nasser's challenge reached its absolute limit, putting to the test the second pillar of the 1956 truce; the US promise to Israel to consider any attempt to blockade the strait as a declaration of war. Nasser reckoned that the blockade of Tiran increased the probability of war by 50%. For the Israeli Chief of Staff, Yitzhak Rabin, it was much more: "the creation on Nasser's part of the *casus belli*".

The remilitarisation of the Sinai Peninsula was a political victory, won without fighting. Why did Nasser jeopardise it by expelling the UN and blockading Tiran? Mejcher, though considering Nasser's conduct "incomprehensible", and though not excluding that he had fallen "victim to his own propaganda", hypothesises a political calculation. Nasser wanted to relaunch his role as a leader, to beat Saudi Arabia's "Islamic alternative to Nasserist Pan-Arabism", to neutralise the pressure of his military leaders, to take the initiative from the Syrian Ba'athist regime, to promote, under his control, the Palestinian cause. The blockade of Tiran, according to Mejcher, prefigured a return not only to the pre-1956 situation but also to the 1949 one, when Eilat was a Palestinian port.

In Israel, a gruelling battle began within the politico-military leadership. On May 23rd, Rabin proposed a pre-emptive attack in order to wipe out the Egyptian air force, followed by an advance on

Sinai; unlike 1956 – he said – Israel could not count on the support of any great power, and surprise was its only resource. The proposal, upheld by the leaders of the Opposition – Menachem Begin, the leader of the right-wing party Gahal, and Shimon Peres, leader of Rafi – was turned down by the head of government Levi Eshkol and by the foreign minister Abba Eban: the USA would not have backed the offensive, while the USSR might have opposed it; a repetition of the Suez crisis, but even worse.

Washington and the "Two Wars"

What would the superpowers do? On May 25th Nasser sent his Defence Minister to Moscow. On the same day, Eban presented himself at the White House. In the Kremlin, the divergences among the Soviet leaders were evident. For the premier Aleksei Kosygin, Nasser had already won politically, and should now negotiate. For the Defence Minister Andrei Grechko, Egypt had the capacity to win a conflict, even if it were attacked; the USSR was on its side. The clash was reflected in *Pravda*, the CPSU organ, and in *Red Star*, the armed forces' organ.

The crisis took Washington by surprise. Eban requested a solemn declaration on the part of the White House that an attack against Israel would be considered an act of hostility against the USA itself; but Johnson already had his own war and could not afford to get embroiled in another. He was categorical: "I am not the king of this country and, since I can command only myself, I will be of no use whatsoever. [...] I have not got even one vote or one dollar to take the initiative". He warned Israel against making a pre-emptive strike and offered the alternative of an international convoy escorted by Anglo-American warships and bombers which would defy the blockade of Tiran in defence of the freedom of navigation; but the "Regatta Plan" turned out to be unviable: neither Canada nor any major European power agreed to take part in it, Iran refused to adhere to it, the White House realised that it would not obtain the consent of Congress, and London advised against an Anglo-American operation disguised as an international one.

Coalition of Arab bourgeoisies

In the Israeli capital there was total deadlock. On May 27th, nine ministers voted in favour of a pre-emptive war and nine against.

Symptoms of a crisis in the executive appeared. Eshkol ordered the demobilisation of 40,000 reservists. The military leaders ignored him and continued to call up reserves. Tel Aviv's deadlock and the absence of any reaction to the blockade led to Hussein of Jordan's shift to Egypt's side. For years the target of assassination attempts and contempt on the part of the Pan-Arabists, Hussein presented himself to Nasser on May 30th to offer him a defence pact. The price paid by Hussein was very high: he undertook to consider any attack on Egypt as an attack on Jordan, to let foreign Arab military forces be deployed in its territory, to reopen the PLO premises and to submit the Arab League to the command of the Egyptian general Riyad.

Nasser's gamble seemed to have paid off. Israel was surrounded: Jordan deployed 56,000 soldiers backed up by 17,000 Iraqis and 270 tanks, Syria massed 50,000 men and 260 tanks on the Golan Heights, Egypt had massed 130,000 men, 900 tanks and 1,000 cannons in Sinai. Even countries that were hostile to Nasser, from Morocco to Libya, from Saudi Arabia to Tunisia, had sent military forces to the Sinai Peninsula. The Arab armies deployed 500,000 men, 900 fighter planes and 5,000 tanks. Israel opposed them with only 275,000 men, 250 fighter planes and 1,100 tanks.

Egyptian defeat

In Israel, with the military leaders' agitation and a strong press campaign against Eshkol's wait-and-see policy, a government of national unity was formed on June 1st. The turning point was marked by the nomination of Moshe Dayan as Defence Minister. The long wait had worn down any alternative, the Regatta plan was an empty shell, and Washington's brake no longer had any pretext. When, on June 4th, Dayan asked the government to authorise the offensive for the following day, neither Eshkol nor Eban objected. The decision was made by twelve votes in favour and two against.

The Israeli air raid on Sinai, on Monday, June 5th 1967, was incredibly successful: it was a complete surprise. No Egyptian commander was at his post. That morning Egypt lost 286 of its 420 fighter planes, almost all destroyed on the ground, and a third of its pilots. Israel lost only seventeen planes: it may fairly be said that it gained total control of the skies and won half the war in just three hours. The moral of this disaster was summarised by the Egyptian brigadier general Tashin Zaki: "Israel had spent years training itself for this war, while we had trained ourselves for military parades". Oren maintains that it was the rapidity of the initial victory, the fierce fighting on the Jordanian front and the entry with messianic fervour into Old Jerusalem that transformed the pre-emptive defensive war into a war of territorial conquest, toned down by some in the formula "territories in exchange for security".

Nasser, overwhelmed by the defeat, made a series of political errors. He signed a hasty order of withdrawal from Sinai that turned into a rout. He tried to drag the USSR into the war, accusing the United States of having taken part in the bombings with an aircraft of the Sixth Fleet. Moscow, angry about the bad impression Russian weapons had made in Egypt's hands, asked instead for a cease-fire. Nasser opposed this, demanding a resolution for Israel's withdrawal, thus giving Tel Aviv time to extend its conquests. On the third day, the war in Sinai, the West Bank and Jerusalem was won. It was also the day of a mysterious Israeli attack by land and by sea on the American spyship "Liberty" in the Mediterranean Sea, despite the flag it was flying, leaving 31 dead and 171 wounded. Mejcher does not exclude that this "error" was the means by which the Israelis cleared the field of any suspicion of American-Israeli collusion and hence of any possible Russian interference.

Armistices with Jordan and Egypt were concluded on June 7th-8th. Only on June 9th did the attack on the Golan Heights take place against Syria which, until then, despite its high-sounding rhetoric, had only carried out intense artillery attacks, keeping its troops safely entrenched. The next day, the conquest of the Golan Heights was achieved and Israel ceased operations, only a few hours after Moscow's theatrical move breaking off diplomatic relations with Tel Aviv, threatening to intervene if Israel did not break off its advance on Damascus.

Failure of oil embargo

On June 6th the "oil weapon" came onto the scene. Saudi Arabia, Kuwait, Iraq, Libya and Algeria decided to suspend supplies to the United States, Great Britain and, partly, Germany. The flow of Arab oil, according to Daniel Yergin, dropped by 60%, removing six million barrels a day from the market; half of the Middle Eastern and North-African oilwells were closed, with pipelines cut off and the Suez blocked. At the end of June, the Nigerian civil war, which broke out over the secession of the Biafra oilfield, removed another half-million barrels a day. Europe rediscovered its energy Achilles' heel: in comparison with the USA that depended on Arab oil for only 3% of its need, France and Italy depended on it for 83%, Germany for 73%, Britain for 69% and Japan for 61%.

But the "oil war" followed the fate of the actually fought war. By July it was clear that the embargo had failed, thanks to increases in production in the USA, Iran, Venezuela and Indonesia, and thanks, above all, to the high logistic capacity of the oil firms and supertankers. In August, still formally under the embargo regime, the Arab States produced 8% more oil than in the pre-war period. The debilitating costs of the lost war had to be covered as soon as possible. Egypt had lost, besides Sinai and Gaza, 85% of its armaments, to the tune of $2 billion. Roughly 15,000 Egyptian proletarians, 800 Israeli ones, 700 Jordanian ones and 450 Syrian ones lost their lives in six days of conflict. About 250,000 Palestinians fled from the West Bank and 95,000 Syrians from the Golan Heights.

The political geography of the Middle East changed. Israel had conquered 100,000 square kilometres, thus multiplying the territory it had had since its birth by three-and-a-half times; Nasserism had been defeated once and for all; in its relation with Washington, Tel Aviv had gained a matchless prestige; Moscow's reputation had come out battered and its relation with Egypt had been mortally wounded; The Palestinian question became the symbol of an all-out revenge for the defeat. Never had such a short war left such far-reaching consequences, or such gaping wounds.

The early 1970s

Prelude to the 1973 Crisis*

The Arab-Israeli war of June 1967 provided living proof of the American difficulty in waging two conventional wars at the same time. Johnson's refusal to honour the defence pledge given to Israel by Eisenhower clearly showed the relative weakness of American imperialism, which was bleeding in the rice paddies of Indochina. France found confirmation of its conviction that the United States would not jeopardise its own interests in order to defend its allies. In December 1967, General Charles Ailleret summarised in the formula "defense tous azimuts" the ultimate military implications of Gaullism: France had to provide itself with a capacity for omnidirectional determent, towards the East as well as towards the West.

During the same period, Harold Wilson's British government made a far-reaching strategic change of tack: totally without influence in the 1967 conflict, prostrated by the devaluation of the Pound – for which the US had denied a lifesaving loan – Great Britain reached the decision to withdraw from east of Suez by 1971, despite President Johnson's threat of a strategic break with London. The "Tet offensive" in Vietnam, in January 1968, took place a fortnight after the public announcement of British withdrawal.

Ambitions of the oil bourgeoisies

At the end of the 1960s the persistence of a strong rate of growth for world capitalism – roughly 5% per annum – and the relative decline of the two superpowers and British power set the scene for the evolution of the oil cycle. In the five-year period from 1965 to 1970 world oil consumption grew by 48% overall, but in the US by 28%, in Western Europe by 60% and in Japan by 127%. The pressure on the price of energy increased.

At the same time, Great Britain's withdrawal from east of Suez left a considerable power vacuum in the Middle East, which the United States could not fill and which whetted the already lively

* Nicola Capelluto, May 2004.

ambitions of the national oil bourgeoisies. OPEC, which had played a minor role until then and which had split over the 1967 embargo, intervened in this singular political-economic conjuncture, to emerge as the new power of the 1970s, i.e., the period between the "Libyan revolution" and the "Iranian revolution".

What sparked off OPEC's rise was the September 1969 coup in Libya led by Colonel Gaddafi, who deposed the pro-Western King Idris. Libya had been greatly favoured by the 1967 war and the long-term closure of the Suez Canal. Libyan oil had a low transport cost as it did not have to circumnavigate Africa, was of high quality and with a low sulphur content. Between 1967 and 1970 the production of Libyan oil doubled, eventually covering a quarter of Western Europe's oil requirements. The main Libyan producer was Armand Hammer's Occidental, which, in just a short time, had become the sixth producer in the world.

OPEC's new power

Libya got the Americans to evacuate Wheelus, one of their airbases, without any difficulty. Henry Kissinger, in the second volume of his *Memoirs*, recalls: "While America was deciding on passivity, Europe decided to use flattery to secure the favours of the radical ruler [...]. Four months after Gaddafi's rise to power, France concluded the sale of one hundred modern jet planes to Libya. [...] Particularly friendly relations were established between Libya and the Federal Republic of Germany".

This acquiescence to the Libyan coup – according to Kissinger – gave the moderate governments of the Middle East "a fatal lesson": "The Western democracies would not protect friendly governments until their radical successors had not challenged access to the oil of the democracies themselves. Consequently, there was no point in trying to secure Western benevolence by lowering oil prices. [...] Radical Libya sparked off a process by which the oil-producing countries gradually discovered, and began to exercise, their dominant power over the world oil market".

In January 1971, the Libyan government launched its oil offensive. It asked the companies for a 20% increase in their list prices, and, on their refusal, responded by striking at Occidental, the strongest but also the most fragile company, because it lacked other Middle Eastern sources.

Libya and the Seven Sisters

Libya imposed a cut in production from 800,000 to 500,000 barrels a day on the American independent company. Hammer asked Exxon, the second producer in Libya, for a supplementary supply, but Exxon refused to help its rival.

In September Occidental gave in, accepting a 30% backdated price increase and agreeing to augment the share paid to the government from 50% to 55%. The other independent companies gave in soon afterwards. The Seven Sisters asked the British Foreign Office and the American State Department to intervene, but both refused to do so. The Seven capitulated in October, agreeing to the conditions already imposed on Occidental.

Persian Gulf and Mediterranean

"Libya's triumph" was, according to BP's historian, James Bamberg, "a decisive moment" for the relations between the Seven Sisters and the OPEC countries. A hail of demands fell on the companies. The Shah asked the Iranian Consortium to accept the Libyan conditions. In December, Venezuela laid down by law that the share of the oil rent due to the State was 60%. In the same month the OPEC summit increased the companies' minimum tax rate from 50% to 55%. In January 1971, Libya asked for another 5% increase in its share.

The oil companies, under Shell's direction, formed a "common front" of resistance. In a "letter to OPEC", signed by the Seven Sisters and another seventeen companies – but not by ENI and the French ELF – they asked for "a simultaneous negotiation with all the governments of the petro-states". The Shah defined the message as "a monumental mistake", because the "radicals" would impose their will during a single negotiation. Iran, Saudi Arabia and Kuwait insisted on the American government's non-interference in the negotiations under any circumstances. The Secretary of State William Rogers took the advice of the "moderates". In place of the "simultaneous negotiation" the companies had to fall back on two negotiations, one with the Persian Gulf exporters represented by Iran, Iraq and Saudi Arabia, the other with the Mediterranean exporters to which not only Libya and Algeria belonged, but also Iraq and Saudi Arabia in that their oil, too, reached the Mediterranean via pipelines.

The first negotiation ended in February 1971, with the Tehran agreement which stipulated an increase of $0.50 a barrel, a yearly price adjustment and a tax rate of 55% for five years. The second negotiation began while Algeria was nationalising 51% of the French oil interests and ended in April 1971 with the Tripoli agreement which granted an increase of $0.90 a barrel and a 55% tax rate. After a year of multiple assaults, Libya had reached the price of $3.45 per barrel. Bamberg recalls that, at that time, the oil industry felt as if it had been hit by a storm, but in comparison with what would happen two years later it was only a light spring breeze.

Non-intervention to the detriment of Europe and Japan

Kissinger [*Years of Upheaval*] denies any validity, in those negotiations, in the distinction between "moderates" and "radicals". "It was a contractual tactic that the following decade would see refined until it became an art form. No matter what the group, within OPEC [...] it laid the blame for the increase in the price of oil on somebody else. [...] The truth, of course, was that all the oil-producing countries favoured high prices; no one was willing to opt out of the cartel".

Kissinger does not hide that in the US government's non-interference in the negotiations there may well have been a good deal more than love of the free market. A 1971 study by his collaborators Fred Bergsten and Harold Saunders listed among the reasons for the non-intervention that "the increase in the price of energy would hit Europe and Japan above all, improving America's competitiveness", that a direct confrontation was a "difficult undertaking in a country convulsed by the Vietnam War" and that there was the risk that the Arab-Israeli conflict would be dragged into the talks. All things considered, "it was our policy of non-intervention that determined the outcome: the companies threw in the towel".

The Texas "Railroad Commission"

The then adviser on national security indicates a second American responsibility: the decision of the Texas Railroad Commission (TRC) to drop all restrictions on US oil production. The TRC, Kissinger explains, had fixed the level of American production until then "greatly below its productive capacity, with the aim of maintaining an internal price of $3.30 – more than a dollar per barrel above the world price – so as to encourage prospecting in the USA". In such a way and through the mechanism of import quotas, "the United States wielded a decisive influence over the world price of oil", because the maintenance of ample unexploited productive capacities induced the Middle Eastern producers to keep their prices low.

The TRC's abolition of the restrictions constituted "a fatal turning point": "No longer able to lower the world price by increasing our production, or even simply to protect ourselves by cutting supplies, we rapidly lost the capacity to act. The balance of power, as far as energy was concerned, shifted from the Gulf of Texas to the Persian Gulf. The OPEC producers took over the driving seat". Daniel Yergin quantifies the consequences of the TRC's decision: from 1967 to 1973 US imports grew from 19% to 36% of US requirements, heavily increasing the pressure on international prices.

Dollar war and energy war

The TRC's historic decision was made in March 1971, just before the Tripoli agreement. Curiously, Kissinger, in both the second and third volumes of his *Memoirs*, shifts the event forward by a year, to 1972. The interests of the American oil-producing states, which thus yoked themselves to the soaring international prices, undoubtedly weighed heavily on the choice; but the turning point probably represented also the first relevant act of the new Secretary of the Treasury and former governor of Texas, John Connally.

Kissinger, who in the first volume of his *Memoirs* qualifies Connally as "really the strongman of the Cabinet", brings him into the scene in August 1971, when Nixon, on his minister's advice, decreed the unilateral suspension of the convertibility of the dollar and a 10% increase of US import duties. That act – Kissinger underlines – was seen by many as "a declaration of war by the United States on the other industrial democracies".

It was in keeping with Connally's style: "like many self-made Texans, he preferred frontal attacks to indirect manoeuvres" and often, "in genuine Texas-style, sought a confrontation for the sheer pleasure of fighting". However, it was also the "fatal turning point" for the Texas Railroad Commission, five months before the "Nixon shock", because it effectively followed in the wake of the hypothesis adumbrated by Bergsten-Saunders, of hobbling Europe and Japan by increasing energy prices: something more than Bill Rogers' "non-intervention", lamented by Henry Kissinger.

The Yom Kippur War

The Oil Weapon in the 1973 War*

In the intentions of American diplomacy, 1973 was to have been "the year of Europe". On the contrary, it was the year of Watergate, of a new Middle Eastern war and of the oil crisis. With the end of a decade of war in Vietnam and with China's entering the game of the balance of power, Washington wished to bring back the centre of gravity of its activity to the Atlantic front, where Europe was acquiring a new importance and identity.

In January 1973, while the United States was signing the peace treaty with Vietnam, the European Community was expanding to nine countries, concomitant with the success of its *Ostpolitik*. American surprise is expressed by Henry Kissinger in the first volume of his "Memoirs": "Brandt's opening to the East had the completely unexpected effect of spurring on the integration of Western Europe. [...] Great Britain's admission to the ECM enabled the European front to regroup".

American political crisis

The US withdrawal from its Vietnam adventure did not put an end to the American political crisis but opened a new chapter of settling accounts. In April 1973 the threads of a variety of tangled skeins began to twist into an infernal knot: the Watergate scandal broke out, Nixon abolished the imposition of a quota on oil imports, Kissinger officially launched the year of Europe and Sadat started to talk about war together with the Syrian president Assad. All of these four events were destined to come to a traumatic end.

The Europeans did not want to sign the new Atlantic Charter – the climax of the year of Europe – with a president lacking credibility. Watergate – writes Kissinger in the second volume of his *Memoirs* – determined "the collapse of a government that just a few weeks before had seemed invulnerable"; the country "seemed to have been seized by a suicidal frame of mind". Kissinger intuited the change of climate towards America in "a nuance" of Willy Brandt's visit on 1th May 1973: "Brandt had become a shade less deferential". He was not the only one.

* Nicola Capelluto, June 2004.

In Japan – writes Daniel Yergin in *The Prize* – the head of the MITI and later prime minister Yasuhiro Nakasone proclaimed the "diplomacy of resources" and an "independent policy" in energy matters: "The era of following blindly is over". The European powers, led by the French Foreign Minister Michel Jobert, rejected the American draft charter and decided to join in discussions with Washington only through the then president of the EEC's foreign ministers, the Danish Knut Borge Andersen. In July 1973, Nixon had to renounce his trip to Europe, reaching the most humiliating moment of his presidency before his impeachment a year later. Almost simultaneously China unilaterally postponed a visit by Kissinger until after the end of the bombing in Cambodia.

The reaction to this double slap in the face from East and West was the appointment of Kissinger as an effectively plenipotentiary Secretary of State and the coup in Chile in September 1973. The world had to know that the American eagle still had talons. In this state of angry weakness Washington faced the new Middle Eastern crisis.

Saudi Arabia's warning

In the Middle East the political geography had remained unchanged since the 1967 war. Israel still occupied the conquered territories and the Suez Canal was still closed to shipping. In the summer of 1973, King Feisal of Saudi Arabia warned the heads of the US petrol companies that were partners in Aramco that the situation was changing and that his country refused to remain isolated from "its Arab friends" because of American inertia; and he threatened: "you will lose everything".

The heads of the oil companies warned the State and Defence Departments, but apathy reigned supreme in Washington. Texaco, Chevron and Mobil publicly took a stand in favour of a change in American policy in the Middle East. Saudi Arabia had taken over the reins of OPEC in its new direction. The strategist was the Saudi Oil Minister Ahmed Zaki Yamani who, in March 1972, had launched the negotiation for the "participation" of the petro-states in the oil companies' property. This countered "nationalisation" and, according to Yamani, would create a link "as indissoluble as a Catholic marriage" between states and companies. Kissinger had opposed OPEC's new line, defining "participation" as a "creeping nationalisation".

The agreement on participation reached in October 1972 immediately conceded a 25% share to the petro-states, rising to 51% in 1983. According to Kissinger, from that moment Saudi Arabia began to "link its oil policy explicitly to progress towards a solution of the Arab-Israeli conflict".

Actually, Saudi ambiguity was a constant in the Middle Eastern panorama, fuelled by Saudi Arabia's dual role as the Muslims' main religious seat and as the Western economies' major oil supplier, but also by the dual American foreign policy, officially pro-Israeli but pro-Arab when guided by the big oil companies. This ambiguity ran right through the regime and the ruling family itself and increased its oscillations in moments of US weakness. Riyadh had already led the unsuccessful oil embargo during the 1967 war. The choice of the Nixon-Kissinger administration in 1972 Sto make Iran its Middle Eastern stronghold by providing substantial military support was also motivated by the uncertainties of its Saudi ally.

In August 1973, Sadat went to Riyadh to inform King Feisal that he was preparing a war against Israel and to ask for his help. Feisal promised half a billion dollars and the use of oil as a political weapon. According to Yergin, the king asked for a longer war than the previous ones: "We don't want to use our oil in a battle lasting two or three days and then stop. We want a war lasting long enough to mobilise world public opinion". Such willingness also reflected the extraordinary market pressure on Saudi reserves. Its share of world exports had risen from 13% to 21% between 1970 and 1973. In just one year, between July 1972 and July 1973, its daily production had increased by 62%, with the risk, according to some experts, of causing damage to the oilfields. The abolition of the American imposition of a quota to oil imports removed the last US influence on the policy of OPEC's prices but concentrated an unprecedented pressure and power of blackmail on Saudi crude.

Sadat's political war

Anwar Sadat had succeeded Nasser upon his death in September 1970. According to Kissinger, Sadat's decision to go to war matured after the May 1972 Russo-American summit, whose final communiqué practically ignored the Middle Eastern question. Sadat's first move was the expulsion of the 20,000 Russian "advisers" in July 1972.

Kissinger gives two interpretations of this. The first is self-congratulatory for a result pursued with the intransigent refusal, "on principle, of any concession to Egypt so long as Nasser or Sadat adopted an anti-Western rhetoric, backed by the presence of Soviet combat troops". The second was self-critical: "We interpreted the expulsion of Soviet advisors with a certain condescension. [...] It did not occur to us that (Sadat) was maybe clearing the way in view of war and wanted to eliminate what seemed to him an obstacle". Sadat was in favour of a separate accord with Israel but could not negotiate it from the awkward position of being the defeated party and without the backing of Syria and the USSR. On the other hand, he knew that he did not have the military power to re-conquer Sinai. "He therefore decided to cut the Gordian knot with war", says Kissinger, but "his aim was at the same time psychological and diplomatic, much more than military. [...] Sadat sparked off the war not to re-conquer territories but to give Egypt back its self-esteem, thus increasing its diplomatic flexibility". Raymond Aron commented in *Le Figaro* of October 10th: "Non-war froze an unacceptable situation, battle broke the ice. Everything became possible again".

The Egyptian offensive was launched on October 6th 1973, the day of the Jewish holiday of Yom Kippur. 220 aircraft and 3,000 cannons hit the Israeli positions on the eastern bank of the Canal and in Sinai, while the Syrian air force and 700 cannons simultaneously attacked Israel's northern frontier. At the end of the day Egypt had established a line along the entire eastern coast of Suez and Israel was on the defensive. "The surprise attack of 6th October" – Aron commented – "was one of the biggest surprises of our times".

Kissinger and "strategic surprise"

The Egyptian leader had seemingly used the fable of the shepherd boy and the wolf in a creative way. He had threatened various times to spark off war and forced Israel to make two costly mobilisations without carrying out his threats. In 1973 the signs of military preparation were numerous but no one took them seriously.

Kissinger's analysis of the Egyptian surprise attack is a lesson given by a political realist to his rationalist self: "It was a classic of strategic and tactical surprise, but the surprise cannot be completely explained either by the 'background noise' or by dissimulation. It was due, instead, to the wrong interpretation of facts that everyone could see; it was not clouded by conflicting information. All that Sadat did was to repeat openly what he intended to do and we did not believe him. He swamped us with information leaving us to draw the wrong conclusions. October 6th was the climax of an error in political analysis on the victims' part. All the Israeli (and American) analyses prior to October 1973 agreed on the fact that Egypt and Syria lacked the military capacity to re-conquer the lost territories by force of arms, hence no war would break out. The Arab armies would lose, hence they would not attack. The premises were correct, the conclusions not. [...] The Syrian and Egyptian armies suffered heavy defeats. However, Sadat achieved his basic aim of shaking the Israelis' conviction that they were invincible and the Arabs' of being powerless, decidedly changing the psychological bases that had led the negotiations to a deadlock".

The recent announcement of a forthcoming American initiative had contributed to the self-deception.

"We knew everything but understood too little"

It was thought that Sadat would wait for Washington's diplomatic intervention, but "the imminence of the negotiations probably accelerated – rather than delayed – his decision to open hostilities; neither could he afford the success of our initiative, which would have compromised his internal position, or its failure, which would have undermined our interest in mediating between the two positions".

On their part, the Israelis, in view of the American diplomatic initiative "had a vested interest in playing down the Arab threats to avoid the United States exploiting the danger of war as a pretext for winning concessions". "The intelligence services had been a fiasco but they were not the only ones to supply wrong estimations. All the statesmen were acquainted with the facts. [...] The concept of starting a war that was impossible to win in order to regain self-respect formed no part of our definition of rationality. Our mental attitude was made even more evident on 5th October when, on waking up, we were given the astonishing news that all the Soviets in Egypt and Syria had been sent away by airlift during the previous 24 hours. It is inexplicable how this development could have been wrongly interpreted. [...] The failure was not of an administrative nature but conceptual. [...] The country's leaders cannot hide behind their analysts when they make mistakes. [...] We were too satisfied with our evaluations. We knew everything but understood too little. And for this the political exponents involved – myself included – must assume responsibility".

Two wars and three partial crises

The real surprise of the war came after the military offensive and was the unprecedented use of the oil weapon both in its extent and in its effects. The military war lasted twenty days, but the oil war six months and it left its mark on the world economy for the whole decade. The double war in the year of Watergate included a partial crisis in Washington, a partial military crisis in the Middle East, a partial economic crisis caused by the use of the oil weapon, but not a general crisis of imperialism. The general balance was not in question, but all the powers fought around these three partial crises.

The Yom Kippur War

Four Strategic Arms in the 1973 War*

A quarter century after the 1973 oil crisis, Henry Kissinger wrote about it – in the third volume of his *Memoirs* – in still-dramatic tones: "In the space of three months, the world's political and economic order found itself face to face with a series of huge problems that threatened its very foundations". "Overnight" the industrialised democracies saw "the cohesion of their societies and, less explicitly, their very political survival" jeopardised. Kissinger – who was writing at the end of the 1990s – deepens the gloom of this scenario by stressing the "topicality" of the crisis: since "oil supplies continue to depend on regions that are among the most volatile on the planet, nothing guarantees that there will not be other oil shocks".

At it tried to buttress its own leadership, Washington feared a catastrophe experienced at first hand and always in ambush, perceiving it as a mortal challenge to its executive in 1973-74. Four strategic arms being employed in the crisis are a measure of its seriousness: military airlifts, the oil weapon, the European dissociation, and the nuclear alert.

Kissinger's policy mix

The Arab-Israeli conflict in October 1973 was a war of attrition with a high consumption of weaponry. Israel, on the defensive, used up all its military stockpiles in the very first week of the conflict. In the first three days of warfare it lost 500 tanks and 49 aircraft. All in all, 3,000 tanks – 75% Arab – were destroyed. Poor maintenance probably caused more damage than enemy shots.

The warring nations turned to their protectors. On the fifth day of warfare – October 10th – the Soviet Union organised a massive airlift to Syria and Egypt: 10 missions a day. The United States hesitated for a few a days. In their *Memoirs* Richard Nixon and Kissinger point to the Secretary of Defence James Schlesinger as the opponent of substantial aid to Israel. However, Nixon's biographer Stephen Ambrose reports another version related by Elmo Zumwalt, the head of American naval operations, according to which aid was delayed on Kissinger's orders. The latter wanted to make the Israeli government

* Nicola Capelluto, July-August 2004.

more malleable and to set up a complex "linkage": the bartering of aid to Israel for the withdrawal of the pro-Israel lobby's support for Senator Henry Jackson's amendment in favour of untrammelled Jewish emigration from USSR. This was imposed as a condition for conceding the status of most-favoured trading nation to the USSR. When the Israeli prime minister Golda Meir informed Washington that her country was on its last legs through lack of munitions, Nixon broke off all delays and – on the night between 13th and 14th October – the USA launched its military airlift.

Nixon's airlift

The Middle Eastern conflict turned into a logistical battle between the superpowers. In his *Memoirs* Nixon boasts of "an operation that was even more momentous than the Berlin airlift in 1948-1949". His evaluation seems exaggerated, but with 550 missions the USA flooded its ally with war-material, enabling it to counterattack. The battle of the airlifts showed America's indisputable logistical supremacy, but also its political isolation. None of its great European allies agreed to put its airbases at its disposal for the airlift. Only the Netherlands and – for just a fortnight – the Federal Republic of Germany supported the USA. Portugal, threatened by Kissinger that it would be abandoned to its fate, offered a base in the Azores.

The oil weapon entered the scene on the third day of warfare, October 8th 1973. Another round of negotiations began in Vienna, and OPEC asked for the official price of oil to be doubled from $3 to $6; the companies offered only a $0.45 increase. The negotiations broke down, paving the way for the cartel's unilateral action. On 16th October, the day after the Israeli counteroffensive, the OPEC delegates in Kuwait City decided on a 70% increase – to $5.11 – in the official price of crude, thus bringing the price into line with the free market.

OPEC and oil

This marked the end of jointly fixed prices by the petrostates and oil companies. OPEC took over the market's reins and declared it would no longer agree to the governments of the consumer countries taking – through taxes – 66% of the end price, against the 9% of the petrostates. The oil companies quickly changed their position. A few days earlier the four Aramco companies (Exxon, Texaco, Mobil and Socal) had sent – via John McCloy – a letter to Nixon, summed up by

Daniel Yergin: "the oil industry of the free world is operating in the red and is practically without any reserve capacity"; any further US aid to Israel could have a "domino effect" of retaliations, even leading to oil supplies being cut off: "the entire position of the United States in the Middle East risks being seriously compromised, to the advantage of the Japanese, Europeans and maybe Soviets, and to the detriment of our economy and security".

On October 17th OPEC's Arab countries – bar Iran – concentrated on how to use the oil weapon. The plan they approved foresaw the participants' cutting their production by 5% every month and differentiating their supplies according to the position of the consumer countries *vis-à-vis* the Arab-Israeli conflict. A secret clause laid down that "the USA should suffer the most consistent cuts". With respect to 1956 and 1967 the novelty lay precisely in the increasing cuts in production which would make bypassing of discriminatory measures more difficult. The actual embargo started on 19th October, after Nixon had made an official announcement of a plan for military aid to Israel to the tune of $2.2 billion. First Libya and then Saudi Arabia suspended all oil supplies to the USA. The vacillating Saudi ally had joined the enemy camp.

Watergate whirlwind

According to Kissinger the Watergate scandal was "the most serious internal constitutional crisis of the century". Triggered by the divisions caused by the Vietnam War – which the former Secretary of State called "our civil war" – its reverberations were felt throughout the entire 1973 crisis. While the Russians were setting up their airlift, the American vice-president Spiro Agnew resigned because he had been found out to be a tax dodger. Two days later the Court of Appeal ordered Nixon to hand over the tapes that could incriminate him to the investigators. On the same day, while Nixon was choosing a new vice-president and talking about whether or not to set up an airlift, Congress passed the War Powers Resolution, "whose aim" – says Kissinger – "was to reduce the president's discretionary powers in the deployment of military forces".

On the day when the Arab countries decreed an oil embargo on the US, the Attorney General Elliot Richardson and his deputy William Ruckelshaus resigned in protest against Nixon's decision to dismiss Archibald Cox, the court prosecutor in the Watergate case. The reaction was furious and Nixon – in his *Memoirs* – admits: "Though

I was prepared for a violent reaction, its intensity took me by surprise. [...] On Tuesday 23rd October there were 21 resolutions for my impeachment at various levels of debate in the Capitol. Six newspapers that had been faithful supporters of the administration called for me to resign".

In the whirlwind of the scandal – like King Lear in the midst of the thunderstorm – Nixon was a king without any powers. Kissinger says in the second volume of his *Memoirs*: "He had not lost his courage, but he was too worried to make decisions; the responsibility passed to me".

European neutrality

Kissinger's strategic objective was to prevent the USSR from exploiting the crisis so as to return to the Middle East in force and above all to avoid independent initiatives on the part of Europe. It was necessary to pour cold water on "our European allies' ebullience" – says Kissinger – "as they might have been tempted to adopt a more unilateral approach". However, this was not possible. "The till then theoretic arguments – whether American and European interests were always parallel – flared up from the very first day". Many Europeans were "sincerely convinced [...] that we had jeopardised Europe's vital interests for American internal reasons".

According to Kissinger "the European position was certainly not superficial; Europe's oil dependence combined with the frustration of being a mere spectator to a crisis in a region where it had once played a leading role".

However, Kissinger was indignant that the distancing of America's European allies meant that "American aircraft coming from Germany were forced to hug the French and Spanish coastlines before reaching the Mediterranean at Gibraltar and arriving in Israel, thus lengthening their flight by about 3,500 km". In the relations among the powers, neutrality is never indifference: it is strategic action. Kissinger rejects the Europeans' "essentially legalistic argument" that NATO obligations did not concern the Middle East.

Nuclear alert against Moscow

The Israeli counteroffensive set up a bridgehead on the west bank of the Suez Canal and surrounded the Egyptian third army on the east bank. Kissinger adopted a delaying tactic that would allow Israel to win a clear victory, while Moscow wanted a rapid truce. From Kissinger's *Memoirs* there emerges a divergence between the Secretary of State and Nixon, who wanted not only a truce but also a rapid peace agreement that would attenuate – through a diplomatic success – the siege at home. Two ceasefires were agreed upon at the UN and broken on the battlefield immediately afterwards.

On October 24th "the Soviet leaders suddenly decided on a showdown". In an urgent letter, Brezhnev asked that the US and the USSR should send "a mixed contingent" to ensure the truce; failing this, Moscow reserved the right "to take appropriate steps unilaterally". 85 Russians ships were already present in the Mediterranean and seven airborne troop divisions were put on the alert. "Nixon's evident weakness was decidedly linked with the blatant challenge that the Politburo had launched at us". If Washington had accepted Moscow's ultimatum, Russian troops would have returned to Egypt and, still worse, "China and Europe would have been shocked at the sight of US and Russian military collaboration in a region of crucial importance". Washington's reply was the declaration of the state of maximum conventional and nuclear alert in peacetime and the warning to Moscow that "unilateral initiatives" would have "incalculable consequences".

Rambouillet directorate

Later on, Kissinger reflected on the danger of that act "at a moment of great weakness" and spoke of a "policy of bluffing" and of a game played in "extra time". Alexander Haig, chief of staff at the White House, reckoned that the Russian move too had been a bluff. This double bluff represented both the height of the Yom Kippur War and the attempt to bring an imperialist confrontation that had become multipolar back within the framework of the bipolar game. All the European governments – including London – dissociated themselves from the nuclear alert, and the Federal Republic of Germany completely withdrew its partial support for the American airlift. Kissinger recalls: we were "enraged by the feeling that we had been abandoned during the crisis and our nerves were on edge". The petrostates were not particularly frightened either; in fact, the embargo continued until March 18th 1974. At the end of December 1973 OPEC, this time under pressure from Iran, increased the official price of crude to $11.65, quadrupling it compared to the eve of the Yom Kippur War.

The inflation of the 1970s was – in part – one of the effects of the 1973 crisis. A second effect was a new reflection on the nuclear deterrent. Yet a third effect was the attempt to redress the balance of the Atlantic relations through an informal "directorate", first of five members and then of seven, launched two years later at Rambouillet.

The Khomeini Revolt and the Iran-Iraq War

The Iran Crisis of the 1970s*

For most of the 1970s the "energy issue" was the main problem in inter-imperialist relations. Military, diplomatic, trade, financial and monetary battles were fought around it.

The jump in oil prices at the end of 1973 led to the acceleration and spreading of the inflation already triggered by the rapid simultaneous expansion of all the major industrial countries in 1972. The prices of non-alimentary raw materials had already risen – according to *The Economist*'s index – by 25% in the second half of 1972 and by over 50% in the first half of 1973. Henry Kissinger denied that the increase in oil prices had any economic objectivity; the prices were artificial and decided for political reasons. He declared to the UN: "What a political decision has done, a political decision can undo".

The Secretary of State's economic obtuseness was only apparent. In fact, in his *Memoirs* he announced that the accusation levelled against him by some of the OPEC countries of waging a "war of nerves" did not lack "a certain pertinence". At a meeting of ministers of finance and central bankers, he explained: "The stakes are more than oil prices and the economy, and include the whole structure of future political relations. If the producers keep on manipulating the prices without the consumers formulating a forceful response, there will inevitably be a handover of power".

Restructuring and oil shock

Kissinger saw a confirmation of his thesis in the 1975 recession. His mantras were: "reduce oil prices" and "break the cartel", but his political objective was to reaffirm American leadership over the Western powers and to break "the perverse alliance between the underdeveloped countries and OPEC", between "a Fourth World" fighting for survival and "an ever more powerful and self-confident Third World", i.e., to prevent the formation of other raw material cartels like OPEC.

The increases in oil price sparked off the restructuring of industrial plants and equipment and of the balance of payment. The battle

* Nicola Capelluto, September 2004.

over energy became a battle over productivity and the diversification of sources. In the five years from 1974 to 1978 the world demand for crude increased by roughly eight million barrels a day, but the production of Middle Eastern oil remained stationary, mostly because of action on the part of the European metropolises, while US oil imports almost doubled. OPEC's credit balance – which had passed from \$9 to \$62 billion between 1973 and 1974 – dropped to \$5 bilion in 1978, only to rise again to \$120 billion in 1980, thanks to the second oil shock, leaving in its wake the glories and misdeeds of the "recycling" of petrodollars.

Currencies and oil shock

According to Daniel Yergin, investments in new oil prospecting avoided the Middle East for many years, concentrating, instead, on North America and the North Sea. There were some notable successes, but also many major disappointments. The Alaskan oil pipeline was completed in 1977 at a cost of \$10 billion, supplying almost a quarter of US oil production. The technological miracle of extraction from the North Sea started production in 1975. In the euphoria of that moment Harold Wilson, the British prime minister, expressed the ambitious wish to become president of OPEC in 1980. Colossal development plans were formulated and then abandoned: a Ford plan for 200 electronuclear and 150 coal-burning power stations, a Rockefeller plan for the investment of \$100 billion in synthetic fuels, and an EEC Plan for 150 nuclear power stations with investments of \$500 billion.

Robert Solomon, the former head of international finance at the American Central Bank, in his history of the international monetary system, underlines the monetary consequences of the oil shock: it imposed fluctuating exchange rates "sine die", thwarting both France's battle for a return to "parity" and the Werner plan's agenda forecasting a complete European monetary union by 1980, replaced by the EMS (European Monetary System), seen reductively by Solomon as "a regional Bretton Woods".

Iran and Saudi Arabia

Kissinger was not the scourge of the petrostates he wished to appear to be. Political calculation imposed the coexistence of simplification for propagandistic purposes and extremely fine distinctions in strategic choices. There was a debate between the Secretary of State and William Simon, Secretary of the Treasury, in 1974. Simon, a former commercial banker, argued that Iran was mainly responsible for the oil crisis; the USA had to stop supplying it with arms and, on the contrary, back the Saudis who were willing to increase their production over and above the ceilings fixed by the cartel.

Kissinger's position was a pole apart: it had been the Saudi embargo that had created panic in the West; Iran was not an Arab country, it had rejected the embargo and refused the USSR authorisation to fly over its territory in order to supply Israel's enemies; the aim of its aggressive line on prices was domestic development. Iran was "the cornerstone of our strategy in the Gulf"; "breaking the back of our most powerful ally in the region, the only one on Middle Eastern soil capable of resisting Soviet pressures, was an absurdity".

In contrast, Kissinger said that it was unthinkable that, in the event of a confrontation, the Saudis might break Arab solidarity on their own: "it would be a mistake to count on them".

In an interview printed in *Business Week* in December 1974, Kissinger drew this conclusion: "The only possibility of lowering prices would be to launch a massive political offensive against Saudi Arabia and Iran in order to force them to compromise their political stability, or in other words their security, if they refused to collaborate. This is too high a price, even for an immediate reduction in the price of oil. If we succeed in overthrowing the Saudi regime and a Gaddafi seizes power, or if we damage the image of an Iran capable of resisting all external pressures, the door is flung open to political currents that risk annihilating our economic objectives".

Kissinger's doubts on the use of force in the Gulf

It was not Iran's incapacity to resist external pressures that led to the Shah's downfall in January 1979, to the rise to power of the ayatollahs' regime and the second oil shock. Kissinger – in *Years of Upheaval* – affirms: "The political theories learnt in the West that led [the Shah] to modernise a feudal, Islamic society and to foster a rapid economic development, were the decisive factor in [his] downfall. [...] The maxims of western liberalism induced the Shah to build a modern secular State on the lines of Kemal Ataturk's reformist model, and to impose industrialisation on a population that had barely moved beyond the feudal stage. For roughly twenty years he seemed to be successful. Iran's GNP's grew at an annual rate of about 10%".

Kissinger denies the "liberal" interpretation that attributed the fall of the regime to its militarisation and repressive policy. He also rejects the thesis of the "neo-conservatives" who, at that time, had taken to attacking the "underlying defect" of the "Nixon Doctrine" that pledged the USA to helping the allied countries in Asia with money and arms but no longer with American soldiers. According to the "neo-conservatives", this doctrine, which had legitimated "Vietnamisation" and US defeat in South East Asia, had prevented the recognition that "only the presence of American forces in the Persian Gulf could be the necessary security umbrella". Kissinger's refutation is important: "For America to create by itself a credible military force capable of defending the Persian Gulf is, even in the best of cases, a task of enormous, perhaps unsurmountable, practical and logistic difficulty".

The former secretary had in mind the "Carter doctrine" of January 1980 which – in response to the USSR's invasion of Afghanistan – proclaimed that "the attempt on the part of any external force to take over control of the Persian Gulf region will be seen as an attack on the vital interests of the USA; and such an attack will be repelled by every means necessary, including military force". However, Kissinger's warning now sounds like an unintended advance reminder to George W. Bush, although this did not prevent the Janus of American diplomacy from backing up as a "statesman" the action he would have avoided as a "professor".

USA and the modernisation problem

In one of his instructive self-critical pirouettes, the former Secretary of State blames "our incapacity to understand that almost metaphysical rebellion against modernisation" that overthrew the Shah.

"Even admitting that we realised the danger, what advice could we give? Do we have a political theory for the transformation of developing countries? Do we know where the balance between authority and liberty and between liberty and anarchy lies in a religious, feudal society? It is easy to say that a more rapid process of liberalisation would have saved the Shah; that progress in parliamentary democracy and a wider participation would have defused the pressures. [...] It is probable, instead, that these "enlightened" panaceas would have accelerated the catastrophe. [...] The fact is that we lack a coherent idea on how to channel the elementary forces freed by the process of development. Mass participation imposed by force more often leads to totalitarianism that to democracy. Nowadays, support of the current regimes in the Persian Gulf is as incompatible with democratic theory as it may be vital to our national interests. In the Persian Gulf the alternative to a friendly authoritarianism is almost inevitably a hostile totalitarianism. Moreover, the political concepts we are trying to transplant into these countries must seem capable only of destroying their social cohesion; if this is the only way out, it is certainly possible that they may prefer to reach a settlement with the extremist currents that swarm in the region. This dilemma is still one of the major intellectual challenges confronting American and Western political thought".

In January 1979 the Shah fled abroad after having to admit that – after 37 years – the monarchy had melted away "like snow in sunshine". The President of the Revolutionary Council that took office in Tehran in February 1979 was Mehdi Bazargan, the political son of Mossadeq, who had appointed him as head of the National Iranian Company in 1951. The Khomeinist revolt deprived the market of almost all Iranian oil exports, amounting to 4.5 million barrels a day. All the other OPEC countries increased their extraction; even so, world oil production lost two million barrels a day in the first quarter.

This 3-4% drop in production sufficed to cause a 150% jump in prices from the $13 per barrel pre-crisis to $34. The "big panic" – says Yergin – led to a frantic buying spree in order to increase stocks, with an extra demand of three million barrels which, together with the lack of Iranian production, raised the daily deficit to five million barrels, equal to almost 10% of consumption.

The second oil shock peaked twice: once with the "hostage crisis" (the kidnapping of 63 employees at the American embassy in Teheran) in November 1979, and the second with the outbreak of war between Iran and Iraq in September 1980, which deprived the market of four million barrels a day, pushing the price up to $42-$45 a barrel.

Doubling of crude prices

In a series of oil prices from 1861 to today, calculated by BP in 2002 dollars, the century's peak price for crude occurred in 1980, at $78.19 a barrel. In order to find similar prices it is necessary to return to the period of the American civil war. During the first petroshock, the price – in 2002 dollars – had jumped to $42.40, while, during the First World War, it had fluctuated between $15 and $24 a barrel and, during the Second, between $13 and $14. The average price – always in 2002 dollars – was $10-$12 in the 1950s and 1960s, $42-$43 in the years of the two petroshocks (1974 and 1981), and $22-$23 in the 1990s.

The seismograph of the prices of crude suggests that – excluding those paroxysmal periods determined by the risk of a rupture of the energy artery – the potential pressure of the demand for hydrocarbons on world oil production and reserves between the 1960s and 1990s led to a – more or less – doubling of the prices rather than their present tenfold increase: enough to increase the role of black gold as a political weapon in every direction, but not enough to justify the doom-and-gloom merchants of the *ecological scam*.

The First Gulf War

Gulf Artery in the 1991 War*

James Baker devotes the first chapter of his diplomatic memoirs [*The Politics of Diplomacy*, 1995] to the "day when the Cold War ended". Surprisingly, he is not referring to the fall of the Berlin Wall but to Iraq's invasion of Kuwait in August 1990. The Soviet Union – says George Bush's Secretary of State – had borne the cost of events passively until then. Now Baker had managed to force the Russian foreign minister Eduard Shevardnadze to condemn "one of (*Russia's*) most faithful allies", committing the USSR to side actively with the United States. This was the real turning point.

Fable of Yalta's non-violent end

More than its historical perspicacity, Baker's judgment reflects his obstinate defence of a policy of joint Russo-American management of the Gulf Crisis, supported by a minority in both Washington and Moscow. However, his thesis has the merit of undermining the thesis of the non-violent overturning of the 50-year-old imperialist order.

By making the end of the Cold War coincide with the outbreak of a hot war that would involve one and half million combatants, Baker unintentionally gives lie to the arbitrary interpreters of "divine providence", but also to his immediate employer. George Bush and Brent Scowcroft, his adviser on national security, introduce their joint memoirs [*A World Transformed*, 1998] with this triumphal, but false, statement: "It is truly amazing to observe that everything has happened – in the main – without any real tragedy. Eastern Europe has thrown off the Soviet yoke, Germany has been reunited and the USSR has collapsed, all without any bloodshed. [...] The biggest change in the strategic balance since the end of the First World War has not caused one death. [...] It was necessary to guide the change without causing either counterblows or rifts. [...] We so managed the situation that there was no loser, only winners".

Saddam's Pan-Arabist ambition

Iraq's attack on Kuwait and the ensuing war took place while the process of German unification was drawing to a close and while the

* Nicola Capelluto, April 2005.

first bloody pages of the break-up of Yugoslav and Soviet federalism in the Baltic and the Caucasus were being written. The long war with Iran had left Saddam Hussein with half a million dead and heavily in debt. He interpreted the centrifugal forces set off by the crisis of the Soviet bloc (including its withdrawal from Afghanistan) as a chance to change the *status quo* in the Middle East. According to some versions, he felt himself encouraged by the United States itself since it had partially supported him during the war against the ayatollahs' Iran, had opened up a line of credit for him at the end of the war and had stated, through its ambassador April Glaspie that "it had no opinions" on his controversy with Kuwait over territory, i.e., Iraq's claim to the rich oilfields of Rumaila and the Bubiyan Islands.

The Hamburg historian Helmut Mejcher [*Sinai, 5. June 1967*] places Saddam's Pan-Arabist ambition within a multi-polar vision illustrated in a speech at the end of the 1970s to the Iraqi ambassadors in Europe and Japan: "China will become an important and influential pole. Europe, where it is France that plays the main role, will form an alternative pole to America. Japan too will play an essential role in Southeast Asia. [...] The Arab world will be at the centre of a similar movement". The Arab world – according to Saddam – had to follow the example of the United States that used oil "as the tool of its world policy and above all as a means of pressure in its relations with Europe and Japan". Whether as an astute adventurer or apprentice strategist, Saddam miscalculated.

Strategic stakes of the Gulf Crisis

In a series of articles Arrigo Cervetto analysed the 1990-1991 Gulf Crisis and War, both as an episode in the energy battle and from the viewpoint of the changing correlations of multipolarism. Iraq's aggression occurred in a period of reduced influence of oil on total energy consumption compared to the 1973 crisis; in Western Europe its share had dropped from 59% to 43%, and in Japan from 76% to 56%.

A series of data from Morgan Stanley gave an even better illustration of the weakened influence of the oil factor on the balance of the major countries: between 1980 and 1989 the percentage of GDP devoted to oil had dropped from 8.1 to 2.3 in the USA, from 6.3 to 1.3 in Japan, from 4.5 to 1.4 in Federal Germany, from 4.2 to 1.5 in Great Britain, from 4.6 to 1.5 in France and from 7.3 to 1.5 in Italy.

Cervetto estimated that "on average, a twentieth of GDP had been recovered".

Unlike 1973, the majority of both the oil cartel and the Arab league took sides against Saddam: apart from the initial impact, neither the oil price nor its supply suffered serious counterblows. Thus the blackmailing power of the oil weapon over the consumer countries had weakened – but not the strategic stakes. Cervetto quoted the American magazine *Fortune*: the first victim of the Gulf Crisis was the idea that the geopolitical centre of the world had moved from Washington to Berlin; now the leadership returned to the United States.

1990's "coalition of the willing"

In Bush and Scowcroft's book the debates of the National Security Council on the Gulf Crisis are amply reported. The then American Defence Secretary (and now US vice president) Richard Cheney immediately showed himself to be sceptical of the efficacy of the oil embargo decided on by the UN Security Council: it was necessary to prevent Iraq from becoming a great oil power overnight. Saudi Arabia and the other Arab allies would make themselves scarce if the USA showed that it was weak. Even without seizing the Saudi oil wells physically, Saddam would impose his influence on the whole region.

According to the CIA representative William Webster, by combining the second and third global oil reserves, possessing the fourth largest army in the world, using Kuwait's immense riches to rearm rapidly and having an outlet on the Persian Gulf, there would not be any Middle Eastern country able to counterbalance Iraq. In Richard Haass's opinion, Washington could not accept the *status quo* imposed by Saddam, because this would accelerate the "violent centrifugal tendencies", would cast doubt on America's "trustworthiness" and would complicate the peace process in the Middle East.

At the end of August, the idea had already matured within the administration not only of military intervention but also of the necessary procedure to arrive at this point, elaborated by Haass himself: it was appropriate to apply to the UN for permission to use military intervention only if the majority of the Arab bloc was in favour and it was certain that there would be the required number of votes; otherwise, it was necessary to abandon the UN approach in order to "create an independent multinational force founded on the participation of Arab friends and allies"; as the legal basis of the war, UN condemnations and the Emir of Kuwait's request for intervention would be sufficient.

The idea of the "coalition of the willing" put into effect in the 2003 war was already ready in 1990. Bush Sr. anticipated his son's "unilateralist" option even though he did not need to implement it: "Although I was ready to manage this crisis unilaterally if necessary, I wanted the UN to be involved in our first reaction". The Powell-Schwarzkopf military doctrine of "invincible force" or of "overwhelming superiority" wanted to erase the paralysing shadow of Vietnam.

Tokyo and Moscow losers

The strategic perspective of the intervention in the Gulf is crucial. Cervetto, referring to the US's bipartisan current most favourable to the war, was, in December 1990, blunt: "When Janus-faced America debates about the Gulf it looks at Europe and at Asia". Cervetto set this judgment inside his analysis of the "uneven development of the post-Yalta period": Germany had unified at a dizzy pace; the pace of European unification was much slower and more contradictory; Japan found itself in the most unfavourable position: the Second World War, over in Europe, was not over in Asia.

Cervetto glimpsed at its birth – in July 1990 – Washington's attempt to use the last of this line of pursuing "*Curiazi*"* to counterbalance the excessive convergence between Germany and the USSR in the concluding phases of German unification. The attempt was a new version of the *Asian card*, but this time it was the *Japanese card* that was used against Germany, while Kissinger's *Chinese card* had been played against Russia. With the outbreak of the Gulf Crisis Washington threw the Japanese card back onto the Middle Eastern table encouraging Japanese participation in driving Saddam out of Kuwait while Germany and, to a certain extent, France dragged their feet. The attempt to draw Japan out of limbo by getting it to join in America's initiative was enthusiastically seized by the prime minister Toshiki Kaifu, but violently opposed by the "nationalist" currents, especially by that of the former prime minister Yasuhiro Nakasone, as well as by Beijing. According to the American ambassador to Tokyo, Michael Armacost, Kaifu linked his line to the aspiration to make Japan a permanent member of the UN Security Council, but he failed miserably and his government resigned in February 1991, even though it had set aside $13 billion to help the coalition.

* "Curiatii", legendary Roman figures. [Editor's note.]

Kaifu was not the only ally to fall victim to the Gulf War. Shevardnazde had preceded him by resigning in December 1990, as he had remained isolated in the Russian government over the programme for reform and had been beaten by the tendency led by Yvgeny Primakov who – says Scowcroft – wanted to bring about Saddam's peaceful withdrawal from Kuwait, thus saving his face and winning a diplomatic victory for Moscow. Shevardnazde's defeat was a blow for Baker who had asked for the Russians to be included in military operations against Iraq. This possibility had been firmly turned down by Scowcroft: "We had worked for decades to keep the Russians out of the Middle East and it seemed premature to invite them".

At the end of January 1991, after the beginning of the offensive against Saddam, the French defence minister Jean-Pierre Chevènement resigned in protest against Mitterrand who had agreed to put the French troops under American command. In Turkey, after Turgut Özal agreed to join the war coalition, the foreign and defence ministers and the chief of staff all resigned. Helmut Kohl, after cashing in on German unification, distanced himself from the military solution, though, in the end, he financed the coalition with almost $10 billion: Bush defined this as "ambiguous and potentially harmful".

A multipolar world

Despite the difficulties, the coalition under US leadership could be launched and approved by the UN because – wrote Cervetto – American imperialism managed to place itself in the centre of a convergence of powers that were, as a whole, favourable to a "momentary adjustment". Henry Kissinger believed at that time that the UN-backed coalition was "unrepeatable", because due to a rare combination of factors, like the crisis in the USSR and its willingness to cooperate with China.

According to Cervetto, with the *"half war"* in the Gulf the US was placing itself "at the centre of every balance of power or, in other words, at the centre of the new world order", even if "military supremacy" masked an important limitation of Washington: "The United States has certainly emerged as the only power able to forge alliances, but it could not have waged war without the financial support" of Japan, Germany and Saudi Arabia.

The world had entered the 1990-1991 Gulf Crisis as multi-polar world and had come out of it – only apparently – as a unipolar world. The new century would open with a yet more tragic version of that ambiguity.

The Second Gulf War

Europe and the War*

The Gulf is oil, but the real war objective of the fighting in Iraq – fighting also carried out by means of oil – is time. Not the handful of days or weeks it will take for Basra, Baghdad, Kirkuk or Mosul to fall or to surrender. The measure of time in question is something else – the years and the decades of the contention between the big powers of imperialism.

Washington has become convinced that the political and economic trends underway will act in its disfavour in the future. It has therefore chosen to play pre-emptively on the timing of its relative decline. Above all this is about imposing conditions on Europe and China, which are changing the great world balances between the powers. Europe is structuring its political power. China is affirming itself as an industrial giant and translating that increased power onto the political-military plane. Washington believes that it must act now in order to condition this change or be forced to endure it tomorrow – directed by the multiplied and perhaps combined power of China and Europe. It goes without saying, however, that the interest of Brussels and Beijing lies in allowing trends which move in their favour to continue.

At the heart of the American conversion to preventive action is this opposite perception of timing. The conflict is a "political war" precisely in the sense that it was planned and carried out by the United States with the explicit intention of influencing the world balance of powers. In the "Bush Doctrine" "preventive war" against terrorism and the proliferation of atomic, chemical and biological weapons shades into the proposition that America will not allow other powers to challenge or equal it. America will keep itself strong enough to "dissuade potential adversaries from pursuing a policy of rearmament aimed at surpassing or matching the power of the United States".

This long time of the strategic confrontation links processes which are in appearance distinct. In fact, it is partly in the Gulf that the destiny of the European Constitution is being decided, because

* Guido La Barbera, March 2003

Washington – by playing ahead of time – has caught the EU in midstream and divided it, conditioning the complex negotiations already underway in the Convention. At the same time the United States – by controlling in the Gulf a vital oil artery for Asia – imposes itself on China and on every other emerging power as the guarantor of an energy *open door* in the region. This is a move which is intended to have the double character of a warning and a tempting offer, with the aim of making negotiation with Washington – in the role of arbiter of the balance between the powers of Asia – inescapable.

The current situation, therefore, is not one divided between an America at war and a peace front opposing war. Rather it is a complex struggle between the great powers of imperialism. The crisis in Euro-Atlantic relations demonstrates this – both the rapid exchange of blows and the emergence of impulses towards mending fences.

If timing is the measure of the contention, then this also puts the internationalist struggle to the test. The concept of the "historical delay" of the revolutionary party might have seemed difficult to grasp, and yet here it is displayed by the "decisive moment" of crisis and war. The capitalist market is global, the classes are global, the game of the imperialist powers is global – a revolutionary strategy can only be global. Instead the consciousness of people – hearts and minds and not, note well, their real existence which is already universal – is a prisoner in little local and national pens, and one needs the peculiar and reactionary *anti-globalization* imbecility to see in them a refuge against the evils of the world.

We can trace in the "Bush Doctrine" the world strategy of American imperialism; in the lines of Chirac or Schröder the objective of European strategic autonomy in the world balance; in the moves of New Delhi or Beijing the eruption of the new powers onto the world market. But if we had to write about a world internationalist party – a minority indispensable for the strategic autonomy of the proletariat, which would make it a power against all the other powers – our pages would be almost entirely blank. Hearts and minds – in America, in Europe, in Russia, in Iraq as in China, in India, in Japan or Brazil and everywhere – are fixed by ideologies to the narrow world of the interests of each single and particular power. They are fixed by Americanism, which preaches that the United States is the universal beacon of liberty and progress but which seeks in war a remedy for decline; by Europeanism, which brags about Europe as a power of peace but equips it for its future wars; by the inept and corrupt nationalism of the Arab bourgeoisies, which turns into religious fanaticism and terrorism a failure fed by rivers of oil and a century of intrigues with imperialism; by the new Hindu, Mandarin or Brazilian nationalisms, which out of old ideologies knead new monsters for new conflicts.

Strategic reflection, keeping the decades in mind, knows how to face today's choices and weld them to principles. "The Main Enemy Is At Home" was the warning of the internationalists of 1914. This was also the title of the first number of *Lotta Comunista* – almost 40 years ago – and not by accident. The political generation of imperialist Europeanism, which is today seated in the parliaments and in the chancelleries, at that time filled the streets and served its apprenticeship in one-way anti-imperialism – fighting Washington, following Moscow and preparing to serve Europe. An internationalist position must be reconstructed literally step by step, but only strategic clarity will tie a new generation to Marxism. Opposition to the war is inseparable from the struggle against European imperialism.

The New Strategic Phase

US "Shale Gas" in the Global Balance*

With the outbreak of the 1973 oil crisis, energy *"self-sufficiency"* became one of the US governments' strategic aims. Richard Nixon was the first to launch the watchword in November of that year, and was subsequently imitated by the incumbent presidents in each of the ensuing Middle East crises.

In the imperialist contention, the prospect of self-sufficiency was used as US omnidirectional leverage on the fossil-fuel-producing countries whose cartel had taken over control of international prices, but also on the other big consuming powers that – with the almost 30-year exception of the United Kingdom – are tied unavoidably to Middle East or Russian supplies. European and Japanese aims were the "diversification" of energy sources and energy "conservation".

Shale gas dimensions

At last American energy self-sufficiency seems to be within reach. Thanks to extractive technologies – fracking, horizontal directional drilling of underground rocks, and the development of extractive chemistry – which combined in an economically efficient way only in the early years of the last decade, it is now possible to obtain large quantities of unconventional gas and oil, whose American definitions – *shale gas* and *tight oil* – are now used internationally. The *unconventional* nature of these products is based on the very low *permeability* (internal fluidity) and *porosity* of the rocks containing them and that generally correspond to older geological sites, the *parent rocks* in which the hydrocarbons were generated.

Between 2007 and 2012, natural gas production in the United States rose by 25% and the estimate of technically recoverable gas reserves doubled. The take-off of *shale gas* availability, added to the consequences of the crisis on Western consumption, has had an unexpected effect: the price of American gas, which had followed that of oil in the previous decade, has fallen per unit of heat capacity (BTU) to one-sixth of the price of crude. According to the study *Fueling Up* by Trevor Houser and Shashank Mohan of the Peterson

---

* Nicola Capelluto, March 2014

Institute, this big difference, making investment in crude more profitable, has catalysed the second stage in the US energy revival, i.e., the application of *shale gas* extraction techniques to *tight oil*, with a number of wells that is four times higher than that of natural gas drilling sites.

The Energy Information Administration estimates that *shale gas* accounts for one-third of US gas production and proven reserves. Measured in billions of cubic metres (bmc), total production in 2011 was about 700 bmc, *shale gas* production accounting for 230 bmc of this; total proven reserves were about 10,000 bmc, with *shale* amounting to 3,730 bmc. Proven reserves are equivalent to 14 years of current production. The EIA puts the existence of non-proven gas reserves at 60,000 bmc, one quarter of this *shale* (16,000 bmc). Natural gas consumption in the United States amounts to 725 bmc (2012 figure). The EIA calculates that the United States will become a net gas exporter after 2015, with 120 bmc of gas exported in 2020, half to North America and the other half in the form of liquefied natural gas (LNG).

There is less *tight oil*. In 2012, according to the EIA, it accounted for 12% of the total supply of every kind of liquid fuel on the US market. Unlike *shale gas* – forecast to grow until 2040 – *tight oil* will peak in 2020 and will then slowly decline. Dependence on oil imports will remain, but it will fall from 40% of total US "liquid" requirements in 2012 to 32% in 2040.

Yergin: the global impact of "shale"

In a January article in *Project Syndicate*, Daniel Yergin welcomed the "unconventional revolution" in US energy with great enthusiasm – because of its abundance (at the end of 2013, it is reckoned that *shale gas* accounted for 44% of all US production) and its "enormous global impact". *Shale gas* is reducing European competitiveness and Chinese manufacturing competitiveness with respect to the United States, and fuelling the American "manufacturing renaissance". American gas prices have fallen to one-third of European and to one-fifth of Asian prices. Germany, which exports half of its GDP, has growing energy costs and, together with the European Union, will have to reconsider its strategies. *Shale* will have important consequences in global energy flows. Five years ago, when an energy shortfall was forecast at the end of the crisis, the United States was seen as a potential market for investment in gas liquefaction. Today,

LNG will have to seek markets in Europe and Asia. China intends to give a high priority to the development of unconventional gas in order to convert its coal-burning power plants. The EIA [2011] calculated that Chinese *shale gas* resources were more than double those of the United States.

US world politics, states Yergin, acquire new flexibility and prove that innovation can change the balance of power. Without *tight oil*, he argues (with some exaggeration), Iran would never have sat down at the negotiating table, since the international oil price rise threatened to undermine the anti-Iranian sanctions: the increase in American production has done away with Tehran's illusion that it had an alternative. Yergin contradicts those that fear *tight oil* could lead to US disengagement in the Middle East. He observes, quite rightly, that it is not oil imports that make the Middle East one of the United States' main strategic interests, but its importance for the global economy and world politics.

Birol: bunch of energy changes

At a CFR conference in December, Faith Birol, the International Energy Agency (IEA) chief economist, placed *shale gas* within a vaster context of energy changes: biofuel development is making Brazil the world's sixth-ranking oil producer and soon an exporter; in order to develop their national grids, many of the big Middle East oil exporters are becoming big oil consumers and will equal China's energy consumption in a few years' time; the stagnation in Europe's energy demand will oblige Russia, whose economy depends on energy exports, to look, in all probability, towards Asia.

American *shale gas*, continues Birol, has led to a price and competitiveness gap between the United States, Europe and Japan that will last for at least twenty years. China, which has only 4% of gas in its energy mix, wants to develop the production of *shale gas*, but will succeed in doing so at a sizeable level only from 2020 on. It is likely that, from 2015 on, the United States will become the world's top oil producer, overtaking Saudi Arabia, but it is "completely wrong" to think that there will be no need for increased oil production in the Middle East: American *tight oil* will be entirely consumed in the United States, but Asia will need to import a further 15 million barrels a day, and at the same time the internal oil consumption of Iraq, Saudi Arabia, and the Gulf countries will increase. Oil investment in the Middle East will have to continue in order to have the necessary oil in 2020.

Peterson Institute prudence

The previously mentioned Peterson Institute study has a more cautious approach. The two authors maintain that it is still to be seen whether the recent increase in American oil and gas production is really the start of structural expansion, as in the early twentieth century, or only a temporary breathing space in structural decline.

Their uncertainty is reflected in the variety of forecasts for American energy import dependency in 2030: 11% for the EIA, 4% for the IEA, 1% for BP, 16% for ExxonMobil, and 10% for Yergin's IHS CERA. According to Citigroup, the United States will become a net energy exporter from 2020 on. America has improved its energy balance, but oil imports still account for 1.8% of its GDP, equal to its trade deficit with China. The decrease in energy import dependency (from the 30% of 2005 to the 16% of 2012) is mainly due to increased energy efficiency: since 1990, energy consumption per GDP unit has fallen by an annual 2%.

The authors reduce some of the evaluations of the impact of *shale* on the US economy: McKinsey & Co. puts it at 2-4% a year. The Peterson Institute estimates its impact on GDP at around 0.2% a year between 2013 and 2020, higher than the effects of the fiscal stimuli during the crisis, but much lower than the effects of the "information revolution" in the 1990s. The *shale*-induced "manufacturing renaissance" will regard only a handful of industries: those that will experience over 5% growth employ only 6% of the industrial employees, and those that will have an over 2% drop in costs employ 5%. In the long term (up to 2035) its effects will be even less, since the *shale* race nibbles investments away from other sectors, and since it will lead to the appreciation of the dollar, which will worsen the non-energy trade balance.

The Ukraine test

The worsening of the Ukraine crisis has caused a number of Washington currents, especially Republican, to propose throwing *shale gas*, in the form of liquefied gas, into the power scales to induce Europe to free itself from its dependence on Russian supplies. This proposal has met with support from some of the American *shale* producers, but also with the opposition of its big consumers, such as Dow Chemical and Alcoa, which want to retain exclusive use of it.

The *Financial Times* has listed some of the reasons why *shale gas* might affect but not completely change the European energy balance. The plants authorised to export LNG have a daily 230 million cubic-metre capacity, half of the gas that Europe buys from Russia. The commercial destination of *shale* is decided upon by private enterprises that have long-term contracts with Korea, Japan, and Indonesia, thanks to Asian prices that are much higher than in Europe. Increasing the number of liquefaction plants is hindered by the cost of $10 billion for each new plant. The suggestion is that the Europeans should purchase LNG on the free market, where it costs 60% more than Russian natural gas.

Philip Verleger, who was the head of the Department of the Treasury's energy policy under the Carter presidency, does not believe in the *shale gas* weapon. He proposes the use of the United States' strategic oil reserves: pouring 500,000-750,000 barrels a day into the market would bring about a $10 per barrel drop, damaging Russia to the tune of $40 billion (4% of its GDP). The geopolitical test imposed on *shale gas* does not do justice to a remarkable development of the productive forces.

Chapter Four

Cornerstones of Internationalist Strategy

Against War, Revolution![*]

As always, capitalism is preparing the conditions for war. We can say more: capitalism is, in and of itself, war, and, since the whole world is capitalist, war is now the permanent condition of the human race. Since the first decade of the century, capitalism has ceased to be relatively peaceful, since it is this development itself that generated imperialism and ensured that the more developed capitalist countries had the economic, and hence the military, strength to impose their interests and their need to expand on the less developed, and hence weaker, countries, or on colonial countries that underwent an inner process of diffusion of capitalism.

Within this framework of the need for capitalist development in the world, every economic tendency (the flows of international trade, capital exports, the industrialisation of backward areas, hegemony over the markets, etc.) has become, since then, the cause of tension and struggle among the various capitalist countries, among the strong and the weak, and especially among the imperialist countries. To conceive of the peaceful, harmonious development of the world with production and trade relations as they are is a pure petty-bourgeois utopia, an ideology that, more or less consciously, seeks to hide a glaring, brutal reality. It is no coincidence that such a flourishing of today's "pacifist" ideologies and "populist" plans for international trade, the "united nations", "mutual assistance", etc. has never before been seen. But what is even more utopian and reactionary is to take the tree for the wood, i.e., to take a particular, isolated effect of imperialism and to point to it as the primary, fundamental and only cause of crises, and of partial or general wars. Those who cannot or do not want to understand the general, global nature of imperialism inevitably end up, or will end up, being accomplices of imperialism, or its propagandists, soldiers and partisans. This is a historical destiny from which no one escapes, and which has seen every political current, even the most apparently left-wing,

* Arrigo Cervetto, May-June 1967.

become a current of imperialism and a "driving belt" in contributing to throwing the proletariat into one or the other trench of imperialism.

Only the rational Marxists, only the Leninists, have succeeded in escaping from this imperialist conditioning and in transforming an imperialist war into a proletarian revolution, because they have taken a firm stand against all the imperialist fronts, against all the capitalist countries whether big or small, and against all the "interventionist" currents, from the "democratic" to the "socialist". But the Bolsheviks could be rational revolutionary Marxists because they were well aware of the nature of imperialism, and because they knew very well that war and peace are none other than the organic manifestations of capitalist life throughout the world.

Decades of prevailing counterrevolution have prevented the Bolshevik patrimony from becoming the patrimony of the working class.

All that it took today for the huge imperialist and counterrevolutionary potential of Italian society to overflow and flood every sector of political life, from the traditional bourgeois parties to the social-democratic, to those that call themselves communist, and even to those that say they are to the "left" of the PCI, was the outbreak in the Middle East of one of the many wars stemming from the capitalist system. Every party and every group was finally confronted with reality, and every party and every group turned out to be, for those who did not already know it, one of the many components of the imperialist system, one of the many loudspeakers of imperialist ideology. We heard about the "Jewish question", the "Jewish people" and "Arab peoples"! The Maoist, Castrist and Trotskyist groups even went so far as to speak about "Arab peoples" fighting against imperialism! Everyone forgot a small detail that the most elementary Marxist analysis allows us to observe today: there is a bourgeoisie and a proletariat in Egypt, and there is a bourgeoisie and a proletariat in Israel!

We therefore find ourselves face to face with two typically bourgeois states that started a typically bourgeois war. The Egyptian bourgeoisie clashed with the Israeli bourgeoisie for economic, territorial and political reasons. The Israeli bourgeoisie fought its war for the same reasons. In this social context, it is of no interest for a Marxist, for a proletarian, to know which was the attacker and which the attacked, since in every war generated by capitalism the attacker is the bourgeoisie and the attacked the proletariat and the poor peasants, sent to kill each other on the rocks of the Karst Plateau*, in the trenches of Verdun, and in the Sinai desert. The Arab and Israeli workers have no conflict of interests; on the contrary, they share the same fate of being exploited by the bourgeois of Cairo and Tel Aviv, which are linked by the tightly-woven web of capital invested in the Middle East. This is channelled through the old and new Meccas of imperialism: Washington, London, Paris, Bonn, Rome, Moscow and Tokyo. Dollars, pounds, francs, marks, yen and roubles are invested in the Middle East, in oil, pipelines, cotton, the Aswan dam, the mechanised agriculture of the kibbutzim, and the textile, iron and steel and chemical industries. The United States and the Soviet Union, France and Britain, Germany and Italy, Japan and the Netherlands invest directly or through the World Bank, trade, lend capital to the various Middle-East states, and sell thousands of planes, tanks and guns. "Democratic" America invests in and lends capital to the Arab countries and Israel; "socialist" Russia sells arms and makes loans at 2.5% to the Arab countries, and at the same time signs economic agreements with Israel. All the other imperialist powers, big or small, do the same. The result is that the Eastern and Western bourgeoisies grow fat on this sordid trafficking, in homage to the "democracy" and "socialism" fed to the suckers, like the classic breadcrumbs, while the Arab and Israeli bourgeoisies that have begun to enjoy the delicious dishes served up at the banquet develop a more voracious appetite for war. As always, the workers pay the price for this system. They pay for it in the imperialist metropolises, and they pay for it in the Middle East.

The Egyptian textile workers have seen their claims ruthlessly rejected, and their revolutionary comrades – the true communists that denounced Nasser's false "socialism" – cruelly imprisoned or killed.

The Israeli workers have had to pay for the serious crisis of the kibbutz "paradise" with strikes and unemployment.

Raised and nourished on intrigues with the European and American imperialists, the Arab bourgeoisie has long added the Soviet card to its hand. The Israeli bourgeoisie played and used the Stalinist card well in 1947, when the Soviet Union and the United States supported Zionism to oust from the Middle East the exhausted Anglo-French powers that were even dusting off Pan-Arabism, arming

* The Karst Plateau is a karstic region on the border between Italy and Slovenia. During the First World War, it was the theatre of bloody confrontations between the Austrian and Italian armies. [Editor's note.]

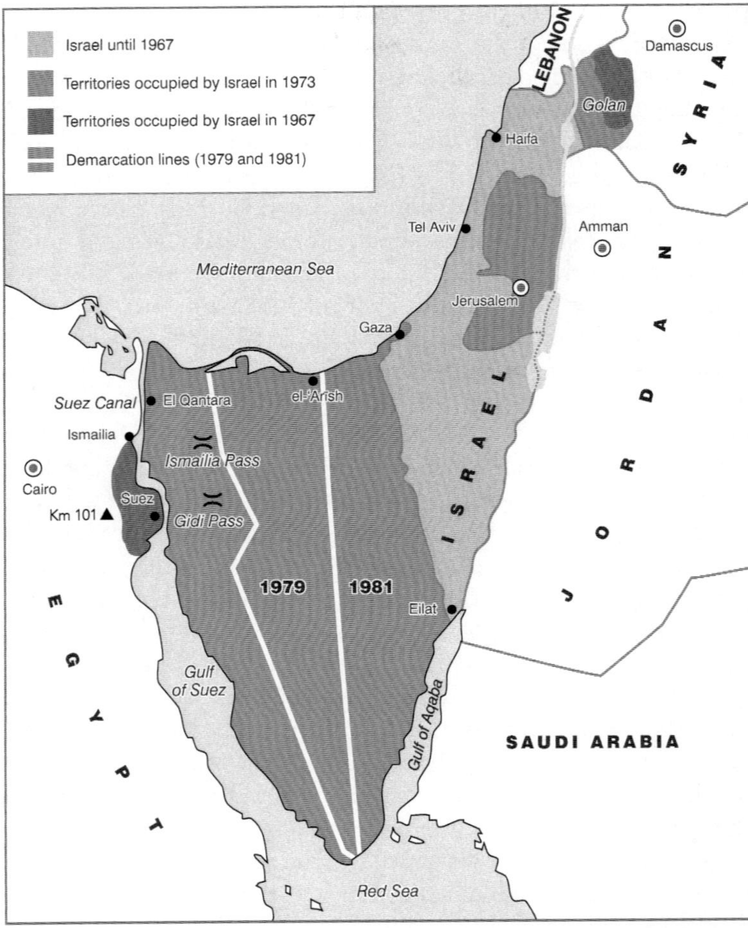

and organising it in order to stay afloat... on oil. The State of Israel was born not with the blessing of Jehovah, but with that of Stalin and Truman. Then, in 1956, it abandoned its godfathers, allied itself with Eden and Mollet, and marched towards Suez. The Sixth Fleet blocked the operation. The Middle East has now become an American sphere of influence, in which the Russians enter only to play the game of the United States. In fact, the Stars and Stripes waves over nearly all its oil. It will take ten years before the reinforcement of European capitalism attempts to return to the Middle East as a competitor and provokes another imbalance in the international and internal relations of the area.

The realignment of the states resumes: the Soviet Union has room for its manoeuvres, and the United States expands the contradictions of its hegemony. The Arab and Israeli bourgeoisies play a secondary but indispensable role in this whole process. Incapable, through weakness and rivalry, of seizing the oil, they can, however, as go-betweens, prepare the troops for a war from which only the great imperialist powers could profit today. Skilled at bartering favours and capital, they are quick to turn both into ideologies with which to stuff the heads of the workers, who are not even different as regards race, but only as regards the opium of their religions.

Only vulgar liars or incurable imbeciles can find a crumb of "socialism" in this comedy of ideas and this tragedy of men! There are also those who have even seen in this war between two capitalisms, tied by a thousand threads to all the imperialist powers, in this war that is the product of imperialism itself, an open struggle against imperialism! This is where the misrepresentation of facts reaches an all-time high. For these people, who have the nerve to call themselves Marxist, it is not the international revolution of the proletariat against their respective bourgeoisies that is anti-imperialist, but the massacre between proletariats in the name of the bourgeoisies that exploit them and send them to their deaths.

This is the aberration to which the abandonment of Marxism and Leninism can lead. These are the political conclusions to which the rejection of the Leninist strategy of the national question and its substitution with the Maoist theory of the "anti-imperialist front" lead. It was more than natural that openly declared social democrats should discover the "democratic" trench and take up their position there, since this is their bourgeois vocation. That the social democrats of the PCI and the PSIUP should in any case follow the imperialist policy of the Soviet Union formed part of their tradition, according to their opportunistic logic. The Maoists and the pro-Chinese were absent, thus confirming the role we had attributed to them since their emergence. Punctually, like the others, they chose not the Middle Eastern proletariat, but the Arab bourgeoisie, not the class revolution that would unite the Arabs and the Israelis, but inter-State conflict, and not Lenin's revolutionary defeatism, but Nasser's national socialism.

The alignment of opportunism is now complete in Italy. These are the incontrovertible facts that every worker can see.

And every worker can see in these facts what fate awaits him as the crisis of imperialism spreads and the struggle between both the imperialist powers and the young capitalist nations that depend on them worsens.

The proletariat therefore has to prepare itself to defend its historical interests by refusing every type of adhesion to its own State or to that of others, and by fighting its way along the highroad of Marx and Lenin's internationalist teaching: "Against war, revolution!"

"Left-Wing Interventionism" by the Side of the Arab Bourgeoisie*

In the previous issue of *Lotta Comunista*** we identified the Maoist, Castrist and Trotskyist groups as one of the components of "interventionism", together with the pro-Israeli social democrats, in the war in the Middle East.

It is useful to analyse this "left-wing interventionism", since it contains all the elements of petty-bourgeois falsification and adventurism that have always been present in the history of the workers' movement, and especially in the Italian case.

In its criticism of reformism and social democracy, revolutionary Marxism has often found the ground occupied by currents that were pushed to formal anti-reformist disagreement by non-proletarian social expectations. Just as often, however, the dynamic of the class struggles in the international field has taken it upon itself to clear the ground and to throw those currents back into their natural channel. When put to the internationalist test, i.e., when the class interests brought into play by the war are huge and the choices no longer permit glib demagogy, the pseudo-left currents inevitably fail it and reveal their intimate "interventionist" nature.

"Revolutionary" in words, they become "bourgeois" when it comes to facts, i.e., they choose war instead of revolution. The internationalist test has always proved infallible, in both the past and today. However, since we do not want our statement to seem unfounded, we give the floor to the "interventionist" groups.

"The struggle of the young Italian revolutionaries is the same struggle as that of the Arab peoples", recognises the *Nuova Unità**** of 17th June 1967. The 24th June 1967 issue goes even further and states, for those who had not yet understood what is meant by "Arab peoples": "Unity among the Arab peoples, which was born when Israel threatened to attack, has become even closer [...] It is a revolutionary storm against aggression that is shaking all the Middle East and engulfing enemies and false friends".

---

* Arrigo Cervetto, July-August 1967.

** See the previous article, "Against War, Revolution!" [Editor's note.]

*** Newspaper of one of the Italian Maoist currents. [Editor's note.]

And in order not to be misunderstood, the pro-Chinese organ announces: "The struggle that the Arab peoples are fighting against the Anglo-American imperialists is a class struggle".

Nuova Unità has applied in the most logical way the Maoist theory of the "oppressed people", conceived of as "oppressed class". It has applied it in a concrete, specific case such as that of the war in the Middle East, and the result could not be clearer. The struggle of such bourgeois States as the Arab states against another bourgeois State such as Israel and against two imperialist states such as Britain and the United States has become a class struggle, a class struggle that has ended up becoming identical to that of the "young Italian revolutionaries"! *Nuova Unità* has suddenly transformed the "peoples" of the various Arab countries into an indistinct, generic, social group, dissolved the various antagonistic classes that make them up, denied the nature of the ruling classes that wield political power in the Arab states, and identified itself with their struggle.

It really wasn't necessary to wait until 1967 to hear such a "new idea"! All the "interventionists", the Arturo Labriola* and the Benito Mussolini, had already expressed it when they identified their cause as "young Italian revolutionaries" with the "proletarian" war of the "Italian people" against the imperialism of the time, "Prussian" imperialism! The other Maoist group, that of *Rivoluzione Proletaria*, did not let itself be outdistanced as it raced towards the "interventionist" finishing line, even if it tried to reach it with a more elaborate line of reasoning, as is set out in issue No. 6 of June 1967. For *Rivoluzione Proletaria*, the tumultuous economic development of the State of Israel "under the control and dominion of American financial capital", shaken by serious internal contradictions and crises, is seeking to find a way out in a policy of expansion towards the Arab countries. The Israeli economy is oriented towards boosting and further developing its arms industry. Israel is therefore a capitalist country with a high level of development "that, for its imperialist expansion, needs to conquer territories that would expand its markets and guarantee it a further

* Arturo Labriola (1873-1959): first a socialist in Naples, after being expatriated to France, he made friends with Georges Sorel; on his return to Italy, he was the driving force in the revolutionary trade-unionist current within the Socialist Party; in 1911, he spoke out in favour of war against Turkey to conquer the colony of Libya, and in 1915 he backed Italy's intervention in the war against the Central Powers. [Editor's note.]

inflow of cheap labour". According to this thesis, the State of Israel itself is emerging as a "new imperialist reality".

According to *Rivoluzione Proletaria*, in the face of this "new imperialist reality", in the face of this imperialist Israeli State, the "Arab peoples' anti-imperialist movement" must not repeat the mistake of seeing its "anti-imperialist war" in the light of conventional criteria, but must acquire the "tactical and strategic conception of a people's war" and open up "a new Vietnam in the nerve centre of the Middle East", "in the heart of the new Israeli State"; i.e., guerrilla warfare that "will be able to expose and exacerbate the most lacerating contradictions within the very context of Israeli society" to the point of liquidating the Israeli State "as a Jewish State". The thesis ends with the statement that "the development of a revolutionary people's war will remove any doubts about the revisionist policy of alliance with the so-called national bourgeoisies, whose sole function is ultimately that of perpetuating imperialist domination in the Middle East via Soviet-American co-operation".

We have given ample space to these positions so that no one can accuse us of having passed over some of their aspects in silence when we say that it would be hard to conceive of anything more contradictory to justify such one hundred per cent "interventionism".

Let's try to untangle such a mass of contradictions, mistakes in analysis and definition, invented and unproved statements, and meaningless words. The State of Israel is a capitalist State, and so is the development of its economy, subject to expansions and crises, pressed, like all the capitalist economies, by the need to find internal and external market outlets. Quite right! But the same characteristics can be found in the Egyptian economy, for instance. *Rivoluzione Proletaria* is very careful not to mention this.

It does speak of "national bourgeoisies", but it says nothing about the social nature of the economy that represents these classes. Is the Egyptian economy, for instance, which represents the Egyptian "national bourgeoisie", capitalist or not? And if it is not, what kind of economy is it?

Rivoluzione Proletaria has recourse to the old stratagem of silence on this fundamental point, the solution to which is indispensable to making even a simple Marxist judgement on such a complex phenomenon as war, even before adopting a militant stance.

The truth is that, by speaking of "Arab countries" and of the "Arab peoples' anti-imperialist movement", *Rivoluzione Proletaria* seeks to conceal the fact that in the Arab countries, as in Israel, there are clearly definable social classes such as the bourgeoisie (upper, medium, and petty), the proletariat, and strata of poor, semi-proletarian peasants.

Thus, Egypt is an "Arab country" in which there is a "people" that, from the Marxist point of view, is a "population" made up of bourgeois and petty-bourgeois classes, a working class, and semi-proletarian peasant strata. Which classes have the means of production, and hence the political power, in Egypt? No Maoist, Castrist or Trotskyist gives a clear answer to this question. They cannot, lest they see their pack of lies exposed for what it is. Reluctantly, and after countless evasions, they manage to say: "a nationalist bourgeoisie", "anti-imperialist".

In Marxist and Leninist terms, this means nothing else than "a young capitalist country" that fights against more mature, i.e., imperialist, capitalist countries.

Israel's economic development is "under the control and dominion of American financial capital". If this is true, Israel is either a "semi-colony" or a "young capitalist country" with a very high level of foreign investment. In no case could it be defined as a "young imperialist country". For all the countries that are "dominated" by "American financial capital", the Maoists, and *Rivoluzione Proletaria*, recommend "national independence" against American imperialism. They even recommend the same aim for Italy, insisting on judging the Italian bourgeoisie as "a slave of US imperialism", and, of course, saying nothing about the imperialist exports of Italian capital to the whole world, as we have long testified in demonstrating that Italy has an "imperialist reality", even though it is not really "new". It is therefore difficult to understand why *Rivoluzione Proletaria* does not apply the same line to the Middle East, and to Israel in particular. Or rather, it is all too easy to understand the Maoists' political seriousness in applying their "general line".

As good opportunists, they say one thing today, and another tomorrow.

Italy is "dominated" by American capital, as is Israel, according to what they say. Italy is a country that must fight for its "national independence" against American imperialism, while Israel is itself an imperialist country! For the Maoists, it obviously matters little that Italy is one of the world's top ten economic powers and that Israel is not even in the top thirty – and the Marxist-Leninist criterion for the definition of imperialism matters even less. Illuminated by the lodestar of the "cultural revolution", the Maoists of *Rivoluzione Proletaria* want to define imperialism when they do not even know the most elementary laws of what makes a capitalist economy work. Mindful of the Maoist motto stressing the priority of "politics", they do not even think of attempting a minimum of economic analysis. They even go so far as to confuse the expansive – hence aggressive – policy of Israeli capitalism with the objective characteristics of imperialism; they confuse the nationalist politics of the Israeli State with the imperialist maturity of its economy.

And they become ridiculous when they point to Israel's arms industry as the sign of this maturity, when everyone knows that the Israeli arms industry exports light weapons and that the Israeli State imports heavy weapons (aircraft, tanks, etc.) to equip its army. In the war in the Middle East, weapons imported from the United States, France, Germany, Britain, the Soviet Union and Czechoslovakia have fired on all fronts.

If a state's expansionist, and hence aggressive, tendency were enough to classify it as imperialist, all the states in the world would be imperialist, and if a state's tendency towards military aggression were enough to call it imperialist, there are very few states in the world that would not be defined as such.

Every capitalist economy is expansionist, by nature and of necessity, and every State reflects its objective trends. This explains why – as the editors of *Rivoluzione Proletaria* should know – a slew of expansionist trends is to be found in the so-called "socialist camp", and why a whole series of hotbeds of tensions and conflicts develops. In the face of such phenomena, we Marxists are careful not to define these states as "imperialist", just as we do not define China as "imperialist", but simply as "capitalist".

Of these states, only the Soviet Union, which has now reached a level of economic maturity that compels it to export capital and to fight for its share of the world market, can be described as "imperialist".

On achieving independence, indeed at the very moment of their constitution, even the states of the "Third World", so dear to the editors of *Rivoluzione Proletaria*, unleashed a series of trends that sometimes led to armed conflicts. One need only think of the Indo-Pakistani war.

The general framework in which these conflicts emerge is that of the imperialist phase, in which the main powers fight for their share of the world market. This means that it is imperialism that historically creates the economic causes and juridical forms (borders, etc.) of the conflicts of the "young capitalist countries". The Middle East is certainly not an exception to this.

However, as Marx and Lenin were well aware, it is ultimately capitalism, with its diffusion of the capitalist relations of production in the pre-capitalist economies, that is the primary cause of the formation of the "young capitalist countries".

In this dialectic, "external" and "internal" causes interweave and create complex and particular situations, so that it may be said that a military conflict between two or more capitalist but not yet imperialist states is both a typical bourgeois war and a product of imperialism: a bourgeois war since it is a conflict of interests between two or more opposing "national bourgeoisies"; and a product of imperialism, since the different imperialist powers, more or less allied with one or another of the "national bourgeoisies", are directly involved in these conflicts, the dynamic of which forms part of their strategy in their struggle for the economic division of the world market.

Since the world entered its imperialist phase, there has been no war without the presence of different imperialist powers. But why doesn't Marxism describe all these wars as "imperialist"? Because, in spite of the inevitable presence of the various imperialist powers, these wars have been characterised by clashes between not yet imperialist bourgeois states.

The Balkan wars that preceded the first imperialist world war were typical bourgeois wars, in which the problems of the various nationalities were translated into the need for the national development of the various capitalisms: this is how Lenin saw them. In his opinion, the position of the proletariat had to be internationalist, not only against the imperialist powers, but also against the national bourgeoisies.

Maoism has not yet explained why this is not applicable to the Indo-Pakistani or the Arab-Israeli conflict. However, the interests of the Chinese State explain what Maoist ideology does not. Seeking to confuse the issue by speaking of "the Arab peoples' anti-imperialist movements" is just a play on words. Objectively, because they aim to become "great", all the "young capitalist countries" are "anti-imperialist", since they aim, in the long run, to weaken the current imperialist powers. However, this is not a valid reason for the proletariat to support them. Only the proletariat is fundamentally anti-imperialist because it is fundamentally anti-capitalist.

What is true of the phase of the struggle for independence from colonial or semi-colonial rule is even truer once independence has been achieved. Nevertheless, in the phase of the struggle for independence itself, the primary condition for a real anti-imperialist impact lies in the proletarian leadership, with a clear Marxist programme and an autonomous class organisation, of the bourgeois revolution itself. In the end, it is only a decisive struggle to obtain this proletarian leadership that allows the establishing of revolutionary hegemony over the masses of poor peasants, most of them destined by capitalist development to be absorbed into the proletariat. A very important moment in this struggle is the demolition of bourgeois ideology and its influence over the worker-peasant masses, an ideology that reveals itself in its concept of "the people" and its denial of class antagonisms within the colonial or semi-colonial society. At its extremes, this ideology goes so far as to deny social classes and to use the concept of "oppressed people" in this sense.

The struggle to ensure proletarian leadership therefore passes necessarily through the denunciation of bourgeois ideology and its conception of "the people". In this respect too, the Maoist, Castrist and Trotskyist currents reveal themselves to be appendages of the bourgeois ideologies of the "young capitalist countries". They theorise an "anti-imperialist" struggle that is none other than the struggle of the "young capitalist countries". Introducing, for the Middle East, "revolutionary war" and "guerrilla warfare" does not change the social nature of the ongoing conflict by one iota. The "revolutionary war" is proletarian when it is led by a dictatorship of the proletariat, i.e., by a class power that is able to use various forms of armed struggle, from the conventional to guerrilla warfare. However, it is the class nature of revolutionary power that defines the forms of armed struggle, and not the opposite. In the second imperialist world war, there were guerrilla movements that were undoubtedly composed of proletarians, but whose leadership was that of bourgeois antifascism. Moreover, the presence and scale of these guerrilla movements did not change the nature of the imperialist war, since only the transformation of these antifascist movements into revolutionary movements, of bourgeois leadership into proletarian leadership, could transform the course, but not the nature, of the imperialist war into a civil war. Hence, it is impossible to see why the Castro-Maoist magic wand of "guerrilla warfare" should change the nature of the war in the Middle East, which remains a bourgeois conflict despite any change in the military forms with which it is fought. And it would remain even more so in the Castro-Maoist plans that limit themselves to "the Arab peoples' anti-imperialist struggle" and do not set themselves the aim of proletarian leadership.

Of course, the war in the Middle East could also turn into a civil war, an authentic anti-imperialist struggle, or a socialist revolution, but only as the result of the initiative of an internationalist communist party that would set itself the aim of destroying the bourgeois Arab and Israeli states, eliminating the Middle Eastern bourgeoisies, unifying the Arab and Israeli working classes, and founding a Middle Eastern socialist State. In a revolutionary transformation of this kind, led by the proletariat and under its hegemony, the military forms of its realisation would play a secondary role with respect to strategy.

The objection raised to our Leninist conception is that class relations do not favour the proletariat in the Middle East. Our reply is that this is true only in part: the proletariats in Egypt and Israel, for example, represent a significant percentage of the working populations; moreover, there are large masses of proletarianised peasants. Secondly, apart from the current relations of force, a class strategy needs to be pursued constantly, even when (as was the case with the very small Bolshevik minority when faced with the "social-chauvinist" Second International) it has no possibility of being realised immediately. Besides, the Maoists, Castrists and Trotskyists have no possibility of immediate realisation of their petty-bourgeois platforms in Italy, and yet they promote them with the aim and result, although extremely limited, of strengthening the various Nassers of the world. Finally, the Leninist strategy applied in the Near East cannot and must not be the work of the Middle Eastern proletariat alone, just as, when it was developed for the October Revolution, it could not and had not to be based on the Russian proletariat alone. The transformation of the bourgeois war in the Middle East into socialist revolution could and should be based on the revolutionary struggle of the European proletariat, and of the Italian proletariat in particular, which operates in a society where the relations of force, because of intense proletarianisation, could benefit it. Undoubtedly, the propaganda of the Maoist, Castrist and Trotskyist positions makes no contribution at all to developing in the proletariat a Leninist consciousness that could make positive changes in the conditions for furthering the socialist revolution in the Middle East; on the contrary, its "interventionism" represents a further element of confusion and reinforcement of social-democratisation within the workers' movement.

The struggle against reformism has to be fought with Marxist clarity. It is impossible to fight social democracy when one reflects certain basic features of it, starting with its lack of theoretical principles. If it is not opportunism, what is that congenital mania for exploiting certain theoretical formulas to justify certain practical positions, from the exaltation of the "Yugoslav revolution" against Moscow the day before yesterday to the exaltation of Ben Bella's outburst against Boumedienne yesterday, and to the support for the same Boumedienne today?

To justify its marked "interventionism", *Bandiera Rossa*, the Italian Trotskyists' official organ, goes to so far as to write that the conflict in the Middle East has seen, on the one hand, a capitalist State, Israel, "integrated into the imperialist system at a regional and global level", and, on the other, "a combination of countries with a colonial or semi-colonial structure".

For *Bandiera Rossa*, Algeria or Egypt are "colonial" or "semi-colonial"!

To account for its "*giri di valzer*"*, *Bandiera Rossa* is even ready to stop the hands of the clock of history, of the formation of nations, and of the development of capitalism in the world. Rather than recognising the bourgeois nature of the Arab States and the development of their economies, it sends them back in time. It is highly likely that the Arab bourgeoisies, the Boumediennes and the Nassers would not accept the social "downgrading" decreed by the imagination of *Bandiera Rossa* – all the more so since those who want to downgrade them to the rank of "colonials" have ended up theorising "permanent revolution" the wrong way round; all they want to push forward permanently is opportunism.

* In Italian political jargon, this is roughly equivalent to "chopping and changing". [Editor's note.]

The National Pretext in the Mediterranean Policy*

Our evaluation of Italy's socio-economic formation and the characteristics of its restructuring is also an evaluation of its trends and level of development.

In a complex political panorama, our theses have long distinguished our organisation, thus confirming what we have always stated: the Leninist Party is the expression of revolutionary strategy, and revolutionary strategy is the expression of the scientific analysis of Marxism. In the present phase of class struggles in the world, there cannot be a solid revolutionary party without a solid science, since every revolutionary movement is destined to be corroded unless it has solid theoretical roots.

Our conception is not one of pure abstraction, but of practical necessity. Our analysis led us to conclude that Italian capitalism had now reached imperialist maturity.

We therefore refused to consider Italy as an "American colony" subject to the multinationals and Atlanticist policy. We judged that Italian imperialism was acting, albeit with less weight, within a framework of alliance with the American superpower, but with its own tendency towards expansion in the Mediterranean.

On the occasion of the Arab-Israeli War in 1967 we wrote that those who did not understand the "general and global nature of imperialism" would end up backing it, and that only consistent Marxists could avoid such a historical destiny. A war in the Middle East was enough to make Italian society express all the imperialist potential with which it was imbued.

All the political currents, including the minority petty-bourgeois intellectual ones, which would fuel terrorism in the following years, sided with the Arab bourgeoisies or, to a lesser extent, with the Israeli bourgeoisie. All the political currents had glossed over the incontrovertible fact of the class nature of the Arab societies and the Israeli society in which the workers were being exploited by bourgeoisies linked to the "tightly-woven web of capital invested in the Middle East", coming from the "old and new Meccas of imperialism: Washington, London, Paris, Bonn, Rome, Moscow, and Tokyo".

---

* Arrigo Cervetto, November 1985.

The metropolises of imperialism invested in oil and sold arms; in many cases, on one side as on the other.

The Arab bourgeoisie, "raised and nourished on intrigues with the European and American imperialists", added the Russian card to its hand. The Israeli bourgeoisie had already played it in 1947, when the United States and the USSR had backed Zionism in order to oust from the Middle East the exhausted Anglo-French powers, which had even dusted off Pan-Arabism to keep on controlling oil.

In 1956, France and Britain – plus Israel which, by joining them, had overturned the alliances – had been blocked by the United States, de facto backed by the Soviet Union. Just ten years later, the European powers, strengthened by the economic cycle, had attempted a competitive re-entry into the Middle East, thus exacerbating its imbalances.

Since 1967, almost twenty years have gone by, twenty years of economic and political history that have exacerbated the trends at work at the time, which, in their turn, had already clearly emerged since the first imperialist world war.

We have little to add to our strategic indications of the time, which are precisely strategic because they go beyond the tactical situation.

In our July 1967 article – written in opposition to a specific version of "left-wing interventionism", inaugurated in Italy by Benito Mussolini and the Sorelian syndicalists – we excluded from our priority tasks the struggle to resolve the problem of the territorial entrenchment of the different ethnic groups in the Middle East. We believed, and still believe, that the priority task in that area should be, and still is, the struggle of the international proletariat, and hence also of the Arab and Israeli proletariats, against the bourgeoisies and the unitary imperialism constituted by the various powers.

This does not mean that the problem of territorial settlement for the Palestinian population does not exist. It means affirming that, only after having carried out its fundamental task of struggle, will the proletariat be able to resolve this problem in the internationalist terms in which it is historically posed. On the other hand, it can also be resolved in nationalist terms, but only within the framework of inter-imperialist competition.

Our position was, and still is, inspired by Lenin's position on the Balkan wars. This denounced the fact that these were conflicts directed by the imperialist powers. Lenin obviously took into account all the national factors involved, but believed they were subordinated to the general course of the conflict among the powers acting in the Balkan area. August 1914 would be the acid test for a correct internationalist strategy and would open the way for the October victory, whereas all the positions of the socialist movement that, in various ways, had run aground on the national factors, would expose them to a historic shipwreck.

This is not a case of indifferentism with regard to the national question, especially as Lenin was the most acute specialist on the national question in the twentieth century. If Lenin behaved in this particular way, it means that we find ourselves face to face with one of the most profound aspects of revolutionary strategy. We find ourselves face to face with an unalterable principle: for Marxism, the national question is not a matter of principle. The Marxist attitude towards the national question has always been, and always will be, dictated by the principle of class struggle. Consequently, those national protest movements that benefit the struggle of the international proletariat will be supported.

The Leninist party that respects this principle cannot be dragged into social-imperialist positions via the driving belt of the "national question". It can be reduced to extreme isolation, but it cannot be denatured.

We have refused to consider the Palestinian "national question" as a starting point based on disinherited masses of poor peasants and on a permanent revolution in the Middle East. Today, we do not side with Italian imperialism in its use of the Palestinian "card", and we remain very firmly on our internationalist position of transformation of the Middle Eastern wars into proletarian revolution.

There are about 2,800,000 Palestinians. 800,000 of them reside in Jordan, 300,000 in Syria, 200,000 in Lebanon, 400,000 in Israel, 630,000 in territories occupied by Israel, and another 70,000 are scattered in other countries. They have no national State and do not form part, as a nationality, of a multinational State. In this, they are not an exception. Dozens of nationalities in dozens of states are in the same condition. There is no State that, in its formation, has not included, often by force, national minorities. Only a few states have recognised multinational forms. This holds true for the states that formed in past centuries in Europe, for example, and holds even truer for the states that have formed in Africa and Asia in the last few decades.

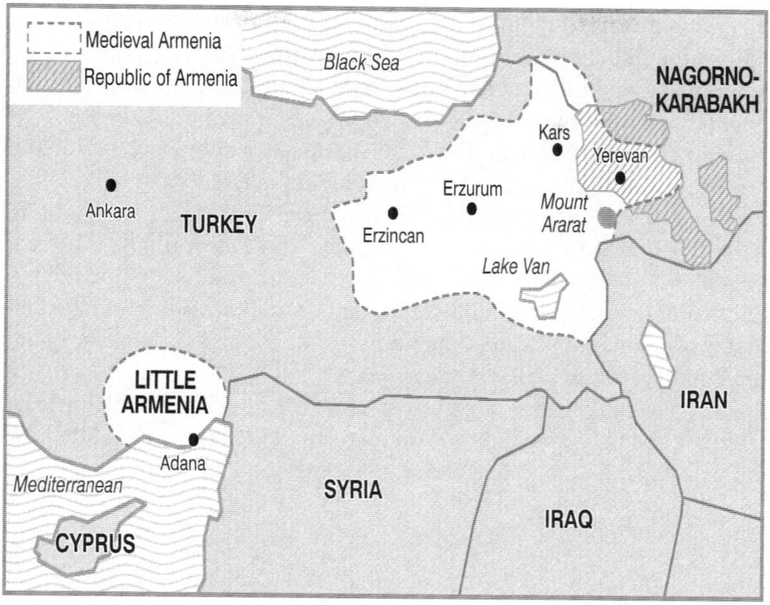
Medieval Armenia
Republic of Armenia
Black Sea
NAGORNO-KARABAKH
Kars
Yerevan
Ankara
TURKEY
Erzurum
Erzincan
Mount Ararat
Lake Van
LITTLE ARMENIA
Adana
IRAN
Mediterranean
SYRIA
IRAQ
CYPRUS

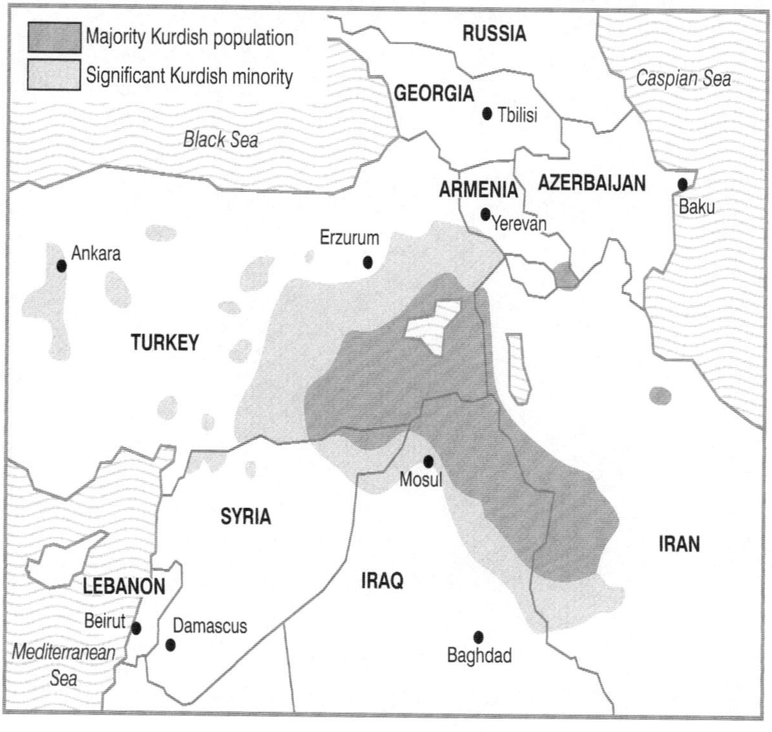
Majority Kurdish population
Significant Kurdish minority
RUSSIA
Caspian Sea
GEORGIA
Tbilisi
Black Sea
ARMENIA
AZERBAIJAN
Baku
Yerevan
Erzurum
Ankara
TURKEY
Mosul
SYRIA
IRAN
LEBANON
IRAQ
Beirut
Damascus
Mediterranean Sea
Baghdad

This means that national factors are used in the inter-State struggle and will be even more used in the future.

The Armenians are reckoned to be about 2 million: half of them are federated with the USSR, but another half forms a diaspora. Massacred by Turkey during the First World War, they have nationalist movements that have resorted to terrorism even recently.

Even more significant is the situation of the Kurds. There are about 18 million of them, i.e., six times the Palestinians. 6 million of them reside in Turkey, 4.5 million in Iran, about 3 million in Iraq, 400,000 in Syria, and 200,000 in the USSR. They also have nationalist movements that aim at an autonomous State and that carry out a harshly repressed military struggle.

Today the various imperialist powers are using the Palestinian "card", but they are ready to use the other cards in the Middle Eastern pack. In Rome, too, there is no lack of players.

Violence and Crises of the Nation-States in the Middle East of the New Strategic Phase*

The Middle East is flaring up in a chain of blood feuds and civil wars that ignore what are by now arbitrary State borders; the sparks of terrorist violence are spreading its flames as far as the metropolises of imperialism, which have always been involved in the area. It is said that the region is set to become the land of "failed States", and that the powers of the "Greater Middle East", the strip of land that goes from North Africa to Afghanistan, are by now the "global Balkans". What is needed is reflection on the Marxist theory of politics and violence that would also include revolutionary strategy, to see how it has dealt with the class and State questions throughout capitalist development for over one and a half centuries.

Facing the task of providing the communist movement with a strategy, Marx and Engels, and later Lenin, found themselves in two different phases when they had to define the terms of a class position on the bourgeois-democratic revolutions and the formation of nation-states. In Eastern Europe and the Balkans, this question interwove with the decline and then the collapse of three empires, the Russian Empire, the Austro-Hungarian Empire, and the Ottoman Empire. Marx and Engels focused on big nationalities that could give birth to big States – Germany, Hungary, Italy and Poland: everything that concentrated the bourgeoisie was favourable to the working class, they would observe in 1866 regarding the "revolution from above" of German unity. By unifying the markets, big polities favoured the development of the productive forces, accelerated the end of the peasants' immobilism and made the concentration of a modern proletariat possible. The strategic concatenation of the "permanent revolution" linked the class and the State struggles; the assault of the democratic bourgeoisie had to be followed by a massive push on the part of the proletariat. The enemy and bulwark of the counter-revolution was the autocratic and semi-feudal Tsarist Empire. The prospect of a revolutionary war against Russia would be the central theme of the strategic hypotheses Marx and Engels would formulate during much of the second half of the

* Guido La Barbera, February 2015

nineteenth century, starting from the 1848 hail of revolutions and going on to the European wars of the 1850s and 1860s.

In this context, alongside support for German unity and the independence of Poland, Hungary and Italy from tsarism and the Habsburgs, Engels would formulate his thesis of "peoples without history". The small populations and the Slav minorities broken up in Eastern Europe and the Balkans by the three wedges of the Russian Empire, Austria-Hungary and European Turkey, had no prospect of becoming nation-states, and the myth that united them was "reactionary Pan-Slavism", a tool of Russian influence and the counter-revolution.

This was not an a priori position or a matter of principle. Marx and Engels attacked Pan-Slavism in 1848 as in the following decades because that myth was the tool of reactionary tsarist Russia. But when the Crimean War broke out in 1853, Engels himself would contemplate the opposite hypothesis – always in opposition to Russia – and would uphold the possibility of an "independent Slav nation" in the Balkan area, dominated at the time by Turkey. The revolutionary wave in Europe would lead in the end to a conflict between "Russian absolutism and European democracy" and capitalist development would deepen the divergence of interests from Russia; furthermore, "the South Slavs and the Greeks of Turkey" already had "far more interests in common with Western Europe than with Russia". When the railway connecting Budapest to the ports of Le Havre, Ostend and Hamburg, on the English Channel and the North Sea, was continued to Belgrade and Constantinople on the Black Sea, "the influence of Western civilisation and of Western trade" would become permanent "in South East Europe".

On the other hand, it remained true, in the thesis of "small peoples", that capitalist development needed big States and big single markets, while the ethnic and religious fragmentation in the Balkans, besides making the principle of nationality and Pan-Slavism a Russian tool, created a tangle that was practically impossible to untangle. This would leave its mark on the entire regional question for decades to come, passing through the Balkan wars, the two imperialist world wars – with the brief independent existence for Czechs, Slovaks and South Slavs between the two conflicts – then through the Yalta division and after its collapse, in 1989, the "new division", with Eastern Europe being gradually absorbed into the European Union. When Czechoslovakia and Yugoslavia were left to themselves in the early 1990s, in the interlude between the two divisions, they ended up with the secession of Bratislava from Prague and the chain of civil wars in Yugoslavia.

Lenin picked up and developed Marx and Engels' strategy about the national question in the political battle between *the Zimmerwald Left*, the internationalist opposition to the 1914 war, when it was a matter of defending the watchword of the "right of nations to self-determination" from the currents that believed it had been superseded. The denunciation of the Tsarist Empire as the "prison of peoples" would be an integral part of Lenin's international strategy during the war, and would flank the political arm of "revolutionary defeatism" in the 1917 October assault. At the same time, however, national self-determination was not a matter of principle for Lenin. Marx "favoured Polish independence in the interests of European democracy"; in his struggle against the omnipotence and influence of tsarism, Lenin wrote in the summer of 1916: "That this attitude was correct was most clearly and practically demonstrated in 1849, when the Russian serf army crushed the national liberation and revolutionary-democratic rebellion in Hungary". The question was "first and foremost" the struggle against tsarism. This is the sole reason why Marx and Engels were at the same time "opposed to the national movement of the Czechs and South Slavs", who had revealed themselves to be "Russian outposts" in 1848-49.

Without contradicting the principle whereby "A people which oppresses another cannot emancipate itself", we can draw two lessons from that battle of Marx and Engels' strategy: "(1) that the interests of the liberation of a number of big and very big nations in Europe rate higher than the interests of the movement for liberation of small nations; (2) that the demand for democracy must not be considered in isolation but on a European – today we should say a world – scale". Furthermore: "The several demands of democracy, including self-determination, are not an absolute, but only a small part of the general-democratic (now: general-socialist) world movement. In individual concrete cases, the part may contradict the whole; if so, it must be rejected. It is possible that the republican movement in one country may be merely an instrument of the clerical or financial-monarchist intrigues of other countries; if so, we must not support this particular, concrete movement, but it would be ridiculous to delete the demand for a republic from the programme of international Social-Democracy on these grounds".

We observe that there were two important criteria for Lenin: the principle of class struggle, which included supporting the bourgeois-democratic revolutions, and international communist strategy, precisely the overall prospect of the "general-socialist world movement". "The Rights of Nations to Self-Determination", a text that preceded the outbreak of the 1914 war by a few months, contains a crucial methodological guideline, indispensable for understanding how Lenin's analysis could be picked up again, developed and applied to the "colonial question" in the post-WWII period, when Arrigo Cervetto would consider the historical phase of the communist movement's support for the bourgeois-democratic national movements to be over.

Lenin counterposed a methodological and analytical consideration to Rosa Luxemburg's objection that the "right of nations to self-determination" was not to be found in the programmes of any of the European socialist parties. What is important is "a comparison of the political and economic development of various countries", since "all modern states are of a common capitalist nature and are therefore subject to a common law of development". We observe that this is the concept of "*socio-economic formation*" and the regularity of its development as a natural law. Futhermore, "such a comparison must be drawn in a sensible way. The elementary condition for comparison is to find out whether the historical periods of development of the countries concerned are at all comparable". Capitalist *socio-economic formation*, we observe again, has its regularities that can be examined in depth with the tool of comparison, but capitalism has a history that gradually seizes the various areas in its creation of the world market.

This is where the comparative analysis of the national question in Western Europe at the time of Marx, in the 19th century of bourgeois entrenchment, merges with that in Russia, Asia and the colonial world at the time when Lenin was dealing with it, at the dawn of the imperialist 20th century. In most Western countries, observes Lenin, this was settled long ago; the important thing is "the difference between countries where bourgeois-democratic reforms have long been completed, and those where they have not":

"The epoch of bourgeois-democratic revolutions in Western, continental Europe embraces a fairly definite period, approximately between 1789 and 1871. This was precisely the period of national movements and the creation of national states. When this period drew to a close, Western Europe had been transformed into a settled system of bourgeois states, which, as a general rule, were nationally uniform states. [...] In Eastern Europe and Asia the period of bourgeois-democratic revolutions did not begin until 1905. The revolutions in Russia, Persia, Turkey and China, the Balkan wars – such is the chain of world events of our period in our "Orient". And only a blind man could fail to see in this chain of events the awakening of a whole series of bourgeois-democratic national movements which strive to create nationally independent and nationally uniform states".

We should note the assonance with Cervetto's thesis in his writing about "colonial industrialisation", in which the young bourgeoisies struggling for independence were at their 1789 moment and waiting for their 1848. It is, in fact, a matter of seeing how our internationalist politics has picked up and developed those theoretical prerequisites for strategy, applying them in the post-WWII period to the final phase of the "colonial question". Our support for the new bourgeoisie's movements for independence in Asia and Africa in the 1950s and 1960s continued Lenin's Third International strategy. But the realisation – in the 1970s – that that phase was over was also a development of it, one that rests precisely on the methodological criterion we have seen always enunciated by Lenin. Let's consider this prediction of Cervetto's, made in December 1960, in a passage we have already had occasion to quote: "The colonial question at a certain stage of international industrialisation – and at the end of the day it isn't a question of many years – will lose its specific importance, since the social forces will polarise around the predominant and widespread relations of capitalist production in very vast economic areas". And let's consider the conclusion to that reflection just over fifteen years later, in December 1977: we communists supported the bourgeois-democratic revolution "because it develops the productive forces", and this gave the democrats the tactical advantage, "because they let themselves be supported with the aim of doing away with us". But "with the end of the movement for independence in all the areas of the world, the tactical advantage also returns to communism, since it is no longer obliged to support democracy".

Lenin's reflection on bourgeois-democratic entrenchment in Western Europe was applied to the new bourgeoisies in Asia and Africa at the end of their anti-colonial struggles. Throughout capitalist development we find first the bourgeoisies of the European nation-states, then those of Russia and the Slav area – with the strategic divide of the Bolshevik attempt overthrown by Stalinist State capitalism – and finally those of the Asian and African world, dragged into the modern capitalist economy also by those European States that had become imperialist powers.

But this is not the whole story. Over the decades, the uneven economic and political development of the new areas has transformed China into an imperialist giant, while the Middle East with its energy resources has remained politically divided and the object of contention. In our December 1985 article "The National Pretext in Mediterranean Politics", we find Engels' formula of the "small peoples" indirectly re-proposed, combined, however, with Lenin's thesis about the Balkan wars, according to which those conflicts saw "the direct conflict of imperialist powers" prevail over national factors. The end of the historical cycle of bourgeois-democratic revolutions did not mean that the question of national minorities had been resolved, stated Cervetto; especially in the Middle East, we may add, where the borders between the states are the direct heritage of the lines of imperialist division, with the overlapping of denominational minorities and fault lines similar to the Balkan tangle.

Cervetto wrote that there was the question of the entrenchment of the Palestinian population, but "only after carrying out our fundamental task of proletarian struggle", i.e., from a revolutionary perspective, "will the proletariat be able to resolve this problem in the internationalistic terms in which it is by now historically posed". In national terms, the question was destined to be seized upon by the "competition among the imperialists". It is here that Engels' criterion is updated with Lenin to the era of imperialism. The Palestinians, without a nation-State or recognition as a nationality in a multinational State, "are not an exception".

"Dozens of nationalities in dozens of States find themselves in their condition. There is no State that, as it was forming, has not included national minorities, often by force. Only a handful of States have recognised multinational forms. What is true of the States that were formed in past centuries – for example in Europe – is even more true of the States that have formed in Africa and Asia in the last few decades. This means that national factors are used in the inter-State struggle and that this will be even more the case in the future".

Examples are the Armenian and Kurdish populations, the latter now in the forefront of the crisis in Iraq and Syria.

Since that "inter-State struggle" regarded both the powers of the area and the great powers of imperialism, how could the question of the unification of the Middle Eastern regional market be posed? Precisely in December 1977, while theoretical reflection argued the end of the cycle of the bourgeois-democratic revolutions in the new areas, Cervetto reasoned about a variation of the "Zollverein solution" in the Middle East.

This was only a "Marxist laboratory hypothesis", motivated by the "very rapid, headlong, Middle Eastern turnaround", we read in his notes for the Party's National Conference. A few days earlier, on November 19th, with a coup de théâtre, the Egyptian President Anwar Sadat had gone to Jerusalem and had spoken to the Knesset, sanctioning the start of the peace process between Egypt and Israel. There was the "objective possibility of a Middle Eastern power": this was Cervetto's key thesis. Around the Egypt-Israel axis, it was possible to think of a "free-trade area with Saudi-Iranian capital, Israeli managers and the disintegration of the 50 million Egyptian and Sudanese peasants". The partial unification of the German area had begun with the "Zollverein", customs union, and had ended with the "Prussian solution", i.e., a military solution, "contrary to Marx and Engels' expectations". In the Middle Eastern area, the Prussian solution had been attempted four times in thirty years, but had ended "in a stalemate in the young capitalist countries and the strengthening of the metropolises". Hence, the solution could be the "Zollverein"; in the area's power relations Saudi Arabia and Iran were "decisive".

This hypothesis surfaced again a few months later in a comment on the conflicts in the Horn of Africa, with more emphasis, however, on the USA-USSR-Europe contention. After the Suez Crisis in 1956, the United States had ended up undermining the positions of France and Britain in the Middle East, we read in a note of June 1978, but the oil crisis had opened the game up to the ECM, the bloc of the European Common Market. The solution of a free-trade area, "instead of the impossible 'Prussian' solution" could open up the space again to the ECM. For the moment, however, it was Washington that was implementing a "balance of power" and a "military balance", and "the Kissinger line" had proved a winner in the Middle East.

That "laboratory hypothesis" remained a reflection that would not be published; if we refer to it now it is precisely because that fruitless strategic variation gives an idea, by contrast, of how the general course of the contention in the Middle East has not only distanced every hypothesis of federation, but also every kind of truce among the regional players. Forty years later, decade by decade, it is precisely the series of regional conflicts and then of civil wars – between Iran and Iraq in the 1980s, with the two American interventions in Iraq in 1991 and 2003, and today with the conflicts in Syria and Libya – that has made America's power games crucial. Something of that old 1977 hypothesis, with its formula of a regional "customs union" as a way for European influence, remains, if anything, in the network of relationships of the Union for the Mediterranean, in the association agreements between the EU and seven countries of its Southern shore – Algeria, Egypt, Jordan, Israel, Lebanon, Morocco and Tunisia – and in the arduous progress of Turkey's EU membership.

This is where the most recent chapter begins, that of the Middle East in the "new strategic phase". Ten years ago, in order to contextualise the "unprecedented strategic event" determined by the irruption of China as an imperialist power, we summed up the three phases of the revolutionary strategy that we sought to expound:

"The strategic axis is no longer the connection between class struggle and bourgeois revolution in Germany and Europe, as it had been for Marx and Engels, or the connection between the inter-imperialist struggles and the bourgeois revolutions in the new areas, as it had been for Lenin. For the first time, with respect to Marx, Engels and Lenin's historical experience, the national question disappears from the framework of the relations that the combined action of the international party has to connect. The global connection of the class and inter-State struggles now takes place entirely in the field of imperialist contradictions, in a world market that is by now complete, and in a world system of States that reflects the global establishment of bourgeois development everywhere".

We excluded at the time, and now we confirm it, that the crises of the so-called "failed States" could again open up the prospect of the support of proletarian strategy for democratic-national demands.

What interests us is that this new chapter, the "new strategic phase" characterised by the continental dimensions of China and the integration of Europe, has two crucial consequences for the contention in the Middle East. First, as we observed in 2004, even for the bourgeoisie "the question on the agenda is no longer the national State as a tool for action". For this reason, "the question of the inadequacy of the national dimension in the contention, in view of the imperialist emergence of the Asian giants" was being posed to the various sectors of European imperialism. And for this reason, the question of the efficacy of their state powers was being posed "to all the powers". The "crisis of sovereignty" is not only European. It is understandable that, for the Middle Eastern bourgeoisies, labouring for decades to stabilise their national set-ups and failing in their search for regional aggregation, the new level of continental state power becomes unattainable, unless there is a catastrophic breakdown in the world order that destroys the imperialist balance.

The second consequence is that the United States' relative decline casts doubt on its capacity to wield and guarantee the regional balance of power, to such an extent that we can read at least the erosion of its capacity to influence – no one knows whether temporarily or permanently – in the contradictory nature of its withdrawal from Iraq and in the crises subsequent to the "Arab Spring". This undoubtedly implicates Europe, caught in the dilemmas of its centralisation in foreign and military policy, but above all it intimates greater importance for China and India, a process, moreover, that is already underway. Not only will all the Middle Eastern contradictions remain unresolved, but they will also be even less resolvable in the new phase of the contention between continental powers, with the unforeseeable oscillations in the balance generated by the open intervention of the Asian giants.

The area will remain the generator and exporter of violence. More than ever, communist internationalism will be a practical necessity.

Crisis in the World Order and War in the Middle East*

"Reactionary terrorism" and "terrorist splinter group of the Middle-East bourgeoisie". It is with these tools that we framed the 9/11 crisis in 2001 with the terrorist attack on New York's Twin Towers; this analysis contributed to our internationalist battle in the wars which sprang from it in Afghanistan and the Persian Gulf.

In 2015, following the terrorist attacks in Paris, culminating a few months later with the Bataclan massacre, we collected in our book *Reactionary Terrorism, Imperialist Europeanism, Communist Internationalism* Arrigo Cervetto's texts on the "The Marxist Theory of Force" and a number of articles which were points of reference in our analysis of the *national question* and the crises in the Middle East. Here we recall three concepts outlined in them.

First, *reactionary terrorism*. This was a scientific evaluation which was inspired by Marx and Engels' opposition to "reactionary Pan-Slavism" – a tool of Tsarist reaction – as well as by Lenin's theses on the Balkan wars. Just as in the Slav area, in the Middle East "the failure of a number of processes of national unification" or "the impossibility of some nations to achieve the critical mass for an independent state organisation" allowed "splinter groups of terrorist violence and the ideological myth" to circulate, subject to every kind of use by other regional states and the powers of imperialism. With the failure of the attempts at Pan-Arab unification, whose champion was Gamal Abdel Nasser's Egypt, the Gulf oil states – where the oil rent "perpetuated the political forms of backwardness" – played a similar role towards Pan-Islamic radicalism to that which Russia played by seizing on Pan-Slavism. This combined with the struggle between the great powers in the region, where "at stake first of all was the carve-up of the area and then the ban, through the balancing game, on its unification under a single regional hegemonic force". The rivalry between "oil-soaked" bourgeoisies also exploited their respective terrorist currents. Moreover, terrorism often arose as the unintended consequence of the power game: Al Qaeda was born as a terrorist splinter group from the guerrilla warfare of the mujahideen whom the Americans and Saudis pushed into Afghanistan in the 1980s

* Guido La Barbera, October 2023.

against the Soviet Union; it is there, too, that we find the origins of the Taliban regime, and ISIS sprang from the disintegration of Iraq after the 2003 war.

Second, the *internationalist class principle* and *the national question*. In the 19th century of bourgeois consolidation, Marx and Engels supported the bourgeois-democratic revolutions in Europe and the birth of big states because this accelerated the development of the productive forces and, with them, the concentration of the proletariat. In the 20th century of imperialism, Lenin brandished the national questions in the Slav area and Asia if and when they served the international strategy of the communist revolution. In the post-WWII period, the cycle of democratic revolutions and the birth of new states out of the anti-colonial struggle – once that process had been completed and the young bourgeoisies were freed from Western domination – has, since the 1960s, left strategic priority to the contraposition between bourgeoisie and proletariat. Faced with the *Six-Day War* in 1967, and opposing both pro-Israeli interventionism and "Left-Wing Interventionism by the Side of the Arab Bourgeoisie" we asserted the *internationalist class principle* which is also our guideline for those crises and wars which somehow leave an unresolved *national question* in play. In Israel there was already "a bourgeoisie and a proletariat". In Egypt and the Arab states there was already "a bourgeoisie and a proletariat". Arab and Israeli workers did not have conflicting interests, but rather "the same fate" of being exploited by their bourgeoisies, which in turn were caught up in "the tightly-woven web of capital invested in the Middle East" by the powerhouses of imperialism.

Cervetto wrote in 1985 that "dozens of nationalities in dozens of states" find themselves in the Palestinian condition: examples were the Armenian or Kurdish populations. The "national pretext" is used in the struggle between the states and between the powers of imperialism:

"This does not mean that the problem of territorial settlement for the Palestinian population does not exist. It means affirming that, only after having carried out its fundamental task of struggle, will the proletariat be able to resolve this problem in the internationalist terms in which it is historically posed. On the other hand, it can also be resolved in nationalist terms, but only within the framework of inter-imperialist competition".

In other words, the only way to oppose every oppression is the internationalist strategy of "transforming an imperialist war into a proletarian revolution".

Third, the *new strategic phase* and the Middle East. We concluded in 2015 that the Middle Eastern bourgeoisies had been "labouring for decades to stabilise their national structures and failing in their search for regional aggregation". In the new condition of the world contention – characterised by the struggle between great continent-sized powers – and even more so for the nation-states of the area, "the new level of continental state power" became "impossible to reach". On the other hand, the erosion of the United States' influence undoubtedly called into question Europe, caught up in the dilemmas of its political centralisation. Above all, however, this erosion revealed "a greater weight for China and India". Not only would "all the Middle Eastern contradictions" remain unresolved, but they would also be "less easy to resolve in the new nature of the contention among continental powers, with unpredictable oscillations of the balance generated by the Asian giants' open arrival on the scene". The Middle East would remain "the generator and exporter of violence". "Communist internationalism" was not a vague pacifist aspiration, harboured in the impotence of good will: more than ever, it would be "a practical necessity".

Crisis in the World Order and War in Gaza*

The *crisis in the world order* is racing ahead, tensions are building up, and hotbeds of conflict are again flaring up. Hamas's terrorist raid on South Israel and the Israeli armed forces' reaction in Gaza have triggered a conflict that may well spread on a regional scale. The conflict could expand if the *war in Gaza* sees the involvement of the Shiite Hezbollah militias on Israel's northern border with Lebanon, and if this brings into play Iran, which, as with Hamas, is their protective power. The points of reference laid down less than ten years ago in *Reactionary Terrorism, Imperialist Europeanism, Communist Internationalism* now need to be integrated and updated.

First of all, we observe that, 50 years after the 1973 *Yom Kippur War*, the *war in Gaza* affair confirms the impasse of the *national principle* in the imperialist era and in the regional contradictions in the Middle East. From time to time, the national principle for the Palestinian populations has been either brandished or cynically abandoned by all the competing Middle Eastern powers, as well as by the great powers, including the use of the various terrorist splinter groups, to the point of degrading it to fanaticism and its reactionary Pan-Islamic variation. In addition, the Israeli bourgeoisie itself is not uninvolved with the consolidation of Hamas: it backed its settlement in Gaza in order to use it to divide the Palestinian front and to oppose Yasser Arafat's Palestine Liberation Organization (PLO) and then the Palestine national authority (PNA). In this sense, alongside the ideologically bankrupt Arab bourgeoisies, there is also a strategic bankruptcy on the part of the Israeli bourgeoisie which believed it could manipulate the transformations of Arab-Palestinian nationalism into Islamist radicalism.

Secondly, in confirmation of our *international class principle* – i.e., there is an Israeli bourgeoisie and proletariat, and there is an Arab bourgeoisie and proletariat – the crisis has also revealed the underrated reality of Asian immigration in the *kibbutzim*: there are a few thousand Thai day labourers, some tens of them among the

* Guido La Barbera, October 2023

victims of the Hamas raid. Social mobility in Israel is similar to that in the Middle East as a whole and in the Gulf monarchies in particular where there are millions of immigrant proletarians. Only communist internationalism can offer a strategic prospect for the unity of all these segments of the working-class, when national and religious myths have divided them and sent them to be massacred for decades.

Thirdly, there is indeed *the crisis in the world order*, the crumbling of the power relations on a global scale as the result of *Atlantic decline* and China's irruption which are opening up old fault lines and stoking endemic regional crises. In this sense, there is a connection between the *war in Ukraine*, the crisis in Nagorno-Karabakh, which has seen 100,000 Armenians overwhelmed by ethnic cleansing met with international silence, and now the *war in Gaza*. The global and regional relations of force are changing; between American decline and the Chinese rise, the margins for action on the part of the middle powers is increasing; critical points are flaring up again and the balances are being redefined with adjustments which Thomas Gomart, the director of the French Institute of International Relations (IFRI), expects will be "brutal".

In an essay in *Foreign Affairs*, Suzanne Maloney, the vice president and director of the Foreign Policy programme at the Brookings Institution, sees in the *war in Gaza* "the end of America's exit strategy in the Middle East". In her opinion, Joe Biden had tried to mediate a new balance of power in the region which would have allowed Washington to cut back on its commitment, "ensuring that Beijing did not fill the void". The almost-concluded historic agreement to normalise relations between Israel and Saudi Arabia promised to align the United States' two main regional partners against their common Iranian enemy, and to "anchor the Saudis beyond the perimeter of China's strategic orbit". Together with these efforts, Biden also sought to ease tensions with Iran. He tried to revive the JCPOA nuclear agreement denounced by Donald Trump, but he failed; as a fallback, he cobbled together a tactic of pragmatic deals and informal agreements.

If the extension of the *Abraham Accords* to Saudi Arabia had been successful, "a new alignment among two of the region's major players might have had a truly transformative impact on the security and economic environment in the broader Middle East". According to Maloney, it is precisely for this reason that that attempt failed.

Biden dramatically misunderstood Iran's interest in making peace. "Iranian leaders had every incentive to try to block an Israeli-Saudi breakthrough, particularly one that would have extended American security guarantees to Riyadh and allowed the Saudis to develop a civilian nuclear energy program".

Israel is being torn apart by the arguments over the astonishing error of judgement that left the border with the Gaza Strip undefended, but this is the direct consequence of the line adopted by the Israeli government regarding Hamas: "a total system failure on Israel's part", in the opinion of the former US Ambassador, Martin Indyk. According to different versions, a second error of judgement is American and regards the *Abraham Accords* undertaken by Trump with Biden maintaining its framework. It is said that that the policy failed because the prospect of an agreement between Israel and the Arab powers that set aside – leaving it unresolved – a solution to the Palestinian question is wishful thinking. This, for example, is the thesis of Beijing, which makes it a cornerstone of its initiative in the region. It is also said, and this is Maloney's thesis, that the policy failed with regard to Tehran which reacted to the threat of an agreement between the United States, Israel and Saudi Arabia. The two versions can be combined: the Palestinian question leaves room for Hamas and the Iranian reaction which wedges itself into that fault line. This is precisely the *national pretext* being seized upon by the regime of the mullahs through its players by proxy.

We observe, however, that if the American aim was to hang onto Riyadh by counterposing China's influence, this allows us to avoid a solely subjectivist interpretation of the "errors" made. If the catastrophic security lapse made by Israel is certain, the American action, in any case, can be explained by its regional policy in relation to China. If this was an error on the part of the USA, it was a *specific error*, part of the battle for influence with Beijing which is destined to continue. We also observe that the American initiative regarding the Saudi Arabians is, by other means, of the same nature as the war waged 20 years ago in Iraq: yesterday to forestall and today to impede the Chinese rise in the Persian Gulf.

The struggle for influence between Washington and Beijing confirms that the *crisis in the world order* is the root cause which is rekindling conflicts that had remained latent. As is highlighted by other fields of the contention – we need only think of American resistance to a modification of the voting rights in the IMF which would be proportionate to China's importance – Washington would like to demonstrate that the old Western order is still working, while doubt is being cast, not only in Beijing, on whether its proposals and forces are enough. The counter-thesis is that no *new order* or a reformed order is possible without China. On the other hand, a proportionate role for China is a major tectonic shift: there is no *new order* without China, but China is so enormously important that recognising it means a strategic downsizing for the powers of the *old Atlantic order*, and it is doubtful that this would be accepted peacefully. It is here that the *crisis in the world order* lets us glimpse its *breakdown* on the horizon.

In the conflagration of the *war in Gaza*, the question is being debated in an unusually explicit way both in Washington and in Beijing. The United States and the European Union exhort Israel to show moderation, writes the *Global Times*, but "the reality that must be acknowledged is that there is currently no powerful force internationally that can substantially promote a ceasefire and end the war". "This requires joint efforts from all countries in this direction, and major powers with greater international influence should set an example".

American leadership, Biden seems to answer from the White House, "is what unites the world". The *Frankfurter Allgemeine* observes that this echoes Madeleine Albright's exceptionalist theses about the United States as an "indispensable nation".

In *The New York Times*, Steven Erlanger has counterposed Biden's mission in Israel to that of Vladimir Putin in China. The two visits demonstrate the extent to which the global strategic panorama has been transformed by the *war in Ukraine* and how that transformation is being displayed in the *war in Gaza*. Russia, China and Iran were already forming a "new axis" over Ukraine. "Together, they find a common ideological cause in denouncing and defying the United States in the name of reforming the existing international order dominated by the West since World War II". The war reveals growing differences between the West on the one hand and China and Russia on the other: these do not only regard the conflict, but also "competing views of the rules that underpin global relations – and who gets to define them".

The direct reply of the *Global Times* to the New York daily needs to be reported because it sets out very clearly a Chinese line which demands a reformed order, albeit not excluding that Washington, Beijing, and also the European Union, may converge on it:

> "History has reached a turning point in the transformation of the post-World War II order, and this period will be marked by turbulence. Old

> conflicts will resurface in different ways [...]. The US views China as a major challenger to its strategic interests, displaying Washington's arrogance and ignorance on a broader, longer-term global geopolitical level. Can the preservation of this order be achieved by pushing China down, containing, and restraining it?
> "Strenuously upholding the existing order through traditional strategic means is one option. But adjusting the current order with a more open mindset to facilitate communication and cooperation between major global and regional powers, between southern and northern nations, as well as between emerging powers and the old great powers in building a new order is another option. The crucial question is: How will the US and the West respond to these changes? Are they willing to relinquish power, and adequately prepared for such a power transition?"

There are undoubtedly signs of a de facto convergence between the USA and the EU on the one hand and China on the other – the former committed to restraining Israel and China to intervening with Iran. Washington openly asked Beijing to intervene with Tehran, and Beijing agreed to do so. Nevertheless, it will not be only the confrontation over the *war in Gaza* that will resolve the question raised by the *Global Times*. The *Financial Times* reports that, according to Emile Hokayem – a senior fellow of the London-based Institute for International Strategic Studies (IISS) – the latest crisis is probably the greatest diplomatic challenge for America since 1990, when the United States "had to put together the coalition against Saddam Hussein". Back then, however, it was the "dawn" of US power in the region, while today "this looks like its sunset".

Again according to the *Financial Times*, notwithstanding China's and Russia's inroads, the United States remains nevertheless "the only power with the diplomatic and military strength to attempt to contain such a crisis". In the opinion of Jon Alterman – a director at the Center for Strategic and International Studies (CSIS) – we could say that the United States is not what it was in relative terms, "10, 15, 20 years ago". "(But) there's no country or collection of countries that comes close to what it can do militarily, diplomatically, or even in terms of intelligence collection".

Washington has deployed two aircraft carriers in the Mediterranean and the Persian Gulf, thus brandishing nuclear deterrence as it did in the 1973 *Yom Kippur War*. Beijing, which has sent two naval squadrons to Kuwait and the Gulf of Aden, plans to have six aircraft carriers, half of the US fleet, by 2035. The battles of the *crisis in the world order* are only beginning.

Chronology

1858 – Following the reforms implemented in the Ottoman Empire, including land reform, foreigners are granted permission to buy land in Palestine.

1882 – After the assassination of Tsar Alexander II in Russia and the subsequent wave of pogroms against Russian Jews begins the first aliyah, the immigration of the Jewish diaspora to Palestine.

1897 – Theodor Herzl founds the World Zionist Organisation and the First Zionist Congress is held in Basel.

1901 – The JNF, The Jewish National Fund, is founded in Basel for the purchase of land in Palestine from local landowners with a ban on reselling it to non-Jews.

1903 – The second aliyah begins, ending around 1914. It will see the influx of 35-40,000 migrants (out of a total Jewish emigration from the Tsarist empire of around 2 million people, mostly arriving in Western Europe and the Americas), with a large number of japonitzki, deserters of the Russian army during the conflict with Japan. They are mostly young urban artisans and poor workers.

1905 – David Ben-Gurion arrives in Palestine as a militant of Po'alei Tzion, founded in Russia in 1903.

1908 – In *July*, the Young Turk Revolution forces Sultan Abdulhamid II to restore the Ottoman constitution of 1876. In Palestine David Ben-Gurion applauds the revolution and demonstrations in support in Jerusalem.

– The PLDC, the Palestine Land Development Company is created with the task of supporting and training Jewish workers for the lands purchased by the JNF, the Jewish National Fund.

1914 – In *October* the European conflict spreads to the Ottoman Empire, which enters the war alongside the Central Empires, Germany and Austria.

1915 – In *July*, a correspondence begins between al-Husayn ibn Ali, Emir of the Hejaz and Sharif of Mecca and Medina, and McMahon, British High Comissioner in Egypt, probing the possibility of an independent Arab state.

1915-16 – Anglo-French offensive on the Gallipoli peninsula which, according to London's intentions, should have quickly put the Ottoman Empire out of action, supported the Russian ally and broken the stalemate on the Western Front.

1916 – *May*. Sykes-Picot Agreement between France and Britain setting out the Allies' war aims in the Ottoman Empire, i.e., an agreed upon partition of spheres of influence between Paris, London and Saint Petersburg. Britain is granted direct and indirect control of an area between present-day Jordan and southern Iraq, with access to the sea via the ports of Haifa and Acre; France would gain Syria and Lebanon, south-eastern Anatolia and northern Iraq; Russia Constantinople with the Straits and Ottoman Armenia. The rest of Palestine is expected to be under international control. In the partition calculations of the powers begins to emerge the crucial importance of the stakes in oil.

1917 – *May*. Declaration by the Secretary General of the Quai d'Orsay Jules Cambon in which France "pledges to assist the revival, through the protection of the Allied powers, of the Jewish nationality" on the lands from which "it has been expelled for many centuries".
– *9th-10th November*. Balfour Declaration. The British Foreign Secretary makes public the declaration in which he pledges to favour the creation in Palestine of a national home for the Jewish people, expressing London's support for the Zionist movement.
– *11th December*. General Allenby's British troops enter Jerusalem accompanied by a delegation of British Zionists. The capture of the city marks the end of Ottoman rule over Palestine.

1918 – *1st October*. Damascus surrenders to an Australian cavalry contingent of the British Imperial Army; a young British officer, Thomas Herbert Lawrence (Lawrence of Arabia) organises a Hashemite "mock conquest" to allow Faysal to proclaim himself king of Syria. Faysal will be the only Arab representative to attend the Versailles conference in order to obtain the endorsement of the victorious powers.
– *30th October*. At Mudros, the Ottoman Empire signs an armistice agreement.

1919 – Po'alei Tzion splits into a left wing and a right wing. From the latter, led by Ben-Gurion, Ahdut ha-Avodah ("Labour Unity") will be born, from which, in 1920, in turn, will arise the Haganah, a paramilitary force and forerunner of the Israeli army, and the Histadrut, the trade union centre of which Ben-Gurion was to become Secretary General.
– At the *end of the year*, the secret Clemenceau-Lloyd George agreement establishes the introduction of mandate regimes over Syria and Palestine, which would be formally sanctioned at the San Remo Conference in April 1920.
– The third *aliyah* begins, lasting until 1923.

1920. *April*. First unrest in Palestine. At the San Remo conference, the Middle East is definitively divided among the European powers according to the criterion of mandates. France is given the mandate over Syria and Lebanon, to Great Britain that over Iraq and Palestine. Within the British mandate, the terms of the Balfour Declaration are retained. Part of the agreement is the cession to France of the Turkish Petroleum Company, the depository of exploration rights in the Ottoman Empire.

– *1st July*. The British military government is replaced by a civilian administration. Jewish riots and terrorist actions begin.

1921 – In *May*, violent clashes break out, first in Jaffa and then elsewhere in Palestine, triggered by incidents during May Day marches between Jewish socialists and communists, with the latter claiming the right to the establishment of a Soviet republic. The clashes between protesters and British police spread to the Arab community causing in six days about one hundred dead and hundreds injured. Herbert Samuel, the first British governor in office, seeing a nationalist confrontation, imposes a brake on Jewish immigration.

– The death of the Grand Mufti of Jerusalem Kamil al-Husseini induces Herbert Samuel to choose a successor from the same family. On *8th May* the chosen successor is Hajj Amin al-Husseini, uncle of Yasser Arafat, who thus occupies the highest religious office in Palestine and comes into possession of financial resources that allow him to play a significant political-religious role.

1922 – London recycles the Hashemites into rulers of the so-called "Sharif Kingdoms" of Iraq, Transjordan and Hejaz, from which they will be removed in 1924 for the benefit of the Saudis. By dividing Transjordan from Palestine, Britain creates de facto the territory of today's Israel and Jordan and one of the dimensions of the "Palestinian question".

1925 – Vladimir Jabotinsky, in opposition to the Zionist leadership, founds Hatzohar (the World Union of Revisionist Zionists).

1928 – *July*. The new Turkish Petroleum sees four main partners (Shell, Anglo-Persian, Compagnie Française des Pétroles and the US consortium Near East Development) holding equal shares of 23.75%. The agreement between the partners indicates the boundaries within which they commit to not carry out separate research activities (self-exclusion clause).

1929 – Violent riots are instigated by the Grand Mufti of Jerusalem Hajj Amin al-Husseini, linked to mutual provocations between Arab and Jewish confessions.

1931 – From splits in the Haganah, the paramilitary organisations Etzel (or Irgun) and Lehi (Stern gang) arise.

1932-33. The Shah of Persia announces the cancellation of the oil concession to Anglo-Persian, which will have to buy back its rights at a high price with minimum royalties of £750,000 per year and the cession of 20% of worldwide profits. Saudi Arabia and Kuwait enter the oil galaxy; the American Socal obtains the first Saudi concession with the exclusion of Iraq Petroleum and Anglo-Persian.

1936-39 – Violent Arab revolt directed mainly against the British occupation and led by the Qassamyun Arab militias, followers of Sheikh Izz al-Din al-Qassam who had borrowed the model of the Muslim Brotherhood in Egypt and had built up a large following among the popular strata of Haifa. The uprising represents the biggest British colonial crisis since that of 1919-21 in Ireland and anticipates the 1946-47 conflict in Palestine, a prodrome of the first Arab-Israeli war.

1937 – The British commission chaired by Lord Peel proposes a partition of Palestine between Arabs and Jews. The proposal is cautiously welcomed by the Zionists, but is rejected by the Arabs. The plan calls for the creation of two States and an international administration for Jerusalem. David Ben-Gurion considers it "the declaration of independence" for the Jewish State since it introduces the formula of "forced relocation" of the Arab population.

1939 – A White Paper is published by the British government led by Neville Chamberlain in which all further Jewish immigration is frozen. David Ben-Gurion, head of the Jewish Agency, states: "We shall fight the White Paper as if there were no war, and the war as if there were no White Paper".

1942 – On *11th May* the Zionist Conference meets at the Biltmore Hotel in New York; it is attended by 600 delegates, including the President of the Jewish Agency in Palestine David Ben-Gurion; the Conference denounces as immoral the restrictions on immigration to Palestine and officially calls for the creation of a Jewish Commonwealth, i.e., a State, in the Palestinian territories; the Conference is regarded as the turning point of the Labour Zionist leadership from a pro-British to a pro-American orientation.

1945 – *22nd March*. The Arab League is born.

1945-1949 – Shoah survivors end up in many cases in camps for displaced persons set up by the Allies in Europe (about 250,000 people in 1947) and, due to immigration restrictions in place in the British Mandate in Palestine, try to reach the region clandestinely; those intercepted at sea by the British end up in prison camps, particularly in Cyprus (around 50,000 people). With the birth of the State of Israel the exodus is unblocked, and, at the end of 1949, the Jewish population reaches one million.

1946 – On *22nd July*, bombing of the King David Hotel in Jerusalem, headquarters of the British military command, by the Irgun. Among the organisers is the future Likud leader Menachem Begin.

1947 – In *February*, London announces its withdrawal from Palestine and in November the UN General Assembly announces the adoption of Resolution 181 for partition. The resolution sees the support of the major powers, but not of London and the Arab League, and provides for the creation of two states, one Jewish and one Arab, and an international regime for Jerusalem. The Arab side rejects partition.
– *7th April*. Syria. The Ba'ath ("Resurrection") party is born, advocating Arab national socialism and Pan-Arabism, with Iraqi, Yemenite and Jordanian branches. From 1954, the Ba'ath will enter into the Syrian executive, marked by strong instability.
– The "Seven Sisters" oil cartel is born between the five major US companies (Socal-Chevron, Jersey-Exxon, Socony-Mobil, Gulf and Texaco) and the European Anglo-Iranian and Shell in three separate agreements in Saudi Arabia, Kuwait and Iran.

1948 – Irregular Arab militias begin to flow into Palestine in January and in March they lay siege to Jerusalem and Tel Aviv. The Haganah begins to receive weapons from Czechoslovakia and the Zionist leadership draws up the Daleth Plan, which provides for the defence of the borders and the eventual destruction of Arab villages inside the Jewish State. The population of dozens of Arab villages is massacred, among them the village of Deir Yassin [9th April] by the paramilitary forces of the Irgun and the Stern gang.
– *14th May*. Proclamation of the State of Israel.
– *15th May*. Official withdrawal of Britain and end of mandate. Five Arab states, Syria and Iraq in the front row, Lebanon, Transjordan and Egypt wage war on the newly formed State: the first Arab-Israeli war begins. For the Palestinians it is the *Nakba* ("disaster"), for the Jews it is the "war of independence". The Arab regular forces, due to poor coordination, less preparation and numerical strength, are defeated.

1949 – Between *February* and *July*, the Rhodes Armistices are signed separately with each of the Arab belligerents, defining the borders of the Jewish State until the 1967 conflict. Israel obtains 78% of Mandate Palestine, the remaining territory is occupied by Egypt and Transjordan. Israel gains a sea outlet in the port of Eilat. The Egyptians occupy Gaza, Transjordan occupies the West Bank.

1950 – *24th April*. The Jordanian parliament votes on the union of Transjordan and the West Bank, annexing it; on the same day King Abdallah ratifies the decision. The Palestinians thus become Jordanian citizens. Egypt takes control of Gaza.

– *5th July*. Israel's so-called "Law of Return" is promulgated, according to which any Jew arriving in Israel is automatically entitled to Israeli citizenship.

1951 – *1st May*. Mossadeq's Persia nationalises the Anglo-Persian Oil Company. A crisis ensues with the British Labour government, which responds with a plan for the military occupation of the island of Abadan, home to the largest refinery in the world, and with an embargo. The American government, ready to exploit British difficulties, attempts a mediation that fails.

1952 – The Egyptian monarchy is deposed by the armed forces led by Gamal Abdel Nasser.

1953 – *19th August*. Persia. The military, in an American-backed coup, overthrows Mossadeq.

1954 – al-Fatah ("The Opening"), a Palestinian political and paramilitary organisation is born.

1956 – Second Arab-Israeli conflict, intertwined with the Suez Crisis. On *26th July* Gamal Abdel Nasser, in response to the US decision to withdraw funding for the Aswan Dam, decides to nationalise the Suez Canal in concession to the Suez Canal Company. France and Great Britain are directly affected by Nasser's decision, France as the owner of the Company, Britain as the main user of the sea route. The British government mobilises 20,000 reservists and the French sends troops to Cyprus. Nasser goes ahead with nationalisation and on 10 September proposes the convening of a conference to amend the Convention of 1888. The US proposes the creation of a "users' association" which is interpreted by the Anglo-French as a means to overcome the nationalisation and use force in the case of Egyptian refusal. On *29th October*, Israel decides to invade Sinai due to the presence of arms deposits of Soviet origin in the Egyptian part of the territory. France and Britain issue an ultimatum for the two countries to withdraw troops 16 km from the Canal and they occupy Suez and Ismailia. To justify the Anglo-French intervention Israel accepts the ultimatum, Egypt rejects it. Counting on the abstention of the US and USSR from the conflict, the Anglo-French bomb the Egyptian airports. On *5th November* Anglo-French paratroopers occupy Port Said while Israel reaches its targets in Sinai. The United States judges the Anglo-French action as a break in the Atlantic front and an act of disloyalty. Nasser is defeated militarily but appears victorious diplomatically. Eisenhower directly invites Eden to halt the operations; England also gives in due to speculation on the pound which makes the country lose 15% of its gold and dollar reserves in the first week of *November* and also because of the US refusal to allow London access to IMF capital. France has to follow. On *7th November* the UN votes for the creation of an international force to replace France and

Great Britain in the occupied territories. Israel must evacuate Sinai and the Gaza strip; Nasser maintains the nationalisation of the Suez Canal and establishes himself as the main Arab leader.

1957 – Enrico Mattei's ENI breaks the golden rule of fifty-fifty profit sharing between the concessionaire company and the producing country and establishes the formula 25-75 in favour of the latter, succeeding in entering the Gulf.

1958 – In *February*, the UAR, United Arab Republic between Syria and Egypt is founded. Damascus, intolerant of Egyptian tutelage, will exit in 1961. In July the pro-British Iraqi monarchy is overthrown by a military coup d'état led by General Abd al-Karim Kassem, a Shia nationalist.

1960 – *10th-14th September*. OPEC, the Organisation of Petroleum Exporting Countries, is founded.

1962-68 – Shia religious guerrilla warfare in Yemen fuelled by the Saudis, British, the Shah's Iranian regime and Israel. Egypt is forced to send 70,000 men.

1963 – The Ba'ath assumes the role of sole party in Syria. In Iraq, General Abd al-Karim Kassem is overthrown.

1964 – *2nd June*. The PLO, the Palestine Liberation Organisation, is born, baptised by Gamal Abdel Nasser's Egypt.

1966 – In Syria, the military component of the Ba'ath led by the Alawite official Hafez al-Assad overthrows the "old guard" of the party, leading to the schism from the Iraqi branch.

1967 – Six Day War. Nasser, alarmed by the possibility of an attack in Syria, after a succession of border clashes and intensified Palestinian guerrilla warfare, deploys 100,000 men in Sinai. After demanding the withdrawal of UN forces, Egypt imposes a blockade of the Strait of Tiran, the Jewish state's maritime outlet on the Red Sea and terminal for Iranian oil supplies. The tension between Israel and Egypt escalates into a sudden rapid armed conflict between *5th* and *10th June* that would become known as the Six Day War. Israeli armoured forces penetrate into Egyptian territory and, after a rapid advance into the Sinai Peninsula, reach the Suez Canal. At the same time, some units occupy Jerusalem and the West Bank. The UN Security Council resolution of *22nd November*, which defines the terms of a settlement of the military conflict remains ineffective and military incidents will continue. With the war, Israel triples its territorial extension, encompassing the Syrian Golan, the West Bank, the whole of Jerusalem, Gaza and the Sinai Peninsula, obtaining an outlet to the Red Sea with the port of Eilat and the interposition of UN forces in Sinai.

– The Khartoum Arab summit takes place in *September*. Nasser obtains the "Declaration of Three No's": no peace, no negotiations and no recognition of Israel, as well as a commitment to the establishment of a Palestinian State accompanied by the so-called "war of attrition" along the Suez Canal.

1967-1970 – War of Attrition. Following the military defeat Egypt, Jordan, Syria and the PLO conduct a low-intensity confrontation along the post-war borders. In *March* 1969, Egypt intensifies military operations along the Suez Canal, with commando attacks, artillery bombardments and air battles over the Canal. From *January* 1970, Israel launches a deep bombing campaign against Egypt. Cairo sees increasing military support from the USSR, including the sending of fighter pilots and anti-aircraft missiles. The confrontation will end on *7th August* 1970 with a cease-fire after a mediation by Washington, fearful of military escalation. Israel will lose between 700 and 1,500 men, Egypt between 5,000 and 6,500 civilians.

1968 – *16th January*. In the House of Commons, the British Prime Minister Harold Wilson announces a withdrawal from the Persian Gulf by 1971.
– The Iraqi regime consolidates around the figure of Saddam Hussein.

1970 – In *September* ("Black September") Palestinian factions in Jordan are expelled from the country for attempting to overthrow the Hashemite monarchy with the aim of establishing a Palestinian State. The repression is violent, with around 4,500 dead, and the survivors are forced to relocate to Lebanon.

1971 – On *17th April* Sadat, who succeeds Nasser, proclaims the new Union of Arab Republics (UAR), joined by Syria and Libya. The expected accession of Sudan, however, arrives late and Syria backs out.

1972 – *July*. Sadat's Egypt expels Moscow's advisers from the country, signalling the pro-American turn in Egyptian policy.
– *August*, Libya and Egypt announce the total merger of the two States within a year. However, the respective leaders are already expressing disagreements over the interpretation of the declaration.
– The OIC, the Organisation for Islamic Cooperation, which groups 57 countries, is founded under Saudi auspices.

1973 – On *6th October*, the fourth Arab-Israeli war breaks out (*Yom Kippur War*). The Egyptians manage to cross the Suez Canal into the Sinai Peninsula. The USSR starts an airlift with 70 daily missions to supply Syria and Egypt. The USA, after some hesitation, floods Israel with 550 missions demonstrating clear logistical superiority. After repelling the Syrian forces and setting up post on the Golan Heights, Israel manages to establish a bridgehead on the western bank of the Canal.

– *16th October*. OPEC delegates decide on a 70% increase in the price of oil. The following day they decide to differentiate supplies based on the position of the consuming countries towards the conflict.
– On *11th November*, at kilometre 101 of the Cairo-Suez road, the ceasefire is signed. Negotiated with the mediation of Kissinger, it allows for the opening of a Conference on the Middle East in Geneva, but does not resolve any of the issues on the table. The war is functional to Sadat's change of alliances that moves Cairo from the Russian orbit into that of the United States. In Israel the war brings about the end of Labour hegemony and the rise of the centre-right Likud party.

1974 – In *October*, the Rabat (Morocco) Congress of the Arab League recognises the PLO as the sole legitimate representative of the Palestinian.

1977 – *19th November*. In a coup de théâtre, Egyptian President Anwar Sadat delivers a speech to the Knesset sanctioning the start of the peace process between Egypt and Israel.

1978 – *17th September*. The Camp David Accords are signed by Begin and Sadat. Egypt becomes the first Arab State to sign a peace treaty with Israel. The issue of the status of Jerusalem is left unresolved.

1979 – *16th January*. *Iran*. The Shah and his family leave the country. Two weeks later, on *1st February*, Ayatollah Khomeini returns to Iran from Paris. On *5th March*, oil exports are resumed, at half the normal pre-crisis level. On *18th March*, incidents occur in Kurdistan, where the Kurds demand an autonomous government. On *8th June*, banks are nationalised; insurance companies follow.
– *4th November*. Protesters storm the US embassy in Tehran, where hostages are taken; following this, President Carter suspends oil imports from Iran from *13th November*.

1980 – *30th July*. With a vote in the Knesset, the Israeli parliament, Jerusalem is defined as the "indivisible capital" of the Jewish State, also claiming the Arab-majority part, East Jerusalem, until 1967 under Jordanian administration.
– *22nd September*. Iran-Iraq War [*First Gulf War*]. The Iraqi army crosses the border into Iran, starting the offensive. The hopes of an easy victory against the Iranian regime, established with the overthrow of the Shah Reza Pahlavi the previous year, prove to be in vain and the conflict enters a phase of bloody equilibrium. After eight years, on *20th August* 1988, a ceasefire comes into force that will put an end to the conflict.

1981 – *6th October*. Sadat is assassinated by a group of Islamic fundamentalists opposed to peace with Israel. He is succeeded by Hosni Mubarak.

1982 – *6th June*. The Lebanese conflict begins, with the Israeli siege of Beirut, aimed at establishing a Lebanese State allied with Israel under Maronite leadership. During the siege of the Lebanese capital on *16th-18th September*, the Maronite Phalangists, in the presence of Israeli troops, are responsible for the massacre of the refugee camps of Sabra and Shatila. The event provokes the resignation of Israeli Defence Minister Ariel Sharon. The war succeeds in the Israeli objective of expelling the PLO from Lebanon, forcing it to fall back to Tunis, but it is among the factors that favour the subsequent establishment of Hezbollah, the Shiite militia party supported by the Islamic Republic of Iran.

1983 – *10th October*. Following difficulties in the Lebanese conflict, Israeli Prime Minister Menachem Begin is forced to pass the baton to Yitzhak Shamir.

1984 – In *September*, Israeli Prime Minister Yitzhak Shamir is forced to launch a coalition government with Shimon Peres' Labour.

1985 – *10th June*. The Israeli army withdraws from Lebanon but maintains its occupation of the so-called "security zone", a strip several kilometres north of the Israeli-Lebanese border.

1987 – Sheikh Ahmed Yassin, a refugee in Gaza since 1948, gives birth to Hamas, the Palestinian offshoot of the Muslim Brotherhood.
– *December*. The first Intifada erupts, a spontaneous movement of the West Bank population that takes both the PLO and Israel by surprise. The movement will be used by Hamas to establish itself as a religious current within Palestinian nationalism, competing with the PLO and al-Fatah.

1988 – *31st July*. King Hussein proclaims the administrative separation of the West Bank from Jordan. The leadership of the PLO recognises the legitimacy of the State of Israel and the creation of a Palestinian State in the West Bank and Gaza. The US endorsement allows the start of direct negotiations that lead to the 1993 Oslo accords.

1990 – *2nd August*. Iraqi troops invade the territory of Kuwait.

1991 – *16th January*. First Gulf War. The United States, in a coalition with 34 other states, attacks Saddam Hussein's Iraq, which had invaded Kuwait. Several Arab League countries are also part of the coalition, among them including Saudi Arabia, Egypt, Syria, Oman, Qatar, Bahrain and Morocco. Libya and Yemen take the opposing side. Jordan declares itself neutral. The ceasefire takes place on February 28th with the military defeat of Iraq.
– *31st October*. Israel-Palestine. The Madrid Peace Conference convenes, held under the auspices of the United States and the Soviet

Union, which brings together the representatives of Israel, Syria, Lebanon, Jordan and the Palestinians.

1993 – Oslo Accords. Arrangements are made to create a single regional market between Israel, Jordan and the Palestinian entity, with diplomatic and financial support from the United States. They provide for the division of the West Bank into three zones, respectively controlled by the PNA, the PNA and Israel and by Israel. However, the Accords will not be followed up because of the creeping colonisation process of Israeli settlers in the West Bank, the competition between Palestinian factions and the difficulty of overcoming the tangled knot of the status of Jerusalem.

1994 – *26th October.* The Israeli-Jordanian Peace Treaty is signed. Jordan thus becomes the second Arab State after Egypt to sign a peace treaty with Israel. Together with the Camp David Accords [1978], the Madrid Conference [1991] and the Oslo Accords [1993], the treaty puts forward a "two-State" solution, which is the same solution as that put forward by mandating Britain in 1937 and 1947.

1995 – *4th November.* The Israeli Prime Minister Yitzhak Rabin is assassinated in Tel Aviv, at the end of a demonstration in support of the Oslo Accords.

1996 – *29th May.* In the elections for prime minister, Benjamin Netanyahu wins over Shimon Peres, thus obtaining his first term in office.

2000 – Second Intifada, which breaks out following the visit of Ariel Sharon, future Israeli Prime Minister, to the Temple Mount, an act considered by Palestinians as a claim to Israeli sovereignty. The Intifada will cause 6,000 deaths among Palestinians and Israelis, consolidate the hegemony of Hamas over Gaza and will end in 2005.

2002 – *29th March.* Operation "Defensive Shield" begins: the Israeli army invades Ramallah and surrounds the Muqata, Arafat's headquarters, which remains barricaded. The military reoccupation of Palestinian cities begins.
– *16th June.* Israel begins the construction of a wall separating Israel from the Palestinian territories.

2003 – Second Gulf War. On *20th March*, an international coalition led by the United States invades Iraq with the declared aim of deposing Saddam Hussein; it is actually a "political" war waged by the USA to deal with Asia and Europe from positions of strength and to anticipate and condition the rise of China and European integration.
– *5th April.* The first US troops reach the centre of Baghdad. The next day, British soldiers enter Basra.
– *15th April.* Italy approves the sending of a military contingent to Iraq.

– *1st May*. US President George W. Bush declares the conclusion of military operations; however, the conflict soon erupts into clashes between local Shia and Sunni factions against the occupiers and between each other.

2005 – In the elections to succeed Yasser Arafat, who died on *11th November* the previous year, Abu Mazen, one of the founders of al-Fatah in the 1950s, emerges victorious.
– In *August*, Israel unilaterally abandons Gaza.

2006 – In the Palestinian parliamentary elections on *25th January*, Hamas wins with 56% of the vote, Fatah reaches 44%.
– *12th July*. Lebanon. Hezbollah launches an attack on Israeli territory; in the following days the Israeli army carries out a large-scale military operation in the south of the country.

2006-07 – Gaza. Palestinian civil war that ends with the consolidation of Hamas and the expulsion of Fatah from the Strip. The result will be the sanctioning of the further division of Palestinian territory between the two nationalist currents.

2007 – *13th June*. Israel. Shimon Peres, former Labour leader, is elected president of the centrist Kadima party.
– *19th September*. The government of Israel formally declares the Gaza Strip an "enemy entity" and cuts off supplies of essential services.

2008 – *19th December*. An armistice declared six months earlier by Hamas expires and is not renewed. In the following days the firing of Qassam rockets from Gaza into Israel intensifies.
– On *27th December*, Israeli raids on the Gaza Strip begin (Operation "Cast Lead").

2009 – *3rd January*. Israeli ground forces penetrate inside the Gaza Strip and encircle Gaza City the following day.
– *18th January*. International peace conference in Sharm el-Sheikh, Egypt. Israel begins its withdrawal and Hamas announces a seven-day truce. The crisis has caused around a thousand casualties.
– *31st March*. Benjamin Netanyahu, also supported by Labour, receives a vote of confidence from parliament and becomes prime minister for the second time.

2011 – *8th April*. Syria. Police fire on Friday protests causing dozens of deaths. President Bashar al-Assad signs a decree on *21st April* repealing the state of emergency that had lasted since 1963, but protests continue. On *31st July*, the army intervenes in Hama, the heart of the rebellion against Assad, shelling the city and besieging it with tanks. On *14th August* the navy is deployed against Latakia, the cradle of the Shiite Alawite minority to which Assad belongs, and machine-guns some neighbourhoods. On *5th October* Syria, Russia and China veto a UN resolution condemning the Syrian regime promoted by France,

Germany, Great Britain and Portugal. On *12th November* the Arab League approves the suspension of Syria and on the 27th a package of sanctions against Damascus. In the meantime the SNC (Syrian National Council), the main organisation of the fragmented opposition cartel and the FSA (Free Syrian Army), its military arm, are formed. Various peace plans will later be proposed, but the bloody civil war will continue between ethnic and religious factions and forces loyal to Assad, with the direct or indirect participation of all powers.
– *31st December* – Iraq. The last 4,000 US troops withdraw. Terrorist attacks increase and political tensions grow between Sunnis and Shiites.

2012 – *14th November*. Israel-Gaza. Israeli bombardment of the Strip in retaliation for Palestinian rocket fire into southern and central Israel. After eight days of clashes, a truce is signed on the 21st; the ceasefire is announced in Cairo by US Secretary of State Hillary Clinton and her Egyptian counterpart Mohamed Kamel Amr.

2014 – *5th January*. Iraq. The city of Falluja is occupied by jihadist militiamen of ISIS (Islamic State of Iraq and the Levant). On *30th April*, in a country devastated by continuous attacks, general elections see the political bloc headed by Shiite Prime Minister Nuri al-Maliki prevail.
– *10th June*. Iraq. ISIS, backed by militias and local Sunni tribes, takes control of Mosul and the next day Tikrit; meanwhile the Kurdish regional government takes control of the oil centre of Kirkuk.
– *20th June*. Iraq. Ayatollah Ali al-Sistani, the country's highest Shia authority, launches an appeal against the violence of ISIS militants. Special units of the Iranian Pasdaran flank the Iraqi officers in the placement of the Shia volunteers who had flocked to the front. On the 29th ISIS proclaims the restoration of the Islamic Caliphate in the territories that have fallen under its control.
– *8th July*. Israel-Gaza. Yet another Israeli military campaign against Hamas (Operation "Protective Edge"). On the 17th the air raids are joined by a ground attack.
– *26th August*. Abu Marzouk, Hamas' chief negotiator in Cairo, and Abu Mazen, president of the PNA, announce the signing of a truce with Israel. The toll of 50 days of clashes is more than 2,000 Palestinian deaths, mostly civilians, and 66 victims among Israeli soldiers.

2015 – *22th January*. Yemen. The Houthi regionalist movement of Shiite confession deposes President Abd Rabbuh Mansur Hadi after an assault on the presidential palace in Sana'a. In February Hadi will be forced to escape, first to Aden and then to Riyadh, Saudi Arabia.
– *17th March*. Israel. Parliamentary elections register a Likud victory. The next day, Benjamin Netanyahu's new government is formed.

– *25th March*. Yemen. Saudi Arabia, leading a coalition of eight Sunni-Arab countries (Egypt, Morocco, Jordan, Sudan, the United Arab Emirates, Kuwait, Qatar and Bahrain), begins carrying out air strikes in Yemen against the Shia Houthi movement, announcing the start of Operation Decisive Storm, which will end on *21st April*.

2017 – *6th December*. US President Donald Trump says in a statement that he formally recognises Jerusalem as Israel's capital, with the relocation of the US embassy from Tel Aviv to West Jerusalem. The State Department hastens to clarify that the move will only take place from 2020.

– *13th December*. The OIC, the Organisation of Islamic Cooperation, approves a Turkish-Malaysian-Iranian motion recognising East Jerusalem as the Palestinian capital.

2019 – Israel. In *March*, at a party with the Likud leadership, Israeli Prime Minister Benjamin Netanyahu says: "The transfer of money (to Hamas) is part of a strategy to divide the Palestinians in Gaza and the West Bank. Anyone who opposes the creation of a Palestinian State must support the transfer of money from Qatar to Hamas".

– *9th April*. Israel. In the parliamentary elections Benjamin Netanyahu's Likud and the Blue and White political alliance led by Benny Gantz obtain the same number of seats (35); neither will succeed in forming a government. On 17th *September* new consultations will be held with the same result.

– *14th September*. Saudi Arabia. Aramco installations and oil fields are attacked with drones and cruise missiles; the attack is claimed by the Yemeni Shiite Houthi militias, but Iran's role in the operation is evident.

– *11th December*. Saudi Arabia. Oil group Saudi Aramco makes its debut on the stock exchange, becoming the world's top company in market capitalisation.

2020 – *28th January*. Israel-Palestine. Donald Trump unveils a peace plan that he anticipated in 2017 as the "deal of the century". The plan envisages de jure recognition not only of Jerusalem, but also of the Israeli settlements created after 1967 and on the Golan, annexed to Israel by Netanyahu before the *September* 2019 parliamentary elections. The PNA would have to cede 30% of the West Bank, including the entire Jordan Valley. In return the Palestinian authority, without Hamas-controlled Gaza, would receive a mini-capital in Abu Dis (a suburb of Jerusalem) and $50 billion in investment; this would include the recognition of a limited statehood, with security in the hands of Israel. A plan that, for the PNA, is worse compared to what was foreseen by the 1993 Oslo accords.

– *15th September.* Abraham Accords. Agreements are established between Israel, the United Arab Emirates and Bahrain, sponsored by the United States, aimed at normalising mutual diplomatic relations. Egypt, Jordan, Morocco and Sudan also participate in the agreements.

2021 – *6th May.* Jerusalem. The eviction of a few dozen Palestinian families in the Arab quarter of Jerusalem, Sheikh Jarrah, claimed by an association of Jewish settlers on the basis of a sales contract signed with the Ottoman authorities in 1876, triggers the "eleven-day war". Intertwining with the affair of Sheikh Jarrah are the demonstrations of the Jewish religious right to celebrate the conquest of East Jerusalem in 1967, with Palestinian counter-demonstrations, culminating in the blocking of access to the Temple Mount and the subsequent clearance of demonstrators by Israeli police, with hundreds of injuries and arrests. The president of the PNA Mahmoud Abbas takes the opportunity to suspend legislative and presidential elections, the first since 2006, in which Hamas had agreed to participate.

– *10th May.* Hamas opens the confrontation with Israel with an initial salvo of Qassam missiles towards Jerusalem and later against major Israeli urban centres, including Tel Aviv; this triggers a military retaliation conducted with drones, air raids and artillery. On *21st May*, Israel and Hamas agree on a ceasefire: in eleven days there will be 260 victims, the vast majority of them Palestinian.

– *15th May.* Palestinians and Israeli Arabs take part in a general strike called by trade unions in Gaza, the West Bank and Israel against discriminatory policies and against Israel's bombardment of the Gaza Strip.

– *13th June.* Naftali Bennett succeeds Benjamin Netanyahu as prime minister. He is the first Orthodox Jew to lead the Israeli government. Decisive in breaking the electoral deadlock that had lasted four rounds in two years is the role of Ra'am, the United Arab List, which thus becomes the first Arab formation to be part of a governing coalition.

2022 – *1st November.* Israel. Likud wins the legislative elections, Benjamin Netanyahu forms his sixth government.

2023 – *4th January.* Israel. Newly appointed Justice Minister Yariv Levin announces the judicial reform project of Benjamin Netanyahu's government, aimed at limiting the power of the Supreme Court and granting the governing coalition a majority in the committee that appoints judges; a protest movement begins that will intensify in the months to follow. The confrontation over the reform will put the Likud itself under strain and will draw criticism from the security and military apparatuses, as well as sparking a clash with the judiciary.

- *10th March.* Saudi Arabia and Iran sign an agreement in Beijing sponsored by China to normalise diplomatic relations. The understanding signals increasing diplomatic activism by Beijing in the area.
- *7th October.* Surprise attack along the frontier between Israel and the Palestinian enclave of Gaza; the Hamas offensive is unprecedented in its modality, a massive incursion into Israeli territory, and brutality, with about 200 hostages and over a thousand vicims: 300 soldiers and several dozen Arab-Israeli, Palestinian or Druze wage earners and Thai, Filipino and Nepalese immigrant workers employed as labourers in the kibbutzim are killed. The retaliation unleashed by Israel starts the Gaza war.
- *9th October.* Israel decides to intensify the blockade of the Gaza Strip and calls up 300,000 reservists.
- *27th October.* During the night, Israel launches a full-scale invasion of Gaza: Operation "Iron Swords" begins. A few days later evacuations begin through the Rafah crossing of holders of foreign passports. For the majority of Palestinians in Gaza the crossing remains closed.
- *November.* Yemen. Yemeni Shiite and pro-Iranian Houthi militias carry out a series of attacks in the Red Sea, particularly targeting ships from countries close to Israel, using missiles and drones. The attacks have a significant impact on trade transiting the Suez Canal, forcing many ships to avoid the Red Sea.
- On *11th November*, the joint summit of the Arab League and the Organisation of Islamic Cooperation is held in Riyadh. Saudi Arabia, faced with the internal split in the League between the more rejectionist anti-Israel positions, led by Algeria, and the more moderate positions of the Arab monarchies and Egypt, dilutes the confrontation by merging the two summits. The assembly pronounces itself in favour of condemning Israel and relaunching the two-State solution. The OIC's joint communiqué effectively reiterates the 2002 plan of Abd Allah, grandfather of Saudi prince Mohammed bin Salman, which conditioned diplomatic normalisation with Israel on the creation of a Palestinian State on the basis of the 1967 borders.
- *19th December.* Yemen. US and Britain launch naval coalition "Prosperity Guardian" in the Red Sea in response to Houthi attacks.

2024 – *3rd January.* Iran. In Kerman, an attack claimed by the self-styled Islamic State results in around 100 dead and 200 wounded among the crowd gathered to commemorate the death of Iranian general Qasem Soleimani, killed four years earlier during a US attack in Iraq.

- *11th-12th January.* Yemen. Anglo-American raid against Houthi positions in Yemen. Countries supporting the attack include Australia, Bahrain, Canada and the Netherlands. Ten countries, including Germany and Denmark, sign a joint communiqué of maximum support for Washington and London's initiative. They do not include Italy.

- *16th-18th January.* Missile exchange between Iran and Pakistan in the border region of Balochistan, an area of irrendentist tensions of the Baloch, a Persian-speaking but Sunni ethnic group. On the Iranian side, the military action is intended to hit the alleged perpetrators of the bloody attack on 3rd January in Kerman, but is also considered an omnidirectional signal.
- *19th February.* Red Sea. France, Germany, Greece and Italy launch the Aspides mission to escort merchant ships in the Persian Gulf, Gulf of Oman, Gulf of Aden and Red Sea with the aim of shooting down missiles or drones launched by the Houthis.
- *1st April.* In Damascus, a targeted attack on the headquarters of the Iranian representation led by Israel leads to the killing of seven officers of the Pasdaran, including some senior officers responsible for logistical coordination with the networks of pro-Iranian Shiite militias operating in Lebanon, Syria, Iraq and Yemen.
- *13th-19th April.* Missile exchange between Iran and Israel. From 7th October, the Jewish State reportedly eliminated 18 Pasdaran officers without triggering an Iranian response. However, the Damascus attack is considered by Tehran as a violation of a "red line": an attack on its own interests and national sovereignty. The Iranian response is massive: more than 300 drones and missiles are launched on the night of *13th-14th April*, but the vast majority are intercepted by the combined action of the US, Israel, Britain, France, Germany and Jordan by activating the MEAD, the Middle East Air Defence set up after the signing of the Abraham Accords. Tel Aviv retaliates in turn by launching one or two missiles towards the Isfahan air base.
- *21-23 July.* Chinese Foreign Minister Wang Yi brings together 14 Palestinian organisations, including Hamas and Fatah, signing the "Beijing Declaration", an agreement aimed at "ending divisions and strengthening Palestinian unity" and under which the PLO is recognised as the "sole legitimate representative" of the Palestinians.
- *30-31 July.* Israel continues the series of targeted assassinations of leading members of Hezbollah and Hamas. On the 30th, in Beirut, Fuad Shukr, Hezbollah military commander, is killed. The following day, Ismail Haniyeh, the political leader of Hamas, is shot dead in Tehran. Iran threatens retaliation.
- *25 August.* Israel's pre-emptive attack on Hezbollah positions in Lebanon, which, in turn, launches hundreds of rockets towards Israeli territory in response to the killing of Fuad Shukr.

Bibliography

Anthology, *Reactionary Terrorism, Imperialist Europeanism, Communist Internationalism*, éditions Science Marxiste, 2017

Abitbol Michel, *Histoire d'Israël*, Perrin, Paris 2024

Abu Iyad - Rouleau Eric, *My Home. My Land. A Narrative of the Palestinian Struggle*, Times Books, New York 1981

Aburish Said, *Arafat, from Defender to Dictator*, Bloomsbury Publishing, London 1998

Acheson Dean, *Present at the Creation. My Years in the State Department*, W.W. Norton, New York 1969

Ayad Christophe, *Géopolitique du Hezbollah*, PUF, Paris 2024

Baker James, *The Politics of Diplomacy*, Putnam, New York 1995

Barnavi Eli, *Storia d'Israele. Dalla nascita dello Stato all'assassinio di Rabin*, Bompiani, Milan 1996

Barr James, *Lords of the Desert*, Basic Books, New York 2018

Bar-Zohar Michael, *Shimon Peres. The Biography*, Random House, New York 2007

Bass Warren, *Support Any Friend*, Oxford University Press, Oxford (UK) 2003

Ben-Gurion David, *From Class to Nation*, 1933

Bensoussan Georges, *Il sionismo. Una storia politica e intellettuale*, 2 vols, Einaudi, Turin 2007

Black Edwin, *The Transfer Agreement. The Dramatic Story of the Pact Between the Third Reich and Jewish Palestine*, Macmillan, London 1984

Black Ian, *Enemies and Neighbours. Arabs and Jews in Palestine and Israel, 1917-2017*, Penguin, London 2018

Bregman Ahron, *Cursed Victory: A History of Israel and the Occupied Territories*, Allen Lane, London 2014

Brizzi Giovanni, *70 d.C. La conquista di Gerusalemme*, Laterza, Rome-Bari 2017

Bush George Sr – Scowcroft Brent, *A World Transformed*, Alfred Knopf, New York 1998

Caridi Paola, *Hamas. Che cos'è e cosa vuole il movimento radicale palestinese*, Feltrinelli, Milan 2009

Cervetto Arrigo, *Opere*, Edizioni Lotta Comunista, Milan 2015-2024

vol. 1, *L'involucro politico*, Edizioni Lotta Comunista, Milano 1994

– "La crisi della teoria politica borghese", *Lotta Comunista*, December 1977

vol. 2, *Forze e forme del mutamento italiano*, Edizioni Lotta Comunista, Milano 1997

– "I semi avvelenati della politica mediterranea", *Lotta Comunista*, gennaio 1986

vol. 3, *L'imperialismo unitario*, Milan 1981 [*Unitary Imperialism* Vol I (2014) – Vol II (2016) – éditions Science Marxiste]

– "Il corso dell'imperialismo nel 1953/54", Relazione alla IV Conferenza Nazionale dei GAAP, Bologna 31st October – 1st November 1954

– "Nel triplice nodo di Suez convergono le contraddizioni dell'imperialismo unitario", *L'Impulso*, 25th September 1956

– "Egitto: Nasser è diventato adulto", *Azione Comunista*, 31st July 1957

– "Medio Oriente: la penetrazione statunitense", *Orientamenti*, September 1957

– "Venezuela: i condizionamenti del petrolio favoriscono l'imperialismo più forte", *Azione Comunista*, 1st February 1958

– "Ruolo oggettivo della Cina nella lotta internazionale della classe operaia", *Azione Comunista*, 31st December 1960

vol. 4, *La contesa mondiale*, Edizioni Lotta Comunista, Milan 1990

– "La nuova contesa imperialistica raggiunge il Sud Atlantico", *Lotta Comunista*, June 1982

– "L'invasione del Libano riapre la sanguinosa partita nel Medio Oriente", *Lotta Comunista*, July 1982

vol. 4, *Il mondo multipolare*. 1990-1995, Edizioni Lotta Comunista, October 1996

– "Bilancia americana del Golfo", *Lotta Comunista*, December 1990

– "La mezza guerra nel Golfo", *Lotta Comunista*, January 1991

– "Primato militare e primato economico nella bilancia in Asia", *Lotta Comunista*, April 1991

vol. 16, "Relazione al Convegno Nazionale", 3rd-4th December 1977

vol. 17, "Relazione al Centro Nazionale Allargato", 2nd June 1978

Cohen Samy, *Israël, une démocratie fragile*, Fayard, Paris 2021

Darwin John, *The Empire Project. The Rise and Fall of the British World-System*, 1830-1970, Cambridge University Press, Cambridge and New York 2009

De Simone Gianluca, *Grande Medio Oriente*, Edizioni Lotta Comunista, Milan 2016

Diner Dan, *Tutta un'altra guerra. Il secondo conflitto mondiale e la Palestina ebraica (1935-1942)*, Bollati Boringhieri, Turin 2023

Eden Anthony, *Le memorie di Sir Anthony Eden, 1931-1957*, Garzanti, Milan 1960

Farsakh Leila, *Palestinian Labour Migration to Israel. Labour, Land and Occupation*, Routledge, New York 2005

Filiu Jean-Pierre, *Histoire de Gaza*, Fayard, Paris 2012

Fromkin David, *A Peace to End all Peace: The Fall of the Ottoman Empire and the Creation of the Modern Middle East*, André Deutsch, London 1989.

Fuller John Frederick Charles, *Armament and History. A Study of the Influence of Armament on History from the Dawn of Classical Warfare to the Second World War*, Eyre & Spottiswoode, London 1946

Gleis Joshua L. – Berti Benedetta, *Hezbollah and Hamas. A Comparative Study*, JHU Press, Baltimore 2012

Gorenberg Gershom, *The Accidental Empire. Israel and the Birth of the Settlements, 1967-1977*, Times Books, New York 2006

Gresh Alain, *OLP. Histoire et stratégies vers l'État palestinien*, SPAG-Papyrus, Paris 1983

–*Israël, Palestine. Vérités sur un conflit*, Fayard, Paris 2024

Gresh Alain - Vidal Dominique, *Palestine 47. Un partage avorté*, Complexe, Bruxelles 1992

Grey Edward, *Twenty-Five Years: 1892-1916*, 1926

Horne Alistair, *La guerra d'Algeria*, Mondadori, Milano 2012

Hourcade Bernard, *Géopolitique de l'Iran*, Armand Colin, Paris 2010

Houser Trevor - Mohan Shashank, *Fueling Up. The Economic Implications of America's Oil and Gas Boom*, Peterson Institute for International Economics, Washington 2014

Jabotinsky Vladimir, *The Iron Wall*, 1923

Kamel Lorenzo, *Terra contesa. Israele, Palestina e il peso della storia,* Carocci, Roma 2023

Kedourie Eli – Haim Sylvia G., *Zionism and Arabism in Palestine and Israel*, Routledge, London 1982

Kennedy Paul, *The Rise of the Anglo-German Antagonism, 1860–1914*, Allen & Unwin, Winchester, Massachusetts 1980

Kepel Gilles, *Jihad: The Trail of Political Islam*, Belknap Press, Cambridge, Massachusetts 2002.

Kissinger Henry, *The White House Years*, Little, Brown and Company, Boston 1979

– *Years of Upheaval*, Simon & Schuster, New York 1982

– *Years of Renewal*, Simon & Schuster, New York 1999

– *World Order*, Penguin Books, London 2014

La Barbera Guido, *L'instabile ordine del multipolarismo. 1995-2001*, Edizioni Lotta Comunista, Milan 2002

– "Ipotetico concerto multipolare delle potenze continentali", *Lotta Comunista*, September 2001

Wars of the Crisis in the World Order, éditions Science Marxiste, 2024

– "Ukraine and Gaza in Europe's Social and Political Cycle", *Internationalism*, January 2024

Laqueur Walter, *History of Zionism. From the French Revolution to the Establishment of the State of Israel*, Knopf Doubleday, New York 2003

Laurens Henry, *Les crises d'Orient. La naissance du Moyen-Orient 1914-1949*, vol. II, Fayard, Paris 2019

Lenin (Vladimir Ilyich Ulyanov), *On the Right of Nations to Self-Determination* (1914), Progress Publishers Moscow, LCW Vol 20. 1977

– *Preliminary Draft Theses on the National and the Colonial Questions*. Lenin Collected Works, vol 31 Progress Publishers, Moscow

Liddell Hart Basil, *The Real War 1914–1918,* Faber & Faber, London 1930

Lockman Zachary, *Comrades and Enemies. Arab and Jewish Workers in Palestine, 1906-1948*, University of California Press, Berkeley 1996

Lowe Keith, *Savage Continent: Europe in the Aftermath of World War II*, Penguin, London 2013

Marx Karl, *Il 18 brumaio di Luigi Bonaparte*, in Marx-Engels Opere, vol. 11, Edizioni Lotta Comunista, Milan 2021

Marzano Arturo, *Storia dei sionismi. Lo Stato degli ebrei da Herzl a oggi*, Carocci, Rome 2017

McMeekin Sean, *The Ottoman Endgame: War, Revolution, and the Making of the Modern Middle East, 1908–1923*, Penguin, London 2015

Mejcher Helmut, *Sinai, 5 giugno 1967: il conflitto arabo-israeliano,* Il Mulino, Bologna 2000

Montefiore Simon Sebag, *Jerusalem: The Biography,* Orion Publishing Group, London 2012

Morris Benny, *Righteous Victims: A History of the Zionist–Arab Conflict, 1881–1999,* Vintage, London 2001

– *1948: A History of the First Arab-Israeli War,* Yale University Press, New Haven 2009

Motosi Giulio, "Tirpitz and Kautsky in Beijing", *Internationalism*, May 2023

Naquet Pierre Vidal, *Gli ebrei, la memoria e il presente*, Editori Riuniti, Rome 1985

Nixon Richard M., *Memoirs of Richard Nixon*, 2 vol., Grand Central Publishing, New York 1979

Oren Michael B., *Six Days of War: June 1967 and the Making of the Modern Middle East*, Presidio Press, Novato 2002

Pappé Ilan, *The Rise and Fall of a Palestinian Dynasty. The Husaynis, 1700-1948*, University of California Press, Berkeley 2010

– *A History of Modern Palestine: One Land, Two Peoples*, Cambridge University Press 2004

– *The Ethnic Cleansing of Palestine*, Oneworld Publications Ltd, London 2006

Pfeffer Anshel, *Bibi. The Turbulent Life and Times of Benjamin Netanyahu*, C. Hurst & Co., London 2020

Primakov Yevgeny, *Russia and the Arabs. Behind the Scenes in the Middle East from the Cold War to the Present*, Basic Books, New York 2009

Quandt William - Jabber Fuad - Lesch Ann, *The Politics of Palestinian Nationalism*, University of California Press, Berkeley 1973

Razoux Pierre, *La guerre Iran-Irak. Première guerre du Golfe 1980-1988*, Perrin, Paris 2013

Reynolds Michael, *Shattering Empires. The Clash and Collapse of the Ottoman and Russian Empires 1908-1918*, Cambridge University Press, Cambridge (UK) 2011

Rogan Eugene, *The Fall of the Ottomans: The Great War in the Middle East*, Basic Books, New York 2016

– *The Arabs: A History*, Penguin, London 2009

Rubin Barry, *Revolution Until Victory? The Politics and History of the PLO*, Harvard University Press, Cambridge (USA) 1996

Rubinstein Danny, *Il mistero Arafat*, UTET Università, Turin 2003

Said Edward W., *The Question of Palestine*, Vintage, New York 1992

Sampson Anthony, *The Seven Sisters. The Great Oil Companies & the World They Shaped*, Viking Press, New York 1975

Segev Tom, *The Seventh Million: The Israelis and the Holocaust*, Picador, London 2000

– *One Palestine Complete. Jews and Arabs Under the British Mandate*, Metropolitan Books, New York 2000

– *1967. Israel, the War, and the Year That Transformed the Middle East*, Metropolitan Books, New York 2007

– *A State at Any Cost. The Life of David Ben-Gurion*, Farrar, Straus and Giroux, New York 2019

Segre Dan Vittorio, *Le metamorfosi di Israele*, UTET, Turin 2007

Shafir G., "Zionism and Colonialism. A Comparative Approach", in Pappé Ilan, *The Israel/Palestine Question*, Routledge, London 1999

Shahak Israel, "A History of Concept of Transfer in Zionism", *Journal of Palestine Studies*, vol. 18, n. 3 (Spring, 1989), Taylor & Francis, Milton Park (UK) 1989

Shindler Colin, *The Rise of the Israeli Right. From Odessa to Hebron*, Cambridge University Press, Cambridge (UK) 2015

Shlaim Avi, *Collusion Across the Jordan. King Abdullah, the Zionist Movement, and the Partition of Palestine*, Columbia University Press, New York 1988

– *The Iron Wall. Israel and the Arab World*, Penguin Books, London 2001

– *Lion of Jordan. The Life of King Hussein in War and Peace*, Penguin Books, London 2008

Solomon Robert, *The International Monetary System, 1945-1981*, Harper & Row, New York 1982

Soutou Georges-Henri, note to Aron Raymond, *Les articles du Figaro, La guerre froide. 1947-1955* (vol. I); *La coexistence. 1955-1965* (vol. II), Éditions de Fallois, Paris 1994

Sternhell Zeev, *Aux origines d'Israël: Entre nationalisme et socialisme*, Fayard, Paris 1996

Tertrais Bruno, *La guerre des mondes. Le retour de la géopolitique et le choc des empires,* Éditions de l'Observatoire, Paris 2023

Thomas Hugh, *The Suez Affair,* Weidenfeld & Nicolson, London 1967

Veidlinger, Jeffrey, *In the Midst of Civilized Europe: The Pogroms of 1918–1921 and the Onset of the Holocaust,* Metropolitan Books, New York 2021

Wall Bennett H., *Growth in a Changing Environment. A History of Standard Oil Company (New Jersey), 1950-1972, and Exxon Corporation, 1972-1975,* McGraw Hill Book Company, New York 1988

Yergin Daniel, *The Prize, The Epic Quest for Oil, Money and Power,* Simon & Schuster, New York 1992

– "The Global Impact of US Shale", *Project Syndicate*, January 8th 2014

Zerthal Idith – Eldar Akiva, *Lords of the Lands. The War Over Israel's Settlements in the Occupied Territories, 1967-2007,* Nation Books, New York 2009

Newspapers and magazines

Al Arabiya – Riyadh
Asharq al-Awsat – London
Avanti! – Rome
Bandiera Rossa – Rome
Business Week – New York
Devar – Tel Aviv
Economist (The) – London
Figaro (Le) – Paris
Financial Times – London
Foreign Affairs – New York
Fortune – New York
Frankfurter Allgemeine Zeitung (FAZ) – Frankfurt
Global Times – Beijing
Grand Continent (Le) – Paris
Haaretz – Tel Aviv
Hindustan Times – New Delhi
Israel Hayom – Tel Aviv
Japan Times (The) – Tokyo
Jerusalem Post (The) – Jerusalem
Kompas – Jakarta
Maariv – Tel Aviv
Monde (Le) – Paris
Monde Diplomatique (Le) – Paris
Neue Freie Presse – Vienna
New York Times (The) – New York
Nikkei (Nihon Keizai Shimbun) – Tokyo
Nuova Unità – Rome
Petroleum Weekly – New York
Pravda – Moscow
Project Syndicate – New York
Reuters – London
RIA Novosti – Moscow
Rivoluzione Proletaria – Milan
Sabah – Istanbul
Red Star – Moscow
Straits Times (The) – Singapore
Times (The) – London
Washington Post (The) – Washington
Yedioth Ahronoth - Tel Aviv

Index of Names

A

B

C

D

E

M

N

O

P

Q-R

S

T

U-V

W-Y-Z

Books published by Éditions Science Marxiste

English

Texts

Arrigo Cervetto	CLASS STRUGGLES AND THE REVOLUTIONARY PARTY
Arrigo Cervetto	THE DIFFICULT QUESTION OF TIMES
Arrigo Cervetto	THE POLITICAL SHELL
Arrigo Cervetto	METHOD AND THE SCIENCE-PARTY
Arrigo Cervetto	UNITARY IMPERIALISM, VOLUME I
Arrigo Cervetto	UNITARY IMPERIALISM, VOLUME II
Nicola Capelluto	THE CRISIS IN GLOBAL RELATIONS
Renato Pastorino	THE UNPRECEDENTED TASK
Renato Pastorino	THEIR POLITICS AND OURS
Guido La Barbera	THE NEW STRATEGIC PHASE
Guido La Barbera	LOTTA COMUNISTA: THE ORIGINS 1943-1952
Guido La Barbera	LOTTA COMUNISTA: TOWARDS THE STRATEGY-PARTY 1953-1965
Guido La Barbera	LOTTA COMUNISTA: THE BOLSHEVIK MODEL 1965-1995
Guido La Barbera	THE CRISIS IN THE WORLD ORDER AND THE PANDEMIC OF THE CENTURY
Guido La Barbera	WARS OF THE CRISIS IN THE WORLD ORDER
Anthology	REACTIONARY TERRORISM, IMPERIALIST EUROPEANISM, COMMUNIST INTERNATIONALISM
Anthology	THE WAR IN GAZA An Internationalist Response

Analyses

Federico Dalvit	EUROPE IN THE GLOBAL COLLISIONS
Donato Bianchi	RUSSIA AT WAR IN THE CRISIS OF THE WORLD ORDER

Documents

David B. Rjazanov	THE ORIGINS OF THE FIRST INTERNATIONAL
G.G. Cavicchioli (ed.)	OCTOBER 1917 100 Years, 100 Militants of the Revolution
G.G. Cavicchioli – E. Gianni (eds.)	1919 THE COMMUNIST INTERNATIONAL 100 Years, 100 Militants of the World Party
Anthology	ENGELS Revolutionary Science and Passion
M. Mancini – E. Gianni (eds.)	1871 THE PARIS COMMUNE 150th Anniversary, The Commune Council Militants

Publications for young people

Arrigo Cervetto	LENIN AND THE CHINESE REVOLUTION Lenin – Inflammable Material in World Politics and other Writings
Friedrich Engels	ANTIDÜHRING & THE ROLE OF FORCE IN HISTORY Arrigo Cervetto – The Discovery of Politics
V.I. Lenin	WHAT IS TO BE DONE? Arrigo Cervetto – The Decisive Struggle
V.I. Lenin	"LEFT-WING" COMMUNISM, AN INFANTILE DISORDER Arrigo Cervetto – The Time of Lenin's Clarity

V.I. Lenin	IMPERIALISM, THE HIGHEST STAGE OF CAPITALISM Arrigo Cervetto – The Marxist Theory of International Relations
V.I. Lenin	THE STATE AND REVOLUTION Arrigo Cervetto – The Restoration of Marxist Theory
Karl Marx	WAGE LABOUR AND CAPITAL / WAGES, PRICE AND PROFIT
Karl Marx	THE CIVIL WAR IN FRANCE Arrigo Cervetto – The Political Form at Last Discovered
Anthology	MAY DAY IN WORKING-CLASS HISTORY
–	OUR INTERNATIONALIST STRUGGLE The Direction of the New Strategic Phase

French

Collection Textes

Arrigo Cervetto	LA DIFFICILE QUESTION DES TEMPS
Arrigo Cervetto	LUTTES DE CLASSE ET PARTI RÉVOLUTIONNAIRE
Arrigo Cervetto	LE MONDE MULTIPOLAIRE 1990-1995
Arrigo Cervetto	L'ENVELOPPE POLITIQUE
Arrigo Cervetto	MÉTHODE ET PARTI-SCIENCE
Arrigo Cervetto	L'IMPÉRIALISME UNITAIRE Tome I, 1950-1967
Arrigo Cervetto	L'IMPÉR IALISME UNITAIRE Tome II, 1959-1980
Arrigo Cervetto	LA CONFRONTATION MONDIALE
Guido La Barbera	LA CRISE DU CAPITALISME D'ÉTAT
Guido La Barbera	L'EUROPE ET LA GUERRE
Guido La Barbera	L'ORDRE INSTABLE DU MULTIPOLARISME
Guido La Barbera	L'EUROPE ET L'ÉTAT
Guido La Barbera	L'EUROPE, L'ASIE ET LA CRISE
Guido La Barbera	CRISE GLOBALE ET RESTRUCTURATION EUROPÉENNE
Guido La Barbera	LA NOUVELLE PHASE STRATÉGIQUE
Guido La Barbera	LOTTA COMUNISTA – LE GROUPE D'ORIGINE, 1943-1952
Guido La Barbera	LOTTA COMUNISTA – VERS LE PARTI STRATÉGIE, 1953-1965
Guido La Barbera	LOTTA COMUNISTA – LE MODÈLE BOLCHEVIQUE, 1965-1995
Guido La Barbera	CRISE DE L'ORDRE ET PANDÉMIE SÉCULAIRE
Guido La Barbera	LES GUERRES DE LA CRISE DE L'ORDRE
Renato Pastorino	LA TÂCHE INÉDITE
Renato Pastorino	LEUR POLITIQUE ET LA NÔTRE Une nouvelle génération de communistes en Europe
Nicola Capelluto	LA CRISE DES RELATIONS GLOBALES
Nicola Capelluto	CRISE DE LA DETTE ET CRISE DE L'ORDRE
Paolo Rivetti	LES SYNDICATS DANS LA RESTRUCTURATION EUROPÉENNE (2008-2015) et en annexe: Considérations sur les luttes politiques en France (2006-2012)
Roberto Casella	BATAILLES ET PRINCIPES POUR UNE POLITIQUE COMMUNISTE
Anthologie	LA GUERRE À GAZA Une réponse internationaliste

Collection Classiques

Marx – Engels	MANIFESTE DU PARTI COMMUNISTE En appendice notes sur les premières éditions du Manifeste et sur sa diffusion
Lev Trotsky	LES GUERRES BALKANIQUES 1912-1913
Friedrich Engels	NOTES SUR LA GUERRE FRANCO-ALLEMANDE DE 1870-1871 Préface de Lev Trotsky

Collection Analyses

Nicola Capelluto – Franco Palumberi	ÉNERGIE ET PÉTROLE DANS L'AFFRONTEMENT IMPÉRIALISTE
Roberto Casella	LE SIÈCLE DES GÉANTS DE L'ASIE – I. LA CHINE (1995-2012)
Roberto Casella	LE SIÈCLE DES GÉANTS DE L'ASIE – II. L'INDE (1998-2012)
Gianluca De Simone	GRAND MOYEN-ORIENT Crises et guerres de la nouvelle phase stratégique
G. Motosi – P. Nardini	LA BATAILLE MONDIALE DE L'ACIER
Federico Dalvit	L'EUROPE DANS LES COLLISIONS MONDIALES
Franco Palumberi	L'AUTOMOBILE ET LE DÉFI ÉLECTRIQUE
Donato Bianchi	LA RUSSIE EN GUERRE DANS LA CRISE DE L'ORDRE
Giulio Motosi	LA DÉMOCRATIE IMPÉRIALISTE EN CHINE
F. Dalvit – J. Van Langenhove	L'EUROPE DANS LA CRISE DE L'ORDRE
Piermaria Davoli	DÉMOGRAPHIE ET MIGRATIONS DANS LE CHANGEMENT D'ÉPOQUE

Collection Documents

G. Munis	LEÇONS D'UNE DÉFAITE, PROMESSE DE VICTOIRE Critique et théorie de la révolution espagnole 1930-1939
Paul Frölich	AUTOBIOGRAPHIE 1890-1921
P. Frölich – R. Lindau – A. Schreiner – J. Walcher	RÉVOLUTION ET CONTRE-RÉVOLUTION EN ALLEMAGNE 1918-1920
Paul Frölich	IMPÉRIALISME, GUERRE ET LUTTE DE CLASSES EN ALLEMAGNE 1914-1918
Anthologie	MARX Scientifique et révolutionnaire
Anthologie	LÉNINE Conscience et volonté révolutionnaires
Anthologie	ENGELS Science et passion révolutionnaires
Anthologie	Le Premier Mai. Dans l'histoire du mouvement ouvrier
G.G. Cavicchioli (dir. par)	OCTOBRE 1917 100 ans, 100 militants de la révolution
G.G. Cavicchioli – E. Gianni (dir. par)	1919 L'INTERNATIONALE COMMUNISTE 100 ans, 100 militants du parti mondial
M. Mancini – E. Gianni (dir. par)	1871-2021 LA COMMUNE DE PARIS 150 ans, Les militants du conseil de la Commune
M. Parri (dir. par)	BÉNÉVOLAT ANARCHISTE ET SOCIALISTE AUX TEMPS DU CHOLÉRA

Bibliothèque jeunes

Anthologie	LE RACISME EST CHEZ NOUS
Lénine	QUE FAIRE? Cervetto – La lutte décisive
Lénine	L'IMPÉRIALISME, STADE SUPRÊME DU CAPITALISME Cervetto – La théorie marxiste des relations internationals
Lénine	L'ÉTAT ET LA RÉVOLUTION Cervetto – La restauration de la théorie marxiste
Lénine	LA MALADIE INFANTILE DU COMMUNISME (LE «COMMUNISME DE GAUCHE ») Cervetto – Le temps de la clarté de Lénine
Lénine	MATÉRIALISME ET EMPIRIOCRITICISME Notes critiques sur une philosophie réactionnaire Cervetto – La critique libérale de Bernstein
Lénine	CE QUE SONT LES « AMIS DU PEUPLE » suivi de LE CONTENU ÉCONOMIQUE DU POPULISME Cervetto – La théorie de la politique de Lénine

Lénine	LE SOCIALISME ET LA GUERRE
Lénine	LA RÉVOLUTION PROLÉTARIENNE ET LE RÉNÉGAT KAUTSKY Cervetto – Le fondement scientifique de la lutte des classes
Cervetto	LÉNINE ET LA RÉVOLUTION CHINOISE Lénine – «Matières inflammables de la politique mondiale»
Engels	ANTIDÜHRING Cervetto – La découverte de la politique
Engels	LA SITUATION DE LA CLASSE OUVRIÈRE EN ANGLETERRE Cervetto – La vision historique de la transformation sociale
Engels	SOCIALISME UTOPIQUE ET SOCIALISME SCIENTIFIQUE suivi de LUDWIG FEUERBACH ET L'ABOUTISSEMENT DE LA PHILOSOPHIE CLASSIQUE ALLEMANDE
Marx–Engels	LA CONCEPTION MATÉRIALISTE DE L'HISTOIRE
Marx	LA GUERRE CIVILE EN FRANCE
Marx	CRITIQUE DE L'ÉCONOMIE POLITIQUE
Marx	TRAVAIL SALARIÉ ET CAPITAL suivi de SALAIRE, PRIX ET PROFIT
Marx	LES LUTTES DE CLASSES EN FRANCE 1848-1850 suivi de LE 18 BRUMAIRE DE LOUIS BONAPARTE
Marx–Engels–Lénine	UNE CAUSE DE L'HUMANITÉ TOUT ENTIÈRE – Anthologie

En partenariat avec éd. L'INTERNATIONALISTE

Anthologie	TERRORISME RÉACTIONNAIRE, EUROPÉISME IMPÉRIALISTE, INTERNATIONALISME COMMUNISTE
Anthologie	LA FONDATION DE L'INTERNATIONALE COMMUNISTE – MARS 1919
Anthologie	ORIGINES ET DÉFAITE DE L'INTERNATIONALISME EN CHINE 1919-1927

Spanish

Textos

Arrigo Cervetto	LUCHA DE CLASES Y PARTIDO REVOLUCIONARIO
Arrigo Cervetto	LA DIFÍCIL CUESTIÓN DE LOS TIEMPOS
Arrigo Cervetto	EL ENVOLTORIO POLÍTICO
Arrigo Cervetto	EL IMPERIALISMO UNITARIO Volumen I (1950-1967)
Arrigo Cervetto	EL IMPERIALISMO UNITARIO Volumen II (1959-1980)
Arrigo Cervetto	EL MUNDO MULTIPOLAR 1990-1995
Arrigo Cervetto	MÉTODO Y PARTIDO-CIENCIA
Guido La Barbera	LOTTA COMUNISTA – EL GRUPO ORIGINARIO 1943-1952
Guido La Barbera	LOTTA COMUNISTA – HACIA EL PARTIDO ESTRATEGIA 1953-1965
Guido La Barbera	LOTTA COMUNISTA – EL MODELO BOLCHEVIQUE 1965-1995
Guido La Barbera	LA NUEVA FASE ESTRATÉGICA
Guido La Barbera	EUROPA Y EL ESTADO
Guido La Barbera	CRISIS DEL ORDEN Y PANDEMIA SECULAR
Guido La Barbera	GUERRAS DE LA CRISIS DEL ORDEN
Renato Pastorino	LA TAREA INÉDITA
Renato Pastorino	SU POLÍTICA Y LA NUESTRA - Una nueva generación comunista en Europa
Antologia	TERRORISMO REACCIONARIO, EUROPEÍSMO IMPERIALISTA, INTERNACIONALISMO COMUNISTA
Antología	LA GUERRA DE GAZA Una respuesta internacionalista

Análisis

Gianluca De Simone	GRAN ORIENTE MEDIO Crisis y guerras de la nueva fase estratégica
Federico Dalvit	EUROPA EN LAS COLISIONES GLOBALES
Federico Dalvit – Jan Van Langenhove	EUROPA EN LA CRISIS DEL ORDEN
Donato Bianchi	RUSIA EN GUERRA EN LA CRISIS DEL ORDEN
Giulio Motosi	DEMOCRACIA IMPERIALISTA EN CHINA

Documentos

Antología	ENGELS Ciencia y pasión revolucionaria
G.G. Cavicchioli (A cargo de)	OCTUBRE DE 1917 100 AÑOS, 100 MILITANTES DE LA REVOLUCIÓN
G.G. Cavicchioli – E. Gianni (A cargo de)	1919 LA INTERNACIONAL COMUNISTA 100 AÑOS, 100 MILITANTES DEL PARTIDO MUNDIAL
M. Mancini – E. Gianni (A cargo de)	1871 LA COMUNA DE PARÍS 150 AÑOS, LOS MILITANTES DEL CONSEJO DE LA COMUNA

Biblioteca jóvenes

Marx	TRABAJO ASALARIADO Y CAPITAL / SALARIO, PRECIO Y GANACIA
Marx	LAS LUCHAS DE CLASES EN FRANCIA / EL DIECIOCHO BRUMARIO
Marx	LA GUERRA CIVIL EN FRANCIA Cervetto – La forma política finalmente descubierta
Engels	ANTIDÜHRING
Engels	LA SITUACIÓN DE LA CLASE OBRERA EN INGLATERRA
Marx-Engels	OBRAS ESCOGIDAS
Lenin	EL IMPERIALISMO FASE SUPERIOR DEL CAPITALISMO Cervetto – La teoría marxista de las relaciones internacionales
Lenin	¿QUÉ HACER? Cervetto – La lucha decisiva
Lenin	EL ESTADO Y LA REVOLUCIÓN Cervetto – La restauración de la teoría marxista
Lenin	EL IZQUIERDISMO, ENFERMEDAD INFANTIL DEL COMUNISMO Cervetto – El tiempo de la claridad de Lenin
Lenin	¿ QUIÉNES SON LOS « AMIGOS DEL PUEBLO » ? Cervetto – La teoría de la política de Lenin
Lenin	EL SOCIALISMO Y LA GUERRA
Cervetto	LENIN Y LA REVOLUCIÓN CHINA Lenin – "Material inflamable en la política mundial" y otros escritos
Antología	EL RACISMO ESTÁ EN NUESTRA CASA
–	NUESTRA LUCHA INTERNACIONALISTA Orientaciones para la nueva fase estratégica
Antología	UNA CAUSA DE TODA LA HUMANIDAD

German

Arrigo Cervetto	KLASSENKÄMPFE UND REVOLUTIONÄRE PARTEI
Arrigo Cervetto	DIE POLITISCHE HÜLLE
Anthologie	UNSER INTERNATIONALISTISCHER KAMPF Richtlinien für die neue strategische Phase

Russian books

Éditions Science Marxiste in collaboration with Prometey Publications, St. Petersburg

Arrigo Cervetto	UNITARNII IMPERIALISM, TOM I
Arrigo Cervetto	UNITARNII IMPERIALISM, TOM II
Arrigo Cervetto	MNOGOPOLIARNI MIR 1990-1995

NOVY PROMETEY Publications, St. Petersburg, Russia

Arrigo Cervetto	TRUDNIY VOPROS VREMENI
Arrigo Cervetto	POLITIČESKAYA OBOLOČKA
Arrigo Cervetto	METOD I PARTIA-NAUKA
Arrigo Cervetto	KLASSOVAIA BOR'BÁ I REVOLIUTSIONNAIA PARTIA
Arrigo Cervetto	VSJEMIRNOJE PROTIVOSTOJANIJE
Guido La Barbera	LOTTA COMUNISTA: GRUPPA, STOYAVSCAYA U ISTOKOV (1943-1952)
Guido La Barbera	LOTTA COMUNISTA: V NAPRAVLENII PARTII STRATEGII (1953-1965)
Guido La Barbera	NOVAYA STRATEGICHESKAYA FAZA
Renato Pastorino	BESPRETSEDENTNAYA ZADACHA
Gianluca De Simone	BOLSHOY SREDNIY VOSTOK. Krizisy i voyny novoy strategicheskoy fazy
Vladimir Nevskiy	ISTORA RKP(B). KRATIJ OCHERK
Lev Trotsky	BALKANI I BALKANSKAYA VOJNA. Pered istoricheskim rubezhom
Ivan Babushkin	RABOČIJ BOL'SHEVIK
Y. M. Steklov	PERVYY INTERNATSIONAL 1864-1872
G. G. Cavicchioli	OKTYABR 1917 GODA. 100 let. 100 bortsov za revolyutsiyu
Federico Dalvit	EVROPA V GLOBALNIKH KOLLIZIJAKH
Antologhija	REAKTSIONNYIY TERRORIZM, IMPERIALISTICHESKIY EVROPEIZM, KOMMUNISTICHESKIY INTERNATSIONALIZM
Antologhija	OBRAZOVANIE KOMMUNISTICHESKOGO INTERNATSIONALA. MART 1919 GODA
Antologhija	KOMMUNIZM ILI VARVARSTVO? NAŠA INTERNATSIONALISTIESKAJA BOR'BA

Greek books

DIETHNISMOS (Internationalism) Publications, Piraeus, Greece

Anthology	Ο ΜΥΘΟΣ ΤΟΥ ΚΑΛΠΙΚΟΥ ΣΟΣΙΑΛΙΣΜΟΥ (The myth of false socialism)
Arrigo Cervetto	ΤΑΞΙΚΟΙ ΑΓΩΝΣ ΚΑΙ ΕΠΑΝΑΣΤΑΤΙΚΟ ΚΟΜΜΑ (Class struggles and the revolutionary party)
Arrigo Cervetto	ΤΟ ΔΣΚΟΛΟ ΖΗΤΗΜΑ ΤΩΝ ΧΡΟΝΩΝ (The difficult question of times)
Renato Pastorino	ΤΟ ΠΡΩΤΟΓΝΩΡΟ ΚΑΘΗΚΟΝ (The unprecedented task)
Guido La Barbera	Η ΕΥΡΩΠΗ ΚΑΙ Ο ΠΟΛΕΜΟΣ (Europe and the war)
Anthology	ΜΙΑ ΥΠΟΘΕΣΗ ΟΛΗΣ ΤΗΣ ΑΝΘΡΩΠΟΤΗΤΑΣ (A cause of all mankind)
Anthology	ΜΥΘΟΙ ΚΑΙ ΠΟΛΕΜΟΙ ΣΤΙΣ ΜΠΑΝΛΙΕ ΤΟΥ ΕΥΡΩΠΑΪΚΟΥ ΙΜΠΕΡΙΑΛΙΣΜΟΥ (Myths and wars in the peripheries of European imperialism)
Anthology	1991-2011 : 20 ΧΡΟΝΙΑ ΠΟΥ ΑΛΛΑΞΑΝ ΤΟΝ ΚΟΣΜΟ (1991-2011. 20 years that shook the world)
Anthology	Η ΕΥΡΩΠΗ-ΔΥΝΜΗ : Ο ΕΧΘΡΟΣ ΣΤΟ ΣΠΙΤΙ ΜΑΣ (Europe as a power: the main enemy is at home)

Anthology	Η ΥΛΙΣΤΙΚΗ ΑΝΤΙΛΗΨΗ ΤΗΣ ΙΣΤΟΡΙΑΣ (The materialist conception of history)
Anthology	ΧΡΟΝΟΙ ΚΡΙΣΗΣ, ΕΠΙΣΤΡΟΦΗ ΣΤΟΝ ΜΑΡΞ (Years of crisis – returning to Marx)
Anthology	ΤΟ ΠΡΩΤΟ ΠΡΑΚΤΙΚΟ ΒΗΜΑ (The first practical step)

Brazilian books

Edições INTERVENÇÃO COMUNISTA Niterói-RJ. – Brazil

Arrigo Cervetto	LUTAS DE CLASE E PARTIDO REVOLUCIONÁRIO
Arrigo Cervetto	LÊNIN E A REVOLUÇÃO CHINESA Lênin – «Material inflamável na politica mundial » e outros textos
Arrigo Cervetto	A DIFÍCIL QUESTÃO DOS TEMPOS
Arrigo Cervetto	MÉTODO E PARTIDO-CIÊNCIA
Arrigo Cervetto	O INVOLUCRO POLITICO
Guido La Barbera	A NOVA FASE ESTRATÉGICA
Lenin	O IMPERIALISMO FASE SUPERIOR DO CAPITALISMO
–	A ASCENSÃO IMPERIALISTA DO BRASIL
–	A NOSSA LUTA INTERNACIONALISTA

Workers of All Countries, Unite!

Internationalism

Journal of Marxist Analysis No. 68 - October 2024 - £2 *Internationalist opposition to the war in Ukraine and the war in Gaza*

Strategic Unprecedented and European Rearmament

The *strategic unprecedented*, a condition never seen in power relations until now, has its main cause in China's irruption as a power of imperialism. This has led to a *crisis in the world order* and to a world contention elevated to the level of confrontation between very large States and *continent-sized* forces. If, on the one hand, the upheaval in the world balance is unprecedented – there has never been an imperialist power with China's dimensions, and there has never been a world contention between giants on that scale – the consequences of the *crisis in the world order* are also *unprecedented tensions*. On the other hand, though, they grasp, combine, and transform already present historical trends and materials, the legacy of other phases of the contention. Ukraine, the Middle East, Taiwan, and the South China Sea were already crisis areas or *nerve centres* of the imperialist confrontation, but it is China's irruption that has rekindled them and turned them into present or forthcoming *wars of the crisis in the world order*.

For this reason, among others, we have defined the conditions of the political struggle and social psychologies in America and Europe as a *new political cycle* or *political cycle of Atlantic decline*, but not as a completely unprecedented factor. The *electoral revolts* of public opinion and the swings, and even convulsions, of America's decline and Europe's political crises are new, but only new with respect to the postwar condition of the rising *phase of social-democratisation*, with the creation of pension schemes and health systems, mass education, and a positive demography fuelled by the *baby boom* of the 1950s and 1960s. The return to state capitalism and to interventionist industrial policies and protectionist measures is also new, when compared with the 30-year-long liberist cycle. Throughout the 20th century of imperialism, before 1914 and in the interregnum of the 1920s and 1930s between the two world wars, public opinion had already been swayed by fanaticisms and mass fears, with historic parties and venerable institutions ending up corrupted, radically changed, or torn apart in ruinous political crises. And the large groups of capital have consistently had cyclical recourse to State power in their relentless competition and for the protection of their spheres of influence, to the point of letting themselves be regimented into war economies.

This also holds true for the new rearmament race. It is an *unprecedented factor* that it is China that is rearming, and that Beijing is aiming to have world-class military forces within the next decade. Similarly, a nuclear order centred on three superpowers: the United States, Russia, and China, with the European Union debating whether to emerge as a fourth pole, has never been seen before. However, it goes without saying that rearmament cycles have characterised the whole history of imperialism, not only in the immediate preparation for the great wars: we need only think of the *new contention* of the 1980s and the rearmament challenge launched by the United States during the Reagan administration.

It is precisely the rearmament of the 1980s that must be considered in an estimation of the missile plans of Japan, Germany and Europe today. At that time, Helmut Schmidt and then Helmut Kohl began to negotiate the terms of a *European defence* with Valéry Giscard d'Estaing and François Mitterrand, while, in Tokyo, Yasuhiro Nakasone envisaged freeing Japan from its postwar *strategic inferiority* by enabling its armed forces to protect the straits around the Japanese archipelago.

In that condition of declining US-USSR bipolarism and amid the accelerating trend towards multipolarism, Reagan's rearmament also leveraged its military competition with Moscow to maintain its military superiority over Germany, France, and Japan. Moreover, since the post-WWII period, *extended deterrence*, offered by Washington to its allies via NATO and the US-Japan Security Treaty, had the precise aim of preventing German and Japanese nuclear rearmament.

The unintended consequence of Reagan's rearmament race – the militarisation of space in the 1980s via the Strategic Defence Initiative, also known as the "Star Wars" program – was the implosion of the Soviet Union, crushed by the weight of its *military-industrial complex* when the flow of oil revenues began to dry up after the tidal wave of the 1970s.

This sudden, unexpected power vacuum allowed Kohl to seize the historic opportunity for German reunification, but today we can conclude that the paradoxical result of that *strategic break* was the weakening of the drive towards *European defence* and of the demands for Germany's full strategic maturity. Undoubtedly, steps were taken in that direction, i.e., the *Bundeswehr*'s participation in the *Yugoslav Wars* and the plans of the European Constitutional Convention for a Rapid Intervention Force, steps that the United States opposed with the two Gulf Wars in 1991 and 2003, which aimed to re-establish American centrality. In the end, what prevailed was the prospect of *peace dividends* – the evaluation that the collapse of the Soviet Union and the end of the Cold War would confirm and favour Germany's leaning towards multilateralism, military-strategic restraint, and the primacy of economic relations in foreign policy. Meanwhile, Tokyo was plunging into deflation and the long stagnation of the 1990s, which triggered a political crisis that, for a while, compromised the unity of the Liberal Democratic Party, the key representative of the Japanese bourgeoisie. Even the prospects of Japan's *strategic maturity* and a rebalancing of the alliance with the United States lost momentum.

What we can say today is that the *crisis in the world order* reopens this double game within the Atlantic Alliance and the US-Japan Security Treaty. Germany and Japan are pushing for missile rearmament and more, which has implications for deterrence balances, *nuclear threshold* conditions, and the European prospect of Berlin sharing the nuclear umbrella of Paris and London. This is *unprecedented*, but it is also a return to the strategic dilemmas that were left unresolved in the 1980s.

(continued on p. 2)

CONTENTS

Cet ouvrage a été achevé d'imprimer en Octobre 2024
par CSC – Viale Sarca 76, 20125 Milano
Dépôt légal: Octobre 2024
Imprimé en Italie